CONTEMPORARY WORLD INTERIORS

SUSAN YELAVICH

CONTEMPORARY WORLD INTERIORS

SUSAN YELAVICH

Phaidon Press Limited
Regent's Wharf
All Saints Street
London N1 9PA

Phaidon Press Inc.
180 Varick Street
New York, NY 10014

www.phaidon.com

First published 2007
© 2007 Phaidon Press Limited

ISBN 978 0 7148 4336 0

A CIP catalogue record for this book is available
from the British Library.

Designed by Jenny 8 Del Corte Hirschfeld and
Mischa Leiner/CoDe. Communication and Design

Printed in China

Table of Contents

Introduction

This is a book about the transition into a new millennium—viewed from the inside out. The interior, whether it consists of one room or multiple rooms, whether open to the outdoors, permeable, or sequestered, gives form to our collective unconscious. The psychological metaphor is deliberate. For even within the realm of architecture and design, the contemporary interior has remained largely unexamined as a legitimate index of culture.

By and large, discussions of the interior have been prejudiced by its perception as a container of ephemera.[1] Popular media coverage of the interior as a leaky vessel of trends has reduced a deeply significant aspect of human behavior to little more than shopping lists. Newspapers and shelter magazines must constantly identify "new" trends and products to meet daily, weekly, and monthly deadlines; television and the Internet have accelerated the pace to a matter of hours and days. With rare exceptions, the emphasis on the consumer (and implicitly on the drive to consume) has disproportionately shifted critical focus away from the ramifications of design on the way we choose to live.

Furthermore, as the American critic Joel Sanders argues in his essay "Curtain Wars," conventional views of the interior are fraught with class bias that flows from its centuries-old relationship with the trades. Reliant on upholsterers, tile-setters, painters, plasterers, and carpenters, the production and conception of the interior is tainted with the stigma of manual labor. Just as insidious, Sanders also observes, is the gender bias attached to the figure of the decorator.[2] Since the profession's beginnings in the late nineteenth century (Edith Wharton's *The Decoration of Houses* was first published in 1897), the public imagination has associated its practice with stereotypes of women and gay men. Undermined and marginalized by social prejudice, it is no wonder that the credibility of the interior as an expression of cultural values has been seriously impaired.

Today, and fortunately for this discussion, the conditions and the light in which we understand culture-at-large have changed. The legacy of the twentieth century's progressive social movements, combined with the as yet incalculable effects of twenty-first-century globalization, has imploded the elitist notion of Culture. The distinctions, for example, between "high" culture and "low" culture are dissipating in a more fluid climate characterized by the cross-fertilization that occurs between the two poles. Translated to the realm of interior design, a window has been opened to admit the breezes of iconoclasm and eclecticism.

At the same time that we are witnessing a democratization of design through the agency of retailers from Ikea to Target, designers are canvassing the vernacular to animate their work: witness the use of graffiti in Kapstein Roodnat's clinic in New York, Pediatrics 2000 (Therapeutic, p. 490). Projects such as Fabio Novembre's Hotel Vittorio in Florence (Hotels, p. 434) and Dorte Mandrup's offices for Cell Network in Copenhagen (Offices, p. 138) are marked by productive borrowings between design and decoration, once considered mutually exclusive. And while the fields of architecture and interior design and interior decoration still have different educational protocols and domains of emphasis, there is evidence of greater convergence between these formerly segregated realms—one example being the recent interest in wall coverings as a narrative and spatial device.

Another way to think of this emergent synthesis is to substitute the triad of "architecture, design, and decoration" with "modernity, technology, and history." One of the hallmarks of the postmodern era in which we live is our awareness of the role of the past in shaping the present. History is no longer understood as linear, but more like the double helix of DNA, with dominant and recessive genes that continually recombine. After a century of ill-fated social experiments in the "new," we no longer discount the role of memory. Just as utopian communist regimes attempted to erase custom and tradition, so ultimately did modernism suppress idiosyncrasy and, in the end, personality—notwithstanding the fact that both movements began as well-intentioned social experiments. In the interior, this valorization of memory manifests itself in a renewed interest in ornament, in evidence of craft and materiality, and in spatial complexities, all running parallel to the ongoing project called modernity. No longer does any one aesthetic language dominate, as the International Style did in the years after World War II. In this new inclusive climate, once-alien styles flourish side by side.

Far more significantly, we see a new elasticity in typologies. Though this book is organized by type of interior—house, loft, office, hotel, and so on—the chapters strain to control their borders, particularly once we leave the confines of home. While the residence has seen the least radical changes to its own program, during the past three decades it has become the catalyst for entirely new ways of thinking about spaces that were once firmly isolated from it–from the secretary's cubicle to the nurse's station to the librarian's reading room. The domestication of such environments is a welcome step in providing more comfort, more reassurance, and more pleasure to spaces formerly defined by prohibitions and exclusions. Unquestionably, the changes we see in public spaces are indebted to the civil rights movements of the late 1960s. Those battles fought against barriers of race, class, gender, and physical ability laid the ground work for a larger climate of hospitality and accommodation.

It is also possible to detect a very different agenda in the popularity of the residential model. The introduction of domestic amenities into commercial spaces can also be construed as part of a wider attempt to put a more acceptable face on the workings of capital. In this view, interior design dons the mask of entertainment in order to conceal the less sanguine aspects of daily life; every interior is fundamentally a stage set. There is nothing new about this charade, nor is it particularly insidious–as long as the actors are complicit in the game. Indeed, it could be argued that transforming work into play is design's ultimate task. Danger surfaces, however, when illusion becomes delusion–when the design of a hospital, for example, overcompensates for the realities of illness with patronizing sentiment, or when offices become surrogate apartments because of the relentless demands of a 24/7 economy.

In these instances, design relinquishes its potential to transform daily life in favor of what amounts to little more than a facile rebranding of space, or worse, an act of deceit. The projects selected here make the case for a range of best practices. Looked at together, they describe the traits (but not the trends) of the contemporary interior. And since, with few exceptions, all of the spaces considered have been realized, this international survey can be construed as a kind of pulse-taking. The interiors have been curated to illuminate ideas that are enduring and to identify potential areas of change. These selections are offered with a desire to ameliorate the limitations of design criticism so acutely diagnosed by architectural historian Kenneth Frampton when he observed:

Despite the vast influence media has on the world … we are still subject to a lack of information with regard to world culture. … Thus, while we are momentarily informed on Japan, we hardly know anything about India, Australia, or South Africa; while we are au courant on Spain, Portugal, France, and Germany, we know less about current practice in Scandinavia.[3]

In response, this book attempts to be catholic in its purview, not by framing design culture in terms of Spain or Scandinavia or Australia but by charting the changes to interiors through countries and across nationalities. Furthermore, instead of offering sociological portraits–for example, of shopping spaces, which would of necessity include phenomena like Starbucks and big-box retail–*Contemporary World Interiors* sets its sights on the achievements that can be said to flow from design. If there is a perceptible bias, it is decidedly toward spaces like Herzog & de Meuron's Walker Art Center in Minneapolis (Culture, p. 315) or Marcel Wanders' Lute Suites in Amsterdam (Hotels, pp. 436-37)–those that make an art out of hybridity, that don't simply mix and match periods but borrow from various episodes in design and refilter them through a contemporary lens. The selection offered here favors those designers who still find wisdom in Renaissance chronicler Baldassare Castiglione's advice:

He who does not avoid … antique expressions, except in the rarest instances, makes no less serious a mistake than he who in his desire to imitate times past continues to eat acorns after wheat has become available.[4]

Today, designers no longer have to choose between a modernist or postmodernist diet. While it is tempting to use the postmodern style–the inflated classicism of the 1980s–as the whipping boy for the acorn-variety of historicism, surely designers would not be as open-minded today were it not for those first excursions into the Pandora's box of style. Likewise modernism survives, indeed, thrives, if somewhat less restrictively, as an ideology of restraint.

Today, the appetite for the new has been replaced by the desire for the different and unexpected. In a time when virtually every style is equally available, form is secondary to formal relationships and to narratives of use. Consequently, each chapter asks, What is this space today? What is the house, the office, the hotel, the museum? How do we think about these interiors? What do they say about us?

It is very likely that one hundred years from now, the answers and the categories for a book such as this one will be quite different. The loft is susceptible to change not only because it depends on a finite resource (vacated industrial space) but also because the sources of its identity–the studio, the gallery, the museum–are themselves no longer tethered to a formal canon of the empty box. Hotels, under the ever-heightening conditions of globalization, show signs of morphing into houses, campgrounds, and galleries. Spaces designed to heal are already superceding those designed to quarantine. As people live longer, all of these spaces will take on different features to accommodate what it means to be human when a lifetime spans four or more generations.

Interiors are, after all, narratives about ourselves, whether we use them self-consciously as such or not. A recent study of our relationships to interiors by the international design consultancy IDEO divides people into "storytellers" (those who decorate), "functionalists" (those who are task-oriented and simply warehouse their possessions), and "campers" (those on the move who barely unpack).[5] But even warehousing–perhaps especially warehousing, whether patients, possessions, or equipment–tells a story about how we think of ourselves. The mistake is to see the interior as a mere container of behaviors or tastes. It participates in those behaviors and tastes. The task ahead is to read them carefully.

Houses

Residential interiors are not confined to any particular type of building. They live within factories, above shops, and within sanctuaries both secular and religious. But when the residence is a house, a freestanding structure whose perimeters are defined by the landscape around it—be it urban, suburban, or rural—design opportunities proliferate exponentially. Exterior walls and apertures become freely malleable elements. Because it need not be integrated with or dependent on the structures that surround it, the freestanding house offers a counterpoint to urbanity and retains an elemental quality of refuge. Not surprisingly, many of the more compelling examples are to be found in the countryside—houses that reverberate with distant memories of ancient villas, summer palaces, and estates. In this Arcadian model, the house is inherently conservative; it suggests lingering images of the chaste wife, innocent children, and familial fortunes protected by household gods—the ideal of the ancient Roman *domus*.[1] Yet, tectonically, it is most open to experimentation. Walls can be erased, roofs raised, and floors folded. Witness the continuing evolution of the open plan, which mirrors the domestic realignments prompted by the various liberation movements of the twentieth century. The idealized wife and innocent children no longer dominate the demographic profile of the average household, which is just as likely to be composed of single parents or same-sex partners, and include no children. Mirroring these shifts in social mores, the modern house has become more transparent, and the story of the contemporary interior has become one of evolving notions of privacy and personal autonomy.

Perhaps the defining feature of urban modernity is the fact that we have become extraordinarily adept at creating private space within exposed settings. Architectural historian Rosemary Haag Bletter points out that after World War I, architects such as Bruno Taut viewed "glass architecture as the sign of a changed, international pacifist society."[2] It was to be symbolic of societies with nothing to hide that had embraced the ideal of peaceful coexistence. Paradoxically, transparent architecture has also evolved as part of the vanguard experiments in the act of retreat, more in keeping with Frank Lloyd Wright's prediction of "lives lived in greater independence and seclusion."[3] Indeed, glass houses set in the countryside, from Mies van der Rohe's Farnsworth House to Philip Johnson's New Canaan House—despite their claims to transparency—have always depended on the seclusion offered by their sites for privacy. The reconciliation of retreat and exposure has become the plot line driving the development of interiors today, as will be seen in this chapter, which begins with the openly naked house and ends with the sheltered and fully clothed one.

The Exposed House

As in the biblical creation myth, where the Garden of Eden is the first home, the contemporary interior embraces nature as a lead protagonist in its narrative. Historian Joseph Rykwert reminds us that "Eden was no forest growing wild."[4] Its domestic pathos and sheltering plantings gave shape to the first rooms, for which the plans have been lost only to be imaginatively recovered within each new house. Where early modernists used landscape views as a surrogate for wallpaper or other artifices of ornament and decoration, today designers are expanding on the idea of the framed view—in some cases by removing the frame altogether.[5] Today, the wall is the window. There is a greater symbiosis, a literal integration with the landscape that both undermines and amplifies the notion of the interior.

The most pointed expression of this ambivalence can be found in the work of Japanese architect Shigeru Ban. The interior of Ban's Wall-less House (1997) in Nagano has been described as a "sandwich of air."[6] Naked, it is the apotheosis of Edenic communal living. But the absence of sybaritic amenities, combined with the discreet presence of self-effacing folding walls, suggests solitude and asceticism. Indeed, the very idea of luxury, integral to the "country" house as a second, expendable home, is critiqued by the design's economy. Architecture and interior are indivisible: A curved slab of concrete serves as both wall and floor. Nestled into the hillside, the entire house is reduced to a single cantilever. Desk, table, and kitchen converge in one volume; the furniture of daily ablutions disappears into sculptural volumes. The only frill in sight (and, one might say, the only conceit, since they echo the fluted cardboard-tube walls of Ban's seminal Paper House of 1995) is the scalloped edges of the chairs, which are of Ban's own design.

The urban doppelgänger of the Wall-less House is Ban's Curtain Wall House (1995). Located in a densely populated Tokyo neighborhood where there is no forest to act as a screen, the house is shrouded by drapes, conflating architecture

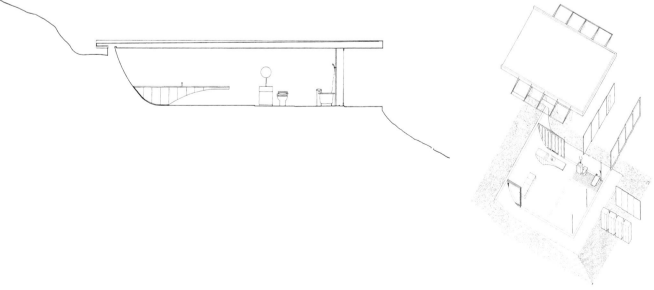

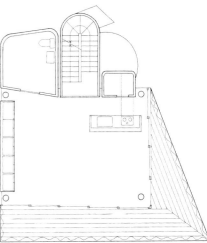

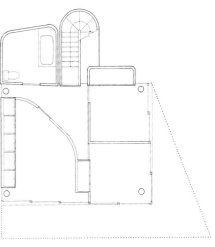

and décor. It is a surreal gesture tempered by cultural tradition. Here the membrane of the curtain stands in for the shoji screens, *fusuma* doors, shutters, and *sudare* screens that are part of the traditional Japanese house.[7] The overall sensation is one of modesty, not exhibitionism—that is, until the curtains are caught in the wind and the house's minimal mien is countered by a baroque theatricality. Here, as in the Wall-less House, Ban plays with the outward signs of twentieth-century modernism to revel in the postmodern contradiction of open shelter and clothed exposure.

The other face of Janus in the transparent house takes the profile of the exhibitionist. Unabashedly hedonistic, Brazilian architect Isay Weinfeld's Alterio House (2001) in São Paulo presents the interior as a *tableau vivant*. When the house's sliding glass panels are open, the entire front facade disappears. Yet a traditional sequence of spaces is maintained, one that departs little from the sequential plan of the ancient Roman *domus*, in which a semi-public atrium leads to a dining *tablinum* and then to a peristyle garden and pool. If

the plan of the Alterio House is inherently traditional, and comparisons to the bacchanalian design programs of the ancients are tempting—after all, the client is a music producer— the elevation has an exuberance and freshness completely of its own time. For one thing, there is no transition into the living room. There is no front door, no foyer, no threshold to cross. Instead, one walks onto a stage. The double-height space dwarfs its furnishings—a mix of pieces created or chosen by Weinfeld, including those by French mid-century designer Jean Royère and contemporary selections from Luminaire in Miami—all of which become Lilliputian props in a spectacle of nightly parties. A single-story central dining area, framed by the living room wall, creates a zone of intimacy that alludes to the private spaces flanking it. The innovation of this house ultimately rests in Weinfeld's skillful manipulation of scale, which grants its owner the dual luxuries of display and discretion.

Operating in the more densely urban context of a narrow street lot, Australian architects Ian Moore and Tina Engelen

also exploit the illusion of the three-sided house, only this time in reverse orientation. With the Price/O'Reilly House (1995) in Sydney, Australia, it is the rear facade that dematerializes. Designed for a professional photographer, this residence is quite literally a stage. A 20-foot-high (6-meter-high) living room doubles as a studio for daylight photography; its domestic furnishings—all on wheels for easy mobility during shoots—are scaled up accordingly. A 16.5-foot-long (5.5-meter-long) kitchen counter establishes a longitudinal proportional system that includes a 10-foot-long (3-meter-long) slab sofa used in combination with low-cost furniture designed by the architects. (The line, called Easy, includes dining table, coffee table, bed, and towel rail.) Above the open-plan live/work space, the bedroom hovers like a balcony, concealing the dressing room/bathroom, which is itself a small, mirrored theater. The most confined room in the house,

the bedroom, also offers the illusion of expansion: One of its walls coincides with the louvered facade of the house's front elevation.

In London, the British firm Future Systems tests the limits of urban privacy protocols by shearing away not just the back wall but also the roof of the Hauer-King House (1994), sheathing it with glass instead of shingles. To further break down the distinction between inside and outside, the white circular ceramic tile floor bleeds out of the house to form an outdoor terrace. Likewise, there are no walls in this interior; instead, brightly lacquered bathroom and kitchen units serve as sculptural objects that define the space without compromising the overall geometry of the house. This is the glass house as greenhouse, both intimate and open, nourishing a distinctly domestic microclimate.

In Montecito, California, Barton Myers presents another point of view on the wall-less house with his own House and Studio at Toro Canyon (1999). Four pavilions, with open plans to accommodate studio, living, and guest spaces, are stepped into the hillside to conform to the contours of the site. With a press of a button, their garage-door facades roll back to offer an unblinkered view of ocean and mountains, framed only by two vestigial columns, the vertical tracks that house the prefabricated doors.

It is one of the paradoxes of contemporary life that the house—once the symbol of protection from the elements—is now a vehicle for exposure to the environment. These efforts to reconnect the house to its surroundings reach far beyond the picture window—they make the house one with the view. Enabled by technology, these houses are also a reaction to technology. Over the course of the last century, the rhythms of daily life have been effectively divorced from the cycles of nature, even from the most basic experiences of weather, by virtue of insulation, heating, and air-conditioning. But by shearing the face off the house, designers have created interiors that offer a compromise between the desire for exposure and the desire for retreat. That they do so by returning the house to its most primitive incarnation—the cave—may be the supreme irony.

The Screened House

The contemporary urge to reconnect the interior to its natural surroundings finds alternate expression in houses that admit the view in gradations through the device of the screen. We see it in the distinct resurgence of the lattice wall—a latter-day brise-soleil. Used by architects with increasing frequency in locations as diverse as Denmark, Australia, Italy, and China, the screen translates the traditional window blind to the scale of a wall. In these projects, views are spliced into cinematic frames by closely spaced wooden bands that filter light and landscape, attenuating but not obliterating the division between inside and out. But something else is evolving here as well. In contrast to the overtly modernist planar features of the houses previously discussed, there is an intimacy and decorative aspect to the lattice approach that reflects the embrace of craft particular to design at the turn of the twentieth century. These regular striations offer continuity with the modernist ethos and at the same time contribute to its gradual fragmentation.

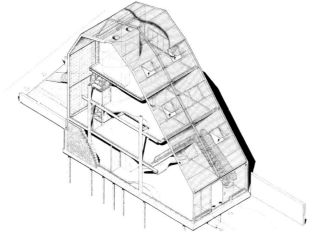

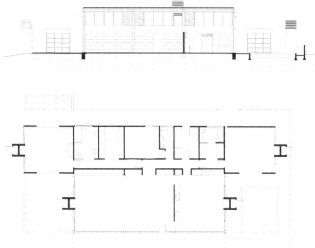

Henning Larsens Studio, Art Gallery and Summer Residence, North Zealand,
Denmark, 2000

An artists' retreat in northern Denmark (2000) by the Danish firm Henning Larsens Studio offers another instance of the facade-as-frame; only here, the house is wrapped in a shed of narrow larch slats. Light enters the interior in much the same way that it does in a barn whose planks have swollen apart. However, the rural quality of this summer studio–a simple volume lined with birch ply panels–is quickly belied by the rigorously elegant lines of the lattice and the clerestory that runs along the floor of the north wall. With an aesthetic of discretion, evident in numerous commissions in Asia, the firm has designed a distinctly modern lantern that flickers on the outside and hints at the warm wood tones within.

Likewise, Sean Godsell's Peninsula House (2002) in Victoria, Australia, is sheathed in finely hewn slats of Australian jarrah wood and speaks not only to a local vernacular but also to the Japanese idea of a space within a space. The Asian influence is most clearly apparent in the bath-cum-rock garden, while the European notion of the sheltered interior is best expressed in the deeply recessed kitchen and living room spaces. Together, they embody "all the archetypal qualities of dwelling: cave, hut, [and] hearth."[8] Where the lattice functions as a canopy for the Peninsula House, it serves as a crate for Godsell's slightly earlier residence in Victoria, the Carter Tucker House (2000), in which every room is dappled with light and the house becomes the equivalent of a giant sundial. Apart from the light, the most distinguishing feature of the interior is its handsome concrete walls, irregularly scored to add yet another layer of striations and to echo the patterns of beach sand.

UdA/Ufficio di Architettura of Turin uses a similar strategy with Levis House (1998) in Biella, Italy, only to accomplish a different kind of transition. A ribcage of timbers stretched like an accordion joins a new house to an existing rural structure. Here again, wall is sacrificed to window in order to offer an expansive view of the Alpine landscape. Passage from the first floor to the second floor is via a semi-exposed, outdoor staircase within the accordion, further fragmenting the idea of enclosure. The furnishings, particularly Gerrit Rietveld Z-Chairs, echo the house's vocabulary of folded surfaces.

In Kengo Kuma's Great (Bamboo) Wall House (2002), the vertical grillwork actually folds in on itself to define interior and exterior boundaries; hence the house's name. For this

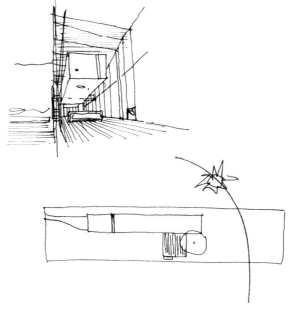

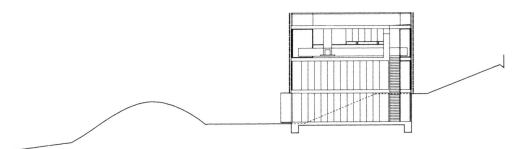

Opposite: SGA/Sean Godsell Architects, Carter Tucker House,
Breamlea, Victoria, Australia, 2000

UdA/Ufficio di Architettura with Davide Volpe, Levis House,
Biella, Italy, 1998

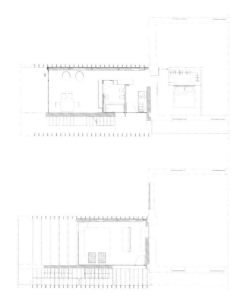

EDGE Design Institute, Suitcase House, Great Wall, China, 2002

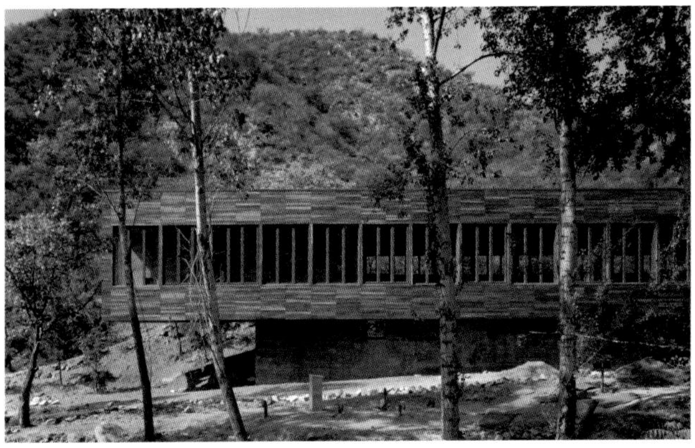

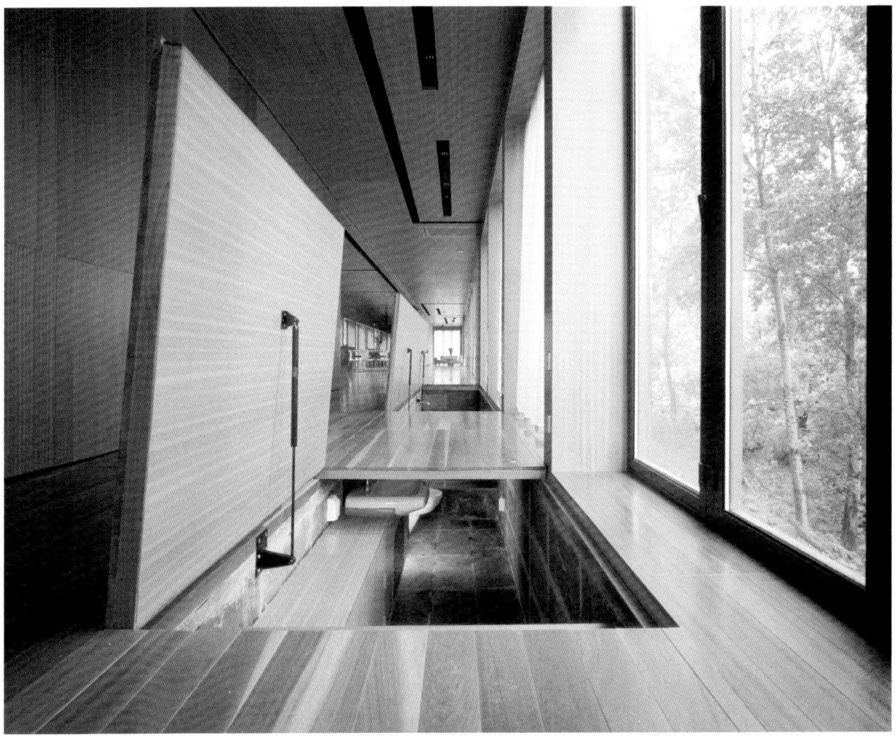

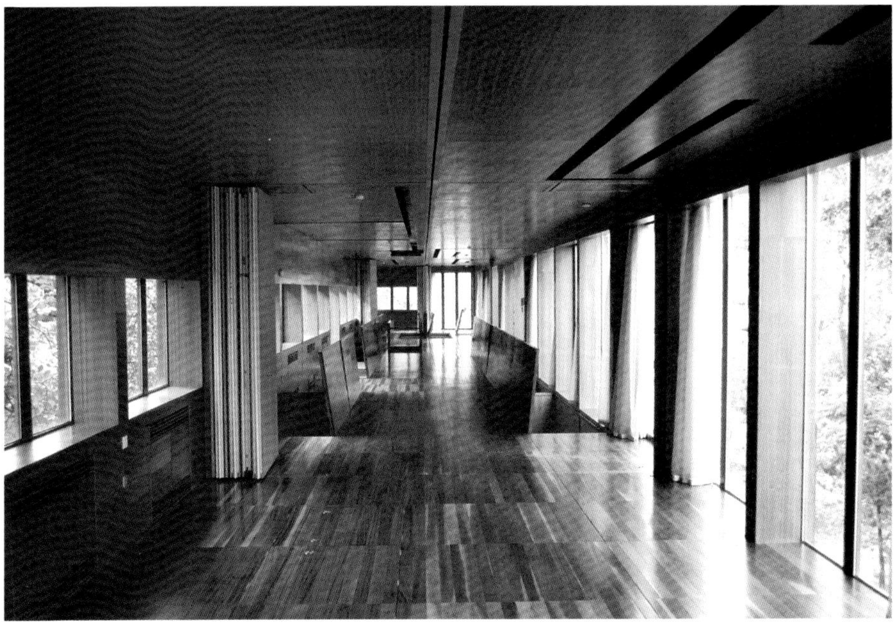

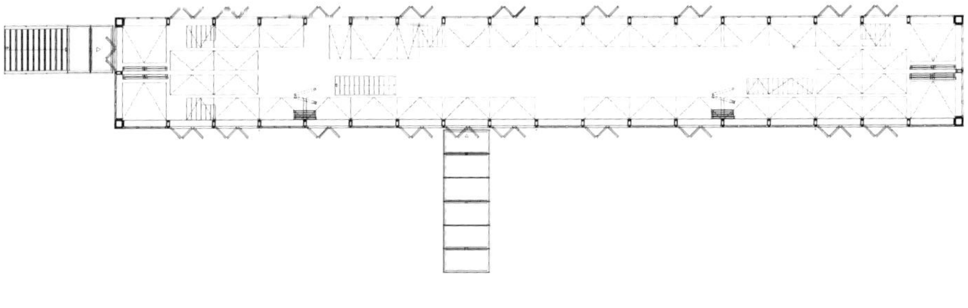

commission–part of a luxury development of vanguard architecture near Beijing called the Commune by the Great Wall–Kuma uses bamboo to create his particular variant of lattice. Drawing on bamboo's strong cultural associations in China and in his native Japan, he evokes ideas of partition–from the Great Wall as fortification to the house as barricade against nature. Colonnades of bamboo of varying thickness become the warp and weft of the house. The space of the kitchen is semi-private, defined by more widely spaced struts, while the stairwell is framed by the open-and-closed rhythm of its vertices. A sitting room–striated on all sides by light and shadow–extends outside like the moon-viewing deck of a teahouse, its view framed by a parted curtain wall of bamboo.

Subterranean Transitions

In the same complex–the Commune by the Great Wall–there is an equally venturesome house that proposes an opposite model of interior-exterior relations. Instead of opening the house laterally to the landscape, Gary Chang's Suitcase House (2002) plays with transition to and from the subterranean level. It is an essay on enclosure, even hiding. Aptly, Chang is the founder of EDGE Design Institute, a multidisciplinary design studio in Hong Kong that produces architecture and products. This is a house that literally has to be unpacked to be understood.[9] Embedded in the floor plane are doors that open to reveal wells of space for sitting, bathing, and storage. Like a jewelry box or a safe with hidden compartments, this house is as much a study in folded space as the Bamboo Wall House. But where Kengo Kuma creates illusory effects with transparency, Gary Chang does so with opacity. The chief distinction between the two has to do with human-scale intimacy, here taken to womb-like extremes. While the Bamboo Wall House defers to the infinite scale of its landscape, Chang's

Suitcase House, with its warren of wooden enclosures, is tailored to the scale of the human body. (In addition to the structural compartments, there are also interior blinds that can be used to further subdivide the main floor.) The house's tightly crafted spaces have a tremendous power that comes not only from its playful premise, a game of traveling in situ, but also from the slightly mysterious quality of a house that is part cellar, part attic. With its drop-down stairs and buried rooms, the Suitcase House constantly alludes to nether regions hidden from view.

Establishing zones of intimacy is an undertaking commonly associated with large residences that must function in a semi-public capacity. However, the same strategy of depressed, recessed space that is the hallmark of the Suitcase House is used to equal effect in a house whose footprint is a mere 800 square feet (75 square meters). Atelier Bow-Wow's GAE House (2003) for Akira and Miyoko Nagae in Tokyo features a partially sunken, book-lined study that is embedded in the core of the house. Founded in 1992, Atelier Bow-Wow is based in Tokyo and known for its conceptual orientation. The arrangement of the GAE House allows Akira, a journalist, to work in semi-seclusion while still sensing his wife's presence. In this latter-day reprise of the sunken living room, the entire space becomes a piece of furniture. The absence of a ceiling transforms the room into a virtual well—part library, part office, part cave. While Yoshiharu Tsukamoto and Momoyo Kaijima, the young principals of Atelier Bow-Wow, designed the GAE House as one of a series of what they call "pet architecture" that inhabits small lots between buildings in Tokyo,[10] it is also possible to view it in light of the blurred boundaries of modern life. Tsukamoto and Kaijima's design is a response to the simultaneity and multitasking that are hallmarks of contemporary living, spawned by technology. Houses like this allow their residents to be alone and connected at the same time, offering an alternative to the much-vaunted home-office. Why replicate the cubicle and artificially cordon off the spheres of work and living when both can coexist in a domestic setting, alleviating the isolation of working independently?

Elastic Spaces

In The Netherlands, Ben van Berkel and Caroline Bos of UN Studio in Amsterdam interpret the compromises and advantages of the family home-office in terms of elasticity. Theirs represents yet a different formal response to the relaxation of borders that characterizes social and architectural practices in the postmodern climate, where hierarchies are suspect and connectivity is prized. Like the GAE House, Berkel and Bos's Mobius House (1998), located in a suburb of Utrecht, is also a meditation on living both together and apart in one dwelling as work and family intersect in the course of a day. Instead of creating discrete spaces that can be opened and closed, UN Studio establishes a sense of flow using a sequence of interlocking spaces that form a continuous loop, twisted like its namesake the Mobius strip, a mathematical figure with one side and one edge. This is a house of reversals and inversions, a house where conventional materials trade places with dividing walls made of glass, a ceiling made of wood flooring, and furniture made of concrete. These suites of tables and chairs offer solid anchors within the animated spaces of the house.

This notion of the interior as a procession through space has received enormous attention at the turn of the twenty-first century. The Mobius House embodies a dynamism that inevitably evokes comparisons with baroque space. But the sixteenth-century baroque aesthetic sought unity through active complexity—disorientation but not dislocation. In contrast, late-twentieth-century interiors make a virtue out of voids and spatial non sequiturs. Los Angeles–based architect Eric Owen Moss has spent the better part of his roughly thirty-year career exploiting these possibilities to invigorate the experience of interior spaces, raising questions about architecture's functionality. Indeed, the steel bridges in Moss's Lawson/Westen House (1993) go nowhere. The irregular rooms of the house consist of interpenetrating, skewed geometries of cone, cylinder, and square. For all the suggestions of dizziness, however, each room retains a feeling of stability, even domesticity, that comes from the Euclidian underpinnings of the house. Sited under the soaring space of the vaulted ceiling, the kitchen becomes a chimney, circumscribed by a Piranesian labyrinth of stairs. Ramps lead off to bedrooms and bathrooms whose slanted walls recall traditional dormers. In the Lawson/Westen House, the fragmenting tactics associated with deconstruction are not used to exclude tradition as much as to rethink it. Indeed, architectural historian Anthony Vidler frames Moss's spatial gymnastics in a specific historical light, observing that "Moss's space, like his geometry, is conceived as shifting, flexing, and jumping,

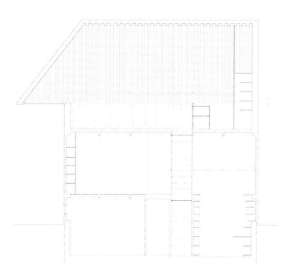

described in gerundive terms that would have delighted
the romantics of the early nineteenth century and given him
a place among the organicists of architecture."[11]

Where Moss creates pockets of intimacy off a vertical core,
Chicago-based architect Douglas Garofalo distributes rooms
along a horizontal axis in the Markow Residence (1998), in
Prospect Heights, Illinois. The house's program respects a
local suburban context of gables, sheds, and dormers without sacrificing its own formal complexity. Indeed, Garofalo
creates his own gables with irregular windows that press
up against the roofline in deliberate but respectful tension
with the surrounding community. Rooms are laced together
by a steel-and-glass-floored bridge that gives a strong feeling of transparency within a house that is otherwise closed
to harsh Midwestern winters and decidedly diplomatic about
its iconoclasm. The interior curtain-wall—a petrified drape
embedded in the living room's warm yellow walls and wood
floor—is both a decorative surrogate and a frozen gestural
element that activates the space.

Like the Lawson/Westen House, the Markow Residence is
ambivalent in its domesticity. Both houses show the influence
of decades of theoretical speculation on the loss of unity and
the legitimacy of forms that impose a false image of whole-
ness on contemporary space, where electronic media like
television and the Internet bring multiple realities into a single
room. (With its radically reconfigured spaces, the interior of

the Markow Residence is especially pointed in its critique and brings a new urbanity to the conventional suburban house.) Deconstruction, the term associated with the philosophy of fractured and layered realities and the architecture that expressed it, did not aspire to completely erase traditional notions of space, as was the case with modernism. Instead, the deconstructionists aspired to dissect them and reassemble their pieces in new collages. Characterized by dynamic form and a visceral sense of movement, these spaces are extremely self-conscious and unapologetically extroverted.

The Scrimmed House

Not all the interrogations of domesticity of this time are quite so confrontational, however. A different response to the tension operating today between the public and private nature of the house appears in experiments with translucence, light, and shadow. In Atelier Tekuto's Cell Brick House (2004)—a 915-square-foot (85-square-meter) residence in suburban Tokyo—conventional windows are replaced by a checkerboard of glazed cut-outs that cover the entire two-story facade. The diminutive domestic interior is patterned by light during the day; by night the exterior is transformed into a glowing box.

The play of shadows in Japanese architect Toyo Ito's T House (1999) in Yutenji, Japan, evokes both the traditional associations of the shoji screen and allusions to virtual reality. Designed for two graphic designers and their son, the T House stands out with its horizontal bands of semi-opaque glass that function as both window shade and facade on a dense urban street. In the simply furnished dining room, the shadow of a tree playing against the luminous window wall relieves the starkness of the space. The branches silhouetted against the glowing wall are the only decorative gesture in the house; evoking both the backlit quality of a computer screen and the outlines of traditional shadow puppets.

Illusion is also the leitmotif of Dutch architect Koen van Velsen's design for the Vos House (1999) in Amsterdam. The Vos House, like Ito's T House, is sited on an extremely narrow urban lot. Simple volumes, sparsely furnished with modern classics, are stacked on top of each other. A glass wall rises through the stories, unifying the floors vertically. A fine mesh grill is used in combination with the glass, offering a kind of pixelated privacy to each floor. Suspended between the side walls of the house, parallel to the facade,

the mesh both reduces each room to a silhouette and offers glimpses into the deeper, domestic space around its margins. Retaining the memory of a curtain, this screen has a calming buffer effect in a house where the front door is situated on the bedroom floor and the facade is essentially a large window. The coup de grace of this exercise in compression and expansion is a tree that rises through the courtyard and terrace to the top of the building, as though it had burst from the soil through the gridded steel floors. Its slender diagonal offers a poignant counterpoint to the house's disciplined asceticism; it is not merely a reflection from outside but rather as much a part of the interior as any other fixture.

The Penetrated House
The intrusion of nature into the realm of the artificial is more than a minor conceit. Rather, it reflects the diminishment–some would say the elimination–of the raw state of nature by centuries of human control. As J.B. Jackson, the noted landscape historian, observes, a "new synthetic version of the forest as the setting for human interaction with nature is evolving a humanized landscape."[12] Not content to contain nature in parks and protected forests or to consign it to peripheral gardens around the house, we bring it inside to both lament our loss and restore some semblance of contact,

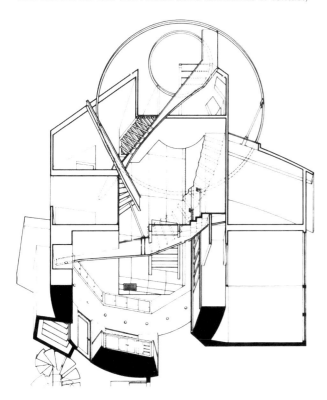

whether by eliminating walls altogether or through the tactics of partial exposure seen so far in houses screened, scrimmed, and pierced.

This aggressive embrace of nature, where trees literally grow through the roof, also occurs in Lacaton and Vassal's House in Lège-Cap Ferret (1998) near Bordeaux, France. Here the tree is less like a found object brought indoors than an extension of a campsite. In contrast to lodges in which rustic furnishings serve as surrogates for nature, here the forest moves indoors, allowing the furnishings to retain the urban character of their owners.

Equally explicit in its relationship to nature is Antoine Predock's Turtle Creek House (1993) in Dallas. Predock extrudes the interior into the landscape with a "sky ramp"– a tensile steel walkway that reaches into the surrounding treetops. Designed in response to the client's passion for birdwatching, the house proper is divided into north and south sections linked by a gallery zone. Here begins an interior trail, punctuated with vantage points for viewing avian habitats, that culminates in a network of roof terraces.

The dramatically attenuated interior is also the primary characteristic of Harry Seidler's Berman House (1999) in Joadja, New South Wales, Australia. Seidler, who died in 2006, was Australia's elder statesman of modernist architecture and was particularly adept at bending abstract sculptural form to the land. Here, the roughness of the landscape is echoed inside with rugged stone walls and fireplaces, which, in combination with the extreme cantilever, hint at a latent

Wrightian character in a house otherwise closer in spirit to Oscar Niemeyer's Brasilia in its sculptural presence. The glassed-in living/dining/kitchen space appears to float on a plane, vertiginously extended over a rocky escarpment on a narrow plank that serves as an outdoor sitting room.

Surrounded by dense vegetation and overlooking the River Plate, Mathias Klotz's cantilevered Ponce House (2003) in Buenos Aires also maximizes the lush landscape through a design that features a glass envelope for a main floor and an upper volume that conceals sleeping quarters. The contrast between the two volumes not only creates a stark separation of public and private spaces, but also gives the bedrooms the uncanny sense of floating in the landscape like a tree house.

The distended balconies and cantilevers in these penetrated houses add a new measure of bravado to the house as a type. The extended perimeters of their interiors yield not just vistas but also the thrill of vertigo. Now that nature has long since been conquered, designers create the illusion of risk within the safety of home. Such features are also unmistakable advertisements for an ideal of leisure, here, with extreme gestures—the architectonic version of extreme sports.

The Autonomous House

Up to this point, the houses discussed can be characterized as testing the limits of enclosure, betraying in varying degrees both a larger cultural anxiety about the viability of the dwelling as a discrete container and a constructive urge to move beyond it. The spaces considered in the pages that follow are marked by a subtly different kind of engagement with their surroundings. In short, they embrace the condition of self-containment and place a greater stress on the autonomy of the dwelling. This isn't to say that these houses are indifferent to their sites, only to suggest that instead of merging with their sites, they inhabit them.

A survey of the autonomous house begins here with the ongoing development of heroic modernism, taken to its most mature expression in the work of Richard Meier. With his practice now in its fourth decade and a highly influential career that has been widely honored (he received the Pritzker Prize in 1984), Meier is perhaps best known to the public for his design of the Getty Center in Los Angeles, often described as a city on a hill (see Cultural, p. 279). His houses are

no less distinct from their settings. Indeed, each is its own urbane microcosm.

Meier sees the house as a public space as well as a domestic environment. It is public not only in the sense that architecture is an art with a public life of its own, but also in his view of the house as a latter-day villa or suburban palazzo, whose domestic functions have always been less prominent than their social functions. There is a quality of scalelessness to a Meier house that insures its monumentality and its autonomy.

In the case of the Rachofsky House (1996) in Dallas, Meier literally puts the house on a plinth. The Rachofsky House contains a private museum with a substantial collection of contemporary art, and, accordingly, its internal grammar is drawn from the realm of the gallery. Furnishings are valued as works of design, as architectural elements in their own right, honored as formally as the client's art collection. A suite

of Mies van der Rohe Barcelona chairs and stools are sited on a gray carpet on the second-floor living room, mirroring the relationship of the house to its platform. Two separate sets of stairs distinguish the public and private sectors of the house. An enclosed private spiral on the south side of the house ascends to the library and the master suite, while a switchback public stair on the north side opens off the gallery foyer and leads directly to the double-height living room on the first floor. The stairway configurations function as geographic cues to the discrete social functions of the public and private realms of the house, which is otherwise characterized by Meier's uniform white palette, linear railings, slender columns, and carefully gridded windows.

By contrast, the Japanese architect Kazuyo Sejima proves that it is also possible to achieve monumentality on a 388-square-foot (36-square-meter) lot in Tokyo. Sejima's Small House (2001) is one of her most notable early commissions, designed before Sejima founded the firm SANAA with Ryue

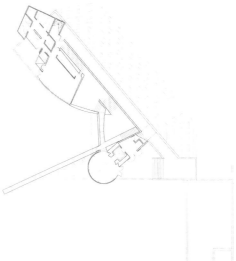

Nishizawa and began garnering international fame. The house
is comprised of three trapezoidal volumes on a recessed
cubic base, and defies normative reference points of scale.
For in spite of its skewed volumes, the house has a strong,
unified legibility. A white spiral staircase, partially framed by
a vertical shaft, penetrates its interior. With its combination
of curving rail, diagonal frame, and fanned steps, all painted
white, this internal spine is at once both optically intricate
and deeply practical, dividing each floor of this family house
that had no room to spare for walls. As a result, the staircase
becomes the house's most important piece of furniture.

New Vernaculars

ARO/Architecture Research Office's design for the Telluride
House (1999) is not only carefully balanced against the
grandeur of its site in Colorado, it also mitigates the hubris
of decontextualized modernism with a new vernacular. ARO's
partners, New York–based Adam Yarinsky and Stephen
Cassell, effectively repurpose one of the modern movement's
signature materials–COR-TEN steel–by cutting it into thin
shingles that clad walls inside and out. At 10,000 square feet
(930 square meters), the mass of the Telluride House is
effectively concealed behind three walls shielding three
separate volumes that step down the mountain, linked by
stairs. However, one only has to turn 180 degrees and
approach the house from the side to see that its interiors
are revealed through staggered window planes, designed to
capture different vistas and to give each room an individual
identity. It is not just the magnificent views, however, that
maximize the presence of the landscape in the interior. ARO
overcomes the passivity of the picture window. With what
amounts to an architectural sleight of hand, the COR-TEN
walls appear to slide like screens in and out of the house.
Their warmly rusted surfaces are evocative of Colorado's
mining history and their pattern functions as a new kind of
woven fabric that ties the scale of the rooms to their furnishings. Just as the coldness of COR-TEN is tempered by the
warm color of the shingles, the clean lines of the house are
complemented by the mid-century French furniture of Jean
Royère, Jean Prouvé, and Charlotte Perriand.

The Tucson, Arizona–based architect Rick Joy likens his Tubac
House (2000) in Tubac, Arizona, to a geode–coarse and rough
on the outside, refined and jewel-like on the inside.[13] The
Tubac House sates the twin desires of retreat and exposure,

here within the extreme conditions of the desert. This is a house defined by a series of incisions. Square and rectilinear apertures frame views both particular and panoramic. Here again, the house appears to be missing a wall (in fact, the void is a covered patio); at the same time, it is encased by planes of richly weathered steel. (The facade evokes board-and-batten facing in the same way that ARO references the shingle.) A refined interior palette—pale maple, sandblasted glass, stainless steel, and polished concrete—supports the contemplative aura of a house designed around the idea of the frame. Even the modernist furnishings defer in their modesty to the chief protagonist: the view.

Contrast is also the hallmark of EFM Design's House on Lake Erie (2002) in Port Colborne, Ontario, Canada. Architect Emanuela Frattini Magnusson exploits the contradiction between the rough stone and corrugated metal of the house's exterior and the restraint of its interior. The strength of the house's flagstone facade reinforces the sense of shelter, appropriate for the cold climate of Canada. Inside, light bounces off white walls and beech floors. Seen from the lakeside at night, the entire house becomes a giant hearth. Daylight reveals a lucid sequence of spaces, including a double-height library, airy enough to unite an eclectic mix of Scandinavian lighting, Adirondack chairs, and Frattini Magnusson's own Fazzoletto chairs.

Simon Ungers and Tom Kinslow's T-House (1992) in Wilton, New York, is not designed to mirror the grade of the landscape; rather, it is insinuated into the ground with a vertical tower that rises like a periscope from the subterranean level and then takes one masterful step out. In designing this house for a writer, Ungers and Kinslow deploy a platonic program with deadpan graphic wit—the house literally forms the letter "T"—in a woodland site that suggests not so much recreation as measured introspection. Virtually every aspect of the house is counterintuitive: a roof you can walk on, a top-heavy shaft that houses a 10,000-volume library, a steel framework of seemingly weightless suspended library shelves. The house is perforated with fenestration on all sides, but an interior shutter system can close off all the views to create continuous, uninterrupted walls. Furthermore, instead of offering contrast to the interior, the house's steel-plate facade reinforces the insistent monochrome of the interior's tongue-and-groove plywood-veneer panels. The

effect is fortress-like, offering solid protection from worldly interference yet open to the ever-elusive muse.

Where the T-House is defined by a taut relationship between its directional axes, the spaces of Rem Koolhaas's House in Bordeaux (1998) in France are literally animated by a hydraulically powered section that courses vertically through all three levels of the house. True to form, Koolhaas celebrates the open plan by puncturing it. For a client who was dependent on a wheelchair, Koolhaas designed a lift that becomes a room, that in turn becomes a mobile stage that glides up the library wall and ends under the ceiling skylight. The three horizontal volumes that comprise the house actually read as two: The main living space is a glass box improbably sandwiched between the ground-level family, kitchen, and dining rooms and the upper-level bedrooms. Furniture is spare and weightless; even the kitchen stovetop functions as a cantilevered concrete extension of the architecture. Silver-foil curtains, designed by Amsterdam-based interior designer Petra Blaisse, shield the south-facing bedrooms. The sensation of movement, both implicit and explicit, is enhanced by circular windows and doors that pivot in counterpoint to the horizontality of the house.

Perhaps the most immediate response to the conflict between exposure and retreat can be found in Alberto Campo Baeza's De Blas House (2000) in Sevilla la Nueva, Madrid, where the Miesian glass box marries the brutalist bunker in a juxtaposition of line and volume. Here, the indoor-outdoor room of the *cortile*, usually located at the center of the traditional Mediterranean house, is placed on top of a concrete block that is the house itself. Half-swallowed by the rugged terrain, its interior spaces have a deeply primal quality that is offset by the spartan purity of their white walls and floors. The ambivalence inherent in the structure–both modern house and primitive cave–can also be construed as an attempt to reconcile artifice and nature, falsely separated by twentieth-century modernism.

Organic Houses

A more obviously conciliatory response to nature can be seen in the revival of organic design, a language that engenders a strong sense of interiority and a symbolic co-dependence between structure and site. In organic design, classical Cartesian space (defined by 90-degree angles) is altered, or sometimes completely subsumed, by convoluted and subtly sensual curves. These spaces are indebted to a formal tradition that extends from the Italian baroque of Francesco Borromini through the art nouveau designs of French architect Hector Guimard to Alvar Aalto's Finnish modernism. The latest iteration of organic design has quickly become a defining characteristic of early-twenty-first-century interiors, stimulated by the use of industrial-design software as an architectural tool beginning in the mid-1990s. Frank Gehry famously pioneered the algorithmic capabilities of computer technology in public buildings as early as 1993 in the Frederick R. Weisman Art Museum at the University of Minnesota. The possibilities for the same technology in residential buildings are just beginning to be explored.

The arcing space that dominates the living room of Hitoshi Abe's n-house (2000) in Tokyo is less a mimetic response to

the natural features of the landscape than a spatial fold occasioned by the constraint of a small site. Designed for a couple who required a series of discrete rooms for themselves and their grown children, the n-house is a chain of boxes pinched to fit onto the buildable portion of the lot. The living room buckles in a dramatic arch that is incised by a pair of skylights. The sensuality of the ceiling's cascading lines is enhanced by the amplitude of the foyer's double staircase.

Despite the predictable effects of the computer on the design process, digital technology has facilitated the production of spaces that are highly idiosyncratic. Craft has become more, not less, important with the advent of programs that yield unique forms that cannot be specified in conventional construction parlance. So, it is hardly coincidental that along with the appearance of digital explorations of blobs and boxes that flourished in the late twentieth century, there has also been a resurgence of more personal and handcrafted houses. These houses make claims to both greater environmental compatibility and greater sustainability.

One hallmark of contemporary organic design—digitally rendered, tail-fin-like forms—found early expression in architect Javier Senosiain Aguilar's fantastical shark-shaped house (1990) for his family in Mexico City. Here, the house explicitly reverts to the cavern. Aguilar carves voids out of ferroconcrete, fitting his home to his family like a well-worn garment. He inserts furniture into floors and walls that grow from a single undulating envelope, lowering the house's center of gravity and bringing its residents in more immediate contact with the floor. An exercise in mixed metaphors, the shark-like exterior houses a warren of cochlear spaces. Echoing the organic functionalism of architects from Erich Mendelsohn to Antonio Gaudí, the design embodies the architect's affinity for the surreal, as well as his aspirations to create an environmental blueprint for living in the land. Another example of this hybrid, hand-crafted naturalism can be found on Great Mercury Island in New Zealand, in a home designed and built in 1997 by architect Savin Couëlle with a team of craftsmen from his native Sardinia. Commissioned by the couple who own the island, the house is a marriage of eccentricity and convention.[14] The mildly hallucinatory effects of the interior's rippled stucco walls are grounded in flat, tiled floors that make no claims to naturalism. Likewise, complex vaulted arches are intersected by rough-hewn wooden

beams. This is both cottage and cave, more a narrative about a coastal site than a merger with it. Throughout the house, stone, tile, and plaster surfaces are accentuated with shards of blue glass, driftwood, and sailcloth to reinforce the romance of a seaside house hewn from the rocky shoreline.

Unlike Aguilar and Couëlle, who bring a homegrown, do-it-yourself ethos to the subculture of the organic house, Kathryn Findlay and Eisaku Ushida bring a finely honed professionalism to the form. Trained, respectively, at the Architectural Association in London and at the offices of Arata Isozaki and Richard Rogers, Findlay and Ushida play with the potential of nonlinear geometry in the Soft and Hairy House (1994) in Baraki, Japan, in a manner that is both familiar and alien. To begin with, the main room of the house is the bathroom, enclosed in the shell of a bright blue pod. Its soft dimpled walls have a distinctly cartoon-like dimension—the complex character of Japanese anime, simultaneously childlike and adult. In a womb-like interior, the house offers the comforting infantilism of retro-future nostalgia. But for all the evocations of space-age fantasy and Salvador Dalí's surrealism, what is really being reinvigorated in the Soft and Hairy House are the possibilities for the sensual and experiential. As with all of Findlay and Ushida's work, the house strives for a continuity between the body and space through a combination of wit, intuition, and mathematical modeling, two seemingly incompatible realms. Here the proto-futuristic dome-spaces of visionaries like Buckminster Fuller are being realized with digital technology that was unavailable to designers of previous generations. Furthermore, instead of transforming the bath into a glorified living room, as so many Western developers have done over the course of the last decade, Findlay and Ushida take it back to its primal state.

The Retreat

Less unorthodox in form, but equally striking, are houses with orthogonal plans designed to satisfy a desire for retreat that is both social and physical. In the examples that follow we see contemporary interpretations of the house as fortress. Even when imbedded in the land, these interiors flow from a design ethos that sees nature not as spectacle but as another layer of insulation. Unlike the houses that opened this chapter, whose design reflects a philosophical predisposition to erasing binary oppositions between nature and nurture, between architecture and its environment, the following

houses are shaped by subliminal, primal antagonisms to
social intrusions (which have multiplied exponentially with
communication technologies) and harsh climactic conditions.
Paolo Zermani's house for his family (1997) in Varano, Italy,
just outside of Parma, is an essay in privacy that draws deeply
on the psychology of protection. Zermani is of the Emilia
Romana school of Italian architecture, which crafts its modernity from the severe regional archetypes of shed and barn, and
which claims the late Aldo Rossi as its spiritual figurehead.

Stepping into the eye of the Zermani house–the entrance is
an enormous oculus–it becomes immediately apparent that
customary sightlines have been called into question. A large
circular window is centered behind the oculus, creating a
series of concentric voids. The interior behind it is oriented
away from the view, its intimacy belied by the massive
geometries of the facade. Behind the twin circles of entrance
and window sits a slender two-story library with room for
just two chairs facing a black steel fireplace. Above the
hearth is an oval portrait of a woman, intended, perhaps, as

OMA/Office for Metropolitan Architecture, House in Bordeaux, Bordeaux, France, 1998

Campo Baeza Architecture Studio, De Blas House, Sevilla la Nueva,
Madrid, 2000

a surrogate to the house's inhabitants, who are otherwise
invisible and protected within. The house presents itself as
a conundrum, a Chinese puzzle of nested geometries, and
repeats the game again on the second floor with a guest
room that is a veritable house within the house. The design
of the interior tempers the iconic symbols of modernity
with the language of the farmhouse. Windows with I-beam
lintels are covered with simple eyelet embroidered curtains;
dark-raftered ceilings meet bright, white-stucco walls that
compensate for the house's extreme sense of enclosure. The
furnishings, too, offer a stark juxtaposition: a combination of
family antiques and Zermani's sturdy but minimalist limited-
edition pieces. This architect's residence is not so much a
professional advertisement as it is a home for an architect
and his family, an observatory directed inside, not out.

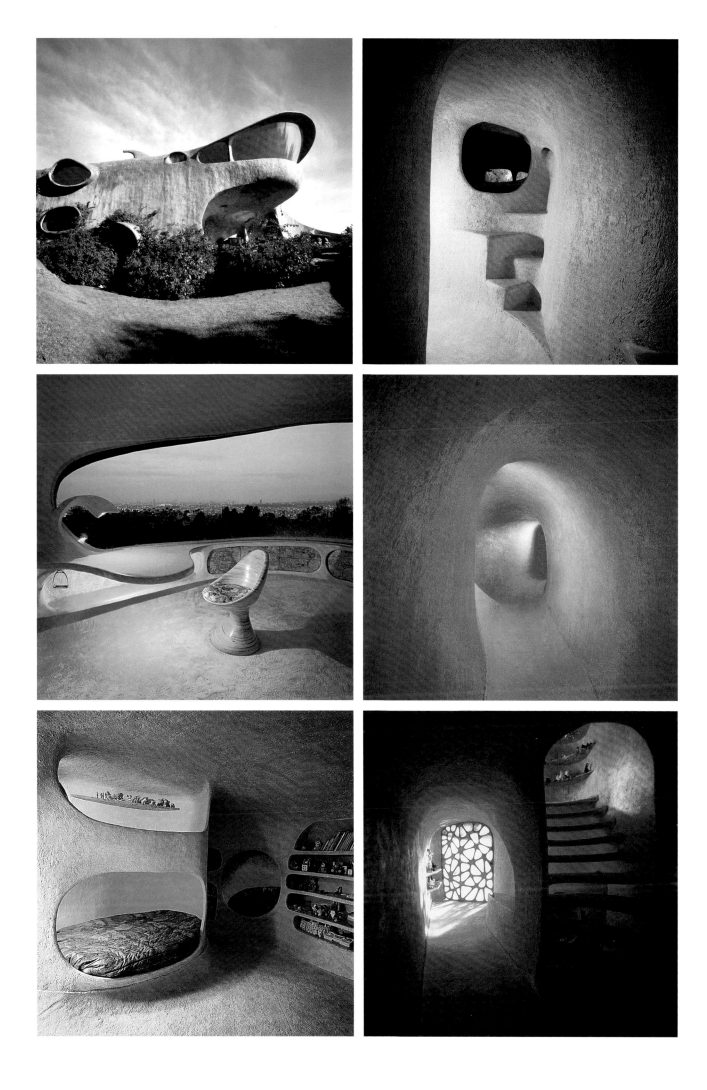

Interiority is also the defining characteristic of the self-effacing Moledo House (1998) in Moledo, Portugal, designed by Portuguese architect Eduardo Souto de Moura. By embedding the house into a rocky hillside, Souto de Moura carves a cave for the modernist box and gives it a regional inflection. The site is landscaped as three enormous stone steps cut out of natural granite. The uppermost step shields the facade of the house proper. Just behind that wall are full-height glass doors that run along the entire front of the house but afford a view only to the centrally placed living/dining room. (Here again, furnishings are positioned for inward-focused social interaction, not window gazing.) All of the other rooms are enveloped by the natural rock formations behind the house or by the massive stone walls in front of it. Natural light enters the house through light wells formed by a narrow wedge of space between the perimeter of the house and its site. The relatively open public area is linked to the landscape by an exterior stone wall that reaches inside and serves as both hearth and partition in the living room and provides a screen for the kitchen. In addition to imparting an almost reclusive sense of privacy, the design accomplishes the additional feat of making a six-bedroom, seven-bath villa seem modest. Indeed, it all but disappears.

The introspective psychology of the Villa Sipione (1995) in Sicily, by the Roman firm Lazzarini Pickering, is both pragmatic and cultural, driven by the extreme Sicilian sunlight and a distinct sense of place. In their renovation of this nineteenth-century villa, the architects inserted a new floor containing three bedrooms, two bathrooms, and a staircase in an existing double-height space beside the living room. Each of these rooms is oriented inward. A fine cut in a central wall that extends up through the terrace admits a blade of light into the vaulted living room, creating an indoor sundial that traces the passing of the hours and the seasons. Windows, coterminous with the facade, have deep interior recesses that accentuate the protective nature of the house's thick stucco walls. The rugged floors of the bathrooms and kitchen are a local sandstone called *pece* that has been colored by subterranean oil deposits; a range of hues—beige, dark brown, light gray, black—can appear in a single stone. Closed but not claustrophobic, the brilliantly white spaces are furnished with family heirlooms and pieces designed by the architects.

Ushida Findlay, Soft and Hairy House, Baraki, Japan, 1994

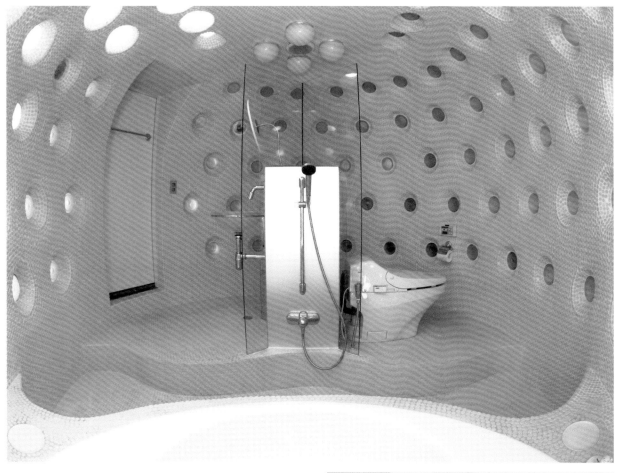

Despite its name and London location, the Dirty House (2002) is not even remotely dark inside, though it is tautly closed in on itself. Designed by British architect David Adjaye for a pair of artists, the house was named for an artwork the clients once made from six months' worth of accumulated trash. Adjaye employs strategies particular to houses that retire from their surroundings, but he uses them here to expansive affect. Windows are set flush with the facade on the first floor and are deeply recessed on the second, suggesting a fortified palazzo, a sense immediately contradicted in the luminous interior. In actuality, this is a glass house hiding behind walls. A system of skylights and channels cut into the interior—the architect calls them "light chimneys"[15]—allows daylight to filter down through the house, where it is reflected by the white walls and ceilings. On the topmost floor, a glass wall wraps all the way around the combined living and kitchen space, where painted planks underfoot recall the rough wood floors of industrial lofts. Windows that could afford a spectacular panorama are reduced to a clerestory by a balcony

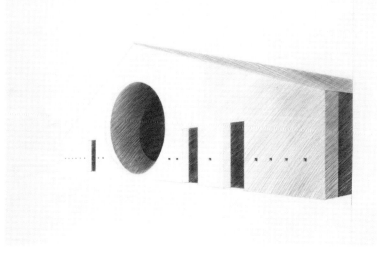

Souto Moura Architects, Moledo House, Moledo, Caminha, Portugal, 1998

that partially obscures the view to reinforce the governing idea of protected exposure.

Historically, the primary impetus for clustering houses together behind walls was protection from siege, as was the case in traditional medieval cities. Today, privacy replaces defense as the justification for walled compounds. With its double-height white entrance wall, Grupo LBC's House on Escondido River (2003) in Mexico City falls into this category of cloistered structures. In contrast to its discrete public facade, the interior of the L-shaped house is unreservedly open with floor-to-ceiling sliding glazed doors enabling seamless indoor-outdoor living. Another interesting example of this typology is the Unfolding House (1998) in Bangkok, where a protective wall conceals a compound of five structures inhabited by an extended family. Designed by Raveevarn Choksombatchai and Ralph Nelson, formerly in partnership as Loom Studio, the house not only offers a respite from the city but also artfully accommodates the need for privacy within a multigenerational household. With the perimeter secured, the spatial metaphor shifts to the more permeable nature of the folding screen. Systems of veiled views and passageways link the residences within the compound. Courtyard facades are composed of brise-soleils, behind which windows open and close like enormous Venetian blinds, admitting light and air as the climate dictates. In contrast, interior and exterior walls are punctured with reveals and narrow incisions that animate the interior with shadow play and contribute a sense of intimacy to the extended complex.

Although Chinese architect Ma Qingyun chose to situate his Father's House in Jade Mountain (2003) around a traditional sequestered courtyard, this intimate interior space was constructed in a very public manner. Near-lying villagers and friends collected stones for two years for the building, which features exterior and courtyard walls constructed of their variegated shapes and colors, while the interior is completely lined in wood. Reflecting pools within the complex echo the jade-green rural landscape that peeks in through lower sections of the stone walls in a poetic play of public and private access. Working in Colombo, Sri Lanka, the late Geoffrey Bawa satisfied an acute desire for psychological and physical insulation in the Jayakody House (1996), designed for the daughter and son-in-law of Sri Lankan president Ranasinghe Premadasa, who was assassinated in 1993 while

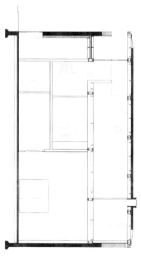

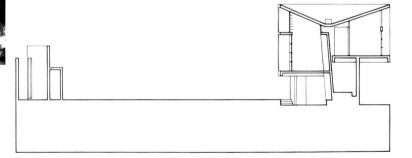

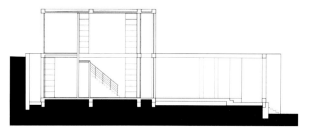

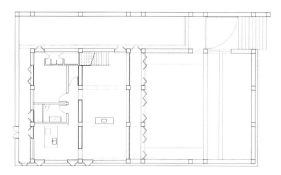

still in office. The house's neutral facade turns its back on the adjacent business district and conceals both a courtyard and a tower that capitalize on the irregularity of the house's 14,850-square-foot (1,380-square-meter) footprint. In counterpoint to the house's solid exterior walls, the interior space is animated by the plan's diagonal axis. The ground-floor reception rooms flank a lush courtyard garden; each room affords oblique views into the next in a way befitting a house based on discretion. The dining room, partly lit by a blue-painted light shaft that also supplies ventilation, suggests an almost aquatic, subterranean environment. Each of the first-floor bedrooms is accorded its own courtyard; the second and third floors have planted terraces and a swimming pool. Though the house is insulated from the city, the inclusion of plants and water emphasizes the idea of refuge in a sometimes hostile urban environment.

Australian architect David Luck's Red Hill House (2001) is an hour's drive from metropolitan Melbourne. Here, Luck joins Souto de Moura and Adjaye in subverting the Miesian glass box in pursuit of meditative space, using extensive glazing to metaphorically turn the house in on itself. This is a house designed for critical reflection: Luck deliberately refuses to commodify the view by framing it. One enters the house via a ramp that becomes a platform for a series of discrete but linked rooms, framed by sliding planes of plate glass and black steel sheets. At the end of the ramp, a fully glazed wall is blocked by a detached section of the building that deliberately cuts off views of the bay below, just as the surrounding woodland limits the house's exposure. The interior clearly conveys the potency of stillness; it is also a critique of the material consumerism of contemporary urban living– all of the furniture is built-in, not bought. This is a house that celebrates seclusion, most notably in the bedroom, where a sensuous gauze-tented bed becomes a room within a room.

The Shed

Houses like Luck's Red Hill are part of an evolving critical regionalism, a way of building and designing inspired by a critique of undifferentiated, international modernism first advanced by architectural historian Kenneth Frampton in the early 1980s.[16] By this time, the social and aesthetic ambitions of high modernism had been bankrupted by insensitive imitation and cheap construction technologies. Even more significantly, the stylistic uniformity of modernism had

failed to take local cultures and local landscapes into account, at the very moment when cultural pluralism was beginning to be acknowledged. The regionalist theory has been seen as particularly relevant in Australia, where culture and climate came together in the vernacular of the rural shed. With its strong, simple lines, the shed proved especially compatible with the economies of modernism. (It is important to note that Frampton's theory did not reject the formal innovations of modernism, like the open plan, so much as it sought ways to modulate those innovations with deference to place.)

The theory of critical regionalism, with its emphasis on local light, materials, and building techniques, influenced some of the earliest efforts to develop environmentally sustainable houses, notably the Marika-Alderton House (1994) in Australia's Northern Territory by Pritzker Prize–winning Australian architect Glenn Murcutt. Designed for an Aboriginal artist and her husband, the simple, open rectangular space does not tap conventional energy resources. With no glass windows, walls function as shutters and vertical metal fins hang from the rafters to direct cooling breezes. Its simple interior, with plywood walls and an exposed corrugated metal roof as the

ceiling, is not atmospheric but an atmosphere, a climate that is manually monitored to mitigate the tropical climate of its site. With a minimalist architectural intervention, exterior and interior become one, honoring the land-based culture of the Aborigines.[17]

A more fully realized example of Murcutt's particular brand of critical regionalism can be seen in his Fletcher-Page House (1998) in Kangaroo Valley, in the southeastern part of the country. Concrete floors and a corrugated pitched ceiling contain Scandinavian modern furnishings and simple white cabinetry within a loft-like open plan. The vernacular shed form accommodates a classical enfilade along the entire south side of the rectangular footprint. On the north side of the house, Murcutt conflates the window and the blind into a triangular structure that opens out at an angle opposite to the pitch of the roof. These window "bellows" not only regulate airflow and reduce energy consumption but also enliven its formal geometry.

The wedge-shaped interior, with cool recesses that seamlessly open onto the vista, is explored more formally in Richard

Meier's Neugebauer House (1998) in Naples, Florida. Drawing less on associations with the working shed than with the regal canopy, Meier creates a butterfly roofline that shelters all but the utilitarian spaces, affording bedrooms and living rooms alike spectacular views of the bay. A delicate brise-soleil casts patterns of shadows that animate the walls and furnishings while providing an elegant, passive solar control.

The interior of Izar House (2002) in Valle de Bravo, Mexico, designed by GA/Grupo Arquitectura, opens like a pair of scissors. To accommodate the site conditions of the steeply sloped property, the architects designed a 1,320-foot (402-meter) steel structure to suspend it in place. Because the roof of the house is supported by the steel pillars of its pre-fabricated skeleton, its walls are released from their structural function. Freestanding, they enhance the floating effect of the angled ceiling while effectively separating the public and private regions of the house. In parallel sequence, the partition walls laterally divide Izar House's rectangular footprint into four bedrooms and a combined living/dining room, all with views into the woodland, all comfortably furnished with contemporary pieces in a neutral palette. Operable glass walls

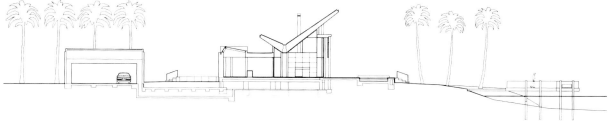

surround the living area, sheltering it from the elements or, in good weather, transforming it into a furnished outdoor room.

In Glade House (2003), a family beach retreat located 45 miles (72 kilometers) north of Sydney, Peter Stutchbury of Stutchbury and Pape breaks up the shed roof into a series of awnings. The house is configured around a courtyard, the central communal "room" of the house. The simply furnished living and dining areas, when not sheltered by a movable wall, function as extensions of the outdoors. In this modernist compound, the kitchen becomes a picnic venue, ready to roll out from under the house's three signature hovering ceiling planes. Behind these communal spaces, bedrooms and baths retreat into the rainforest under another gently sloping roof.

The Domesticated Shed

Each of the three final projects embrace domestic interior conventions at the same time as they test them. The first inserts a modern aesthetic into the shell of the shed; the second creates a new shed while embracing a do-it-yourself

ethos; and the third treats the house as a found object that in turn becomes a cabinet of curiosities.

In the case of a country house for designer Ingegerd Råman and her husband Claes Söderquist (2001) in Southern Sweden, the shed is an old school house that was converted into a home by the Swedish firm CKR/Claesson Koivisto Rune. The volume was stripped down to reveal the roof line and gracefully reconfigured with steel-and-glass-framed doors, new interior walls, and exposed bleached-pine floorboards. Storage is concealed behind the walls on the second floor, eliminating further visual distraction and reinforcing the sense of quiet that pervades the light-filled house. The minimalist interiors accentuate the compatibility of peasant chairs, Alvar Aalto pieces, and custom furnishings like CKR's own 13-foot-long (4-meter-long) dining table.

The renovated schoolhouse is exceptionally beautiful in its graceful accommodation of the past into its designers' Scandinavian modern sensibilities, but doesn't stray far

from canonical modern design: its furnishings and surfaces still acquiesce to the demand for "pure" space. By contrast, the next two projects—the Harris Butterfly House by Rural Studio in Alabama, and the Holtzman house in upstate New York by interior designer Joseph Holtzman—welcome the idiosyncratic, valorize the personal, and are antithetical to codified notions of style. Both interiors honor the intuition of the amateur and the expertise of the professional. Moreover, they are symbolic of a new openness and eclecticism that has been building momentum since 1971, when architects Robert Venturi and Denise Scott Brown first coined the term "decorated shed." At the time, Venturi and Scott Brown were referring to any building "where systems of space and structure are directly at the service of program, and ornament is applied independently of them."[18] Early champions of the emotional function of ornament in transforming unadulterated spaces into homes, the architects' critique of the late International Style opened a Pandora's box of stylistic pluralism, a box whose lid has never been closed. Indeed, in every interior typology examined in this book,

there is growing evidence of a new appetite for the crafted and the decorative.

Today, the term "decorated shed" has begun to take on a new- and more literal-meaning. No longer is there a single canon to be modulated, as in the case of critical regionalism or classicized postmodernism or even Venturi's populism, but a rich history of ideas spanning the centuries. Venturi must be duly credited for his critical role in recognizing the tremendous social value attached to everyday design, for making it "possible to accept the casual and the improvised in the built environment."[19] However, the influence of product designers like Hella Jongerius and Marcel Wanders of the Netherlands, as well as fashion designers such as the Belgians Martin Margiela and Ann Demeulemeester, has been reinvigorating design with wit, craft, new materials, and intelligent appropriations.

The terms "casual' and "improvised" are almost too tame to describe the ebullience of the Harris Butterfly House (1997),

one of the first design-build houses to come out of the late Samuel Mockbee's Rural Studio at Auburn University in Alabama. The clients for this and all of the studio's projects are poor residents of Hale County who are in need of new housing. The structures are designed to be as energy efficient as possible and are built with inexpensive and recycled materials with a locally inspired aesthetic that never condescends or resorts to kitsch. Rather, they are recognizably modern in their architectural sensibility.

The Harris family's Butterfly House in Mason's Bend, Alabama, has a striking, raked roofline that covers a generous screened porch (in lieu of air conditioning) and gives enormous presence to an interior whose flowing space and high pitched ceiling belie the house's modest footprint. The architectural virtues never overshadow the furnishings and personal possessions of the elderly couple who live in the house; these include a trove of homemade collages and a permanent installation of indoor Christmas lights. Nor

were the clients mere recipients of architectural largesse. They actively participated in the design process. It was the client's concern over wasted space that led to the suspension of a loft in the living room's pitched ceiling, a move that created another set of views within and without. The synthesis of personal decoration and formal architectural space is complete and respectful; neither censors the other.

Joseph Holtzman, a designer and the former publisher of *Nest* magazine, shows no such deference to built reality when, as both client and designer, he creates decoratively surreal effects in his summer home—called Camp Nest (2002)—in Ghent, New York. Holtzman sees Camp Nest as a work in progress, an incubator of the new iconoclastic interior. Here, decoration is concentrated on every surface of the proverbial shed, in this case an undistinguished 1950s gabled house. There are countless surfaces to read, from baseball-themed walls imprinted with beeswax, to marijuana-leaf patterned chintz upholstered chairs, to a room that is delineated by a

Samuel Mockbee/Rural Studio, Harris Butterfly House, Mason's Bend, Alabama, 1997

Joseph Holtzman, Camp Nest, Ghent, New York, 2002

drawing of a room. Ceilings are not simply lids on boxes, but canvases to be striped, patterned, or scored—an optical reward for merely lying down. Each room is endlessly hospitable and entertaining to the eye. The house's furnishings are almost compulsively eclectic and never static or frozen in display like their conventional glass-house counterparts.

Like the Butterfly House, Camp Nest is also the product of student contributions, a collective endeavor by interns working under Holtzman's direction. For all its oddity, however, the house is not an isolated phenomenon. Camp Nest shares in a growing culture of iconoclasm that has profited from the permissiveness—if not the formal languages—of postmodernism. Camp Nest is a polemic of possibility. Uniquely adventurous, Holtzman's approach engages architecture but is just as likely to deny it with illusion and optical games. It is an approach more familiar to designers of apartments and lofts, considered in the next chapters, where architecture is by and large received, not invented.

Apartments

The success of the apartment has become so associated with the advent of the elevator and the evolution of the city that it is often mistakenly thought of as a nineteenth-century phenomenon. In fact, the apartment building as we know it today is less an invention than an innovation–a refinement of a dwelling type that dates back to imperial Rome. Typically three or four stories tall, but sometimes rising as high as eight stories, the Roman archetype–an apartment block called an *insula*–was arranged around a courtyard, with shops on the ground floor and residential quarters above. Though they were plagued by structural inadequacies and fire, substantial remnants of *insulae* dating from the early second century AD still survive at the mouth of the Tiber River in Ostia. Remarkably little has changed in the actual living arrangements within the apartment since their time. Two millennia later, at the Unité d'Habitation (1952) in Marseille, France, Le Corbusier used essentially the same floor plan, placing bedrooms at either end of the rectangular volume and connecting them with a functional spine.

For all the continuity observed in the interior layout of his apartments, Le Corbusier has been credited with promoting the only substantial change in the concept of stacked dwellings: the three-dimensional, detached high-rise, set apart in the urban landscape–the proverbial tower in the park. Architectural historian Vincent Scully theorizes that Le Corbusier's intent was to give the apartment building its own privileged architectural status and to eradicate any lingering social stigma. For, despite its venerable history, by the nineteenth century the apartment had become associated with loose morality and slums, and was viewed as another symptom of urban ills– particularly in the United States. In his claims for the apartment tower's essential humanism, Scully goes so far as to posit that that the Corbusian apartment building was "like a Greek temple [in] ... its sculptural scale," offering "an image of human uprightness [that] ... dignifies all its individual units."[1]

Ironically, it could be argued that the precedent for Le Corbusier's freestanding apartment building was built on decidedly undemocratic foundations. For centuries, the raison d'être of communal architecture was the concentration of power and prestige, the most famous of which was the palace of Versailles. A very different kind of tower in the park, by 1710 it contained 226 dwellings, twice as many single rooms, and some 10,000 residents.[2] Such congestion was tolerable

as a necessary condition of court life, but it became intolerable when it devolved into urban tenement houses. The apartment regained its respectability in the mid-1900s by offering the aristocratic amenities of the full-service hotel–a move intended to offset the indignities of a collective dwelling and to erase any lingering whiff of the workhouse or the tenement. In New York, for example, Henry Hardenbergh based his design of the Dakota (1881–84) on Parisian models first introduced by Richard Morris Hunt in his 1869–70 Stuyvesant Flats.[3] The Dakota was specifically meant to appeal to affluent tenants who would find its amenities and luxurious appointments handsome compensations for apartment living. Those still harboring qualms about living under a shared roof were appeased by the spectacular privileges of the penthouse. Even today, the freestanding apartment tower with views on all sides remains synonymous with luxury. Certainly it affords the architect and designer more latitude in manipulating the framework of the space, whereas most apartment design is generally restricted to lining the envelope.

Whether working in the model of the regal palace or the republican *insula*, today's designers not only personalize space with décor but also increasingly address the psychology of personal space. The interior is the critical realm where architects, designers, and clients challenge the inherent limitations of standardization to reflect individual preferences, tastes, and social patterns, as well as to explore purely formal, aesthetic conventions. This chapter will explore two broad categories of apartment design: first, that seen in newly constructed apartment buildings, in which new approaches to the interior are integral; and, second, that of apartments in pre-existing structures. These two general rubrics encompass a tremendous variety, given the highly personal and transitory nature of apartment life. What matters here is the designer's intent. Is it to mirror the client's personality? To create a narrative from other contexts? Or is it, perhaps, to eliminate any suggestion of narrative outside of those supplied by the client's sheer physical presence? These are the questions that drive this chapter's explorations.

Apartment Towers

At the opening of the twenty-first century, the free-standing apartment tower has become associated with the most prominent names in design and architecture. Where the first principle of real estate was once "location, location, location,"

today apartment sales are just as likely to be driven by an
architect's signature, be it the engineering tour de force of
Santiago Calatrava's Turning Torso in Malmö, Sweden, the
pristine glamour of Richard Meier's Perry Street apartments
in New York, or the sensuous luxury of Philippe Starck's
international chain of Yoo Apartments. This is not an isolated
phenomenon, but part of a broader consumer pattern in which
value is generated by celebrity endorsement; the novelty is
that entire buildings are now perceived as objects, much the
same as cars or clothing or sports equipment. Partly to mitigate
this preoccupation with the building's facade and form, and
partly to achieve the ideal of a fully integrated environment,
architects have become increasingly involved in the interior
design of their buildings. By bridging the aesthetic languages
of interior and exterior, these designers don't dictate décor
but offer residents cues for articulating the blank slate of
the apartment.

In a housing complex in Fukuoka, Japan, New York architect
Steven Holl draws on Japanese cultural traditions and his own
preoccupation with what he calls "porous space" to mitigate
the impersonality of the generic apartment. In a thoroughly
contemporary interpretation of *fusama*, the sliding partitions
of traditional Japanese architecture, the Void Spaced/Hinged
Space Housing (1991) is designed around the hinge–both the
device and the idea. Twenty-eight interlocking apartments
on five floors are splayed off a single spine to admit natural
light on three sides of each unit. The footprint of each unit is
identical to that of the next, but interior walls pivot to allow
maximum freedom; residents can expand the living area during the day to include the spaces used for sleeping at night.
In addition to allowing for such day-to-day modifications, the
design also takes a long view toward family life, permitting
rooms to be added or subtracted as children are born or leave
home or when elderly parents move in. In a deft synthesis
of design and culture, variously colored walls, judiciously
introduced, reinforce the planarity associated with Japanese
interiors while at the same time deferring to individual tastes.

In an apartment block called The Grid (2001) in Sydney, Tina
Engelen and Ian Moore of the Australian firm Engelen Moore
use richly hued wood panels for doors and closets to establish
chromatic distinctions within each apartment. A decade after
the completion of Holl's Fukuoka housing, this firm takes
up similar issues of flexibility by deploying floor-to-ceiling

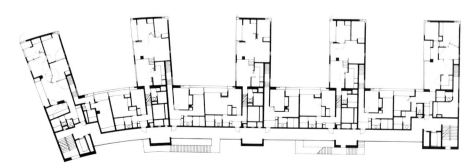

sliding screens to delineate corridors in each apartment
and give privacy to the bedrooms that are passed en route
to the central service pods. These pods, which contain the
kitchen, laundry room, and bathroom, are clad in dark gray
polyurethane and read as large furniture elements within the
apartment's white walls and ceiling planes. In the Honeysett
penthouse apartment, Engelen Moore produced a fully realized interior using a neutral palette of tan, gray, and white
furnishings, including Tulip family tables and Womb chairs
by Eero Saarinen. Such normative modernism certainly contributes to the commercial appeal of the apartment, neither
threateningly idiosyncratic nor overly tame in its design.

In GA/Grupo Arquitectura's Terremoto Building (2003) in
Mexico City, the concept of fluid boundaries derived from
the East works in tandem with the Latinate model of the
outdoor room—specifically the terrace, the private microcosm
of the public plaza. Each standard apartment in the Terremoto
Building boasts a single balconied terrace—a relatively
conventional means of testing the limits of confinement in
an apartment building. But in the two duplex penthouses,
whose interiors were also designed by Grupo Arquitectura,
the terrace assumes a new dimension as a full-size room—23
by 56 feet (7 by 17 meters)—equal in stature to the other
public spaces of the apartment. As if to accentuate the luxury
of the additional space, the upper level is accessed via a
fractured set of stairs: a block of travertine steps separated
by a reveal from a slightly narrower wood staircase hovering
above it. Here, a large hearth brings an indoor motif outside
in a subtle game of reversed expectations. Below, in the
dining room, green-tinted glass echoes the blue sky, offering
a cool contrast to the brown-and-white palette of the walls,
floors, and furnishings.

Though they are designed for specific clients, Engelen Moore
and GA/Grupo Arquitectura's penthouse interiors are, in a
sense, model apartments, intended to illustrate the architects'
ideal scenario. In contrast, the modular interiors of Philippe
Starck's Yoo Apartments—real estate ventures in London
(2002), Hong Kong (2004), and Miami Beach (2005)—offer
choices that transcend mere color palettes but stop short
of a full range of actual furnishings (though that, too, is an
option). Starck's approach is rooted in thematized marketing
strategies traditionally used by furniture companies. For
example, in the mid-twentieth century, American families

bought suites of furniture with names such as Mediterranean, Colonial, or Contemporary, and inserted them into indeterminate spaces. For the twenty-first century, Starck reverses the equation by theming the space itself with materials, colors, and fixtures that suggest complementary furnishings. "It is not healthy for people to live in the fantasy of their interior designers," says Starck, who describes his design brief as helping people "figure out what type of person they are: nature, culture, classic, or minimal."[4] These four ideas constitute the menu of options in apartments Starck has designed and co-developed. These options, however, are so open-ended as to defy distinction: Polished chrome is intended to cue "culture," wood paneling suggests "classic," oak references "nature," and clear white marble conveys "minimal." (Only "culture" is altered in accordance with the market.) For anyone desiring a sharper focus, Starck proposes lamps, carpeting, window blinds, and furniture, much of which is of his own design.[5]

Similarly, Conran & Partners' Roppongi Hills Residences (2003) in Tokyo are designed to give inhabitants a choice of interior plans, palettes, and materials synchronized with the furnishings marketed by Conran stores. Instead of offering personality profiles, however, the apartments' appointments are meant to suggest different affinities with nature–a strategy that counterbalances the decidedly urban character of the five high-rise towers. "Forest" is the name given to a two-story plan with a double-height living room that offers dramatic views of Tokyo; this plan is executed in three different woods: cherry, walnut, and oak. "Desert," fittingly, has the most open plan and offers extensive sandstone shelving, oak floors, and brown gradations on white walls. With black limestone floors and blue nubuck-clad shelving, "Mountain" aspires to hipness but borders on grandiose. While the premise for the Roppongi Hills Residences is similar to that of the Yoo Apartments, the Conran apartments are not condominiums but rentals that cater to long-term business stays. The furnished Roppongi Residences are, in essence, an alternative to a hotel. In that respect they are part of a growing trend in residential interiors that replicate the aesthetics and amenities of the luxury hotel–a clear case of history repeating itself.

Even more common than partnerships with home furnishings companies are synergies between real estate developers and

high-profile architects who bring assurance of a known aesthetic and the rationale for a higher market value. Two recent projects by Pritzker Prize–winners show how the relationship between design and development can transcend expectations while still remaining commercially viable. In the case of the 178-foot-tall (54-meter-tall) Céramique Tower (1998) in Maastricht, The Netherlands, the Dutch government invited Portuguese architect Álvaro Siza to design a high-end rental complex as part of a master plan for the city that included the participation of such internationally recognized talent as Mario Botta and Herman Hertzberger. Siza designed all of the penthouse apartment's furnishings himself: tables, chairs, desk lamps, even the welcoming red figure painted on the wall beside the front door. Significantly, the apartment is also intended as a short-stay business rental, again loosely

conforming to the hotel model. The other 34 apartments, housed in two towers for maximum light, benefit from Siza's floor plans and communal amenities. It is notable that Siza's designs, and his considerable reputation, have succeeded in attracting upmarket renters in a country that promotes home ownership.

With 173/176 Perry Street (2002), Richard Meier has created a pair of luminous, 16-story glass-and-steel towers along Manhattan's West Side Highway. Befitting his modernist pedigree, Meier eschewed the historicist models favored by most New York developers. Architecture critic Herbert Muschamp described the towers' interiors as "neutral but aesthetically charged environments" that have the pure "radiance" of the art gallery loft.[6] Indeed, as in the typical

Conran & Partners, Roppongi Hills Residences, "Mountain," Tokyo, 2003   Álvaro Siza Architect, Céramique Tower, Maastricht, The Netherlands, 1998

loft building, there is one open-plan apartment per floor.
Floor-to-ceiling windows in each apartment offer breathtaking,
almost vertiginous views of the Hudson River. Apart from
space planning, Meier's involvement with the interior was
minimal: The glass walls themselves become panoramas of
the exterior, and rooms are saturated with sun- and starlight.

By contrast, in the 165 Charles Street apartments, a 16-story
project completed in 2006 just south of the Perry Street
towers in New York, Meier designed both the exterior and
the interiors. The material palette conforms to Meier's well-
known minimalist ethos: jet-mist granite, wengé wood floors,
and exquisitely understated white Surell kitchen and bathroom surfaces. The expansive nature of the building's western
views is complemented by ceilings that range from 11 to 16
feet (3.5 to 5 meters) in height. But the most interesting
aspect of the apartments is their refined informality. The
layout of a one-bedroom apartment, for example, comprises
a loft-style combined kitchen/dining/living space facing the
Hudson River. The bedroom needs no door, as it is positioned
at the rear of the space and is accessed along a fully fenestrated hallway. Opaque glass reveals between rooms allude
to connectivity without breaching privacy. Still, Meier's
design, which balances the constraints of predetermined
fixtures against the freedom of the open plan, refrains from
anticipating the needs and desires of tenants who provide
their own furnishings.

Individual Apartments

To the extent that the branded apartment building becomes an intentional community of like-minded residents attracted by a singular designer, it contradicts the nature of urban life. Just as cities are defined by the random encounters of their polyglot populations, so apartment buildings are more typically a mix of radically different interiors reflecting the individuality of residents who might have little more than a floor plan in common. While it's true that the period and location of an apartment building do influence the makeup of its tenants to some extent, rarely do those tenants' tastes conform to any aesthetic model, as would be expected in the interiors, for example, of a Richard Meier building or the Jean Nouvel tower (under construction at this writing) at 40 Mercer Street in Lower Manhattan. If anything, the opposite is true. In a post-Freudian age, the apartment interior becomes a surrogate for the "examined life," an extension of the life-long pursuit of self-actualization. The process favors

definitive acts of addition and subtraction that result in a formal whole. Design by accretion is a luxury largely outside the parameters of most commissions. Only in their own homes can designers afford to approach the interior as a work in progress.

Designer Self-Portraits

It is not a completely unfair generalization to say that Europeans, with their long experience of dense urban living, have learned more adroitly than others to live with overlapping layers of history without either sacrificing the respect for the new or being constrained by cultural constants. Andrée Putman, the doyenne of French interior design, has made her own home a model of the virtues of disciplined acquisition. She recognizes that "Doing one's own home is dangerous if you fail at making your own self-portrait."[7] It is telling that she has been in the same apartment in Paris since 1978, choosing to alter it in 1994 rather than move, and that it

still looks prescient. Case in point: The gauze netting that enshrouds her bedroom hints at the return of the veil to interiors, a gesture most recently reprised by Dutch designer Petra Blaisse and the late American designer Mary Bright.[8]

Contemporary modernism has now matured enough to have caught up with the intelligent eclecticism pioneered in France by interior decorators like Madeleine Castaing (who died in 1992) and Putman. However, where Castaing was promiscuous in mixing styles and epochs, Putman is considerably more disciplined in her choices, decidedly more faithful to the history of modernism—particularly to France's seminal contributions, from Le Corbusier to art deco. Pieces by Eileen Gray and Jacques-Émile Ruhlmann dominate but also accommodate. Putman says she likes to "group objects very close to each other, as close friends, although they were never assembled before."[9] To wit, the French modernists play host to other periods and regional styles, from an eighteenth-

century carved-mirror German grandfather clock to contemporary art by Julian Schnabel and Lucio Fontana to ancient Egyptian tomb sculpture. Putman believes "the mutual relation between objects—even with violence—gives an incredible energy to a room."[10]

One of the challenges in considering such personal spaces is their resistance to aesthetic theory, to codified movements and style, and their susceptibility to mere description. They are neither wholly modernist nor emphatically historicist stage sets that can be struck at any time. Designers like Putman, however, make the case for a critical approach that is anchored in culture. They have the ability to absorb unrelated but compatible elements into a convincing whole and to create a personal sense of place with its own specific geography.

The same might also be said of Mario Bellini in the design and redesign of his palazzo apartment in Milan, in 1974 and

2004 respectively. Certainly, the overriding context is Italian, from the frescoes of Milanese architect Piero Portaluppi (1888–1967) that Bellini inherited with the space, to the furniture of his own design, to his collection of Novecento paintings, Gio Ponti lighting, Venini glass, and Venetian mirrors. But here again, nationalism is tempered in Bellini's study by an Anglo-Saxon work ethic embodied in Norman Foster's Nomos table, in the living room by gargantuan German Avantgarde Acoustic speakers, in the bathroom by pony-skin-clad Tom Dixon chairs, and in the bedroom by a sixteenth-century Aubusson tapestry. Where Putman relies on her acute formal sensibilities, Bellini, the pioneer of product semantics (a facet of postmodern expressionism), puts his trust in language and memory.[11] Furnishings are carefully placed so they speak to each other, beginning in the foyer, where the rationality of an Aldo Rossi architectural model squares off against the surreality of a Memphis table by Ettore Sottsass. To enter the public space of the living room–which Bellini likens to a city–one steps through an architectural portal designed by Bellini's friend and colleague Gae Aulenti in the first renovation. On the second floor are more intimate spaces for dining, sleeping, and bathing– zones where the social gives way to the private, all beneath American artist David Tremlett's newly commissioned ceiling frescoes. Because the evolution of the design of the

Bellini apartment essentially mirrors that of a family– specifically the Italian idea of *famiglia*, which embraces both the personal and the cultural–formal cohesion is secondary to the telling of a personal history.

By contrast, Lee Mindel of Manhattan's Shelton, Mindel & Associates, furnishes his New York penthouse (2000) with the critical eye of a curator and the dedication of a committed collector. There is an integral relationship between the lucid architectonics of the apartment and his collection, which includes furniture by Charles and Ray Eames, Jean Prouvé, Josef Hoffmann, Hans Wegner, and Alvar Aalto, as well as art by Richard Serra, Robert Ryman, and Alexander Calder. There is one bold exception to the classically modern ensemble: the glass chandelier created by Syrie Maugham for Venini in the 1930s over the Shelton, Mindel & Associates dining room table. Mindel's is a postminimalist aesthetic, with clean lines and "access to things that make you feel good [but] … not a victim to those things."[12] Objects, like the chandelier, are on view as though in a gallery; they are never treated as set decorations. Public rooms are arrayed around a central spherical structure, creating a sense of movement that subliminally suggests the directional flow of a museum space. Compounding the sense of momentum, a dramatic stainless-steel staircase rises up through the

steel-and-glass cylinder to a rooftop pavilion that offers a panoramic view of the city.

In their duplex on New York's Central Park West (1995), Calvin Tsao and Zack McKown of Tsao & McKown Architects deploy the romance of the spiral staircase to different ends. Instead of leading to the public space of a rooftop deck, the staircase takes on a domestic role, separating the social spaces from the private quarters upstairs. With this single structural element, the architects confer the attributes of a house onto their apartment, without sacrificing the residence's essential urbanity. The spiral's voluptuous curve cantilevers out into the living space, revealing the graphic edge of the stairs, like piping on a bespoke suit. Throughout the apartment, Tsao and McKown deploy rich materials—a silver-leaf wall in the living room, Brazilian-cherry floors—with a uniquely architectural approach to ornament. Furnishings, like the black-and-red needlepoint Napoleon III chairs in the living room, are chosen exactingly and sparingly to echo the color, tone, or finish of elements elsewhere. With a deft weaving of space and materials, the architects have transformed the mundane idea of space within a space—the definition of an apartment—into qualities of enclosure and intimacy that are synonymous with home.

Architect Marta Laudani has created an autobiography in microcosm in her 360-square-foot (33.5-square-meter) apartment in Rome (2002). Forced to keep the long corridor that consumed one-fifth of the apartment, Laudani turns it into a library and illuminates it like a street with Seminara industrial lamps. Instead of settling for a hallway closet, she makes a sculpture out of hangers, suspended opposite the Sixties beaded bench/light designed by Laudani and Marco Romanelli and a square of Gio Ponti tiles. "We are so accustomed to putting every last centimeter of space in our homes to deliberate use," says Laudani, "that we forget other factors that can shape interiors."[13] Accordingly, her apartment is full of modest but ingenious gestures. Custom kitchen cabinets bear holes punched into their doors to create domestic constellations. Wardrobe doors pierced with small rectangular cut-outs reveal glimpses of their contents while creating a pattern on the walls. In this way, even everyday tasks take on an element of surprise, and design is fully integrated with the rituals of daily life, as it has been in Italy for centuries.

Opting for a more vibrant form of personal expression in her London apartment (2004), Hong Kong art dealer Pearl Lam employs Op-Art graphic wall treatments, magnifying them with a profusion of mirrors, and contrasting their hallucinatory

geometries with curated furnishings. Where Laudani uses graphic punctuations for functional ends, Lam accentuates their surreal affects by layering oversized patterns on an intimately scaled labyrinth of hallways, walls, and doors.

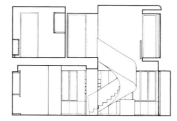

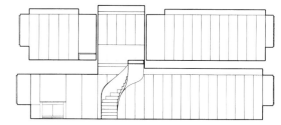

Portrait of the Client

Just as the architect's home is a kind of self-portrait, the commissioned apartment has the potential to take on the aspect of portraiture. This is particularly true today. In the aftermath of postmodernism, when design theory is weak and practice is pluralistic, the subjective and the personal grow even stronger. And when there is absolute clarity about the brief, when client and designer are empathic, the interior becomes, if not a mirror, then a window into the psyche.

Such is the case in an apartment on the Upper East Side of New York (2002) that 1100 Architect and interior designer Tony Ingrao designed for collector and Democratic party activist Lisa Perry and her family. Perry's immersion in the theatrics of 1960s futurism–so complete that it extends beyond her prodigious collection of Pop Art to her wardrobe, makeup, and hair–became the de facto brief. Two ornate

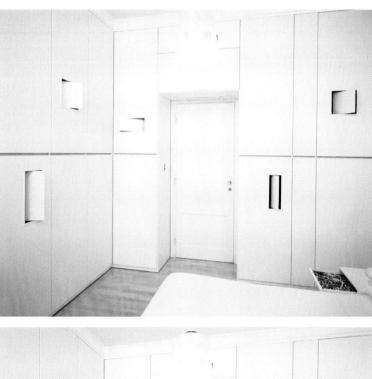

ballrooms, and the dark service corridor connecting them, are now a series of linked penthouse pods hovering over the East River. 1100 Architect partner David Piscuskas transformed the suite into a gleaming vessel befitting a devotee of the Space Age. Brilliant white walls meet the ceiling in a curve to give a gravity-free feeling to the soffit-lit rooms "so you have this kind of atmosphere of infinity," Piscuskas explains. "The Perrys are very optimistic people, and I think the whole place has that sort of feeling."[14] Windows open to stellar views, and white epoxy floors studded with marble chips reinforce the sensation of floating in space. Backlit acrylic walls line the library, where books arranged by the colors of their spines punctuate the room in much the same way as the intensely hued Pop paintings offer focal points in the seemingly limitless space of the apartment. Following the plot line developed by the architects, interior designer Tony Ingrao fleshed out the interior's cool sci-fi ambience with pieces as iconic as Eero Saarinen Tulip chairs and as idiosyncratic as the multi-legged Japanese seats in the foyer.

Ingrao masterfully reinvents the conversation pit by treating the living room sofa as a room-size composition enclosing an island of space within it, making it clear that this is the command center, the social hub of the apartment.

If the Lisa Perry apartment has the scale and aura of a mothership, the Monte Carlo apartment (1997) designed by the Rome-based firm Lazzarini Pickering is a retro-futuristic time capsule compressed into 412 square feet (38 square meters), including a terrace. The difference between the two apartments, however, is not simply a matter of size. For Carl Pickering and Claudio Lazzarini, the "retro" part of the equation entailed slipping quotations from the eighteenth, nineteenth, and twentieth centuries into a 1960s script. In the living room, for example, two partially stripped Louis XV armchairs face a Magister sofa by Antonio Citterio. In its literate brand of futurism, the ensemble pays homage to Stanley Kubrick's *2001: A Space Odyssey*, Pickering's favorite film.[15] Here, closets perform double duty as translucent

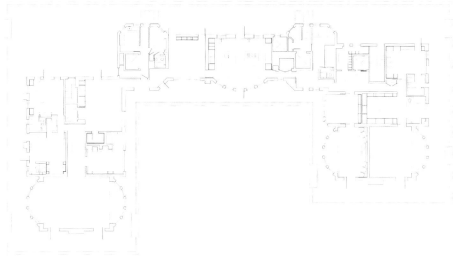

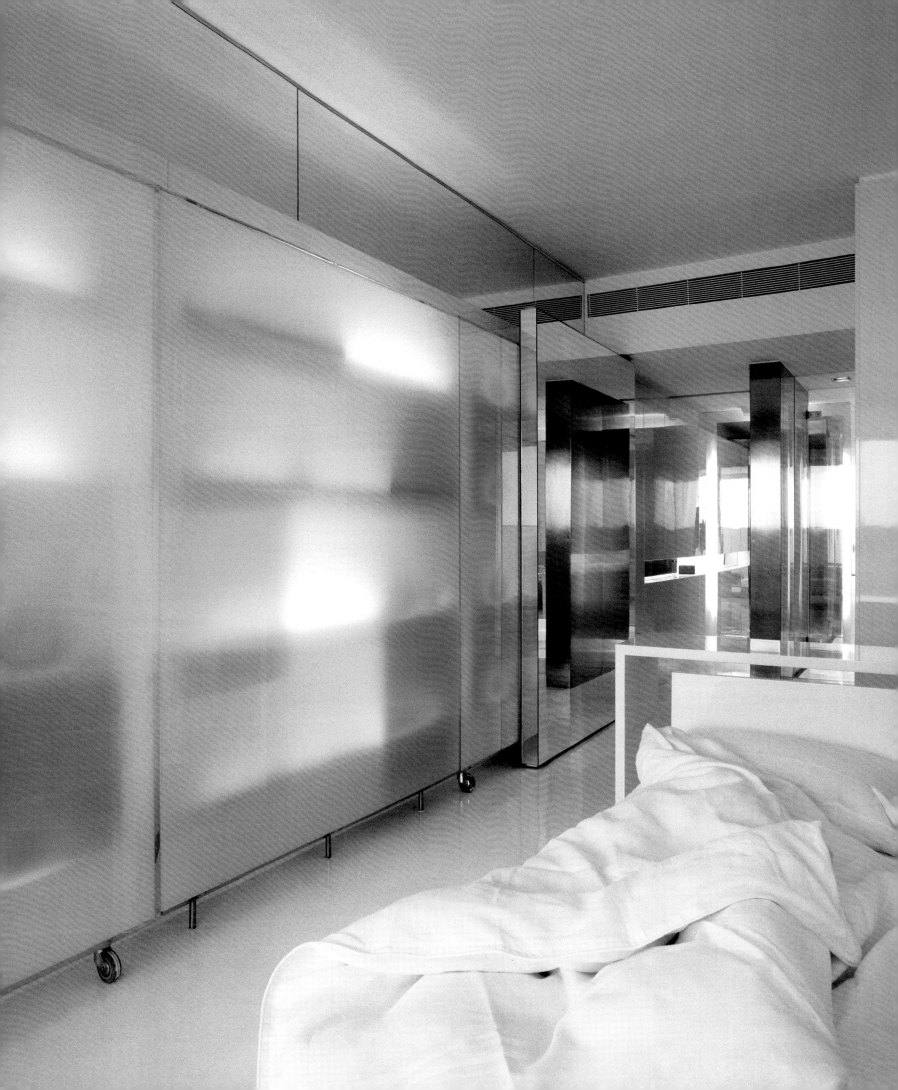

walls, with proportions that lend gravitas to the stage-set glamour. A custom-designed white steel headboard glides over the bed to become a breakfast table. The balcony window frames the ocean vista like a portal on a spacecraft. Designed for a businessman who spends his work week in Monaco alone, Lazzarini Pickering has not only provided the client with a handsome alternative to a hotel room, but also fabricated a glamorous alter ego for a temporary bachelor.

Using a parallel strategy, Hong Kong–based architect Gary Chang's Edge Design Institute condenses the urbanity of the loft into a 322-square-foot (30-square-meter) apartment in Hong Kong (1998) by folding the living room and bedroom into one multipurpose space. As with the Monte Carlo pied-à-terre, the client is a man who lives alone and, accordingly, Chang plays with the theatrics of the single's pad. The dramatically curtained living/sleeping space faces a window that, with the press of a button, becomes a movie screen, turning the apartment into an intimate cinema. Blue fluorescent lights bathe the floor; white lights make the ceiling appear to hover; and the physical confines of this small apartment all but disappear in a filmic vapor.

Kevin Walz's design for the Manhattan apartment of importer Amy Napoleone (2004) might be best described as a double portrait. The residence's defining features are drawn from both the designer and the client's enterprises in home furnishings, but more so from their mutual regard for tactile, hand-crafted interiors and the design traditions of Italy, where Walz lives. Structural considerations left little latitude to alter the apartment's layout, so Walz and Napoleone's favorite surfaces and materials—cork, marble, silk, alabaster, and wood—took on an especially critical role in transforming a relatively unforgiving L-shaped shell into a home. The Italian limestone that covers the floors—and, in the bathroom, the walls and ceiling—is subtly incised with arcing lines; silk curtains hand-loomed in India are buttoned over valence rods; the master bedroom's walls are rendered in a tone on tone pattern painted onto wet plaster; cork tiles make an unexpected appearance on a wall in the guest room; and the ceilings' waxed lacquer surfaces are deliberately rough. Walz also designed the living room couch (upholstered in linen velvet and shearling), the light fixtures, the cork side chairs, the walnut cocktail table, and the blanket-like carpets, integrating them with Napoleone's eclectic lamp collection and a mix

of vintage and pedigreed modernist furniture. Such a rich material palette, says Walz, allowed him to "explore the idea of texture rather than pattern."[16] But perhaps the signature artifact is the illusory wall that delineates the dining room: a screen, custom made for the apartment, crafted from brass tubes held together by knotted rope. The slender columns create a visually permeable divider that characterizes the apartment's overall design. Flattering in its personal attentions but never overly controlling, this is an apartment that acknowledges the life of the home as a work in progress.

A pied-à-terre for an extended family in a high-rise in downtown Hong Kong presented an entirely different set of conditions for French designers Elizabeth Garouste and Mattia Bonetti. Once dubbed the "New Barbarians" for their eccentric furniture design, Garouste and Bonetti are iconoclasts of the first order, and their obsessive-compulsive design process was ideally suited to the commission. Like the Napoleone apartment, the Woo Apartment (2002)–Garouste and Bonetti's last collaborative venture–places a premium on the customized and the hand-crafted, but takes these attributes to even greater lengths. There is not a surface, fixture, or furnishing in the apartment that was not made specifically by the designers for this residence. Each room in the apartment is a complete environment unto itself–from the lushly moderne living room, papered in stripes of gilt

paper, to the fantastical bedrooms, each tailored to the personality of a different family member. (The apartment is designed for the elder Woos, their son, and visiting grandchildren.) Beyond creating stage sets for daily life that might be mistaken for scenes out of *Camelot* or *Alice and Wonderland*, Garouste and Bonetti bring an unprecedented level of invention to their furniture design. In the living room alone, there is an aluminum bar, a mink upholstered chair, and a table ornamented with hundreds of pressed butterflies. Yet there is never a breakdown or dissolution into chaos. On the contrary, a strong sense of control flows from the fetishistic attention given to the design of each artifact and its role in the room.

The Apartment as Lifestyle

In designing a modest 231-square-foot (21-square-meter) apartment for a filmmaker in Milan (2002), Marco Romanelli focuses less on his client's tastes than on living patterns, using the space to prioritize leisure, work, and domestic activities. A central cube divides the space into a casual home theater on one side (furnished with bright red Harry Bertoia Diamond, Large Diamond, and Bird high-back chairs) and on the other side a compact home office, with custom-made white painted ash desks with dark brown linoleum tops. The cube itself contains the domestic functions–a kitchen and bath, with a loft bed on top of it. In a characteristically Italian design spirit, Romanelli infuses the utilitarian with

the philosophical, describing the central cube as the means of separating "where you go to watch and where you go to think."[17] But for all Romanelli's emphasis on program, perhaps the most original aspect of the design is his formal response to the demands of storage. Walls, cabinets, and even desktop surfaces are sheathed in strikingly asymmetrical planes of brown, white, and red linoleum, wood, and plastic laminate. Here, form is inspired—but not dictated—by function; the result is intelligent entertainment for the eye.

It is one of the ironies of late-capitalist society that Russia is now the locus of a burgeoning market for consumer luxuries. The end of Communist austerity unleashed a pent-up appetite for material pleasures, a fact most vividly manifested in the grandiose villas of the new oligarchs. In contrast to such flagrant excesses, Alexey Kozyr of Arch4 Studio demonstrates a finely honed sense of proportion and a particular sensitivity

to the structural possibilities of craft. In an apartment in a retrofitted mansion in downtown Moscow (2003), Kozyr introduces ornament into the conventions of modernism by using a judicious mix of orthodox and unorthodox materials. A glass, steel, and aluminum staircase made of 2,000 finely chiseled pieces acts as a high-tech foil to an opulent onyx ceiling. The dining room is open to the living room but is demarcated by massive black concrete piers that subtly reference imperial scale within a grid that is undeniably contemporary. Drawing from a reservoir of memory, Kozyr has created a hybrid interior—one that looks back at Russian history while at the same time articulating a new generation's quest for identity.

Of all the changes in lifestyle evident at the turn of the millennium, the most pervasive is the dismantling of the boundaries between work, play, and rest. A global economy and a continuous stream of digital information have created a round-the-clock work ethic. Even those with corporate offices now need space to work at home or, as in the case of Marble Fairbanks's client for the Vertical Townhouse (2000) in New York, space to think about the very nature of working at home. The client was the founder and owner of a company that provides in-home healthcare. In response to his philosophical interest in evolutionary versus determined spaces—spaces that can adapt as people's needs change, whether for reasons of health or taste—Marble Fairbanks created an open plan. However, instead of the customary horizontal plan, this interior opens up vertically through a thirteen-foot-wide Manhattan townhouse. (Since they aren't free-standing buildings, townhouses present the same constraints as multi-floor apartments; however, they do offer greater latitude for interior spatial reconfiguration.) Here, on the top three floors of the townhouse, the architects created a residence with spaces that are all visually connected by glass floors and open-tread steel stairs cantilevered from a party wall. When privacy is called for, a horizontal metal partition can be pulled out of the wall to intersect the stairs and completely separate the top floor from the lower two. (Each floor also has an independent means of egress to the lobby.) There are also translucent mesh scrims that can be pulled out under the glass floors to create a more subtle sense of separation. Moreover, when guests arrive, the second floor can be divided in two with a custom-designed, folding wood screen that has been sheathed in vinyl and milled into a handsome dot-matrix pattern. With these simple alterations, the client can create multiple permutations of living and working, and—especially important—working out, given that the largest piece of furniture in the townhouse is a rowing machine.

Austrian architects Lichtblau Wagner move beyond behavior accommodation toward full-fledged behavior modification in a housing project called solar.dach.wien.5 (2002). In the attic of a nineteenth-century building in Vienna, the architects created four apartments for four separate residents, each measuring 540 square feet (50 square meters), that are not only energy efficient but also promote a lifestyle that cheerfully forgoes conventional comforts in favor of the collective good. Solar cells provide hot water, mobile panels replace fixed walls, circulation corridors have been eliminated, and storage and laundry facilities are communal, as is an additional room that can be used by one resident or another by mutual

agreement. In one of the apartments, a bright yellow mobile unit serves both as a closet and as a staircase to a loft workspace, in an elegant feat of hybridization that recalls the room-as-furniture prototypes designed in the late 1960s by Italian designer Joe Colombo. By virtue of its color alone, the structure offers vibrant proof that sustainable design requires no aesthetic sacrifice. In fact, the architects make a point of it by including glazed slits along the length of the roof ridge. They say the small loss of energy is more than compensated for in the experience of light in unexpected places indoors, an experience to remind the apartment dweller that "the roof over their head is more than a functional coffin-lid."[18]

The Apartment in Context

Like the proponents of nurture over nature, who argue for the primacy of environment over biology, certain designers find external conditions–culture, place, history–to be more potent design catalysts than the illusory subjectivity of personal taste. These designers draw their inspiration from subjects more enduring than the ever-changing apartment dweller.

Two duplex apartments with centuries of history ingrained in their fabric–one designed by Finnish architect Pekka Littow of Littow Architects in a seventeenth-century building in Paris (1999), the other designed by Lazzarini Pickering within a sixteenth-century building in Prague (1999)–offer examples of how to retain the character of a garret without succumbing to facile romance. Both apartments occupy their building's uppermost floors, and both designs make a virtue of exposed ancient wooden rafters. Littow attached bands of oak lathing to existing irregular ceiling beams to create an undulating wave overhead, while Lazzarini Pickering created an architectural vitrine of steel and glass over the original structural supports as a counterpoint to their geometry. The

Littow Architects, Private Apartment, Paris, 1999

Lazzarini Pickering Architects, Prague Apartment, Prague, 1999

designers' treatment of the original fabric is not entirely parallel, however. In the Paris apartment, Littow has arbitrated between old and new by contrasting the found color of the wood with minimalist white walls and furnishings; Lazzarini Pickering opted to paint the original beams white so they can be better seen against the exposed-brick walls and a more catholic range of furnishings.

The five architects of Sweden's Koncept Stockholm addressed a similar space—consisting of two top-floor apartments in a nineteenth-century building in Sweden's capital (2001)—but instead of stripping away layers to reveal the past, they literally wallpaper over it. The most striking feature of the space is the hallucinatory floor-to-ceiling mural of magnified grasses by Roger Andersson in the media room. Like traditional

scenic wallpapers and frescoes, the prototypes for today's immersive environments, the mural is a clever pun on the virtuality of film and video—and no doubt a welcome antidote to Stockholm's long winters. With grass blades 16-inches wide (41-cm wide), it is, according to project architect Nils Nilsson, "as if you're an ant on someone's Sunday outing."[19] The faux foliage is also a lush interlude in a handsome but otherwise familiar modern landscape of layered open spaces, variously appointed with a Boffi kitchen, Antonio Citterio and Antonello Mosca sofas, and Swedish pine floors. By reintroducing the trope of the wallpaper panorama, Koncept Stockholm signals that it is part of a new generation interested in enriching the idiom of the clean white box by rethinking the possibilities for imagery and doing so with warmth and humor.

New York–based architects David Leven and Stella Betts
also play with the idea of illusion–that of the cinema. Instead
of masking the interior perimeters of a nondescript low-
ceilinged apartment in a Manhattan high-rise (2002), they
use them as a neutral foil for the only redeeming feature
of the space: its spectacular view. The result is an homage
to the city and the cinema–specifically Jacques Tati's 1967
classic *Playtime*, a satire of modern Paris in which monuments
like the Eiffel Tower and the Arc de Triomphe are reduced
to fleeting reflections in the glass facades of International
Style buildings.[20] In the work of Tati, Leven and Betts found a
way to bring the cityscape inside. They positioned a slightly
angled glass wall between the entrance and the north-facing
window, so that at different times of day, as the angle of
light changes, a mirage-like reflection of the Empire State
Building appears in the apartment like virtual wallpaper.
Playing along with the game of reversals, there are no window
curtains but an interior curtain of parachute fabric that
divides the space to make guest rooms when needed or disappears in the gathers of its folds. Like Tati, Leven and Betts
celebrate the city with subtlety and wit, without resorting
to cliché or defaulting to sentimentality.

The Apartment Stripped Bare
Although there is a definite revival of the decorative within
many contemporary interiors, the Platonic ideal of the clean
white box continues to exert its appeal. Just as the Greeks
saw physical objects as conduits for transcendent ideas,
today's technology allows designers to achieve unprecedented
lucidity in their designs. Virtuality and miniaturization are
rendering cumbersome cables and bulky appliances increasingly unnecessary, freeing up space from obvious signs of
mechanical intrusions.

Gabellini Associates' design for an apartment on the forty-
ninth floor of the Olympic Tower (2003) on Fifth Avenue in
New York is a minimalist spatial construction that features
a seamless integration of advanced technology. Michael
Gabellini describes the 1,800-square-foot (167-square-meter)
interior as an "envelope"–a commonly used but particularly
apt metaphor for the effects of lightness and containment
he achieves within the membranes of the apartment. Indeed,
the architect says that "light is our first material in every
project."[21] Audio-visual systems are located within a central
pier fitted with a flush-mounted video screen on a revolving

panel. Mechanical and digital systems constantly monitor the environment for safety and comfort; magnetic sensors give access to blind panels, eliminating the need for traditional hardware on closet and cabinet doors. Technology is not reified, but rendered as invisible as the electrons that feed it. Nothing distracts from the serenity of white plaster, marble, and optical-glass walls that respond automatically to control natural light. As for wallpaper, there is the panorama of Manhattan itself.

Taking the reductivist model even further, Claudio Silvestrin's 990-square-foot (92-square-meter) Girombelli Apartment (1999) in Milan is almost a ghost of an apartment. Living space is reduced to day and night zones separated by a 46-foot-long (14-meter-long) satin-glass wall that silhouettes the apartment's residents as they move on either side of it. Custom-designed matte stone benches and bathroom fixtures conceived by the architect take on a charged presence in this monastic environment. Windows are gauzed with solar veils, contributing to the indeterminate nature of the space. There is the sense of living within a cloud—a space of lightness in which an almost complete absence of detail offers a comforting contrast to the cacophony of the city. In that sense, Silvestrin has captured the essential feature of the apartment—a space that conceptually floats within a space, a home stacked between or on top of others, where facades are mere masks for the multiple personalities that make up the urban dwelling.

In the case of the MEM Building (2004) in the Tokyo suburbs, Makoto Yokomizo creates thirteen opportunities in thirteen spare apartments for residents to realize their own notions of just what constitutes "home." Accordingly, each of the apartments in the ten-story building has a different layout. They are, however, linked by such spartan details as a stripped-down staircase that floats in midair (each step attached singularly to the wall) or a glassed-in bathroom situated in the middle of a shiny wood floor. The Yokomizo apartments bring this chapter full circle to the architect-designed complexes it began with—in this case providing the barest of frames for an exercise in serial portraiture.

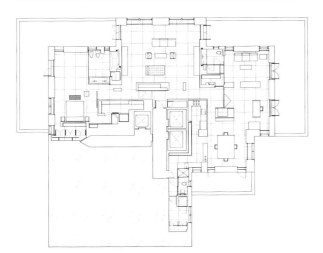

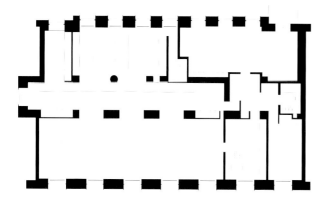

Lofts

LOT-EK, Morton Duplex, New York, 1999

The history of the interior is a testimony to the human capacity for adaptation. Whether as a result of conquest, abandonment, or conversion, the continual process of reinhabiting old shells and giving them new life—by gutting and refurbishing them and ultimately rethinking their programs—has been part of human history since ancient times. The basilica, for example, has become so synonymous with ecclesiastical structures that few recall it was a Roman meeting hall before the fourth century, when Emperor Constantine made Christianity the state religion and the basilica evolved into a house of worship. (Worshippers never actually entered the ancient temples of the gods; rituals were conducted outside them. Christianity, following the Judaic tradition, brought its congregations inside, generating a whole typology of ecclesiastical interiors.) Conversely, in seventeenth-century Japan, under the influence of samurai lords, the Shinto tea house transcended its religious role to also function as a secular space where treaties and business arrangements were negotiated. (Arms were forbidden in the tea house, just as in churches and temples, so it became a neutral space in which combatants and rivals could meet and social classes could mix.) More recently, the cathedrals of secular culture—nineteenth-century banks and train stations, even skyscrapers—are being repurposed as retail outlets, malls, and apartment buildings.

The residential loft was also uniquely a New York phenomenon, at least in its earliest incarnation. In the years following World War II, as New York replaced Paris as the art capital of the world, Manhattan was Mecca for artists. Coincidentally, a growing exodus of light-manufacturing from Manhattan created a surplus of vacant factories, sweatshops, and warehouses. These vast interiors offered ideal studios for the new influx of ambitious painters and sculptors. Though the notion of loft-living was soon to follow, at the time there was little about these raw spaces to hint at their vast potential.

Lofts became the twentieth-century equivalent of the cold-water garret; as early as the mid-1960s landlords began to rent them to painters and sculptors whose work far exceeded the scale of the easel and who often needed heavy equipment to make their art. Sewing machines moved out and over-scaled canvases and welding gear moved in, quickly followed by the bare necessities for sub-rosa residences. (Existing conditions in these spaces were often very crude; indeed, the live-work loft was illegal in New York until 1975.[1]) What began as an informal economy driven by landlords adapting to the decline of urban industry, had, by the 1980s, blossomed into a full-fledged real estate romance fueled by bohemian ardor and a space-hungry residential market. Many artists' lofts had as much, if not more, square footage than a suburban house.[2] Today, the loft is a staple housing type almost as remote from its gritty origins as the parish church is from the Roman civic center. In fact, the idea of the loft has been so widely interpreted that it is frequently hard to distinguish it from other kinds of apartments.

What's more, the loft is no longer an exclusively urban species—lofts appear in abandoned mills and manufacturing sites well outside city limits—and its pedigree, while populist, is no longer purely industrial. For more than two decades, developers have been building open-plan condominiums with faux factory windows and exposed brick walls and marketing them as lofts in response to changing residential tastes, social trends, and real estate realities. Chief among these trends are the growing popularity of an urban lifestyle and its remove from the specificity of place, an increasing tendency to work at home, and the limited number of industrial buildings available for reclamation. So widespread is the appeal of the loft that it has also been widely adopted as an architectural typology for corporate offices, retail establishments, restaurants, and hotels. (These nonresidential uses will be considered in the chapters devoted to those programs; the focus of this chapter is the residential loft.)

The loft has become both a design theme and a physical entity with its own specific, if malleable, conditions—a fact that makes categorization difficult. To distinguish the loft from other residential types, this chapter applies a rudimentary criterion that allows for a degree of flexibility: the fact of conversion—usually from an industrial space, but also from older forms of residence. In Milan, for example, where zoning ordinances still prohibit residential occupancy in industrial buildings, designers adapt older apartments to create loft-like spaces. Ultimately, the distinction between apartment and loft is subjective, dependent on both pre-existing conditions and the designer's stated intentions. The loft is yet another index of the fluidity of form and meaning that pervades every realm of the interior. In our postmodern era, not only do we reclaim buildings, we also reclaim ideas, for what has really happened is that the century-old modernist ideal of the open

plan has been made palatable in the sheep's clothing of history. Modernism's hard edges weren't so much softened as roughened by the patina of found spaces.

Having insinuated itself into the residential canon by subterfuge—landlords and artists generally shared a "don't ask, don't tell" policy when it came to illegal living arrangements in early lofts—the early loft resisted shedding its industrial trappings and was little more than an indoor campground. However, as it took on an aura of respectability with its rising stature in the marketplace, the loft became less beholden to its blue-collar background and was free to invent its own pedigree. Two examples from the 1980s—the decade in which the residential loft definitively became a real estate staple both in and beyond New York—illustrate polar archetypes of the genre: disciplined asceticism on the one hand and, on the other, libertarian playfulness. The first is Frederick Fisher's Vena-Mondt Studio (1983) in Los Angeles; Fisher collaborated with California artist Eric Orr to create a live/work loft for a lawyer and an artist, and their collection of painting and sculpture. What started as an investigation of the role of art in architecture became a paean to the loft as a work of environmental art in its own right and an implicit tribute to the artist-led rejuvenation of derelict urban spaces.[3]

By contrast, a loft by the late architect Alan Buchsbaum in a former hat factory in New York's Greenwich Village for the actress Ellen Barkin (1984) was unabashedly draped. Like other postmodern projects of the 1980s, the space was cloaked in the subjective realm of narrative. Buchsbaum wrote that "the chairs and tables look as though they were set down by the movers and might be moved to some other spot, should the whim arise."[4] Here the architect broke with the perceived authenticity of the bare box, offering another model for the loft in which the domestic supersedes the raw and the personal takes precedence over the prescribed.

These two lofts bring the history of design and art to the empty space of the loft. On the one hand, there is the model of stark, utilitarian beauty that traces its lineage to the Bauhaus. On the other, there is the time-honored practice of collage and assemblage, of using cultural discards to create new narratives—a strategy that dates to the time of Picasso. These two traditions, exemplified by Fisher's modernist purity and Buchsbaum's postmodernist layers, are now blurred by

cross-pollination, swiftly rendering old categories obsolete. In this respect, the loft interior–a virtual blank slate–has been especially accommodating. For at its essence, the loft is itself a hybrid–a hybrid of the culture of industry and the culture of art. Not surprisingly, artists and designers, regardless of their stylistic preferences, are often more likely to expose the evidence of these pieces of urban history so critical to their own identities.

The Artist's Loft

In deference to the primal nature of the loft, New York-based architect/designer George Ranalli created a house within a house for an artist couple and their son in lower Manhattan. In the K-Loft (1993–95), the bedrooms, bathrooms, and kitchen are contained in discrete volumes set within the stalwart brick ceiling and walls of a former sewing factory. Common birch plywood on internal walls, doors, and customized furniture animates the new rooms and invests them with an organic presence that gives them the appearance of growing out of the floor plane. The ziggurat pattern of the birch panels creates a self-conscious contrast to the industrial lingua franca while at the same time paying discreet homage to Ranalli's architectural mentors, Frank Lloyd Wright and Carlo Scarpa (both of whom were masters at creating a sense of place through architectonic detail). The sequential aspect of the plywood pattern visually links the disparate rooms. Without disowning the loft's essential character–the walls do not meet the ceiling and the perimeter remains raw–Ranalli succeeded in converting the former factory floor into a domicile with minimal concession to bourgeois domesticity.

The structural bones of a former spinning mill in Barcelona encase a studio and home (2000) designed by architect Carol Iborra and interior designer Mila Aberasturi for an artist's family. The Catalan name of this loft is La Nau, which literally means "the factory," and, in fact, its designers capitalize on the rhythm of the old mill's original buttressed arches to create a white rib cage for the loft. (In the living room, the arches do double duty as a decorative scalloped "valence" above the starkly gridded window.) The double-height space accommodates a second tier that comprises the artist's workshop and the master bedroom, both contained on a platform behind a railing, open to the views outdoors. The main living space below is equally fluid, separated from the kitchen and bathroom by partial walls. The main-floor bedrooms are

casually cordoned off by translucent partitions made of fiber-glass attached to a wood frame with exposed studs. From the immediacy of the construction to the hand-painted mural in the child's bedroom, the space retains the inherently playful, ad hoc nature of the artist's loft throughout.

Of course, the artist's loft has never been the exclusive domain of painters and sculptors (though such associations persisted because of the preponderance of art gallery lofts in lower Manhattan). In fact, the live/work loft is a uniquely ecumenical space, equally hospitable to musicians, actors, dancers, videographers, performance artists, architects, and designers. It is a typology especially amenable to those whose practice consists of making things and running a small business, who have created a sequel to the loft's manufacturing history.

Given the distinctly urban nature of the iconoclastic furniture of Brazilian designers Humberto and Fernando Campana, it was only natural that Fernando was drawn to a commercial space in the center of São Paulo (1994). Two concrete structures, formerly a warehouse, proved commodious enough to serve as a dwelling, a workshop, and an exhibition space for a burgeoning design practice.[5] Where there had been a common lavatory linking the two buildings, Campana created a courtyard garden–an understated outdoor room that retains the factory's original concrete stairs. Steel-framed windows, including a new glazed wall in the living room, reinforce the spaces' industrial character while providing decorative, graphic punctuations for the brilliant-yellow plastered walls and waxed-concrete floors. The calculated and the crude sit in complementary tension, echoing the sensibility of the Campana furnishings scattered throughout.

By no means, however, is the appeal of the loft restricted to people engaged in prototyping or modeling. It is an equally compelling environment for designers whose processes are virtual. Indeed, most of the work conducted by designers in the live/work spaces of today is done electronically. Mike Latham–a designer of high-tech furniture who was trained as an architect–makes transparency the subject and object of his own loft in Brooklyn, New York (2001). Not only do its rooms float, but its walls are transparent. Glass boxes on industrial casters serve both as cabinets and as translucent screens that can be used to reconfigure areas for working,

eating, and sleeping. Despite the loft's futurist flourishes, the model is medieval: The mobile furnishings conceptually recall interiors of the Middle Ages in which worldly goods were merely temporarily unpacked as feudal lords moved from one castle to another.[6] In Latham's loft, every possession is on view as part of an aesthetic language caught between architecture and industrial design, between the 1950s glass box and the 1970s transparent telephone. A Danish-modern sofa and Latham's own TV Table (comprising a television, a VCR, and a tire jack) embody a playful attitude toward technology that suits a loft designed as a kit of parts. With a sly wink, Latham subverts modernism's desire to celebrate "less" by filling its glass boxes up with more.

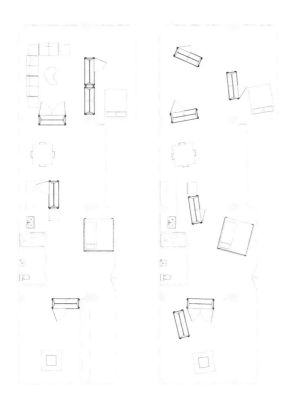

In their conversion of the basement and ground floor of a five-story loft building in Lower Manhattan serving as their office and family home (2003), Sandro Marpillero and Linda Pollak of Marpillero Pollak Architects were more literal in their interpretation of "less is more." By moving a section of the rear wall of the structure forward, they reduced the building's footprint and gained a 16-foot- deep (5-meter-deep) urban garden. Capitalizing on the space they gained, the architects created a 25-foot-high (7.5-meter-high) atrium with a rear wall of glass that looks out onto the garden and channels generous amounts of natural light into the center of the long narrow loft. Adjacent to the atrium, a two-story volume contains the bedrooms, which overlook both the garden and the interior space below. The reconfiguration is so successful that, according to Pollak, "When people descend into the living room/atrium, they immediately forget that they're in a basement. I think this comes from the counter-intuitive move of making such a high window look out onto such a restricted space. Usually big windows are oriented towards big views."[7] The living zones are separated from the work zones along a meandering vertical axis established by an innovative bookshelf/staircase that rises up through the building; the street-front rooms are devoted to business, and the garden-facing rooms to the home, in a taut compression

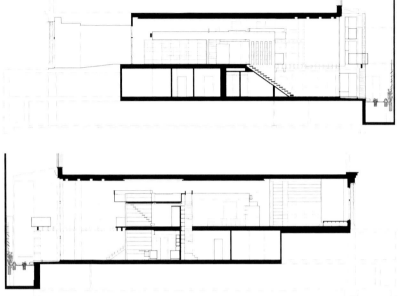

of city and country. Cantilevered balconies within the residential atrium, as well as a mezzanine in the 15-foot-high (4.5-meter-high) office space, create an artful complex of spatial layers, a layering echoed in the remnants of the building's industrial past that have been incorporated in the interior. Salvaged timbers serve as railings, steps, and countertops; wrought-iron window shutters, still covered in blistered red paint, are reused as pantry doors. Columns and piers, excavated in the walls, are partially revealed, noticeable only when lights are turned on. (Marpillero grew up in Italy, where the frescoes of churches are often like votives, illuminated by coin-operated lights). Throughout the loft, the process of "making" is palpably evident from the details of the cabinetry to the deployment of the structural beams and platforms. Its character is archaeological, revealing the rich stratigraphy of the urban loft.

The Loft as Art Object

Just as the artist's loft is freighted with the history of labor, the purely residential loft is inflected with the memory of the art that brought it into being. At its most exploratory, the loft becomes a surrogate art object, engaged in the poetics of perception through self-conscious and unexpected manipulations of space and light, for their own sculptural value. With an acute sense of the surreal, architect Attilio Stocchi animated a defunct factory building in Bergamo, Italy (2002), to create a thoroughly bizarre home. The result is a loft that floats within a slender forest of canted steel poles. Floors, tables, and beds are tethered to the columns as if frozen in motion. A glass plane in the floor of the main living space reveals an undulating "fish" made of twenty-one large iron rings–envisioned by the architect as a captured animal at the heart of the house. Radiant in the darkness, the subterranean "aquarium" amplifies the strangeness of the tilted columns that pierce every level of the loft and of the cloud of metal mesh suspended above the living room. The bathroom, hovering above the dining area in its own box, conjures the image of an automaton poised to walk through the room. Within the chaste gray-and-white spaces of the loft, these insertions illustrate what architectural historian Anthony Vidler interprets as the uncanny nature of contemporary architecture—the unsettling quality of its fragmented forms that are deliberately "unhomely."[8] In the context of the abandoned factory, the suggestion is especially convincing. Stocchi himself states that he "always thought that architecture should be alive and it's always seemed natural … that this life should come from the soul of an animal, its shadow."[9]

The work of LOT-EK is nothing less than a monumental collage, and New York—so integral to the history and identity of the loft—is its subject. Partners Ada Tolla and Giuseppe Lignano craft their interiors by dismembering and reassembling the artifacts and arteries of the urban landscape. In the case of the Morton Duplex (1999) in Manhattan, they cut a petroleum truck's tank in two to create enclosures for the loft's private spaces. One section, containing two sleeping pods, is suspended horizontally over the living room; the other rises vertically, encasing two bathrooms stacked on top of each other. The taxi-yellow pod interiors, their silvered exteriors, fire-engine red furnishings, and a bright blue painted-concrete floor pick up the colors of the working city. But the loft's proletariat legacy is most evident in its hardware, from the pods themselves to the exposed plumbing to the fire-escape ladder that leads to the grate-metal mezzanine. And while the salvaged parts evoke Robert Rauschenberg's combines and Andy Warhol's icons, the loft is unquestionably the product of a new generation's preoccupation with the aesthetics of appropriation and the pragmatics of sustainability.

The Minimalist Loft

Coincidental with the evolution of the residential loft was the emergence of the minimalist and conceptual art of the 1960s and 1970s. Minimalism grew out of a desire to distill art to its most essential nature, an optical experience of color, light, and space, without references, without narrative. These artists went beyond the abstraction of reality to the straightforward exhibition of material reality—and, ultimately—with conceptual art, its dematerialization. The "detachment and presence" of this work was intended to raise questions, as

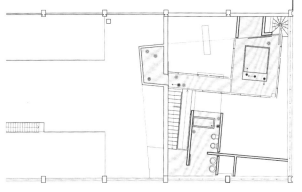

Below and opposite: LOT-EK, Morton Duplex, New York, 1999

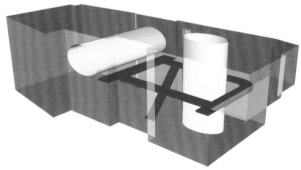

Moore & Pennoyer, Zoran Loft, New York, 1988

art historian Lucy Lippard wrote at the time, "about what there is to be seen in an empty surface."[10] And, by extension, a seemingly empty space.

The rejection of the precious, extraneous, and superficial associated with these movements proved an ideal complement to the modernist ethos as it was adapted to the loft. The loft's primal feature–sheer space–was inherently conducive to the language of the open plan. For designers inspired by the spatial freedoms granted by Mies van der Rohe and drawn to the asceticism of artists like Donald Judd and Robert Ryman, the task was to minimize the impact of necessary domestic insertions while also mitigating the incongruity of the loft's vestigial industrial features. In the ensuing years, the minimalist ethic's manifold interpretations, which have long since become unmoored from artists' manifestoes, have ranged from the brutally severe to the sleekly seamless.

By the 1980s, the luxury of space, once a cheap by-product of loft living, had become a true economic luxury–and what better way to signify that largess than to keep the loft open. The paradox of hedonistic minimalism–of spatial excess and

a poverty of objects–found early expression in the 1988 Manhattan loft of Czech-born fashion designer Zoran, whose interior scheme was executed by Peter Pennoyer and Peter Moore. The pedestrian rituals of daily living were deliberately split from their customary spatial domains and, in the case of cooking, eliminated altogether. (There was no kitchen here–food was ordered in.) The fully exposed bed and bath are separated from the rest of the space only by a series of low risers. Every surface in the door-less space is painted white; the sole pieces of furniture, apart from the bed, are a long Japanese-style table and a series of cabinets fused into the wall. In spite of the design's totalizing aesthetic, the character of the original space is magnified, not muted; indeed, the few remaining indigenous elements–namely, the windows and columns–take on even greater prominence within the amorphous white volume of the loft.

Few lofts have embodied such startling extremes of purity and exhibitionism since. Shock is no longer a value consistently associated with art or the loft now that both have fully been absorbed into mainstream culture. Twelve years later it is clear in conversions such as that of the Canal Building Loft

Claudio Silvestrin Architects, Canal Building Loft,
London, 2000

Johnson Chou, Yolles Loft, Toronto, 2001

Claudio Silvestrin Architects, Canal Building Loft,
London, 2000

(2000) in London, designed by Claudio Silvestrin, that the reductivist aesthetic had become less about the subtraction of amenities than about their rationalization and concealment. Closets and bookshelves abound, but because they are hidden within a 40-foot-long (12-meter-long) wall and are indicated only by a pattern of linear reveals, the sense of frugality is maintained. Opposite these, a bare white wall hides a children's bedroom, a generous bathroom, and stairs leading to the mezzanine, where a study and a sleeping area are located. The spartan character of sheer space is softened by an uphol-stered couch designed by Silvestrin and by his choices of natural materials: pear wood for the dining table and staircase and Lecce stone for the floor, the basins, and the kitchen island. With these grace notes, the architect transforms the 1920s warehouse without sentimentalizing family or factory.

Canadian designer Johnson Chou's renovated Yolles Loft (2001) in a Toronto warehouse accommodates the desire for comfort and privacy without sacrificing the discipline of "less." The client's tongue-in-cheek design directive– "think penitentiary"–yielded a loft that is rigorously edited but hardly punitive.[11] Aptly, Chou concentrated his attention on the regions of retreat: the bedroom and the bathroom. A cantilevered aluminum bed hovers in mid-air, stainless-steel walls shimmer over concrete floors, and carefully propor-tioned aluminum closets set up a serial rhythm in the space.

Architect Florian Beigel, working in London, gravitates toward the more humble face of minimalism, using and exposing simple materials in environments with few distractions. Beigel converted one floor of a 1930s shoe factory in Clerkenwell into a residence (1999) by setting three planar volumes (for sleeping, bathing, and eating) at an angle to the original columnar grid. A timber laminate, specially developed for this project, is used on walls, doors, and counters in the bedroom, bathroom, and kitchen. Set against a field of whites and grays, these striated panels and planes take on the quality of ornament. The one truly sybaritic note is concealed in the bathroom, where the walls and floor are painted Yves Klein blue. But the real energy of the apartment is in the tension of its convergent axes, echoed in the network of high-frequency fluorescent lights that zigzag across the ceiling.

In his conversion of an attic in a historic house in Lucerne, Switzerland, architect Gus Wüstemann created The Glacier

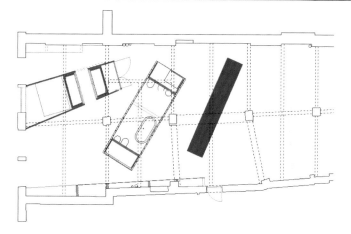

(2005), a loft that is both rich and spare, warm and icy, using the tactic of subtraction in the service of tranquility. To Wüstemann, the reductivist aesthetic is more than just a stylistic preference; its spatial economics are a wellspring of design opportunity. Disinclined to waste even interstitial spaces, hallways, staircases, and closets do double duty as sculptural and functional elements. Wüstemann makes a staircase to the rooftop terrace into a complete landscape unto itself. Steps of varying widths—some wide enough to lounge on—cascade down to the living area like a shiny white glacier. Surfaced in lacquered particle board, the staircase is also designed to draw light down from the roof into the window-deprived living spaces below. The snow-white geometry continues in the kitchen, where two clean, Corian-clad volumes all but conceal the oven and storage cabinets while serving as both counters and a cooktop. A seamless floor of high-

gloss white polyurethane extends through the entire loft. The floor is so reflective that the bed in the master suite almost appears to levitate above its fluorescent-lit platform. Wüstemann carefully balances the Alpine glare with generous spans of honey-colored oriented strand board and discrete sections of exposed structural walls. The furnishings similarly alternate between the ragged and the smooth. Shaggy sheep-skin rugs and pillows play counterpoint to Flos lamps, Vitra desks, and Verner Panton chairs. Here, aesthetic poles of stringency and indulgence come together with unusual grace and an enviable sense of balance.

Buschow Henley & Partners' formal language in the Michaelides Apartment (1999) in London also pays homage to the masters of minimalism. Two new walls with can-tilevered concrete planks are arranged in a sawtooth pattern

that subliminally recalls the work of Donald Judd, while Flavin's is echoed in the linear tungsten tubes and concealed fluorescents that mark the joints and corners of the complex perimeter of the existing brick walls. Such allusions to art world icons like Judd and Flavin are likely unconscious ones, secondary to the carefully calibrated proportions of the new concrete insertions and their functional role as screens for bathing and storage. Surely, however, these allusions testify to just how strongly lofts continue to be connected in our collective imagination to the legacy of the artists who saved them in the first place.

The Hybrid

By the mid-1980s, the luxury loft, was no longer an oxymoron. A commonplace in US real estate markets, the loft became attractive to the affluent-hip and began to migrate abroad

mirroring the itineraries of an increasingly global citizenry. New York architect Emanuela Frattini Magnusson of EFM Design was asked to design an American couple's pied-à-terre in Paris, in the Place des Vosges, a complex of aristocratic residences commissioned by Henry IV and built between 1605 and 1612. In this rarified setting, Frattini Magnusson capitalized on the space's noble pedigree without sacrifice to her own modernist principles: She stripped the space to its seventeenth-century shell and replenished it with contemporary and antique furnishings. Under the 400-year-old ceiling beams a bright yellow cube housing a kitchen is parked like an alien from another planet, complete with its own hieroglyphic: an arch and a pendulum that respectively constitute the top and the leg of a semicircular folding breakfast table. Flanking the yellow Siena-marble antique hearth in the living room are two Brigadier couches designed by Cini

Boeri and a Kioto table by Gianfranco Frattini. A Belgian tapestry presides over the Knoll granite dining table and its suite of Breuer chairs. Paintings by modern masters hang companionably in the living room, which, though open in plan, has none of the formal characteristics of a gallery. By mixing the tropes of design and décor, of flexible walls and fixed objects, Frattini Magnusson designed a loft that would appeal to the collector as much as to the artist.

Clearly, the loft has come a long way since it first emerged as the new urban turf of fledgling and impecunious artists and architects a full generation ago. That it has indeed been an evolution is born out in Massimo d'Alessandro's loft (2000) in Rome–a mature hybrid that reflects a lifetime of collecting and designing. D'Alessandro is an architect and a collector married to a prominent fashion designer, and their home, in a former electrical plant, represents the confluence of their combined talents and tastes. Its balconied plan, as well as the absence of windows on the ground floor (originally intended to minimize distractions for plant workers), evokes a space no less canonical than Le Corbusier's Esprit Nouveau Pavilion

for the 1925 Exposition Internationale des Arts Décoratifs et Industriels Modernes in Paris. At the same time, the loft is consummately personal, assembled over time rather than in a single moment. Today, the space, painted uniformly white, is both intimate and airy. The living room is simultaneously protected from and warmed by the strong Roman light that pours across the terrace garden and through the second level's clerestories. Bentwood chairs ring an Alvar Aalto table in the dining area; the adjacent living room is arranged around an antique Chinese rug. Here, a pair of pink upholstered couches and a pair of curvaceous leather armchairs exert a feminine presence. Still, no single element dominates–though one could make an argument for the art, which is dispersed throughout the residence (though it, too, is various in scale and subject). This is a space whose organic arrangements hark back to early loft encampments but whose generous stylistic range reflects the sophistication of a seasoned marriage.

In the case of one loft space in Bruges, Belgium (1995), William Sweetlove and Linda Arschoot of the Non Kitch Group literally took the lid off an old tin factory, essentially

making half the ceiling disappear by replacing the northern faces of the building's sawtooth roof sections with glass. In so doing, they not only exponentially increased the light that travels through the three-story loft, but also created a curiously ambiguous interior that feels both inside and outside at once. The sensation is most acute in the triple-height living room, where a suite of colorful Philippe Starck chaises are laid out on a planked floor that seems to be suspended beneath the fragmented tiled roof. Around and above this convivial space, which is the social center of the loft, a mezzanine houses the kitchen and dining spaces. On the lowest level–belowdecks, as it were–are the private rooms, as well as a gymnasium and a pool. With this loft, hybridization is not just a matter of marine metaphors or a deconstructed roof; it is a savvy blend of design sensibilities, from the engineered quality of the exposed structural elements, to the playfully animated furniture, to the classic-modern planarity of partition walls, free of the ceiling.

A former photography studio housed in a 1940s apartment building in Milan was already a live-work hybrid when the Milan-based firm of Caturegli and Formica transformed it into a loft in 2002. The designers not only exposed the pillars and beams that were previously concealed and inserted industrial metal-framed windows, they also layered the space with a set of international references that transcend the loft genre. The open living room became a piazza, with a central pier set into a tiled base that doubles as seat and table, like a piece of public park furniture. Japanese interior traditions are also freely quoted, from the sliding pocket doors of the bedroom, with its tatami mat, to the translucent polycarbonate panels that turn the orange laundry room into a lantern. Scandinavian-pine floorboards unify the loft, climbing the wall of the living room like a gently arcing wainscot. With this small blurring of an edge, the designers remind us that the loft is always, by definition, a space in flux.

The Permissive Loft

The loft has always been a space of promiscuous borders. Because its beginnings coincided with the counterculture movement of the 1960s, its uninhibited open spaces and do-it-yourself approach to décor became synonymous with

alternative lifestyles. Even today, as sociologist Sharon Zukin observed in her 1982 assessment of loft living, "the physical layout of most lofts, interrupted by a few doors or walls, opens every area and every social function to all comers."[12] A product of industrial abandonment, nurtured in a spirit of adventure, the loft is imprinted with the memory of its libertine past.

In the 1990s, a new kind of permissiveness entered the picture when the notion of beauty—long disparaged as bourgeois and discounted as antithetical to the aims of modernism—was rehabilitated. The decade witnessed a revival of its literature, triggered by art critic Dave Hickey's famous 1994 treatise *The Invisible Dragon: Four Essays on Beauty*,[13] and a sanction of its presence in exhibitions like the Hirshhorn Museum's "Regarding Beauty" in 1999. What began in the fine arts as a rebellion against the aridity of conceptually driven work soon infiltrated the realm of design, launching a new appreciation of craft that coincided with technology's new capacities to realize complex curves. The same software used by filmmakers and animators (to

render the dimensionally realistic dinosaurs of *Jurassic Park*, for example) now allows designers and architects to create buildings and objects with multiple turns and twists, opening up a host of new design gestures. As a consequence, the decorative, once banished, is undergoing reappraisal. No single ethos or aesthetic has emerged, because beauty is by nature anti-theoretical; it is emotional, visceral, and subjective. Its manifestations are diverse, and its expressions are cloaked in languages both ornate and restrained, for beauty goes beyond taste. As the Italian philosopher Gianni Vattimo writes, "Beauty is ornament ... the extension of life's worlds through a process of referrals to other possible life worlds."[14] In short, it is expansive and permissive. Where modernism had a singular (minimalist) quality, this postmodern notion of beauty is inherently plural.

In New York's Davol Loft (1999), the young Madrid- and New York–based firm Moneo Brock exploits the virtues of heterogeneity with a wide-ranging material palette. Architects Belen Moneo and Jeffrey Brock preserved the essential openness of the columned space, insuring that light would reach its

center by using an array of translucent sliding partitions. The directness with which the panels are hung from their tracks, like the simple Plexiglas light diffusers attached to the ceiling on a pattern of wood framing members, is an explicit tribute to the raw loft. However, it is a tribute that is deliberately contradicted by the glow of the mica and silver-leaf cladding on the new walls introduced at opposite ends of the loft. More than compensating for the absence of windows on the walls that they cover, their shimmering iridescent surfaces introduce an exotic presence that is as foreign to the loft's original state as the artificial branches of the birch-bark kitchen table and twig-style bed.

In making their home in an old leather factory in London, Amanda Levete and Jan Kaplicky, partners in the British architecture firm Future Systems, put a premium on the pleasure principle, but with a vocabulary decidedly more Pop than opulent. Intensely pink wall-to-wall carpeting works as a radical color field for the lemon-colored walls that curl around the kitchen and master bedroom of the partners' Hillgate Street Residence (1996). Kaplicky cites

Le Corbusier and Oscar Niemeyer as major influences, and here, Le Corbusier appears in the white gridded ceiling, Niemeyer in the elliptical rooms. But there is also a bit of the Beatles' *Yellow Submarine* in the loft's gigantic, round matrimonial bed and in the cartoon-like pink raft that doubles as a guest bed and sofa in the 29-by-16-foot (about 9-by-5 meters) open space upstairs. (Except for the Eames dining chairs, all the furniture was designed by Future Systems.) In their pursuit of new ways of living, intuition and emotion are as integral to the partners' work as the architectural legacy of their modernist heroes. As Levete says, "Designing is also about the *quality* of a space."[15]

In 21st-Century House (2002) in downtown Manhattan, New York architect Diane Lewis used a 16-foot-long (about 5-meter-long) divider of pivoting wall/doors to turn a long narrow space (90 feet long by 30 feet wide, or about 27 meters by 9 meters) into a sort of three-dimensional chess board on which all the pieces are white. Lewis sees the loft as "a direct response to a Miesian vision where the necessary storage elements define districts of orientation and the only volumes

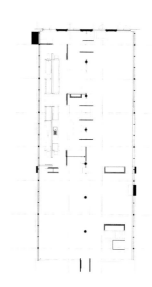

are for storage but do not reveal that they can be opened."[16] Indeed, these volumes play a disappearing game: The painted plywood partition wall folds into doors that reveal the bedroom, kitchen, bath, and a floating "guillotine" daybed for guests. But for all its invention and references to classical modernism, this loft respects the raw-loft vernacular: the line of original cast-iron columns extends into the living room; natural light comes only from windows at either end; the floor is bare, its dark painted boards emphasizing the length of the space; and furnishings are spare or built-in. Only the chairs by Arne Jacobsen for Fritz Hansen and by Harry Bertoia for Knoll, and the lamps by Poulsen, inject the occasional note of color. In her rationally articulated geometries—which also extend to an ingenious ceiling grid for lighting and climate-control systems—Lewis exploits the paradox of the open plan's permissiveness by inventing rules and regulations where there are none. And in this respect, the loft is aptly titled.

Where Lewis's modus operandi is rooted in modernist abstraction, architect Johanna Grawunder openly alludes to other environments. Borrowing from the cabana, Grawunder gives the working-class loft a holiday, transforming an industrial space outside Milan into a second home named Beach House (2003). A former associate of the renowned Italian designer Ettore Sottsass, Grawunder—who divides her time between San Francisco and Milan—reinvigorates the space with saturated color. California hedonism is matched with the sleek, modern sensibility associated with Milan. Matte-black structural beams and columns parse out the dominant architectural rhythm of the space, supporting a ceiling painted light blue. Under this perpetually cloudless "sky," a steel picnic table announces the dining area in a wry twist on the modernist dictum to bring the outdoors in—a principle more conventionally expressed by the loft's ample fenestration. Grawunder designed the lamp hanging over the table—a fluorescent tube shaded in vivid red plastic—as well as the sunny yellow platform bed in the adjacent sleeping area, which can open up to the rest of the house during parties. A sense of leisure permeates the loft, which its architect describes as "open, relaxed, airy, and bright by day, at night a bit sexy but not hung up on prestige."[17]

Where Grawunder introduces sensuality through light and color, architect Kazem Naderi uses water as the leitmotif for his own Tribeca Loft in downtown New York (1990). In another instance of cultural cross-pollination, Naderi takes his inspiration from the Persian courtyard gardens of his native Iran. Just as the architectural centerpiece of those gardens is the *hawz* (small pond), the centerpiece of the Naderi Loft is a deep blue-mosaic bathing pool surrounded by pure white walls, floors, and ceiling. Naderi's eclectic but meticulously

curated collection of objects and furnishings introduce a discreet but distinctly decorative sensibility to the otherwise pristine spaces of the loft. Among these are an Eames bentwood screen, gilded eighteenth-century Italian stools, chairs by Jean Prouvé and Josef Hoffmann, a Chinese platform box, African sculptures, and, fittingly, Persian paintings and textiles. Naderi moved the original exterior steel shutters indoors to seal the loft from the noise of the city and create an urban oasis of his own.

Playfulness and sensuality shed their exoticism and are treated as essential components of daily life in another New York Loft (2004), this time designed for a couple by Ali Tayar. To the Turkish-born architect, these are familiar cultural values and are expressed in the loft's casual mien. Yet there is nothing unconsidered about the space, from the orchestration of the orthogonal and diagonal thrusts in the plan down to the custom bronze door pulls designed by Tayar himself or the family of furnishings chosen by the owners. Without a trace of the self-conscious, the loft's lighting and furniture are comfortably integrated; pieces by Achille Castiglioni, Karim Rashid, Ingo Maurer, Frank Gehry, Ayala Serfaty, Droog, and Kartel are treated like the good friends they are. The kitchen, in particular, demonstrates the affinity between Tayar's architectural sensitivities and his clients' personality and lifestyle: The clients loves to cook and socialize, and the

architect obliges them with an asymmetrical peninsula that gives command of the kitchen and oversight of the living and dining room. Outlining the peninsula's modest dimensions is a lush green Indian-marble countertop that serves as an elegant bar before turning the corner. The kitchen cabinets, enameled in a complementary celadon, subtly curl at one side to soften their edge. These small gestures all contribute to the welcoming spirit of the loft and its clients.

In lieu of domestic intimacy, ARO/Architecture Research Office's SoHo Loft (1999) in New York opts for urbane glamour. Here, a grand, cascading staircase stages a gravity-defying coup of tectonic craft. The result of ARO partners Stephen Cassell and Adam Yarinsky's collaboration with Guy Nordenson and Associates structural engineers, the loft is a sophisticated structure in every sense. Risers made of stainless-steel tubes ripple between the two upper floors, hemmed in by a banister embroidered with delicate cabling. Stabilized by floor-to-ceiling sheets of laminated glass, the staircase is structurally impervious but visually spare. Indeed, it is the centerpiece of an interior landscape in which the play of light is carefully choreographed with opaque and transparent planes. Materials are used in their largest practical sizes so that their texture, color, and pattern become the ornament for the space. A wall of blue Bahia granite divides the kitchen from the dining area. Large panels of sandblasted glass in the master bedroom

catch and amplify daylight; the warm red bubinga wood of the library accentuates the color of the setting sun. A massive baroque glass sculpture by Dale Chihuly hanging from the living room ceiling is an exuberant foil to the loft's Miesian elegance. The Hans Wegner Ox chairs and ARO glass side tables in the living room, and the Mario Bellini Cab chairs in the dining room, are invitations to linger.

This chapter has traced the trajectory of the loft from a site of improvised living arrangements, with loosely curtained walls and beds on the floor, to fully orchestrated dwellings, palatial yet proud of their populist histories. (To erase them completely would be to lose the very status of the typology.) In this sense, the loft epitomizes the double challenge of interior architecture: to shape an ideal within highly considered spaces and, at the same time, remain open to evidence of lives lived.

Offices

Over the past century, the unspoken contract between employer and employee that guaranteed lifetime security in exchange for lifetime loyalty has begun to unravel. Job security has become a thing of the past, and with it, unswerving allegiance to a single company. The terms of agreement between employer and employee have changed; a new courtship process has replaced old methods of recruitment. Not only do employees need to be fleet and flexible, but employers need to make themselves and their environments as desirable as possible. In the process, the office is no longer gray, and the workplace, along with other institutional settings—hospitals, schools, and government buildings—has taken up the plot line of the domesticated interior, but with an interesting twist. What appeared to be a logical progression of enlightened planning, in the shift from factory floors of desks open to supervisory surveillance to variations on the theme of the semi-private cubicle, exploded in the 1990s with the birth of the virtual office.

In the utopian but short-lived "new economy," the workplace seemed to be evaporating, or at least morphing into something closer to a conglomeration of home, hangout, and clubhouse. In this through-the-looking-glass inversion of play, the walls of the office were reduced to shells around cell phones, Palm Pilots, and laptops. As design critic Véronique Vienne has observed, the workplace of the late 1990s and early 2000s "became a three-dimensional web site–a portal into the electronic world."[1] The frenzy to attract talent and investors for the new dot coms in Silicon Valley and Silicon Alley led to hasty real estate grabs and expedient office solutions in quickly furnished rental spaces.

Organizationally driven office design appeared increasingly irrelevant in light of new working behaviors. The long-held adage that the best ideas surface at the proverbial water cooler–where managers and workers mingle informally– became a core principle of innovation-driven businesses, leading to experiments in communal working that echoed the previous generation's experiments in cooperative living– except that now the utopian ideal had shifted from anti-capitalist to hyper-capitalist.

Common to both archetypes–the cushion-strewn coffee house of the 1960s and the conference room/basketball court of the late 1990s–was a veneer of effortlessness, beneath which

lurked an impending disillusionment. In an eerie premonition of the economic downturn that would come at the turn of the millennium, dot com workers, deprived of their own designated workspace, were beginning to express feelings of homelessness. And when virtual capitalism imploded with the collapse of the dot com boom, twenty-first-century designers were left to pick up the pieces and reassemble the contemporary office.

As with every radical movement, the pendulum has swung back–not all the way, of course; it still hovers off-center. The genuine idealism of radical workplace design experiments is now being absorbed into more normative office spaces. The fact is, flexibility–frequently touted as a new feature of the workplace–has long been an ideal of corporate-office design, as even the most abbreviated history of the late-twentieth-century office reveals.

Modularity was already established by the mid-twentieth century as a core principle of modernism. In the 1950s, SOM/ Skidmore, Owings & Merrill–credited with inventing the modern office landscape, beginning with New York's Lever House (1952)–brought modularity to the office with the introduction of movable partitions of variable heights and colors. The intent, however, was not to disrupt traditional office hierarchies or to create adaptable spaces for workers, but rather to insure that the architects' visual and spatial schemes could not be corrupted by the expediencies of facilities managers. SOM's Gordon Bunshaft believed that "social welfare workers were wonderful, but they shouldn't be called architects."[2] It is also worth noting that at the time, corporations were less prone to rapid and drastic realignments; businesses were more monolithic, jobs more stable.

By contrast, in Europe, where offices have traditionally been more communal, the seeds of a truly progressive workplace were being sown. In Germany in the late 1950s the Quickborner Group, in reaction to the International Style, developed the first open-plan office, known as *Bürolandschaft*.[3] The literal translation of *Bürolandschaft* is "office landscape," and the design scheme was, in fact, modeled on the organic properties of nature, with free-flowing spaces and loose arrangements of plants and screens as spatial dividers. Ahead of its time, Quikborner's success was short-lived. The plan, it turned out, was *too* open; employees felt overly vulnerable to supervision

MoveUp
LACKIEREREI

Kommunikations-Forum
KAROSSERIEBAU

plantings from North America, Asia, and the Mediterranean, the gardens also serve an environmental purpose, bringing daylight and fresh air into the central atrium that rises through the entire height of the building.[5] Arranged along all three sides of the triangular building, individual offices offer views outward toward the city and inward toward other offices across the atrium, underscoring the idea of a city within a city by visually linking the personal and collective spaces of work.

In the Genzyme Center (2003) in Cambridge, Massachusetts, the German architectural firm Behnisch, Behnisch & Partner extrapolated on the idea of a central atrium that functions as a vertical boulevard rising through stacked "villages" of open workstations and offices. The atrium of this 118,250-square-foot (11,000-square-meter) building, which accommodates 920 workers, is not an unbroken column of space, however. In keeping with the firm's ongoing explorations of organic expressionism, the building bifurcates like a tree through twelve stories and branches horizontally from the center of the building to create a variety of distinct spatial situations. Individualized office "dwellings" with views of the public areas and interior gardens extend through the full height of the atrium. As with the Commerzbank, the internally focused design eases the isolation of work. The Genzyme Center also boasts an interesting decorative component that typifies the crossover of residential and commercial vocabularies in large office buildings and goes beyond the now requisite assemblage of mid-century modern furnishings. "Chandeliers" of sparkling acrylic panes, hung from stainless-steel rods, seem to float randomly throughout the atrium, dispersing the sunlight that pours in through its prismatic sky-lit ceiling.

A city unto itself, the Telenor building (2002) in Fornebu, the headquarters of Norway's biggest telecommunications company, contains 2.75 million square feet (more than 255,000 square meters). Designed by Seattle-based NBBJ, headed by Peter Pran, with interior architecture by Spor Dark Design of Norway, the complex brings together more than 7,000 employees once dispersed across 35 different locations in the Oslo area. Like the Commerzbank and the Genzyme headquarters, the Telenor building breaks up the enormity of the space into work zones (in this case, 200 "pods" that accommodate thirty to forty people each). It, too, has multistory glazed restaurants and an exhilarating atrium that serves as an indoor winter garden.

Unlike the previous examples, however, the Telenor building is not surrounded by an urban landscape but is sited on a fjord six miles outside of Oslo. Resembling a docked ship, it is configured horizontally in two arcing glazed forms, one three stories tall and angled backward to draw in more light, the other five stories tall and angled forward to cut glare. The building's design can be seen as an interpretation of the fluid nature of telecommunications—what the eminent Spanish economist Manuel Castells has termed "the space of flows."[6] All the offices are open-plan, punctuated here and there with glass-boxed rooms that respect the occasional need for privacy while still remaining transparent. Half the employees have no fixed workspace, as the building is wired to accommodate them anywhere. The backpacks of peripatetic workers can be hooked to the underside of communal desks, which can be raised and lowered at the touch of a button to accommodate the different needs of changing teams. The eclectic mix of office furniture, including irregularly curved work tables, is as seriously playful and democratic as the building itself, where in-between spaces—curving boulevards and cascading stairways—are given special attention to encourage chance encounters. All these elements create a balance between the ever-shifting microcosms of teams and individuals and the fathomless macrocosm of Telenor's interconnected corporate universe.

Swiss architects Jacques Herzog and Pierre de Meuron have tested the tensions between the personalized and the generic, the individual and the corporate, on a more intimate scale in their addition to the head office of the insurance company Helvetia Patria (2002) in St. Gallen, Switzerland. Office stations are paired in rooms with floor-to-ceiling windows that transform the four-story building into a serialized, transparent tableau. Seen from the outside, office workers are silhouetted like actors in a Robert Wilson performance piece, their silent movements captured inside the building's graphic window frames, each tilted at a slightly different angle to give every office a subtly varied orientation. In this performance, the props could be said to upstage the actors: Pipe lamps designed by the architects hang from the ceiling like wriggling alien plant forms and can be twisted in any direction to provide customized illumination; red and yellow plastic Panton chairs provide calligraphic notes of color in the otherwise brilliant-white spaces. By inserting such gestural furnishings and fenestration into the predictable modularity of a conventional office, Herzog & de Meuron have pulled off an unlikely

merger of idiosyncrasy and conformity that even the most conservative of industries can embrace.

Although there is nothing intimate about Zaha Hadid's widely publicized BMW Central Building (2005) outside Leipzig, Germany, its design does much to bridge the often-alienating gaps between workers and management. Conceived as a "communication knot," the space connects the various hangar-like buildings of the car plant with its office and meeting areas, including a democratic cafeteria where all of the company's employees eat. The synthetic nature of the design takes on particularly dramatic proportions in the building's enormous lobby: Pierced by a diagonally projecting second floor, the space is animated by cars gliding by on a conveyor belt above as they circulate from one department to the next. The multivectored interior, outlined with long strips of glazing, gives handsome expression to speed and motion while the mass of its intersecting volumes communicates a substantive sense of authority.

The Office in the Garden

Whereas offices like Commerzbank, Genzyme, Telenor, and BMW are urban hothouses designed to stimulate productivity by putting it on display, an alternative approach stresses the benefits of tranquility. Architect Koen van Velsen conceived the Dutch Media Authority (2001) in his native Hilversum as a series of serene spaces that look outward to views of the forest. Trees literally poke through the entrance canopy, and patios have been cut out of the building volume around several existing trees, which provide the focal points for each office. Instead of placing offices along the perimeter of the building, van Velsen gathered them in the center of the building in interior courtyards that become outdoor rooms. Fully glazed common corridors, arrayed along the length of the north and south facades, are stepped to conform to the site's topography, allowing employees to take a walk in the woods, as it were, throughout the working day. Rendered in a language that pays homage to the Japanese roots of classical modernism, the Media Authority's exquisitely detailed interiors are defined by their irregularly spaced windows and predominantly white walls, which are judiciously interrupted by planes of saturated color. Furnishings are minimal and elegantly graphic, modest punctuation marks for a state agency whose role is to edit and monitor the media.

Enrique Browne & Associates Architects, Pioneer Offices, Paine, Chile, 1998

More literal in its relation to the landscape is Chilean architect Enrique Browne's office for Pioneer (1998), a company in Paine, Chile, specializing in the production and marketing of seeds. Appropriately, the office is embedded in the landscape, bunkered in part beneath a grassy mound. Browne carved natural-light channels into the building's grass roof and placed a courtyard garden between its two parallel wings. Natural illumination is diffused through the office spaces by handsomely articulated partition walls of translucent glass. The translucent screens, which stop several feet short of the angled ceiling, appear all the more delicate against perimeter retaining walls of rusticated stone and the ceiling's timbered joists. Pride of place is given to the two-story lounge, a tall, luminous space paneled in blond wood with an inclined wall whose windows offer views onto the garden. Despite being partially below grade, every worker has contact with nature; in essence, Browne has brought the outside in—from above.[7]

The New Shed

When Enrique Browne positioned the office as a seedling, he subconsciously tapped into the agrarian roots of the history of work. When New York architect Ross Anderson took on the design of the corporate headquarters for clothing retailer Abercrombie & Fitch (2001) in New Albany, Ohio, he put that history front and center by creating a series of six shed-like structures housing offices, studios, and a refectory. Together they seem less the product of a corporate campus construction project than a twenty-first-century barn-raising.

The memory of manual labor is evoked by the preponderance of timbered construction—nowhere more dramatically than in the up-lit two-by-fours that frame the entrance hall of the campus's main building. In the commons, a grain hopper–like structure shelters a cafeteria; employees lunch at long benches under chandeliers that resemble wagon wheels. An assembly hall, open to the outdoors, continues the rural theme and its celebration of rugged entrepreneurship. Remarkably, the complex remains free of the more cloying aspects of theming, partly because Anderson doesn't parody rural architecture but instead combines its language with sculptural gestures like the rake-cum-chandelier in the dining hall and the massive fireplace in the assembly hall. More to the point, his design skillfully fuses the mythology of the family farm with the individualistic urbanity associated with the company's brand.

The design studios and offices, situated between the social spaces, vary in mien from mid-century modernism to the stripped-down industrial vernacular of chicken-wire office pens and standard metal garment racks.

Abercrombie & Fitch's headquarters is evidence of an increasingly common strategy to place a design premium on the communal and the recreational, particularly at companies that bank on the fruits of creative employees' random conversations and are concerned with sustaining their creative energies. For the new headquarters of Pixar (2002)−Steve Jobs's renowned digital-animation studio in Emeryville, California−BCJ/Bohlin Cywinski Jackson, designers of the Apple Stores in New York, Chicago, and Tokyo, were commissioned to create situations that enliven the often solitary work of digital animation with

a spatial configuration that increases the frequency of social interaction among directors, producers, animators, and the host of consultants who work with Pixar. Thus, the centerpiece of BCJ's brick, steel, and glass loft is a two-story atrium−Pixar's giant living room−that everyone must pass through en route to one of the buildings' three theaters, its espresso bar, or its post office. (Employees also enjoy such perquisites as a lap pool, a basketball court, and a fitness center.)

To further offset the isolation of closed-door work, BCJ configured the animators' offices in U-shaped pods centered on a lounge containing bars, couches, and even a putting green. For the public areas, interior architects Garcia + Francica of San Francisco mingled pieces from Ligne Roset and Cassina with others by Charles Eames, Alvar Aalto, and Warren Platner.

Opposite: BCJ/Bohlin Cywinski Jackson, Pixar Animation Studios, Emeryville, California, 2002

Pentagram Design, Muzak, Fort Mill, South Carolina, 2000

Eight specially commissioned hand-woven Tibetan rugs create vibrant islands of color and add another level of comfort to ease long working days. BCJ also understood that, as with any home away from home, spaces had to be adaptable to ad hoc personalization. Pixar's facilities director, Tom Carlisle, reports that two years after the building opened, ten prefab "sheds" have been inserted in the pods, which animators have personalized with their own painting and siding. These interventions are understood to be temporary, but they are a clear illustration of the nesting instinct encouraged in today's offices.

In an era when manual labor has been reduced largely to strokes on a keyboard, the reprise of the factory-office goes well beyond the spatial freedoms that these loft-like environments afford. Equally important is the image they project, particularly for corporations that want to appear hip and casual, but also seriously industrious. At Muzak's headquarters (2000) in Fort Mill, South Carolina, the factory shed provided a highly visible symbol of a brand reborn. Following on the heels of a new graphic identity designed in 1997 by Kit Hinrich of Pentagram, Muzak commissioned James Biber, also of Pentagram, to design the company's relocated headquarters. In repositioning itself as "audio architects," as opposed to packagers of "elevator music," Muzak needed an interior that would reflect the scope of its ambitions.

Giving an urban edge to the business of "canned" music, Biber's brand-new industrial loft sets up the social dynamic of a small city for the 300 employees who work there. Biber based his design on medieval Italian town plans; a graphically syncopated reception area performs the function of the central piazza, with two-story workspaces radiating outward from it. And just as medieval dwellings had no fixed furniture, all the desks, by Vitra, are on wheels, and the office corridors are, in principle, infinitely reconfigurable. All offices are open-plan, including the CEO's. Here, stepping onto a carpet replaces a knock on the door as the protocol for initiating a conversation. Beyond fostering collegiality, the design was conceived to work as a visual analogue of a soundtrack, "scoring" color and materials in the same way Muzak relates the emotional properties of sound to place. Biber uses vivid blue, green, and orange cabinets (also by Vitra) to offset the gray tones of concrete walls and cement floors with lively notes of color. The huge space is punctuated with numbered "street

BRT Architects/Bothe Richter Teherani, Office Building for Tobias Grau,
Rellingen, Germany, 2001

BRT Architects/Bothe Richter Teherani, Office Building for Tobias Grau,
Rellingen, Germany, 2001

corners" and each zone has a conference suite built out of a
different material to give it a distinct character–a soft area,
a wood area, a translucent area, a metal area–that, in turn,
echoes the variety of instrumentation and sounds on which
the business is founded.

The idea that a corporate space might have more than a
symbolic or conceptual relationship to the corporate product
has been pursued even more explicitly in Rellingen, Germany,
where BRT Architects/Bothe Richter Teherani designed the
headquarters of the German lighting manufacturer Tobias
Grau as two glowing aluminum-and-glass tubes. (Built in
1999, the first structure houses workshops, a café, offices,
and display rooms on two levels; the second, built in 2001, is
used for storage.) Here, BRT not only created an *architecture
parlante*–the building as flashlight–but also achieved a potent
conflation of contemporary and ancient notions of workspace.
The Grau headquarters' curving walls, clad in aluminum,
speak to the new appetite for organic spaces, while the wood
ribs that support them recall the craft of shipbuilding (once
a mainstay of nearby Hamburg). Moreover, at a company for
which energy consumption is a central concern, the design
is decidedly energy-conscious. Southern facades are fully
glazed and shaded by solar panels tinted blue; along the east
and west walls, giant louvers of green glass move automatically
with the sun's position. Conference rooms, sheathed in
massive sheets of clear glass, admit natural light that mixes
with the artificial illumination of the company's products. The
entire project is an exercise in precise calibrations of light,
so it follows that every interior element–from the concrete
staircase in the entry lobby to the ribbed wall of the cafeteria–
is articulated by the taut lines of light and shadow.

No less striking is the glass-and-steel lozenge that forms TEN
Architects/Taller Enrique Norten's Televisa Service Building
(1995) in Mexico City. The swooping, ribbon-like sheath that
defines the structure's ceiling curves around to become walls,
which in turn enclose the television media giant's corporate
offices. An enormous glazed facade provides an airy and
light-filled common space for workers on break or visitors to
the conglomerate.

In contrast to the ground-up construction of the previous
examples of "factory" offices, the curved container for Cell
Network (2001) in Copenhagen was a defunct seaplane hangar

Dorte Mandrup Architects, Cell Network / Seaplane Hangar H53,
Copenhagen, 2001

built in 1921. Dorte Mandrup-Poulsen, a principal of Dorte Mandrup Architects, believes that a "renovation should tell the story of a historic building's past life,"[8] and has achieved that goal here by preserving the architectonic properties of the structure and contrasting them with a diaphanous modernity. Three interior towers, constructed of steel columns and stairs (all painted white) and birch floors, rise up lithely under the original vaulted concrete ceiling. Gathers of white parachute fabric cordon off offices and conference rooms, allowing for rapid changes of spatial configurations while also serving as projection screens for presentations by Cell Network's Internet designers and strategists.

late Jay Chiat (1931–2002). In partnership with Guy Day, Chiat founded the advertising agency Chiat\Day in 1968. In the process of growing the firm and garnering international acclaim with campaigns for clients like Apple and Energizer (he made the Energizer Bunny famous), Chiat began to question the way his own company worked. His preoccupation with the potential of digital technologies to free his staff from their desks to spend more time with their clients led to one of the most famous ventures in office design of the twentieth century.

The saga began with Frank Gehry's 1991 Venice, California, office that included a giant pair of binoculars designed in collaboration with artists Claes Oldenburg and Coosje van Bruggen. This was Chiat\Day's first warehouse-style office, a big, informal open space on a single floor that gave the staff a vital sense of common purpose. Along with the radical advances in wireless technologies that would soon follow, the Gehry building was the catalyst that led to Chiat's most notorious experiment in the communal office.

In 1995, the firm's New York branch, designed by another iconoclast, architect Gaetano Pesce, opened without a single assigned desk, without secretaries to answer phones, and ⸱t personalized business cards or corner offices. Here, ɩy personal real estate allotted to workers–whether employees or new hires–was a locker. Even laptops ɔhared. Quoted in *Wired* in 1994, Chiat said that he rying to structure things more like a university, rather ike an elementary school. Most businesses are run ɩementary schools–you go to work and you only leave ɔffice when you have to go to the bathroom. That sort ng breeds insularity and fear, and it's nonproductive."[9] 's poured-resin furnishings and floors and padded ure provided a characteristically uninhibited answer to 's brief. It was almost a literal reflection of the meltdown ɔollowed when employees found themselves craving a ɔlance of routine in their workday.

ɾestingly, the opening of the Pesce-designed New York e coincided with a growing movement among educators ɹiticularly at the elementary-school level) to promote a t from assignment-driven learning, signified by rows of ks, to participatory learning, with fewer structured lessons more open spaces and mobile furnishings. Since then, however, both the office and the classroom have seen a return to "basics." But not without profound influence from Jay Chiat and others who championed the idea of the deskless office. (It is worth noting that the practice of assigning office space on an as-needed basis was pioneered as early as the late 1980s by several large consulting firms, including Ernst and Young, Andersen Consulting, and Price Waterhouse Coopers.[10] Motivated more by the economics of real estate than curiosity about the social life of the office, this office arrangement, also known as "hoteling," is still used today, primarily to provide minimal working accommodations for itinerant sales forces.) Perhaps what was most prescient about Pesce's design was its utopian goal of merging the tools of work with an environment coded for leisure. The problem with the Pesce office wasn't its soft, domesticated edges or its formal eccentricity–traits that proved highly influential, as will be seen–but its relentlessly public nature.

Realizing that not everyone in Chiat\Day was as nomadic as its CEO and that even risk-taking individuals often need to work privately before sharing publicly, Clive Wilkinson designed the Los Angeles office (1999) of the successor firm, TBWA\Chiat\Day, by sublimating Gehry's loft and Pesce's surrealist lounge into his own view of the office as a layered, boulevarded city. (Chiat\Day was acquired by Omnicom Group in 1995, which resulted in the merger with TBWA, best known for its Absolut Vodka campaign.) Wilkinson restored individual offices and created clearly (if unconventionally) delineated meeting rooms. Taxi-yellow shipping containers, stacked three stories high, serve as conference rooms for art directors and copywriters. Teams assigned to specific corporate accounts meet in tent-like structures made of veils of white translucent fabric tautly stretched from the building's 27-foot (8-meter) ceiling. Workstations were given particular attention: Wilkinson designed a customized system–rendered in chlorophyll green, California blue, and matte black–called NEST (Nice Environment for Sitting and Thinking). With this jarring mix of vocabularies, sometimes bordering on the cacophonous, Wilkinson brought a messy creativity to the LA office, ideal for the hyperactive nature of the advertising business.

In contrast to Wilkinson's urban industrial interior, Marmol Radziner's design for the San Francisco base of TBWA\Chiat\Day (2002) draws its narrative from the site's Barbary Coast history. Dramatically curving walls and a palette of cork floors, sea grass mats, burlap wall panels, maple, and Douglas fir transform the interior of a boxy 1880 warehouse. Indeed, Radziner's maritime metaphor is based on the fantasy of recovered parts from a shipwreck. Voluminous hulls rise through the space, shaping corridors on the first floor and holding conference and project rooms on the second. The vertical thrust of the hulls is also a remnant of Chiat's ethos of anarchy, expressed in his legendary, if apocryphal, exhortation: "We're not the Navy; we're the pirates."[11] Now, open-plan offices are balanced by a series of low enclosures in

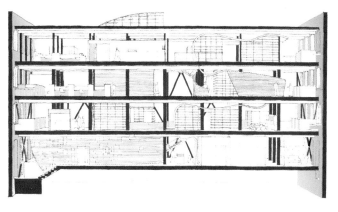

different sizes that admit light and glimpses of co-workers while still affording privacy. Here, and in the LA office, as well, the designers have definitively shifted away from schemes that try to change workplace behaviors to those that are guided by them.

That said, behavior in the workspace has itself undergone something of a revolution. Office politics may be a constant feature of business, but office decorum is widely variable. In companies that prefer to be perceived as ateliers or studios, materials and spaces are less likely to be precious and more likely to be rough and ready, indifferent to sneaker scuffmarks and compatible with the youth culture they want to attract. Traces of past occupancy are kept, lending a bohemian cachet.

Lofts and Other Conversions

Loft spaces, like those occupied by the staff of *Time Out New York* magazine in New York, offer both expedience (open volumes for quick occupancy) and the romance of raw industrial space. When the magazine set up shop in a 10,000-square-foot (929-square-meter) loft in NoHo (just north of SoHo) in 1996, architect Margaret Helfand capitalized on both qualities, finessing a crude palette of corrugated fiberglass, oriented strand board, and wood studs into a handsome, unvarnished study in constructivist geometry.

When the magazine decided to move in 2004, Helfand was given the opportunity to extend her vocabulary over two floors of a 1914 building in West Chelsea whose huge spaces have made it especially attractive to designers. (Richard Meier and Charles Gwathmey have their offices there.) More than just a warren for frenzied editorial work, *Time Out*'s offices regularly receive visits from advertisers, models, directors, and actors. Here, they are welcomed by vivid orange, yellow, and violet upholstered seating by Patricia Urquiola poised on two colorful planes of carpeting by Interface. Access to the mezzanine conference rooms is via a cantilevered steel staircase that rises above the seating area amid an informal thatch of suspended fluorescent tubes. Both spaces—the staircase and reception area—signify a coming of age, a celebration of the magazine's phenomenal success. In the case of *Time Out New York*, a publication whose success depends less on the perception of maturity than on street credibility, Helfand's custom-crafted design lends a palpable credibility to the brand.

Despite the fact that industrial spaces have been re-appropriated as offices for more than a generation, the perceived "honesty" of raw spaces and off-the-shelf building materials continues to exert power, particularly when they are as exquisitely honed as in the offices of the Cisneros Television

Group (1998) in Miami Beach. With tectonic precision, New York–based architects John Keenen and Terry Riley capitalized on the unpretentious nature of their materials to create a luminous, modern office for the group and its four Latin-American affiliates. Its defining element is an irregularly curving wall of acrylic sheets, mounted on an aluminum frame and "stitched" together with basswood fins. This modest but elegant "necklace" loosely encircles a reception area while separating offices on the north and south sides of the floor. By and large, the handsomely executed workstations and offices are conventional in their organization and layout, but like the reception area, the offices' communal spaces are specifically textured by a variety of fixtures and furnishings– from star-shaped fiberglass lamps by Robert Lewis to curtains by the late Mary Bright to pendant lights of the architects' own design.

Morphosis's design for the headquarters of SHR Perceptual Management (1998)–a major advertising firm with such clients as Coca-Cola and Volkswagen–is defined by an irregular curving figure. Morphosis's interior breaks the banality of the firm's otherwise nondescript office building, which is located in an unexceptional neighborhood of Scottsdale, Arizona. A serpentine wall slices through the upper two floors of the three-story 15,000-square-foot (1,393-square-meter) space, serving as both scenography and seam between private offices and communal spaces. While vestigial aspects of industrial structural elements are exposed–the building's concrete ceilings, pillars, and ductwork are left in plain sight– the overriding sensibility is of a vanguard futurism that becomes graphically explicit in the aluminum pods that hang above the company's central meeting room, which rises vertically through all three stories of the office. Clients and staff confer around a 16-foot-long (4.8-meter-long) steel-and-glass table that, in a small feat of engineering, floats suspended from cables within the 30-foot-high (9-meter-high) shaft.

The unconcealed sinew and bones of repurposed commercial space have long since been co-opted as a badge of corporate creativity. By now, exposing any part of a recolonized shell, whether new or old, telegraphs this creativity. Such is the balance and the bargain struck by Lee H. Skolnick Architecture + Design Partnership in its interior for Global Crossing (2001), a telecommunications company housed in a Lower Manhattan high-rise designed by I.M. Pei in the 1970s.

In a reversal of fortunes, the modernist open office, replete with spectacular floor-to-ceiling views, is stripped back to reveal its bones, effectively converting it to a loft. To achieve the desired industrial sophistication, Skolnick removed the suspended ceiling to reveal structural concrete beams and air ducts, using them as muscular supporting actors in a performance dominated by lithe, bundled strands of fiber-optic cables. The glowing, mesh-covered lanterns whiplash through the space, signaling its governing feature: light. (These ethereal snaking forms–thirteen in all–also serve as a marquee for a company dedicated to digital electronics.) Sandblasted walls around the boardroom become transparent toward the top; freestanding glass panels and honeycombed aluminum doors create scrims for semi-private offices; the open-plan layout delivers ample daylight to workstations; and the stairs connecting the two floors are made of translucent, tinted resin. By contrast, the core mechanical area is sheathed in a custom-developed rubber flecked in yellow and blue–the colors of the company's logo–that indicates the central power plant of the operation and also the infinity of space.

The Village

While the architectural envelope of an office establishes the baseline for its interior language, it is also sometimes the case, as with Global Crossing, that the envelope's aesthetic and physical perimeters may usefully recede in the face of other priorities. This is particularly true when the nature of work requires that the parts of the office become greater than the whole. Fifty years ago the solution would have been a ring of conventional offices separated by floor-to-ceiling walls and closed doors. But even though the same functional requirements apply today–quiet, privacy–what has changed is office culture. The perception, if not the physical fact, of openness is sacrosanct. So now discrete workspaces are justified not by authority but on the grounds of creativity. A new generation of "villages" within boxes, nesting like Russian matryoshka dolls, offer a compromise between walled-off rooms and open floors. (Ironically, the open office suffers from the same problem that afflicted the office modeled on the factory. The difference is that now all employees, not just the secretarial pool, are constantly in full view. The return to privacy may well be, at least in part, a consequence of the new office democracy–ostensibly gender-blind and hierarchy-free.)

In the case of Kostow Greenwood Architects' design for the Dallas office of Mad River Post (2002), a film and video post-production company, the impetus to create discrete spaces within space was driven by the requirements of the industry. To accommodate the nature of the work done at the studio and also to mitigate the isolation of days spent in the darkness of the editing room, the architects created a series of editing "cabins" in the vernacular of a summer camp. Editors, alone or in small groups, work in 320-square-foot (30-square-meter) houses sided with corrugated sheet metal. Furnished with vintage furniture and objects found on eBay, these freestanding dwellings are capped with pitched roofs and have large picture windows with opaque pull-down shades. Producers work in spaces tented with sailcloth and absent of doors. They are partially shielded by wood-slat partitions that effectively channel light from the window-lined perimeter corridor into the center of the 15,000-square-foot (1,393-square-meter) space. To offset the distributed nature of the work spaces, the architects carved out an "open" space between the editing rooms and the offices–an interior patio with outdoor furniture, a kitchen, and a lounge for visitors and staffers. No matter that the 18-foot-high (5.5-meter-high) space has the bona fides of an industrial loft–the 1938 structure was once a munitions factory–its cinderblock walls and oak floors are now the stage set for shelters once associated with the rugged outdoors, all designed by the Manhattan-based architects.

For the San Francisco advertising agency Kirshenbaum Bond & Partners West (2001), architects Mark Jensen and Mark Macy of Jensen & Macy Architects have also designed a building within a building; here, however, the goal wasn't to facilitate

Kostow Greenwood Architects, Mad River Post, Dallas, 2002

individual performances but to maximize joint endeavors. Less a village than a collective, the space is the result of the architects' skillful navigation of the client's desire for both openness and privacy. The three-wing structure looks like a cluster of giant televisions with enormous viewfinder windows. Designed to accommodate a movable feast of meetings and conferences, the sculptural forms are the center of gravity in a highly activated space; the architects have flanked the closed volumes of the central core with an indoor garden and a broad staircase where staff congregates for company-wide meetings. Workstations and dining area are on slightly skewed diagonals within the 21,950-square-foot (2,039-square-meter) space.

The exterior surfaces of the office's conference wings are coated with chalkboard paint, and the traces of previous meetings' notes and diagrams lend a decorative calculus to the interior equation. One wing of the conference suite features a ceiling and wall treatment of white acoustical foam used in recording studios—both stylish and absorbent—as well as a custom wraparound couch of royal blue leather reminiscent of the furniture of a 1970s sunken living room. Flos globes hover over the other two conference tables, which are flanked by Herman Miller Eames chairs in a rainbow of colors. (The three wings can be open to each other or separated by folding acoustical doors.) A bright green, carpet-clad structure has cocoon-like spaces carved into it where employees can retreat and make private calls. For all the tongue-in-cheek elements of the design, Kirshenbaum Bond & Partner's San Francisco offices never succumbs to kitsch; they remain playful, in large part because of the child-like thrill of entering a house within a house.

In an age when companies like to make claims to transparent business practices, the successful insertion of private rooms often relies on a sense of humor. They must appear to be witty, not secretive—a sign that management doesn't take itself too seriously. Today, few merchants want to be perceived as stodgy purveyors of goods; instead they sell pleasure. In Nike's London Headquarters (2003)—a hub for marketing, retail, sales, and design staff as well as visiting celebrity athletes—the youthful and aptly named Jump Studios took a shot at the company's ethos of serious play and scored by transforming the swoosh logo into a series of glossy blue aerodynamic shells. These Pop lozenges announce the

reception area and make it clear where the action is—in the meeting spaces, sales rooms, and "war rooms" where confidential product development takes place, and in the offices of key senior management. Glimpses of these spaces are visible to staff working in the surrounding workstations, reminding them that "something exciting is happening just around the corner,"[12] in the words of Jump's Sean Pearson.

The trope of the enfilade—the suggestion of endless space and endless possibility that is achieved in the Nike office's repeated convexities—is the hallmark of another London office, that of Corinthian Television (2003). Designed by Gensler, the world's largest architecture and interiors practice, the space is dominated by a sequence of editing booths—a series of white elliptical pillars sliced on a diagonal by blue lenses and surrounded by footlights—that definitively secure the office's retro-mod credentials. Between these booths and the exterior wall is another, more conventional, series of private spaces; these give editors the option of working in daylight, which can alleviate the strain of long workdays. Similarly, the transmission suites that communicate with cable and satellite networks (located in two large elliptical rooms, one on each side of the floor) were designed as segmented glass wedges that enable communication between video crews while maintaining acoustical integrity. As Kostow Greenwood did with the Mad River Post offices, Gensler acknowledges the necessity of isolation in media-production work, but offers relief from it as well: the firm has created discrete "houses" with their own distinct architecture and functions and, at the same time, introduced pockets of flexible space, furnished with mid-century classics—Warren Platner chairs in the café and beanbags in the lounge. Both Gensler and Kostow Greenwood base their designs on exploration themes: In the case of the Dallas office, it's the great outdoors; in London, it's a *2001: A Space Odyssey* fantasy of outer space.

Two final examples in this section, each extraordinary in its own way, illustrate how the notion of the sculptural office landscape—the clubhouse within the club—has been pursued to opposite ends. The first, by Frank Gehry, deals in monumentality; the second, by Amsterdam-based interior designer Kho Liang Ie, places a premium on dispersion.

The conditions that led Gehry to arrive at his design for the DZ Bank Building (1995–2001) in Berlin had less to do with

the changing nature of work than with the changes taking place in post-reunification Berlin. Sited on historic Pariser Platz, next to the 1788 Brandenburg Gate, the bank building had to conform to newly legislated restrictions on height, proportions, and materials that augured against any expressionist gestures. So Gehry built a "Gehry" *inside* the building's enormous, ten-story atrium. The architect has always blurred the lines between architecture and sculpture, and here he erased them altogether, taking the prosaic conference room and remolding it in the shape of a prehistoric horse's head.[13] Clad in an armor of two-millimeter-thick steel plates, the form is both awesome and oddly moving in the way it is confined in the case of the building. Under its magnificent, netted glass canopy, however, the head loses its brutality (and its inevitable *Godfather* associations) and takes on the quality of a Fabergé egg encased in a box of Douglas fir that houses the perimeter offices. Looking down on the curtain of steel is a perk for employees whose desks ring the windowed atrium, a practical response to German regulations stipulating access to daylight for every office.

Those who enter the interior of the horse's head find it is pure sinew and muscle, woven of slender bands of American red oak, finely perforated to create optimal acoustics. No microphones are needed in the space, which holds up to 85 people. As conferees enter and leave, they look down through another convex glass roof—a doppelgänger of the one above. The view of the reception space below is faceted by triangular mullions and further enhanced by an elegant "cloud" of hanging glass rods by the sculptor Nikolas Weinstein, set in relief by brilliant red carpeting.

Just as the animistic presence of Gehry's structure is made all the more astonishing by the corporate nature of the building around it, the severely modern twenty-two-story office high-rise designed in 1996 by Dutch architect Abe Bonnema in Tilburg, The Netherlands, gives no hint of its radical interiors commissioned by the Dutch insurance company Interpolis. In this case, however, iconoclastic design is taken out of the lobby and put to work. Almost ten years after the failed Chiat\ Day experiment in New York, in 2003 Interpolis revisited the idea of the mobile office worker by keeping its conventional spaces as meeting rooms and creating an addition that would allow its 500 employees to work in environments of their choice. To accomplish this, Kho Liang Ie, the interior designer in charge, brought in eight disparate talents to create eight completely different spaces: designer Marcel Wanders, artist Irene Fortuyn, furniture designer Piet Hein Eek, architect Ellen Sander, designer Bas van Tol, artist/designer Joep van Lieshout, designer Jurgen Bey, and theater designer Mark Warning. Employees are given a choice of which of the eight "clubhouses," as the designer terms them, they wish to work in.

The eight clubhouses are exuberant expressions of individuality; together they implicitly honor the corporal in corporation with their emphasis on the personal. Wanders's contribution, which he calls *Steenhuis* (Stone House), reprises the house-within-a-house idea, with huts nestled together closely in a space painted black to suggest an enchanted wood. The huts, painted on the outside with folk art and flora, contain an eclectic range of contemporary furnishings, including chandelier lighting by Jurgen Bey. Bey's own space, *Huiskamer* (Living Room)—features his Oostoel chairs, with oversize "ears" for private conversations, amid fantastically florid wallpaper and frilled lampshades that reclaim the parlor for the office. Bas van Tol's *Weefhuis* (Weaver's House) leaves the forest for the bazaar. With a nod to the openness of ancient markets, he loosely contained the space with a curtain wall of strands of rope; textile patterns from Persia, Morocco, and Flanders provide a decorative foil for yellow Lucite chairs and silver barstools. With her *Spoorhuis* (Railway House), Irene Fortuyn created a train club car but managed to avoid the pitfalls of theming by admitting the absurd. Here, a scattering of felt splotches on the floor, meant to suggest ink drops (vestiges of the pre-digital age), read equally well as abstract non sequiturs that gleefully disrupt the linear corridor. In the same topsy-turvy spirit, computer screens rise above a tabletop covered in thick brown carpeting in Ellen Sander's *Wijsheid* (Wisdom) conference room. And in Marc Warning's *Lichthuis* (Light House), a smorgasbord of chairs, lamps, and exposed electrical connections are grounded by a red rubber floor. Piet Hein Eek insured the credibility of his *Boshuis* (Wood House), another cafeteria, by designing its chairs and tables of recycled wood. Joep van Lieshout's *Tuinhuis* (Garden House) pokes out from the building's pilotis into the garden and boasts a giant blob-shaped fiberglass television lounge in a trailer, which sits

adjacent to a series of split-level wooden structures housing desks and conference spaces. The overall result at the Interpolis offices is a design that refuses to take itself too seriously and remains open-ended–an ethos echoed by the company's management, which gives employees the choice of working in their old offices if they choose or, in some cases, even at home.

While the degree of customization embraced by Interpolis may not be economically feasible for many companies, the desire for personalization is nonetheless growing. It has even affected the realm of office systems, as can be seen in two product lines by Herman Miller and Knoll International. In 1999, Herman Miller launched the Resolve Office System, designed by Ayse Birsel, a Turkish-born product designer

based in New York. Resolve, in the words of critic Steven Skov Holt, "uses 120 angles to build constellations that eliminate the maze-like grid of cubicles."[14] Instead of wood or metal, tautly stretched scrims cordon off zones in the office, to a much softer effect. Individual workstations are sheltered under petal-like canopies that give the system a distinctive identity without compromising its chief virtue: the potential for customization offered by a kit of parts.

Likewise, Knoll's A3 Office System (2000) by Lise Anne Couture and Hani Rashid of Asymptote is another rejection of the hard-edged office environment. Bright-orange desks and accessories are housed within cocoons of translucent fabric whose stretched dot-matrix pattern accentuates the enclosure's

womb-like curves. It is an especially expressive visualization of the psychic membranes that workers construct around themselves in the highly sensitive social system of an office. Like Resolve, A3 draws on a formal language that is organic. Given that the reception of these two systems has been mixed, it appears that such experiments in extreme customization may be premature for the mass market, though welcome catalysts for future invention.

The Domesticated Office

One might expect that a survey like this one, written after the turn of the millennium, would of necessity devote considerable attention to the home office–the much-vaunted office of the future. But, in truth, the home office is still largely a sociological phenomenon without a discernible design profile, and for now remains primarily in the context of residential design–annexed into houses, apartments, or lofts. Of greater interest in the context of this chapter are offices that take their cues from the home.

While it is true that offices have long been decorated with drapes, massive furniture suites, rugs, lamps, wet bars, and so on, such amenities were almost always the exclusive prerogative of the executive suite. Such residential comforts– along with their connotations of prestige, personal ownership, and leisure–were carefully segregated from office culture at large. This model has lost credibility in today's working world, where companies draw their energies from teams and claim

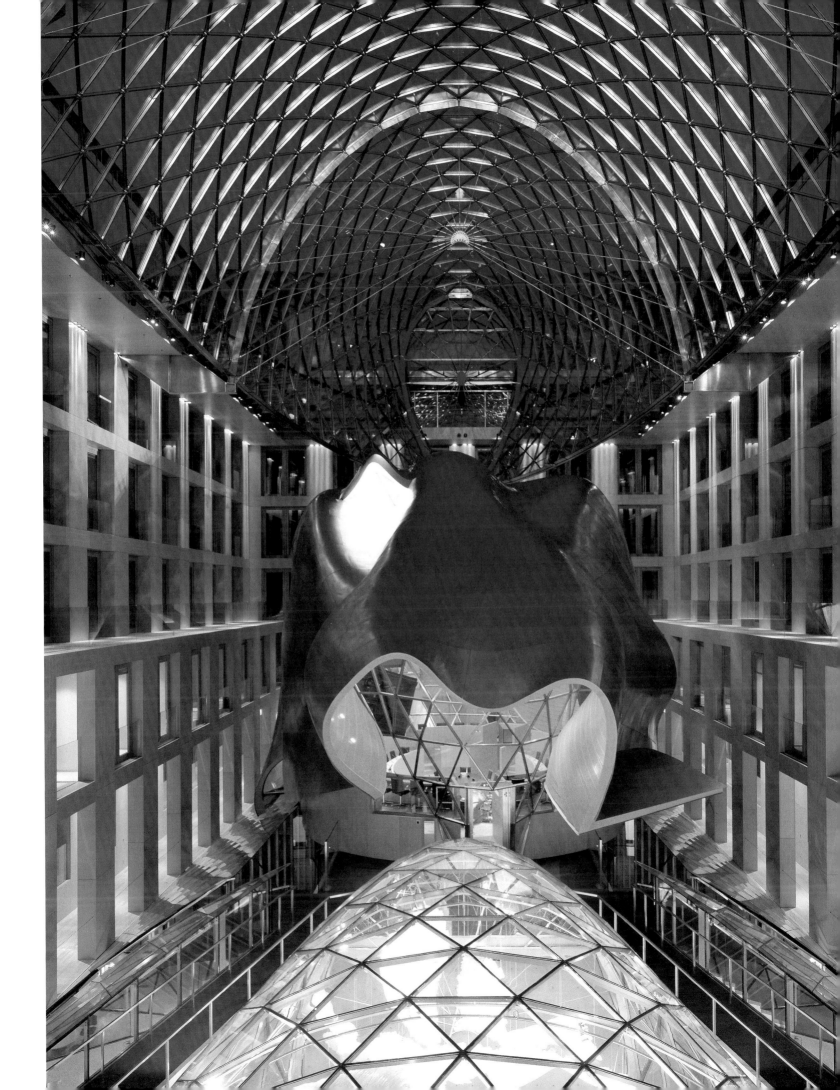

Below and opposite: Kho Liang le Associates, Interpolis, Tilburg,
The Netherlands, 2003, with interiors by (clockwise from top left)
Bas van Tol, Jurgen Bey, Atelier van Lieshout, Mark Warning, Marcel Wanders,
and Ellen Sander.

to view hierarchies and their symbols as counterproductive. Now, it is not unusual to find curtains, lamps, sofas, and lounge chairs spread liberally throughout even the most conventional of business settings. Furthermore, designers' choices are no longer dictated by the presumption that the office environment should be masculine–a presumption generally interpreted by past generations of designers to spec furnishings that were either of a sturdy, massive historical style or severely modern, preferably in the spirit of Mies van der Rohe or Le Corbusier. The gradual rise of women in the professional work force certainly can be credited for opening up options beyond these two extremes, but it is also arguable that the recent popularity of organic mid-century modern furniture, with its softer edges and informal spirit, made it possible for the office interior to cross gender lines.

An important harbinger of the feminized office can be seen in a project by Emilio Ambasz from the early 1980s, the Financial Guaranty Insurance Corporation (1983) in New York. Here, glamour makes an entrance on the modernist stage, and not just in the boardroom. Ambasz, the industrial designer and architect who curated the Museum of Modern Art's influential 1972 exhibition "The New Domestic Landscape," distinguished the interior architecture for Financial Guaranty with a single

device, the curtain. Ambasz used panels of silk strings as the sole form of partition between executive offices—a strategy that both conceals the occupants and subtly reveals their presence. Emanating from the ceiling like laser beams, the gauzy string curtains also provide a lush source of illumination in the way the light bounces off the fibers. The exterior walls behind them are painted a gradated blue that gradually intensifies from bottom to top, giving the illusion of a far horizon.

Similarly, the examples that follow place a premium on visual pleasure, banking on the theory that the nonquantifiable can be used to great benefit in a bottom-line context. For businesses that sell services and information, the design of offices become a surrogate product. These projects are linked not by any explicit image of home but by an emphasis on aesthetic innovation over management theory. Such an approach had hitherto been the exclusive domain of the house; here, it crosses the threshold into the office.

In what became an iconic early-1990s interior—the offices of D.E. Shaw & Co. (1992), a New York investment firm—Steven Holl transformed a lobby into a northern version of a Latin courtyard, introducing windows that admitted not views but a warm light reflected off white sheet-rock walls painted on

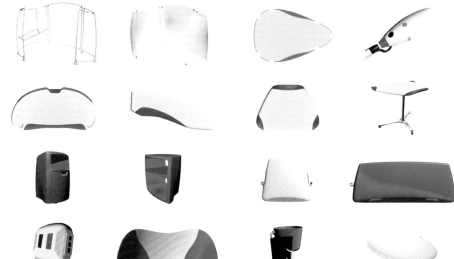

the reverse with a range of fluorescent colors and backlit with natural and artificial light. The project has been described as a parallel exercise in invisible elements—the virtual brains of the investment company's computers and the architect's delicate insinuation of color—as there is not a fixture in sight.[15] But one is not the literal expression of the other; each is merely a catalyst for Holl's ongoing investigations with light in architecture. In fact, the space is a rich compost of formal ideas whose geometries can be variously traced to Russian Constructivism, the de Stijl movement, and the colorful modernism of Luis Barragán, all of which enjoyed renewed interest in the 1980s. This is no last gasp of a facile post-modernism, however, but a cogent synthesis that resulted in a paradoxically warm minimalism. If the lobby customarily serves as the "parlor" of the office—a formal place where guests are received and introductions made—Holl has reconceived it as a meditative space that soothes the tension of anticipation and waiting.

Mecanoo, an architectural firm based in Delft, The Netherlands, didn't have to invent any metaphors for hospitality when it was asked to design the office for organization consultants Andersson Elffers Felix (2000) in Utrecht. The company was already in residence in an 1897 mansion, originally designed by architect S.J. de Rooy as his own home. Over its history, the interior of the Villa Maliebaan, as the house came to be called, had changed ownership many times, and the most recent renovations had left it a warren of cramped, low-ceilinged rooms. Without resorting to a restoration—neither the client nor the architect were interested in a period piece—Mecanoo strengthened the house's inherent residential qualities while creating a series of open work spaces. The firm rescued the spatial virtues of the original mansion by inserting a new staircase where the original one once stood, bringing light back to the core of the building. Deeply set windows hint at the villa's age, but immaculate white walls are wholly contemporary. The architects gave each level a different floor treatment, much as might be done in a residence. The partially subterranean conference room floor is made of ship's oak, which softens the effect of the room's cool, gray concrete walls. The attic offices are paved with stainless-steel plates whose high industrial sheen is tempered by the delicate wallpaper that covers the ceiling and upper half of the dormer walls. Further blurring the languages of home and office, lamps were custom-designed, as were the tables in the main office and conference room. The only obvious signals of work are the computer monitors and office chairs.

The sensitive modernization of historical buildings is an especially European phenomenon, and one that has particular resonance in former eastern bloc countries like Hungary, which until recently had significant architectural structures but little money to restore, much less update, them. The opening of physical and economic borders in the past two decades, however, has meant an influx of Western business interests, which has in turn begun to change the look of the capital city's urban landscape.

A case in point is a series of historical renovations—as well as new builds—commissioned by the Dutch bank ING in Budapest. Hired by ING, Dutch architect Erick van Egeraat (formerly of Mecanoo) first renovated and modernized a Neo-Renaissance palazzo on the city's grand Andrassy Street (1994), adding such new elements as a two-story organically shaped glazed boardroom embedded in the building's roof, which he dubs "the whale" for its biomorphic bubble shape. This startlingly contemporary intervention—a modern baroque gesture in a nineteenth-century architectural context—not only broadcasts the company's presence but also introduces much-needed space and light into an otherwise dark building. Van Egeraat also had the opportunity to restore the capital's only remaining modernist building (2001), which once housed the Hungarian Trade Union for Builders, and design a new office annexed to the 1949 structure (2003). Here again, an expressionist glass facade translates into light-flooded interiors, while symbolizing the openness of a once-closed city.

When Capital Z Partners, which calls itself an "alternative asset management firm," decided to situate its headquarters in SoHo instead of Midtown Manhattan or Wall Street, the company gave Stephen Cassell and Adam Yarinsky of ARO/ Architecture Research Office the freedom to create a light- and art-filled residence (1998) for the company's nine partners, eighteen principals, and numerous support staff. The first priority was to drench the interior of the four-story warehouse with light without resorting to fluorescents (or any other conventional solutions), so ARO partitioned the offices and common rooms with a custom system of extruded-polycarbonate panels and transparent glass sliding doors. Framed with blackened steel and cherrywood, the doors and partitions impart a Zen-like serenity, diffusing natural light and providing a shimmering backdrop for carefully curated suites of furniture. Here, contemporary and classic-modern pieces—ranging from Gerrit Rietveld Zig-Zag chairs to bright-red Vermelha rope chairs by the Campana Brothers—do more than merely telegraph taste; they impart the relaxed atmosphere of a private home, particularly in the common rooms, furnished with pendant lighting, area rugs, and contemporary artwork. In every respect, the Capital Z office goes beyond the generic—even in the bathroom, which is covered with a hallucinogenic wallpaper specially commissioned from the artist Christine

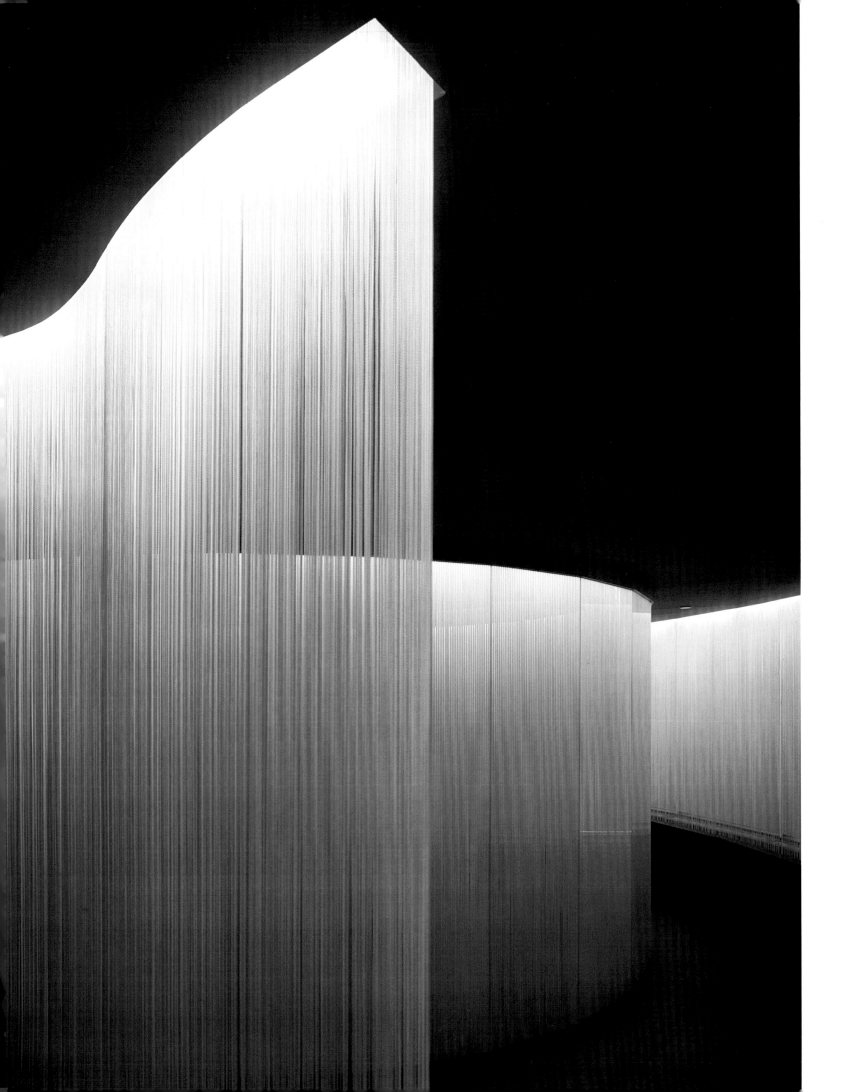

Opposite: Emilio Ambasz & Associates, Financial Guaranty Insurance
Corporation, New York, 1983

Steven Holl Architects, D.E. Shaw & Co., New York, 1992

Tarkowski. But more than any specific residential conceits, it is the level of customization and ARO's preoccupation with craft that make the space so hospitable and blur the distinction between the personal and the institutional.

Such iconoclastic interiors are not merely evidence of an inconsequential trend; they are the result of nearly a half-century of mounting resistance to and, ultimately, repudiation of, modernism's binary oppositions. It is important to point out here that modernism is not rejected but integrated into design history; hence its precepts are no longer considered irrefutable. Formerly antithetical notions—public and private,

function and decoration, rationality and intuition—are being reassessed and brought together in virtually every sphere of culture and design.[16] Furniture is no exception. When architects and clients set out to create office environments that reflect our equivocal feelings about the nature of work, they can now look to a burgeoning crop of furniture designers who also refuse to be held to type. For the offices of the award-winning Parisian advertising agency BETC Euro RSCG (2000), Frédéric Jung of Jung Architectures designed both open and private workstations for the firm's 360 employees. Jung invited Plum Bureau partners Catherine Geel and Indiana Collet-Barquero to select a panoply of vanguard pieces to ward off the client's allergy to all things institutional. The ad agency's president and creative director, Rémi Babinet, who collaborated closely with the designers on the project, set the brief by asking: "Why should people be worse off at the office than at home?"[17] The answer he got rivals most homes for sheer pleasure.

To wit: Erwan and Ronan Bouroullec's carpet, with its slender bands of color, sets a variegated tone and is matched in invention by pieces from the French collaborative Radi Designers, including benches with images of whippets on either end. Frédéric Ruyant was commissioned to create communal cubicles that integrated low-slung sofas in fuchsia, raspberry, cobalt, and emerald. The list goes on to include Konstantin Grcic's turquoise document-storage system, Piero Lissoni chaises, and Enrico Baleri poufs. Even the workstations in the open-plan office have a mix of design sensibilities, all held together by a few repeated elements: Everyone, even the directors, works at the same Jean Nouvel desk, and has the same tilting Enzo Mari wastebasket and Grcic lime-green-and-white hanging lamp. And everyone shares the light that pours in from the floor-to-ceiling window, a result of Jung's decision to move one of the building's sidewalls inward twenty feet and replace it with glazing.

Among the most striking aspects of the Capital Z and BETC Euro RSCG interiors are their episodes of highly keyed color. Banished are the rules that once limited such exhibitionism to fashion and the home. Today, fashion and femininity are increasingly valued commodities in the office. Walter Camagna, Massimiliano Camoletto, and Andrea Marcanto, partners in UdA/Ufficio d'Architettura in Turin, Italy, would add another quality to that list: ephemerality. Their design for a Milanese advertising agency, D'Adda, Lorenzini, Vigorelli (1999), is a tribute to the temporal and the seductive—two cardinal traits of the ever-changing landscape of advertising imagery. Color becomes the defining feature of rooms flooded with projections that are synchronized with the lighting system. Closets are backlit to reveal the outline of the clothes and objects inside. A reception room floats in a field of white—the sum of all color. Anchoring these illusions is a Ruhlmann-esque staircase of exceptional delicacy.

If D'Adda, Lorenzini, Vigorelli used intense color to convey the drive of ambition, Ushida Findlay all but converted it to

electricity in the design for a marketing communications agency in South London. In the Claydon Heeley Jones Mason office (2001), ribbons of steel—bright orange on one side and metallic silver on the other—snake through the lobby, serving simultaneously as reception desk, seating, and support for video screens. This swath of functional calligraphy wends its way from the reception area into the office proper, where it outlines zones of occupancy.

Hard edges are virtually nonexistent in the London office; they would be an impediment to the corporate ethos, which is built around flow. Brightly colored modular tabletops replace standard desks and are laid out in a loose pattern to encourage interaction. In the conference room the curls of the steel ribbon are echoed in the ghost of a Hokusai wave etched into the room's glazing. Here, sheer curtains striped in green, orange, and blue have magnetic strips ingeniously woven into the fabric for presentation displays. (The firm's staff use magnets instead of thumbtacks to post their work.) In the center of the room sits Kathryn Findlay's custom conference table surrounded by playful orange chairs manufactured by

Allermuir. In sum, the office represents a new, forward-looking organicism, rich in layers inherited from Art Nouveau and Surrealism across the chasm of a century, without the saccharin aftertaste that comes from facile imitation. Here, decoration becomes another sign of the desire for independence and autonomy still struggling to find its way into the culture of work. This is the next generation's vision of the workplace: nonthreatening, unpredictable, and optimistic.

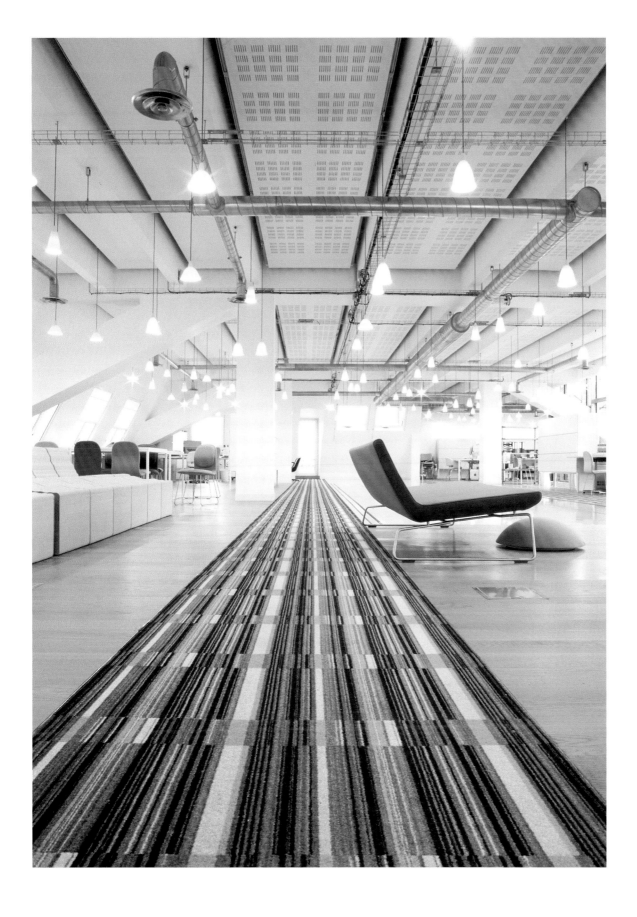

Opposite: UdA/Ufficio di Architettura, D'Adda, Lorenzini Vigorelli,
Milan, 1999

Ushida Findlay, Claydon Heeley Jones Mason, London, 2001

Civic

Over the past century, public skepticism of institutional authority in the West has become the rule rather than the exception. Beginning with the rebellions of the 1960s and continuing through the end of the Cold War, social contracts between figures of power and their constituents were sent back to the drafting board. In recent decades, heightened prosperity and an increasingly demanding consumer culture have produced a sense of entitlement unimaginable just fifty years ago, when the decisions of politicians, doctors, and clergy went largely unquestioned. New pockets of power and advocacy and streams of information through digital publishing and broadcasting have made transparency of process—be it judicial, legislative, or educational—essential to the credibility of those who would claim to serve the people. It has also become a critical aspect of the spaces in which their services are rendered.

Bureaucratic inconvenience and intimidation, still a fact of life in many parts of the world, is increasingly rejected in prosperous societies as counterproductive to the common good.[1] Bureaucratic dispensations—whether in the form of postage stamps, library books, court sentences, or diplomas—are no longer considered in isolation of the environment in which they take place, and the social climates those environments foster. Though libraries, schools, courthouses, and government offices have distinct design traditions, they now frequently share the broader role of community center, leading designers to search for ways to accommodate expanded social ambitions while still respecting conventions of use and meaning established centuries ago.

What were once considered luxuries of the private sector—comfortable seating, access to communications media, cafés, generous lighting—are now all but mandatory in the design of public environments. Conversely, private schools and institutions are increasingly making their facilities—swimming pools, meeting rooms, classrooms—available for public use as a way to diminish social strain and insure good community relations. Furthermore, nonprofit entities, from libraries to schools to cultural embassies, now must compete with commercial enterprises that have co-opted the traditional amenities of the public sector, whether they be reading rooms in bookstores or indoor parks in shopping malls. Furthermore, there is an increasing tendency of libraries, schools, and government agencies to emulate each other, even absorb each other's func-

tions, in response to developments in psychology, education, information science, and the social sciences over the course of the last century.

Schools and Universities

Schools, once modeled on factories and prisons, have over the past century been increasingly recognized as places of discovery, not just assembly lines of rote learning. The progressive reforms of the twentieth century—which opened with educator Maria Montessori's pioneering recognition of the power of self-directed inquiry and closed with the widespread embrace of Howard Gardner's theory of multiple intelligences (visual, verbal, musical, social, psychological, and physical)—have begun to produce a new generation of educational environments.

Early childhood education, now safely distant from the demands of the working world that schools are perceived to ultimately serve, has fostered an especially lively laboratory for design experimentation. Here, there is room for the fantastic as a legitimate impetus for learning. Günther Behnisch, the German architect who has pursued the organic functionalism of his fellow countryman Hans Scharoun (designer of the Berlin Philharmonie), has made educational and civic buildings central to his practice—most notably the German Parliament in Bonn, which will be considered later in this chapter. Among his many innovative school designs—marked by the skewed planes and angles of their interiors—the Kindergarten Ship (1990) in Stuttgart, Germany, stands out as the most playful in its use of space to encourage discovery and stimulate learning. Conceived as a stranded ship, the school has portholes, a narrow and steep staircase, and a large "mast" dividing the group rooms. Leaning decks and canted walls imaginatively reinforce the nautical theme. Behnisch describes the school as "a piece of the world ... that was missing and has become rare in our everyday existence."[2] Here a gentle spatial disorientation, combined with fragments of a mythical voyage, effectively restore that sense of adventure.

By contrast, Peter Hübner's firm Plus + Bauplanung designed a kindergarten (1990), also in Stuttgart, that makes an educational value of structure within a more conventionally orthogonal plan. The interior is divided into modules, each approximately nine feet square, just large enough to hold about twenty children sitting in a circle. The timbered modules

impose a tacit order on each floor: on the first floor they are
interconnected to create a large group space; at higher levels
they enclose rooms for children to nap. The regularity of the
spatial system is offset by the room's improvisatory furnishings: There are no fewer than twenty types of chairs, desks,
and tables, chosen from different manufacturers' catalogs.
The result is a decorative scheme—which critic Peter Blundell
Jones describes as "wonderfully inconsistent"— actively
promoting exploration and antithetical to the traditional
imposition of discipline.[3]

In his simple tube-shaped structure for a daycare center linked
to the Imai Hospital (2001) in Odate, Japan, Shigeru Ban
has taken cues from local craft traditions and the universal
childhood desire for a warm enclosing environment in which
to play. Using a regional bentwood technique normally used
to create bento boxes, Ban crafted nineteen sheets of laminated
veneer lumber into a tunnel punched through with regularized
cut-outs that admit light into the simple room's blond wood-
lined interior. A steep roof of fiberglass and folded steel plates
allow for snow to slide off during winter and provide a
striking geometrical contrast to the tubular interior.

Recognizing that the first years of formal schooling represent
a rupture between structured and unstructured learning and
play, the Seoul-based firm ISON Architects have created
Kindergarten Angel (2003) in Anyang, South Korean, that
combines a warm and safe sense of interiority with moments
that afford outward-looking glimpses into nature and the
world beyond. Located on a triangular site in the midst of a
high-rise development, the school's classrooms are adjacent
to gardens that attract the flora and fauna the students
learn about in lessons.

In the majority of school projects, designers must make the
most of limited budgets and less-than-ideal conditions, so when
the results exceed expectations it is all the more gratifying.
Such were the circumstances the young British firm DSDHA/
Deborah Saunt David Hills Architects faced when commissioned to create a nursery outside of London. An addition to
the John Perry Primary School (2004), the project was the
firm's first freestanding building, and it is remarkable for a
simple gesture of wit and economy: windows that become
customized viewfinders, staggered at different heights (child
and adult) in a translucent polycarbonate facade. Deborah

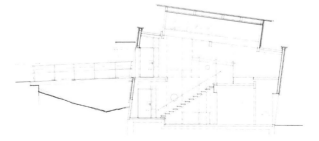

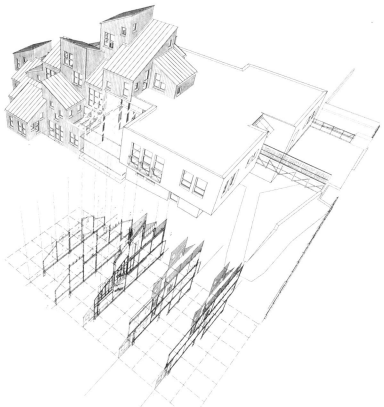
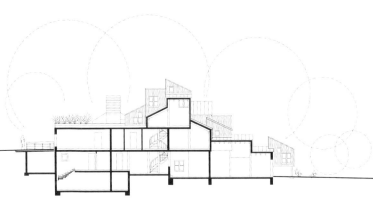

Saunt of DSDHA explains: "When you're small, a really big
vista isn't as interesting as a spy hole."[4]

In Santa Monica, California, Julie Eizenberg and Hank Koning
of KEA/Koning Eizenberg Architecture rebuilt and enlarged
the constricted urban campus of Pluralistic Elementary School
No. 1 (1999) to include seven classrooms, a multipurpose
activity space, an extended-care space, a library, and administrative rooms. Widely regarded for architecture that is both
socially and environmentally sustainable, Koning Eizenberg
created a school that is child-centered and family-friendly
through a collaborative design process that involved the
students, parents, teachers, and administrators. More than a
mirror of progressive educational values, the school also
represents a social contract in which architects share, but
do not entirely relinquish, authority in the design process.
The result is not merely improved community relations, but
also physical spaces that transcend generic functionality to
become what architecture critic Aaron Betsky calls "jewels
of expressive practicality."[5] At Pluralistic Elementary School
No. 1, the classrooms themselves offer students a tutorial in
the science and art of architecture—from the graphic nature
of their exposed ceiling trusses, which tell the story of the
roof, to the colorful covered passages, which demonstrate the
environmental interdependence of "indoors" and "outdoors."

There is a growing consensus among educators—not just among
designers—that a school's furnishings, interior surfaces, and
palette make as much of an imprint on a child's psyche as the
building itself. In choosing a modernist idiom (still synonymous
with progressive values), schools reinforce their own philosophies
of openness. For the Little Red School House & Elisabeth Irwin
High School expansion (2003) in Manhattan, the New York firm
1100 Architect tapped into the Scandinavian vein of modernism
to create a welcoming domesticity that nonetheless refuses to
condescend to students with adult clichés of childhood. Blond
wood and contemporary furnishings and lighting fixtures were
chosen over "playful" mosaics or murals. The design, developed
by 1100 Architect principal David Piscuskas and his team, also
reveals a critical educational priority. The first thing a visitor
notices on entering the 10,000-square-foot (929-square-meter)
addition is the library, set on a pedestal two feet above the lobby
floor level and on full view behind glass, drawing the eye as a
shop window would. The two-story library has pride of place
as the school's social and intellectual hub, with bookshelves

and comfortable chairs on the first floor and a computer lab
on the mezzanine. The addition also yielded a new cafeteria
with an undulating wood-slat ceiling and clerestory windows,
three new classrooms (including a luminous, sky-lit art studio),
and a welcoming entrance plaza that completely reorients the
school toward the more open urban boulevard on the west.

Erasing the last vestiges of the punitive nature of education—
often felt most acutely in high school, where adolescent drives
often conflict with educational imperatives—was uppermost
in Thom Mayne's mind when his firm Morphosis set out to
design Diamond Ranch High School (1999), a public school
in Pomona, California. Mayne had little latitude in the way of
budget for furnishings that would match the school's vanguard
crags of corrugated galvanized steel, but what the interior
may lack in small amenities is made up for by multiple points
of orientation, a plan that works in tandem with the contours
of the landscape, and a strong sense of interiority generated
by outdoor corridors and intimate courtyards wedged irregularly within the complex. Red-painted trusses pierce the
interior of the classrooms in the three wings that project out
over the valley. The upper levels hold classrooms as well as
spaces for art and music, all under ceilings of suspended
perforated metal. For such a large school—there are 2,000
students—Diamond Ranch achieves a sense of community
because it gives its teenage student body a clear sense of
spatial autonomy.

While Morphosis's design compensates for the suburban
dislocation from the city, Herman Hertzberger's design for
the Montessori College Oost in Amsterdam (1999) mirrors
the behavior of a city within a city. Recognizing that secondary
schools are "populated by children of an age when … they
prefer to get out of the house to hang out," Hertzberger says
his intention at Montessori College Oost was to make pupils
"feel as much at home … as in their familiar stamping
ground: the city."[6]

Balconied classroom galleries are staggered in half-stories
that overlook a single communal hall that reads like a plaza
within an urban block. At Montessori College Oost, however,
"hanging out" is not restricted to the hall. This quintessential
teenage pastime is the a priori design consideration of the
entire space, from the diagonal sightlines across the balconies
to the amphitheater-like stairs between floors that encourage

students to congregate. Hertzberger understands the nomadic routines of high school students—constantly moving from class to class—and made an event of their movement by introducing multiple stairways. Interspersed between these gestural spans of metal and wood are red, yellow, and blue columns that offer vertical punctuation marks (with a subtle nod to the palette of Dutch modernism), echoing the animated sociability of the school.

Just as Hertzberger's design can be seen as a product of Dutch culture, which places a premium on social cooperation in a densely populated and geographically constrained country, BOORA Architects' work reflects the value put on pragmatism and natural beauty in the western United States. Working in the socially progressive state of Oregon, BOORA has designed several public schools premised on principles of environmental sustainability, proving that green design is not beyond the reach of public-sector budgets. A case in point is the 260,000-square-foot (24,154-square-meter), 1,800-student Clackamas High School (2002), which was selected by the Energy Foundation, a US advocacy group, to serve as a national model for exceptional energy performance.[7] Because the school's four academic houses are organized along an east-west axis, students enjoy high levels of natural light—particularly in the generously glazed library—and teachers report a marked decline in "sleepy behavior."[8] Even the locker-lined hallways are illuminated by clerestories and skylights. Ceilings received special design treatments that go beyond their practical functions of distributing light and sound: In the cafeteria, crisply angled planes hover dynamically overhead, and in the auditorium, fiberglass baffles matched to the color of the

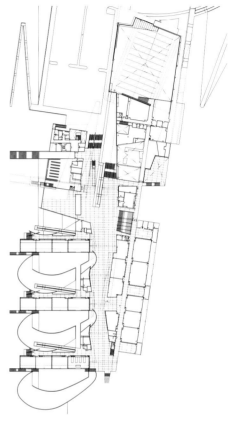

Architecture Studio Herman Hertzberger, Montessori College Oost, Amsterdam, 1999

BOORA Architects, Clackamas High School, Clackamas, Oregon, 2002

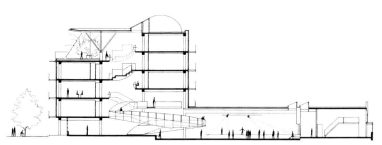

room's maple veneer ripple above the space, creating elegant silhouettes against the dark ground of the theater's ceiling. Grace notes in an economically prudent design, these graphic details shift the experience of school, as well as the argument for sustainability, from a matter of duty to the pursuit of pleasure—a wholly American value.

Using an entirely different design strategy, Santiago Calatrava revisits the notion of the school as a cathedral of learning. The commission to design additions to Wohlen High School (1988) in Wohlen, Switzerland, came relatively early in Calatrava's career, and its scope is quite modest in comparison to his now internationally renowned portfolio of bridges and buildings. Nonetheless, the school is notable for its aspirational language and as a portent of work to come. Calatrava designed for the school's entrance canopy, lobby, library, and assembly hall, distinguishing each space with the iconography of its construction system: A ribbed arched entry canopy joins the two wings of the existing school, sheltering the students who pass through it; a radial canopy over the lobby echoes the act of gathering; a vaulted concrete ceiling, resting on a single central column, hovers over the two-story library, which

Calatrava likens to an open book or a bird in flight. And adjacent to the library, five parabolic arches support a web of slender slatted pine boards that filters light into the assembly hall. The tectonic confidence of each space has the additional advantage of exerting a strong unifying force that makes them coherent as strata in the school's interior architecture.

In higher education, where competition for students and resources is fierce, increasingly this same sculptural strategy is used to create landmarks of prestige. Contextualization within wholly unified architectural schemes (which often devolves into theming) no longer has to be literal. Stylistic conformity thwarts the full capacity of design to explore new programs through new forms and is, in fact, antithetical to the needs of the university.

The University of Utrecht, in The Netherlands, has described the purpose of Rem Koolhaas's Educatorium (1997) as making "the university … visible to the outside world" while at the same time acknowledging that the interior program must offer more than "suitable accommodation to scientists and students [and] encourage the university to function as an academic

community."[9] Engendering that sense of community becomes the paramount task of the interior, leaving the facade to function as a billboard.

In Utrecht and also in Chicago, at the Illinois Institute of Technology's (IIT) McCormick Tribune Campus Center (which opened in 2003), Koolhaas insinuates a neighborhood mentality into an architecture of big, curvaceous forms. The Dutch Educatorium is a freestanding building whose interior is shaped by an attenuated S-curve that yields a lower-level restaurant with a canted ceiling that forms the sloping floor of the theaters above it. The structural curvature is reinforced internally by interior wood veneer that gives the illusion of being pulled up from the floor and twisted and turned to form the arc of the ceiling.

The presence of the IIT Campus Center is signaled outwardly by a massive, shining elliptical tube ingeniously designed both to accommodate the elevated train that cuts through the site and to form the roof of the student center underneath it. The program includes a welcome center, dining facilities, the studios of the campus radio station, an auditorium, a meeting room, and a variety of stores and services. Laid out along the shortcut paths used by students on the site prior to the center's development, the interior is conceived as an indoor city, a distinct enclave within the greater campus, which was designed by Ludwig Mies van der Rohe in 1956. Tropes familiar from Koolhaas's New York SoHo Epicenter (see Retail, p. 356) are evident in the built-in bleachers and stairs that overlook the sunken two-story recreation and dining area and in the murals designed by Michael Rock and Susan Sellers of the New York design studio 2x4. Here and in their other collaborations with Koolhaas, 2x4 turned information into décor with graphics that behave as furnishings, from the large digital clock near the entrance to the maps embedded in the floor to the portrait wall honoring IIT's founders. Together, these constitute a new definition of decoration in an architectonic interior—this one distinguished by layers of translucent and transparent glass, a glowing red computer lounge corridor, a revealing glimpse of the belly of the train tube, and "boulevards" studded with Mies's signature black I-beams.

It is worth recalling that until recently educational environments, like other public places, were largely considered inappropriate venues for the expenditure of resources on interior design per se. Decoration was acceptable only if it was exhortatory or pedagogical, actively preaching or implicitly instructive. This explains why, even today, apart from the appearance of cushioned chairs and couches, amenities in schools are largely didactic, as with 2x4's digitized image of Mies at IIT, or intrinsic to the architecture itself, thus avoiding the perception of superfluity.

For these cultural reasons, as well as for purely practical ones—specifically the flexibility required by rapidly changing curricula, student populations, and research requirements— campus interiors continue to be bifurcated into lounges more residential in nature and laboratories and classrooms that hew to the monastic. But where heavy curtains and leather club chairs once defined the lounge or common room, now open spaces reflect the egalitarian nature of the college campus. Furthermore, these spaces are no longer considered purely social, and their value as places of informal learning is reflected in their design.

This shift in perception is clearly evident in the immense glazed atrium of Rafael Viñoly's Lewis-Sigler Institute for Integrative Genomics at Princeton University (2003) in Princeton, New Jersey. It is a place where scientists can come down from their laboratories to enjoy a break in a café furnished with Ron Arad's Tom Vac chairs, or meet in the intimacy of Frank Gehry's horse-head-shaped conference room.[10] The atrium's 30-foot-tall (9-meter-tall) window is "curtained" by perforated louvers that follow the movement of the sun, thereby reducing the load on the building's cooling systems and also creating a lattice of shadows that gives visual texture and scale to the vast room. The Institute's research spaces, designed through extensive collaboration with the faculty, were no less carefully considered. The loft-like open spaces contain movable lab benches and easily configurable partition systems whose chief amenity is their flexibility.

Just as designers of scientific research facilities are placing a new premium on social space, dormitories are now conceived as holistic residential environments, not just with cafeterias and lounges, but also with gyms, theaters, computer labs, and game rooms. This new model of collegiate housing, which brings once disparate facilities and activities into the same social matrix, proved an ideal vehicle for

Steven Holl's ongoing explorations of porosity. In point of
fact, Holl's design for Simmons Hall at the Massachusetts
Institute of Technology (2002) in Cambridge was inspired
by the physical and metaphorical properties of the sponge.

The deep-set fenestrated facade of the ten-story residence
features 18-inch deep (46-cm-deep) windows and keeps an
open relationship to the larger campus while affording its
residents a multiplicity of views of the Charles River. Each
room has nine operable windows, and the perforations in
the facade are echoed in the punctured grills of the stainless-steel stair railings and the circular cutouts in the
dormitory furniture, designed by Holl's office. The random
Swiss-cheese patterns cut into the desks and bookshelves
are microcosms of the calculated irregularities Holl uses to
disrupt his own grid; the most provocative and unexpected
of these are the common rooms' freeform gray walls, which
fold and curve upward toward Structolite skylights. While
they employ distinctly different form languages, the organic
common rooms and the rectilinear dorm rooms both contribute to the idea of the dormitory as an illuminated cavern,
both a place to retreat and a place to meet.

On a larger level, Holl's building is a critique of the modernist tendency to use vast, open areas to eliminate any
sense of closed interiority. In distinction, Holl proposes an
active give-and-take between inside and out. In this he is
not alone. One example of the same volumetric push-pull
appears in Henning Larsens Studio's new building for the
IT University of Copenhagen (2004), a small graduate school
where rooms are cantilevered into an interior courtyard like
open drawers of various sizes. Their white, cubic surfaces
are animated by digital artworks created by American artist/
designer John Maeda (who also happens to be the director
of the Physical Languages Workshop at MIT).

But unlike the Danish IT University, which resides in a
single (and singular) building, MIT is a sprawling campus
that is currently enjoying the fruits of a billion-dollar building program launched in the 1990s. Its stature secured,
MIT is not as concerned with establishing its presence as
much as with creating a greater sense of community with
built expressions equal to the genius of its occupants. Significantly, the new commissions at MIT resume a tradition
of innovative architecture on the campus that includes Eero

Steven Holl Architects, Simmons Hall, Massachusetts Institute of Technology,
Cambridge, Massachusetts, 2002

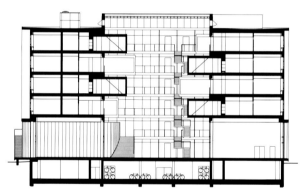

Gehry Partners, Ray and Maria Stata Center, Massachusetts Institute of Technology, Cambridge, Massachusetts, 2004

Saarinen's Kresge Hall (1955) and Alvar Aalto's Baker House (1948). One of the most celebrated pieces of the new campus configuration is Frank Gehry's Ray and Maria Stata Science Center (2004), which houses the departments of artificial intelligence, computer science, philosophy, and linguistics. In keeping with the new model of the multitasking ivory tower, the Stata Center also includes a child-care facility, a cafeteria, and a fitness center.

Designed from the inside out, the Stata Center comprises two towers linked by a common area called the "town center" that contains a long "student street." Beyond offering familiar metaphors for a university town, the building models a notion of scientific inquiry and intellectual exchange. Its spaces are in constant conversation with each other. Bridges and walkways generate what Boston architecture critic David Eisen describes as "ever-changing vistas of colleagues across the way and clouds passing overhead."[11] With its canted walls, many of them vividly colored, the building looks upon and leans in on itself, even pulling some of the exterior surfaces inside, heightening the sense of an inwardly focused community. World Wide Web inventor and Stata Center occupant Tim Berners-Lee, a senior research scientist at MIT, has likened the building to the Internet in that it's not rigidly structured and offers multiple ways of getting information.[12] The architectural character of the Center—Gehry famously referred to it as "a party of drunken robots"[13]—is reflected in the absence of uniform furnishings. In contrast to Holl's **gesamtkunstwerk**, desks, chairs, and other furnishings were selected by the Gehry office, but their placement is intentionally ad hoc. Students and faculty can reconfigure their labs and offices as needed. (Furthermore, wiring is embedded in the floors, not the walls, for maximum flexibility.) As with all of Gehry's buildings, there is a joyous freedom that comes from the absence of predictability and the suggestion of possibility—supremely fitting qualities for a center that sits on the former site of the famed Building 20, otherwise known as the Magical Incubator. (Building 20 was built after World War II as a temporary wooden structure but stood until 1998; it was the site of Noam Chomsky's research in the science of linguists, the canvas for Timothy Leary's painted murals, and the base for many of the first generation of computer hackers in the 1960s.)

In Santiago, Chile, a young architect named Alejandro Aravena has created a similarly unconventional—if more economically modest—solution to housing the Mathematics Faculty of the Catholic University of Chile (1999). Rather than design a new building, Aravena grafted two pre-existing structures together with a series of zigzagging hallways meant to inspire off-grid thinking for the mathematicians who tread its paths. In fact, the corridors reflect the misalignments between the floors of the two buildings. Aravena's choice to celebrate their disjunctions is not only an honest expression of two different structural conditions, but also a mirror of the nonlinear nature of contemporary logic and thought.

The problem of architecturally linking the past with the present was addressed in an entirely different way at RMIT, one of Australia's premiere design and architecture schools in Melbourne. Formerly based out of an elegant but antiquated neoclassical building built in 1887 by the city's Hibernian Catholic Community, the progressive school wanted a way to update its civic identity and expand with

lecture facilities and auditorium space. Rather than take aesthetic and material cues from RMIT's pre-existing building—the predominance of vivid green is the only nod to an Irish heritage—Ashton Raggatt McDougall created a state-of-the-art, six-story structure called Storey Hall (1995). Its brilliant prismatic skylights and windows are directly inspired by Oxford mathematician Roger Penrose's work with tessellation (known to cognoscenti as his "fat and skinny tile" invention). The complex geometry of the fenestration is carried through in faceted interior walls that seem to ripple through the building, finding sensual counterpoint where they meet with sloping stairwells and tapered columns. The result is a series of iconoclastic spaces uniquely hospitable to the work of mathematics in the digital age.

Not all expressions of science and technology are so literally gregarious. Tod Williams and Billie Tsien set up a call-and-response relationship between their buildings and the landscape surrounding them to craft environments of serenity. Two of their projects—the Neuroscience Institute (1995) in La Jolla, California, and the Williams Natatorium at

Cranbrook (2000) in Bloomfield Hills, Michigan–reveal this relationship to be a consistent thread in their work. In the case of the highly lauded Neuroscience Institute, the architects designed the outdoor rooms and the promenade that link the three basic structures–laboratories, offices, and auditorium–in a complex for usually incompatible types of scientists: theoreticians and laboratory empiricists, or those looking to prove their ideas and those seeking to discover them. The Institute's interior carries fragments of the earth inside in walls made of Texas fossil-stone and heavily blasted concrete that reveals a green stone aggregate. Redwood is used in large wall panels; the furniture, designed by Williams, is made of cherrywood. A tapestry depicting the California coast, designed by Tsien, graces the dining room. Designed as a "monastery of science," each office is a private refuge within a unified whole, and offers expansive views of the Pacific and the surrounding landscape. The auditorium, clad in pyramidal panels with "light pipes" embedded in the seams, pursues the idea of the illuminated cloister, complementing the atmosphere of retreat and communion that infuses the entire program.

Sited on the grounds of the Cranbrook Educational Community designed by Eliel Saarinen, the Cranbrook Natatorium not only has a specific relationship to its site– Michigan's lakes and the campus's fountains and water- ways–but also offers constant views of the cosmos with two 32-foot (10-meter) oculi cut through the roof and ceiling. Athletes, regular students, and members of the surrounding community do their laps beneath the open sky. Even inclement weather becomes an aesthetic event, as swimmers stroke through snow and rain showers gracefully funneled through the elliptical voids. (Should the need arise, the openings can be sealed by sliding roofs.) Though the Natatorium's oculi are dramatically angled into a flat roof, the experience of swimming through its concentrated weathers suggestively recalls the open dome of the Pantheon. (Both architects have spent considerable amounts of time in Rome; Tsien is on the board of the American Academy in Rome, and Williams was a Fellow there in 1983.) The building's tension with the sky is strengthened by the fact that the structure is literally embedded in the landscape. One enters at the level of the observation deck, surprised to find the pool sunk below the visible facade of the building. The Natatorium's interior walls are articulated

Tod Williams Billie Tsien & Associates, Neuroscience Institute, La Jolla, California, 1995

Opposite: Tod Williams Billie Tsien & Associates, Williams Natatorium, Cranbrook Athletic Complex, Bloomfield Hills, Michigan, 2000

with green, blue, and dark iron spot-glazed brick, in a subtle nod to the craft tradition on which Cranbrook was founded. Mahogany is used for wall and window panels to offer warmth, and the ceiling is painted a rich, dark blue. The walls and floor of the pool are warm-toned concrete block.

Inserted into rich architectural contexts—the Neuroscience Institute is adjacent to Louis Kahn's Salk Institute, and the Natatorium is surrounded by Saarinen's art deco campus, as well as new buildings by Steven Holl and Rafael Moneo—both buildings' quietly expressive programs embody a deeply internalized design history and a thoughtful response to the character of the surrounding landscape. Their interiors are marked by a distinct humanism, evident in surfaces that invite touch, seen in closely hued palettes, and discernible in narrative elements, like the Neuroscience's tapestry or the Natatorium's oculi.

It is worth returning to two lower schools here for their similar sensitivities to landscape. Operating in more isolated conditions, architects Antoine Predock and Valerio

to terms with greater demand for access to their resources: books, periodicals, video, film, and web journals that are multiplying daily.

There are those who would argue that the evolution of the "soft," or virtual, digital library eliminates the need for physical buildings—other than those required to house giant servers—and theoretically they are right. But the purely electronic library is essentially a utopian vision that neglects the role of memory stimulated by touching and looking at books, not to mention the chance social encounters libraries have always provided. In fact, at the same time that the Internet has become encyclopedic, the social role of libraries is growing exponentially. Lounges that were designed to offer a break from the isolation of reading are growing into entire wings. Indeed, these expanded facilities can be seen as a direct response to the physical isolation of individuals connected by computer cables.

Even as the digital library outpaces the physical library with sheer volume of information, it is hard to imagine that it could replace the physical library's role as a tangible demonstration of civic pride. Working behind the facade of a historic structure, Alberto Campo Baeza reprises the archetypal model of the monastery for the Orihuela Public Library (1992) in Alicante, Spain. Books and reading rooms are sequestered behind three-story-high walls cut with deep openings to signify the building's relationship to its thick-walled historic palazzo. These rooms are accessed via three levels of walkways, along the wall opposite the arched entry, that overlook the public space below. Campo Baeza's real achievement, however, is the courtyard, where he has designed interior walls that are finished in polished stone and has set them as diagonal planes into the orthogonal space, echoing and framing the unfolding rhythm of the main stairs. A white painted-metal structure of telescoping columns and triangular trusses supports a glazed skylight. Together these elements not only mitigate the sense of fortification implicit in broad expanses of stone, but shift the axis of the space 90 degrees. In reorienting the space away from the palazzo's facade, Campo Baeza doesn't turn his back on the building's history, but creates an interior confident enough to absorb its information in a mimesis of the library itself.

On a wholly different scale, but in the same spirit of synthesis, Egypt's Bibliotheca Alexandrina, the Great Library of Alexandria (2002), is defined by millennia of history and an acute sense of place in the city and in the world. Out of a field of 500 competition entries, Snøhetta, an international architectural collaborative based in Oslo, was chosen by the Egyptian government and UNESCO to create a contemporary equivalent to the ancient library that thrived some 2,000 years ago in the same city–the library where Archimedes and Euclid studied, where the poet Calimachus first devised the notions of classification that became the basis for libraries as we know them today. The enormity of that legacy insured that beyond being a critical repository of knowledge, the Bibliotheca would become a symbol of international cultural awareness. Snøhetta's design, which claimed first prize at the 2002 World Architecture Awards, secured that stature, aptly imbuing the form and symbolism of the circle with new purpose for a new era.

Within the Bibliotheca's immense tilted disk–528 feet (161 meters) in diameter–is the largest reading room in the world. Its floor rises in a series of fourteen concentric terraces to accommodate more than 2,000 readers and researchers. The library's overwhelming presence is lent human scale by seating areas that create personal space and by the rhythmic presence of concrete columns that grow out of the cascading interior landscape. The furnishings within the reading hall were conceived as a totality so that all of its component sections come together as a complete design when seen from the entrance balcony and the room's high terraces. The library's overall composition is further animated by delicately designed wooden chairs, whose graceful curves contrast with the

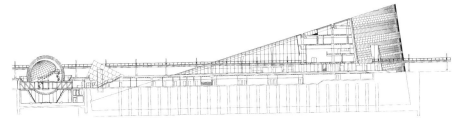

straight lines of the desks and shelves. Like the banded
capitals of the slender columns, these high-back seats
make effective but subtle reference to historical Egyptian
design. These artful differentiations effectively eliminate
the monotony of repetition that often occurs in such vast
spaces by texturing and articulating the segments of the
circular volume.

Conversely, the faceted underside of the library roof, which
is delineated by a diagonal pattern of triangular clerestory
windows, unifies a grand space dominated by small-scale
objects. Echoing the patterns of light created by the clerestory,
the reading room's pre-cast concrete walls are pierced with
small rectangular cutouts that create a swirling pattern of
their own and also work acoustically to absorb ambient
noise. The interior's otherwise neutral palette is animated
by splashes of blue and green light (colors long important
to Egyptian and Muslim culture) that emanate from glass
blocks inserted in the roof. These details all participate in
what amounts to an integral vocabulary of tectonic ornament that textures the vast space, signaling a renaissance
of craft and an embrace of complexity, both of which are
fast emerging as hallmarks of design in the early twenty-
first-century.[14]

Given the fragility of their holdings, even modern libraries
cannot be wholly transparent. They must find other means
of announcing their presence. Hence, the tradition of grand
edifices seen in the Bibliotheca Alexandrina's hieroglyphic
cladding and taken to literal extremes in the four "open
books" that make up France's Bibliothèque Nationale (1995),
designed by architect Dominique Perrault. Located on the
banks of the river Seine in Paris, the library is one of former
president François Mitterand's *grands projets* of the 1990s.
While on the exterior Perrault flirted with the idea of transparency as a paradox—the 264-foot-tall (80.5-meter-tall)
L-shaped glass towers reveal wooden shutters, not books—
his interior is a model of clarity. With impeccable detailing,
Perrault established an elegant coherence throughout using
an industrial palette of red carpeting and gray steel and
concrete, modulated by the warm wood of the furniture,
floors, and, of course, shutters. Necessary for energy conservation, the movable window shutters also domesticate the
corporate overtones of the towers, confirming the institution
as the home library of all French citizens—and fulfilling

a cardinal requirement in the brief: that the library be "neither a temple nor a supermarket."[15]

The British Library (1998) at St. Pancras in London, designed by Colin St. John Wilson, reflects a more conservative approach to the prestigious commission of the national library. The building is a model of good citizenship in its legibility—no mean feat for a library containing more than 150 million volumes and serving 16,000 visitors a day—but its interiors are compromised. True, the design does successfully alleviate the monotony of the sheer volume of reading tables and shelves (all designed by the architect) with multistory spaces whose ceilings are painted brilliant white in contrast to the blues and greens of the carpeting and table surfaces. And it's also true that, as architecture critic Samantha Hardingham points out, "the gulf between the sheer size of the building and the scale of its human users [is] bridged by ... balconies ... short flights of steps and escalators, and ... a grid pattern in the stone and brick paving."[16] But the overall aesthetic of the grid—seen most clearly in the latter-day baldachin that dominates the humanities reading room—speaks more to a dated postmodernism than to the turn of the millennium.

Underlying the entire project is a larger awkwardness, an unresolved tension between the gravitas of such a commission and a genuine desire to be user-friendly. In his book on the library, Wilson alluded to the source of the tension—

the collision of archetypes: "[T]here is one type of building which is profane yet in fulfilling its proper role touches the hem of the sacred: the great library."[17] The uncomfortable resolution of these two archetypes may have been as much a consequence of the project's lengthy gestation (commissioned in 1974, the library was beset by numerous delays) as it was a factor of changing social values.

Indeed, by the 1990s, comfort, entertainment, and transparent access, once considered soft luxuries in institutional settings, were being seriously re-evaluated in light of their ability to encourage learning, reading, and participation in the civic realm. At the same time, designers, having closed the chapter on the heavy-handed historicism of the 1980s, were becoming nimbler; they began searching for less predictable responses to accommodate the ever-faster flow of incident and accident in contemporary life. One of the more interesting examples from the transitional period of the early 1990s is Hodgetts + Fung's Towell Library (1992) for the University of California, Los Angeles, a temporary structure intended to be used for only five years. The designers took the liberty of creating a tented structure of woven polyester that would have been unusual for a permanent building but which nonetheless proved seminal in the long term. Bright-yellow floors and stacks introduced an element of exuberance into the monastic order of the library. Traditionally circular reading rooms were unconventionally ribbed in aluminum. The Towell Library was both literally and conceptually raw, but it was more than a piece of high-tech machismo: Its exposed fasteners, cables, and functional elements were signs of a growing conviction that, as architectural historian Kurt Forster observed, "nothing holds together any longer but what has been joined and bound together by artifice."[18] Not only the artifice of materials, but the artifice of ideas. This notion that there can be no pre-ordained style or spatial program because all styles and programs are fictions—even in institutions dedicated to the preservation of history and information—had the profound effect of liberating the library from its image of order. Soon to follow were new libraries crisscrossed by stairs, bridged by ramps, and otherwise opened up and sewn back together in unexpected ways.

Bolles + Wilson's design of the City Library Münster (1993) in Münster, Germany, not only offers the surprises of an

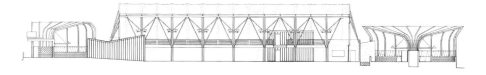

aesthetic derived from designing from the inside out, but
is also a prime example of the new sociability of public
libraries. (Admittedly, it is a sociability driven as much
by the firm's commitment to the citizens of Münster as
the anxiety about the comprehensiveness of the library in
an age of mass-market bookstores). Australian Peter Wilson
and his partner Julia Bolles, a native of Münster, where
the firm is based, looked at the activities the library would
support and came up with two distinct spaces, linked above
and below ground, that declare the library's split personality.
A long rectangular slab—unself-consciously celebrated as
a supermarket of information—houses the library's café,
auditorium, and two-story newspaper reading room. A
curved structure—a fragment of the archetypal circle—
serves the more traditional library function, with stacks
interspersed among quiet reading areas.

Both wings are sky-lit, their ceilings partially encased by
massive ribs of white laminated timber that support warm
wood acoustic panels. The massive scale established by
the structural elements is mitigated by windows sized for
individual views. Another indication of their commitment
to provide personal space in a communal environment is
the fact that the architects never lost sight of the relation
of furniture to room. The place of the reader was always
carefully considered, as evidenced by the deep windowsill
seating niches and multiple intimate spaces. Bolles and
Wilson also recognized that the reader is now also a listener,
a viewer, even a flâneur enjoying the scene; accordingly,
they introduced customized furniture, such as the whimsical
wheeled newspaper "wagons" and the "vehicles" in the
Mediathek that allow visitors to listen to tapes, as if they
were sitting on carnival floats.

In his 1974 book *A History of Building Types*, Nikolaus
Pevsner notes that the original library was first a piece of
furniture—the book cupboard—and only later a building.[19]
Where Bolles and Wilson play with the relationship between
the two, Will Bruder's Phoenix Central Library (1995) in
Phoenix, Arizona, conflates them entirely. Based on a simple
orthogonal grid made up of square bays based on library
stack modules, the library is colloquially referred to as
"saddlebags for books." Bruder's functionally driven design
quickly became a national icon and brought new attention
to the cultural and design potential of civic libraries in the

United States. (Its impact as an urban icon can be seen in the major commissions that followed, among them Moshe Safdie's Salt Lake City Public Library and Rem Koolhaas's Seattle Central Library, the latter of which is discussed later in this chapter.) The biggest innovation that Bruder brought to the library's interior is its exposure to light and landscape—a resonant factor in a Western state that prides itself on wide-open spaces, and a practical benefit to the readers dispersed throughout the building's 280,000 square feet (26,012 square meters). The library is literally book-ended in glass: The south wall is outfitted with automated solar tracking devices to minimize heat gain and glare; the north wall is shielded by "shade sails" to optimize views in the face of summer sun. Designed for display as well as protection, the glass facades proudly showcase the library's books and its patrons to the community. The concern for natural light and sightlines was not confined to the building's edges, however. To insure that daylight reached the heart of the library, Bruder situated a five-story light well at its center. Within this monumental atrium, automated sun-tracking skylights ration acceptable amounts of natural light into the interior. Paired with a sequence of tapered concrete columns, the skylights helpfully orient visitors as they thread their way through the spatial grid. The attention to lighting is even carried through to the yellow reading lamps of the architect's own design. Beyond providing additional artificial illumination, the lamps also create a pattern of horizontal slashes that brightly punctuate the cavernous space of the Great Reading Room.

Instead of stressing the gravitas of the library—the weight and authority of its holdings—designers like Bruder project a view of knowledge as light. Mecanoo's design for the library at the Delft Technical University (1998) in Delft, The Netherlands, brings both illumination and wit into its precincts with saturated color, slender proportions, and playful geometry. Sited partially below grade, the library's most distinguishing feature is the conical form that thrusts through the structure's grass-covered roof and is the crown of the library's interior. Capped in glass, the luminous white cone, balanced on splayed steel columns above the library's huge hall, creates an interior room of its own. Four rings of study space hug its periphery, permitting light to flow down to the main floor. Flanking it are two steel-framed cases suspended from the ceiling holding multistoried shelves of books that are silhouetted against a field of ultra-marine. These massive cases, which seem to flow endlessly upward, are accessed by diagonal stairs that also lead down to an informal reading area containing pod-shaped tables and stools. In an increasingly computer-driven library culture, Mecanoo put a premium on the pleasure of being able to touch and smell the books from the open stacks to the processional axes that connect them. The result is an atmosphere both ethereal and sensual, an environment wholly appropriate for a library devoted to the technical and natural sciences.

If Mecanoo's library, with its conical dome and soaring bookcases, is full of suggestions of the cosmos, Italo Rota's Anzola dell' Emilia Library (2000) on the urban fringe of Bologna, Italy, is tightly homebound. Conceived as a series of living rooms, brightly colored translucent boxes create discrete niches for readers embedded in the white-walled geometry of the space. A unique solution to the perennial problem of creating intimacy in an institutional setting, the rooms occupy a scale between the carrel and the reading hall. Visually rich and totally unexpected, Rota's design seems, in the words of *Abitare* magazine critic Beppe Finessi, to have "fully assimilated Bruno Munari's observation … 'if you give a child a boring book, it will find books boring for the rest of its life.'"[20]

Long denigrated by conservatives as distracting and counterproductive, entertainment is now widely understood as a critical aspect of learning, valuable in reducing inhibitions,

encouraging free association, and reinforcing the relational nature of knowledge. In the largely silent context of the library, entertainment has often been confined to the children's story hour. More recently, however, libraries are placing greater emphasis on the haptic and visual aspects of design, and we now see libraries seeking and serving broader constituencies, particularly those for whom literacy is a goal and not a given. Accordingly, libraries are taking on more extroverted personalities, not only in their public facades but also in the narratives that unfold in their interiors.

In South East London, an area undergoing regeneration, SMC Alsop designed the Peckham Library New Media Center (1999) as an inverted L and, in the process, upended almost all typological expectations. Visitors enter the library under a cantilevered block and emerge into a double-height entrance foyer where, before seeing a single book, they encounter the One Stop Shop, which offers community information and advice. A glazed elevator, offering spectacular views of London, brings visitors to the horizontal block of the lending library itself. Here, the whole notion of the reading room is catapulted to the future and reconfigured as three huge, timber-clad pods that contain a children's activity area, an Afro-Caribbean literature center, and a meeting room. Lifted up from the library floor on stilts, these spaces are a cross between tree houses and spaceships. Running like a steady bass rhythm throughout the design is a sense of craft, detected in the patchwork cladding of the pods, the woven-steel braiding of their lighting fixtures, and the building's colored window panes, variously clear, yellow, blue, and green. But not once does the space pander to some facile notion of community. Rather, its distinctly contemporary, expressive form (the building was awarded the 2000 Stirling Prize) challenges preconceptions of institutions and cultures.

This is the same challenge taken on by the sixteen architecture firms engaged by the Robin Hood Foundation's L!brary Initiative for elementary school students in New York. Putting design on a par with building staff and collections, the foundation has engaged these firms, working on a pro bono basis, to design interiors for libraries in at-risk public schools in spaces that range from 1,300 to 2,000 square feet (121 to 186 square meters).[21] Further underscoring the importance of words, the foundation persuaded graphic designers at Pentagram to do the signage for every project.

At PS 42 (2002) in the Far Rockaway neighborhood of Queens, Weiss/Manfredi Architects celebrated the library as an active, kinetic place by introducing red seating into the space that rocks and wheels, and a rippling "worm wall" of curving wood bookshelves. A story-telling area is defined by a translucent white curtain inscribed with words chosen by the students and rendered by Pentagram in handsome, playfully scaled gray characters—a subtle but sure signal that this is a project that takes young enthusiasms seriously.

At PS 1 (2004) in the borough of Brooklyn, local architects Marpillero Pollak Architects saw an opportunity to make a figurative element out of the reading tables, and created a customized system of lamps and desks to make a playful,

interlocking zigzag that snakes through the space. Each
table is incised with a capital letter so that children can
easily find or claim a place. Other opportunities presented
themselves underfoot and overhead. Instead of carpeting,
sound-absorbent cork covers the floor; and overhead, Jasper
Morrison globe lights play a game of peek-a-boo behind the
ceiling's Swiss-cheese perforations.

The remarkable aspect of the Robin Hood libraries is that
they are respectful and playful at the same time. They

exemplify in microcosm the new liberties being taken with the identity of rooms devoted to the act of reading. While ancient archetypes will always exert considerable power, all signs point to a more interactive and extroverted role for libraries of the future. And there is one library that, at the outset of the new century, definitively makes the case for the library as a social, intellectual, and civic hub.

If any question lingered as to whether the library had to adhere to a fixed form to capture the public imagination, it was settled when Rem Koolhaas's Seattle Central Library, opened to nearly universal acclaim in 2004.[22] Writing in the *New York Times*, architecture critic Herbert Muschamp called it "a big rock candy mountain of a building" whose exuberance and visual delights flow directly from the interior's social program. Muschamp writes: "This is the meaning of the Central Library. It thinks its way beyond our dualistic tendency to polarize social and aesthetic values. Who says we need to take sides? The interplay between them can be beautiful."[23] Indeed, every aspect of the 412,000-square-foot

(38,276-square-meter) library–designed by Koolhaas's firm OMA/Office for Metropolitan Architecture in tandem with an intense public process–is filtered through a quintessentially Dutch vision of design that extracts the extraordinary from the ordinary. So synthetic is the result that it is virtually impossible to tease apart the functional from the formal aspects of the library's design. For example, the choice to stratify each activity of the library in separate layers– beginning at the base with parking and, in order of ascent, entrance lobby, community meeting rooms, stacks and circulation desks, and administrative offices–led in turn to the decision to devote the top level of each layer to reading rooms and terraces. But the logic of stacking, in and of itself, would have been nothing more than a librarian's cliché were it not for the fact that the volumes of each layer were skewed and clad with a diagonally gridded glass sheathing. The structural ornament of the facade and the canted interior volumes cast a harlequin pattern of shadows across the vast interior public spaces that serve each level, while offering distinctive views of the city outside from all of the building's floors.

The formal acrobatics reach a crescendo in the famed Spiral, the central and largest volume of the ten-level building, which holds all of the library's books and consumes thirty-two percent of the entire interior. Conceived as a practical solution to accommodate unforeseen areas of growth in the collection, it is also a model of democratic wheelchair access. In the Seattle public library, users are not confined to reading rooms but are encouraged to wend their way

through the library's core. Beyond its clear functional and social roles, the form of the Spiral is also a metaphor for the library's unending accumulation of knowledge and the Sisyphean task of trying to contain it.

Of equal consequence are the building's smaller gestures, such as the rubber floor mats printed with Dewey decimal system numbers that act as signposts in the Spiral. Practical and unexpected, the oversized numerals were the work of graphic designer Bruce Mau, but in spirit they are typical of Koolhaas' appreciation for the latent power of the mundane. Instead of fluorescents, induction lamps–like the kind used in Europe as streetlights–illuminate the first floor of

the library. The floors of the stacks are concrete, but where wood could be used, the architects specified a handsome composite of recycled Douglas fir scraps. On level ten, inexpensive panels covered in rip-stop nylon, a fabric normally found in sports arenas, hide utilities and give the ceiling a soft, quilted aspect. Even the furnishings, by Europe's most innovative designers, work in the spirit of OMA's adaptive vernacular, like the .03 chairs by Maarten van Severen and the Joyn tables by Ronan and Erwan Bouroullec that were specially customized for the children's library. Petra Blaisse, the creative consultant for the interior, designed digitally printed rugs patterned with plants and grasses as well as an acoustic auditorium curtain, green and yellow on one side with a bear-fur motif in vinyl on the other. Chartreuse escalators and lipstick-red stairs move visitors through the building's iconoclastic spaces, which turn an ordinary trip to the library into a powerful design initiation.

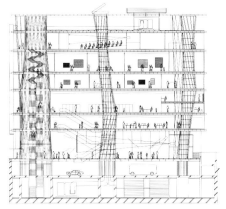

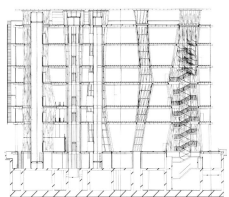

That Seattle should be the beneficiary of such forward-thinking design is not surprising; after all, this is a city famous for nurturing many of the entrepreneurial forces that transformed the cultural landscape of the late twentieth century—most notably Starbucks and Microsoft. It seems, however, nothing short of miraculous to find such architectural brilliance in Cottbus, a quiet, nondescript town in eastern Germany. To counter the flattening effect of the region's Communist architectural past, Swiss architects Herzog & de Meuron turned the local university library in to a lace tower. Set on a man-made rise, the Information Communication Media Center–rendered in German as the acronym IKMZ–at Brandenburg Technical University (2005) gives Cottbus a badly needed focal point and its citizens a level of visual excitement whose only precedent may be in Seattle.

As powerful as the undulating facade may be, the library's true gifts lie within: the interior of the IKMZ is unusually open and gregarious. A lush palette of fuchsia, deep purple, emerald, and lime green interrupt the institutional whisper of the library's white spandrels, chairs, and slender coiled light fixtures. The library's innate institutional reticence is flaunted by corkscrew stairwells and undulating balconies. No matter how immersed library users become in their searches, they are never totally isolated, since each of the building's seven floors are cut through to yield double- and triple-height reading rooms that look out in all directions. The most seductive feature, however, lies in the building's skin, which is etched with overlapping upper- and lowercase letterforms, like a bourgeois lace curtain rendered in contemporary typography. Here, Herzog & de Meuron extends the notion of literacy, making the case for contemporary ornament as resonant with meaning as any illuminated manuscript.

Community Centers

Factors such as urban revitalization, the growth of extracurricular activities, and increased user amenities have raised the social profile of the library to the point that there is growing evidence of an impending role reversal. The library is now positioned as an ancillary function of the community center much in the same way that social spaces like cafés and meeting rooms have become ancillary functions of the library itself. This union of two formerly distinct civic spaces is not necessarily a response to economic constraints imposed by limited public funds; if anything, this tendency represents a loosening of typological constraints accelerated at the turn of the millennium by the restless undercurrent of the digital revolution.

One of the prime examples of this development can be found in Japan. The cyber café-cum-library follows the logic of hybrids like the gallery/department store, common in a country where hierarchies of aesthetics and function have traditionally been absent and cultural apprehensions about technology virtually nonexistent. However, even in this context, Toyo Ito's Mediatheque in Sendai (2001)–a library, media center, performance venue, and gallery space–is a remarkable instance of poetic synthesis. Its most dominant feature is the internal clusters of bending columns that Ito claims were inspired by seaweed swaying under water. The metaphor suggests that as we navigate uncharted digital waters our institutions require openness–not only to literal demands of changing technology but also to new purpose. In short, the library is morphing.

Unlike the pop facade of Renzo Piano and Richard Rodgers' 1976 Pompidou Center in Paris, a distant but interesting precedent of umbilical transparency, Ito's columns all but erase the separation between the building's utilities and the spaces they serve. These elegant (and structural) utility conduits, girded by white steel pipes, keep the floors free for reprogramming and constitute a strong graphic presence cutting through each floor of the seven-story building. Custom furniture is dispersed throughout the building, including Karim Rashid's red reception desk and yellow chairs, Kazuyo Sejima & Associates' clover-shaped seating (on the second floor), and Ross Lovegrove's chartreuse snaking tables (in the audiovisual center on the seventh floor). Along with K.T. Architecture's red bench-and-counter units in the casual seating areas, the furnishings complement the sculptural quality of the interior and forge a unique visual identity for each level without permanently fixing the activities assigned to them.

Though far more intimate in scale and modest in program than Ito's Mediatheque, Dorte Mandrup Architect's design for a Neighborhood Center (2001) in Copenhagen evinces the same desire for flexibility. Involving new construction and an interior renovation, the young Danish firm's design for this center in the Holmbladsgade section of Copenhagen resulted in a closely integrated library, town hall, and café. A new foyer, gridded by open bays of white columns three stories tall, houses the café and the book lending area, but can be closed off after library hours to be used for other purposes. (Stacks are housed in an adjacent nineteenth-century structure.) The new addition is an open communal

hall, designed like a tree house on trunks of oblique
concrete columns and simply furnished with red-and-white
Spring chairs designed by Susanne Fossgreen. The room's
glass walls are double paned by an interior floor-to-ceiling
wood screen configured like oversized bookshelves, as if to
introduce the library's spirit of informed discourse into a
space for public affairs.

For reasons both structural and symbolic, wood and glass
were also the materials of choice for the Tomochi Forestry
Hall, a small community center in the forestry town of
Tomochi, Japan (2004). Asked to build a structure that
would serve as a combination meeting center/sports hall

and symbol of the town, architect Taira Nishizawa conceived
an artfully engineered composite building of wood and steel
that looks from outside to be a chrysalis or bush growing
inside a glass hothouse. The lattice-like structure is so light,
in fact, that it did not need a concrete foundation. The
building's meeting room is the size of two mini volleyball
courts and can accommodate both civic and athletic functions.

In contrast to the Calvinist restraint of Mandrup's
Neighborhood Center and Nishizawa's essentialist Tomochi
Forestry Hall, the Marion Cultural Centre (2001)–a library,
café, and theater located in the suburbs of Adelaide,
Australia–is openly flamboyant and proudly narcissistic. The

gigantic letters M-A-R-I-O-N form the building's facade
and its interior, literally fusing the identity of the township
to the functions of the library, theater, meeting rooms, café,
and art gallery. Fully three-dimensional super graphics, the
monumental letters that announce the building also shape
its reading niches, corridors, and rooms. The vibrant center's
designers, the Australian architectural firm Ashton Raggatt
McDougall, have embedded countless references to language
throughout the structure's brilliant orange-and-purple interior.
Braille, Morse code, sign language, and hieroglyphics are
etched into windows; oversize hands function as wayfinding
icons. Deliberately garrulous, the design responds to a
library policy that welcomes—rather than discourages—
conversation. In physically unifying these different entities
under a vast ceiling of hanging plywood panels, the architects co-opt the attraction of a mall experience—one-stop
shopping—and make it truly public. As such, the Marion
Cultural Centre is a provocative example of using the architecture of retail to reinvigorate civic life.

Government Buildings

Of all the civic spaces considered in this chapter, government buildings—namely courthouses, municipal buildings,
houses of parliament or congress, and embassies—are most
likely to represent the greatest concentrations of power
and history. They also tend to be conservative in design,

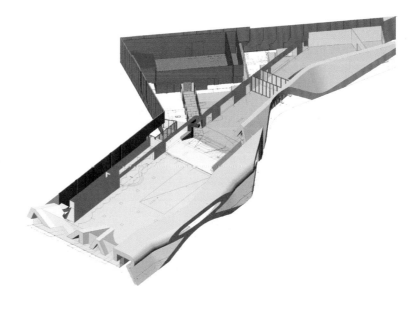

Ada Karmi-Melamede Architects with Ram Karmi, Israel Supreme Court, Jerusalem, 1995

particularly in societies whose leaders are highly accountable to their constituents and are reluctant to risk alienating mainstream taste or to appear less than circumspect in the expenditure of public funds. In these cases, design that doesn't pattern itself on convention is viewed as a liability. The exceptions to this rule tend to occur during periods when civic fervor and architectural fecundity coincide. This may be one of those moments. Having seen what architecture can do for museums and concert halls and, in turn, the communities they serve, the slower-moving forces of government are beginning to view their national and regional buildings as icons of place, not just warehouses of bureaucracy.

Up until the late twentieth century, official architecture tended to fall into two broad categories: Beaux-Arts classicism, flamboyantly revived by Michael Graves's Portland Building (1980) in Oregon, or the more severely tailored, stripped-down classicism of high modernism, brutally articulated in Paul Rudolph's State Health, Education and Welfare Services Center (1970) in Boston. In both cases the civic investment was largely confined to their imposing facades. Today, however, buildings of the state are becoming harder to identify as they take on the garb of their civilian counterparts, and as their interiors begin to follow suit.

It would be too simplistic, however, to suggest that the polarization of historicism and modernism that marked the last century has disappeared. Rather, the poles have moved closer and designers are internalizing the traditions and forms of the past and importing ideas from other design contexts. In the process, postmodern contextualism becomes less a matter of overt historical quotation (as with the Graves courthouse in Oregon) than an opportunity for hybridization.

Given the particular sobriety of dispensing justice, Ada Karmi-Melamede and her brother Ram Karmi used a subtle amalgam of convention and invention in their Israel Supreme Court building in Jerusalem (1993/95). The complex includes a library, an administrative building with judges' chambers, and a wing containing five courtrooms that extend like five fingers from the main hall. Here, design traditions are not emulated but honored through a series of contrasts that begin at the entrance. In the main foyer, a marble floor with a typical Middle Eastern pattern, designed by Ram Karmi's daughter Tal, is illuminated by light descending from the apex of the entry's sharply pyramidal roof. The courtrooms' basilica-inspired ceilings find a contemporary complement in simple wooden bench-es, which in turn benefit from decorative acoustical walls at the rear of each room. Like the walls in Arab homes,

these permit views outside but not in. In the library, curved
wood bookshelves line a three-story arcing corridor that
receives indirect natural light through deeply recessed
windows. The judges' chambers surround a courtyard that
is accessed through cool gray-and-white vaulted corridors.
Paul Goldberger, writing in the *New York Times*, said of the
courthouse, "The sharpness of the Mediterranean architectural tradition and the dignity of the law are here married
with remarkable grace."[24]

Issues of context, both literal and metaphysical, define the
City Hall of Utrecht renovation (1999) by EMBT Associates
Architects/ Enric Miralles Benedetta Tagliabue. (This was
Miralles's last commission before his untimely death at
the age of 45; it was completed by his partner, Benedetta
Tagliabue, who continues the firm's work.) It is indicative of
recent shifts in design currents that, in this project, rather
than mimic the historic elements on site or set them apart

for contrast, the architects thoroughly integrated the historic
fabric to create a new but layered city hall. Working within
a labyrinth of ad hoc additions made over the course of five
centuries, the architects did not aim for a unified interior,
but instead achieved what Miralles called a "conglomerate
of the diverse houses of the city."[25] EMBT salvaged what
historic fragments remained and connected them with
hallways and walls articulated with a timber-and-beam
framework that graphically outlines windows, defines stairwells, and, in the case of the city council room, cantilevered
overhead. The irregular bands of dark wood against white
walls evoke medieval architecture without remotely succumbing to any faux historicism. Instead, the structural
asymmetry and the suggestion of craft become a metaphor
for the construction of contemporary communities that is
particularly pointed in the design of the marriage room.
Here, facing an orange wall with an off-center hearth, couples
getting married sit on benches with two different backs and

under two different chandeliers, each resolutely individual
but comfortable sharing the same space.

In point of fact, EMBT view its design process as "a psychological approach,"[26] and more recently have brought it to
bear on the new Scottish Parliament Building (2004) in
Edinburgh. The architects' stress on iconoclastic forms
speaks to a view of government as a collection of individuals,
signified in custom-designed desks, Gaudí-like chairs in
the debating chamber, and private seating alcoves outside
the general assembly. At the same time that EMBT's design
reflects the sensitivities of a modern democracy, it also
reflects a profound understanding of Scottish history:
Gargantuan Celtic crosses are carved into the lobby ceiling
and cement piers rise in interstitial spaces like trees in an
ancient forest.

The graphic sensibility of EMBT's Utrecht renovation
surfaces again in the Scottish Parliament building, particularly in the committee rooms' timbered windows and walls,
but the design also departs from EMBT's typically angular
aesthetic. Here, EMBT introduced organically shaped plaster
ceilings in the committee rooms and fin-shaped metal
clerestories in the garden lobby. The concavities and convexities are not fully integrated into a singular aesthetic,
but rather collaged and layered in counterpoint to the
orthogonal rooms they inhabit—a subtle visual parallel to
the work of argument so crucial to the democratic process.

Similar parallels are evident in Gunther Behnisch's civic
buildings—the cornerstone of his Stuttgart-based practice
since it began in the late 1950s. While not as extreme as,
for example, the Kindergarten Ship discussed earlier in this
chapter, the Plenary Complex of the German Parliament
(1990) in Bonn is full of deliberate imperfections and complex interactions, traits Behnisch associates with individual
freedoms and democracy.[27] The parliamentary chamber's
circular form confers equality on representatives from all
parties and sits in tension with the rectilinear viewing
galleries suspended above, where the press and public are
given oversight. Outside of this centralized, highly symbolic
space, asymmetry prevails. Lobbies are crisscrossed by
cantilevered stairs and illuminated by irregular lines of
light. It is particularly in these elements, as well as in the
"bird's nest" staircase leading to the chamber's viewing

galleries, that we see a relationship to the vectors that define the Scottish Parliament.

The reconstruction of the Reichstag (1999) in Berlin placed a different burden on its designers, given the difficult history inflicted on the 1894 Paul Wallot edifice, bombed as Hitler's headquarters, occupied by Soviets, and abandoned until Christo's wrapping of the building in 1995. Foster + Partners' solution eschewed fine-grained complexity for monumental form, but with a sharp semantic reversal. With a dome of glass, Norman Foster created a literal tribute to transparent democracy placed in the center of Germany's reclaimed capital city. In so doing he transfers emphasis from the representatives to the represented. Citizens and tourists course through the Reichstag's grand glass globe on helical ramps that lead down to an observation platform situated above the circular governing chamber. At the core of the cupola, a "light sculptor" reflects natural light into the chamber while also inflecting the interior with a visual complexity. Here, and in the merger of the Beaux-Arts base and the glass dome, bombast is deflated without sacrificing the power of scale.

Today, these flickering spaces are increasingly replacing the weightier appurtenances of governmental pomp and circumstance. Oratory podiums, judicial benches, and other trappings of officialdom tend to pale in the light of these new interiors; flags and insignias, though still present, are truly incidental to the beacon of form. Richard Meier's United States Courthouse and Federal Building (2000) in Islip, New York, epitomizes the platonic ideal with light-filled court-

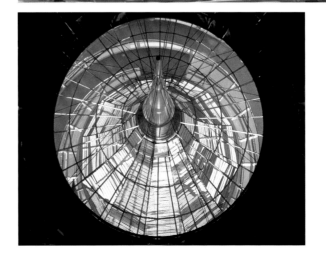

Richard Meier & Partners, United States Courthouse and Federal Building,
Islip, New York, 2000

rooms that flank a massive interior courtyard. But this courthouse reveals ambitions that go well beyond the formal.
Recognizing the fact that such massive interior environments
are, in fact, climates, Meier took into account the psychological effect of sunlight, and offered expansive views of the
Long Island landscape to ameliorate the long periods of waiting involved in the judicial process. (It is worth pointing
out that newer civic buildings, including Meier's, are increasingly becoming test cases for sustainable interior
environments. Thom Mayne of Morphosis designed the San
Francisco Federal Building, completed in 2005, so it could
be vented naturally, allegedly cutting energy consumption
by 50 percent.)

The interior of Meier's Sandra Day O'Connor United States
Courthouse Federal Building (2000) in Phoenix, Arizona,
reaps the benefits of an innovative passive climate-control
system, but it also introduces a new material presence:
a lens-like ceiling, designed by the artist/designer James
Carpenter for the cylindrical Special-Proceedings Court-
room, which sits at the heart of the transparent six-story
building. Scored laterally and longitudinally like a globe,
Carpenter's inverted dome exerts a satisfying ceremonial
presence without contradicting Meier's minimalist sensibility,
which is articulated in the broad horizontal bands of beechwood that encircle the room. (The dome, like most of the
designer's architectural commissions, conceals its practical
function; in this case, it contains a sprinkler system required
by fire code.)

In contrast to courthouse designs meant to be a source of
calm to patrons who need no further stress in their lives,
there are civic buildings whose program it is to project an
active climate of change. Such was the ambition of the
young Slovenian firm Sadar and Vuga in its design for the
Chamber of Commerce and Industry of Slovenia (1999)
in the capital city of Ljubljana. The design reflects the new
liberties of a burgeoning capitalist system in the young
state. Divided into two volumes—the front of the building
comprises boxes stacked on slightly skewed axes, and
the back is staidly orthogonal—it also reflects a certain
ambivalence common in emerging democracies.

Like Meier, Jurij Sadar and Bostjan Vuga recognized that the
occupants of their building would likely spend a lot of time
waiting for the wheels of bureaucracy to turn. Instead of
offering meditative views, however, the architects created
a warren of intimate spaces that cut across and down the
dizzying vertical channels created by the skewed volumes of
the facade. Fundamentally urban, this is a building of myriad
distractions. Its spatial fluctuations ideally complement the
institution's mission to stimulate the flow of capital, but
they also reinforce the social nature of those transactions.
Less abstract than the flow of capital is the flow of people,
who move across the variously colored planes in a kaleidoscopic interior of interlocking views and voids.

Transparency and tension are also leitmotifs in the young
American-Irish firm Bucholz/McEvoy Architects' design for
Fingal County Hall (2000) in Swords, a town in County

Sadar Vuga Architects, Chamber of Commerce and Industry of Slovenia,
Ljubljana, 1999

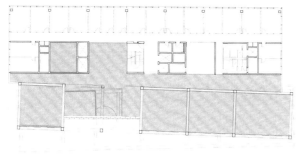

Dublin. A fully-glazed, five-story atrium lobby offers both a view of the ancient townscape of Swords and a window onto the public debates that will shape the country's future. Inside its arcing wall, visitors walk beneath an intricate, trapeze-like system of cables that partners Merritt Bucholz and Karen McEvoy describe as a symbol of Ireland's phenomenal tech revolution in the last two decades. There is nothing sterile, however, about the tensile cabling that suspends the 120-foot (36.5-meter) perimeter glass wall from the roof; instead it has the crafted character of a massive sail-ship's rigging. A similar character carries over into the precisely articulated office wings. Here, grids of windows and vents (the complex is naturally ventilated) create a pleasing weave of cross-views that offset the simply furnished open offices. The most important symbol of the collective ethos of the County Hall is found in the council chamber room, where semicircular glass-topped tables hold out the promise of clarity within the complexity of bureaucracy.

Throughout the Fingal County Hall, neither rationality nor expressiveness is allowed to dominate or overwhelm. This balance is indicative of a larger trend toward the erasure of traditional aesthetic polarities that is being made possible by technologies that know no difference between them. Once-conflicting sensibilities are now being melded to achieve a seemingly paradoxical equilibrium.

Of course, paradox is inherent in any governmental structure, which must express a confident sense of authority on one hand while assuring the public of its accountability on the other. In Spain, the Madrid-based Sancho Madridejos Architecture Office grappled with just such a duality in its design for the San Fernando de Henares Town Hall (1999), a cubic complex of voids and solids built on the remains of an eighteenth-century tapestry factory. The three-story building—which includes council chambers in one wing and public spaces in the other—features translucent walls of onyx, a poetic reference to the material's architectural history and a strategy similar to that employed by Alberto Campo Baeza in the Caja General bank in Granada (see Offices, p. 125). Here, the virtual geometries are as changeable as the public opinions aired within the rooms of the Town Hall.

Perhaps the strongest indication that the optical illusions, asymmetries, and non sequiturs of cutting-edge contemporary design have filtered into the mainstream—in projects ranging from the Scottish Parliament to the San Fernando de Henares Town Hall—is the degree to which the pleasures of the unpredictable are now welcome in the forums of diplomacy. A look at two acclaimed embassy buildings, built a decade apart from each other, reveals two different design sensibilities and cultural biases, to be sure; but such a comparison also reveals the trajectory of design as it has come to embrace iconoclasm. At first glance, the Embassy of Finland (1994) in Washington, DC , designed by the Helsinki-based firm Heikkinen-Komonen Architects, gives all the appearances of hewing to established modernist protocols. Its glazed walls dissolve into a view of nature and its rooms are furnished with Eames chairs and the architects' trademark gray-stained-plywood desks. But the space also admits the surprise of gestural elements like the downward curve of its baroque staircase and, tracing a line above it, a ribbon of exposed halogen light bulbs. And while the interior's dominant palette of steel, glass, and wood stays within a context established by Mies and Aalto, the two conference rooms sheathed in copper bend the rules of restraint. Not only does the glowing material introduce an extroverted presence, but also the rooms themselves are theatrically suspended within a sixty-foot-deep (18-meter-deep) "canyon" cut through the core of the building.

A decade after the completion of the Finnish Embassy, the ratio between the rational and the expressive was reversed in Rem Koolhaas's design for the Netherlands Embassy (2003) in Berlin. Koolhaas wrapped the building with what he calls a "traject," an enclosed glass promenade that lets visitors walk out over a small patch of Berlin while remaining inside Dutch territory. Apart from the frisson of seemingly standing in midair, and of being both inside and outside the building at once, the passageway fulfills a larger purpose

by giving visitors a medley of unexpected views into the workings of the embassy as they traverse the building up to the roof garden and a cantilevered "sky box." Inside the embassy's working and ceremonial spaces, the refrain of exchanged glances continues. Partitions of glass and perforated aluminum delineate the communal offices, and reception areas are afforded a greater measure of privacy by Petra Blaisse's lemon-yellow-and-silver lace curtains. In the windowless conference room, Gijs Bakker's Peepshow wall covering offers views of a different sort, as does the glazed hole in the floor (affectionately dubbed the "Rem hole"), which reveals the foyer below.

Yet, instead of provoking a sense of disequilibrium, the embassy's complex spatial composition yields a sense of domestication, which is enhanced by the furnishings—a mix of contemporary pieces and traditional Persian rugs. (Dutch history is, after all, distinguished by Protestant materialism.) Yet Koolhaas avoids the suffocating excesses of a bourgeois interior. In creating a domicile for a nation, he's put vanguard values in the service of diplomacy. Less formal than the Finnish building in Washington, the Koolhaas embassy sets the stage for even bolder freedoms in civic design, and is yet another indicator of this generation's comfort with a fusion of types (residential and public) and an intersection of formal languages (orthogonal and organic), both of which are quickly becoming a hallmark of the new millennium

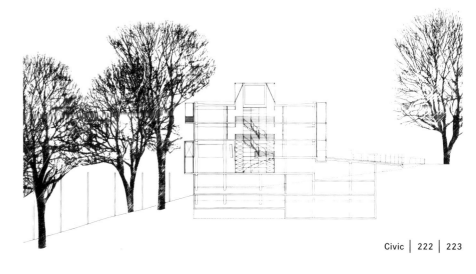

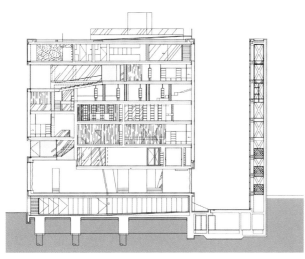

Religious

Sanaksenaho Architects, St. Henry's Ecumenical Art Chapel, Turku, Finland, 2005

It is ironic that modernism—with its own secular canon—found its most enthusiastic converts in the realm of religious architecture. It is no coincidence that churches, synagogues, and temples wholeheartedly embraced the Modern Movement's expressive geometries at the very same moment that the mass media began to openly speculate about the existence of God. When the editors of *Time* famously paraphrased Friedrich Nietzsche on the cover of the 8 April 1966 issue by asking "Is God Dead?" the question was no longer a matter of philosophy.

In the 1960s, almost a century after the publication of Nietzsche's *The Gay Science*, his famous pronouncement characterized the crisis of faith plaguing Western culture, in the midst of a counterculture revolution that had become critical of any kind of authority, temporal or spiritual. Organized religion was experiencing the same institutional vulnerability that was affecting governments, universities, and corporations. The reflexive rigidity of mainstream religion was being questioned by younger and more socially conscious congregants. In response to their agitation for change, architects and designers were called upon to create new symbols, new spires, and new spaces for new liturgies. Broad shifts were taking place in the major religions, from the Reform movement in Judaism to the liberalizations of Vatican Council II on the Roman Catholic Church.[1] A generic ecclesiastical style, epitomized by the exaggerated arcs, sharp angles, and swooping canopies of suburban synagogues and churches, flourished as religions looked for relevance in style and substance.

The pace of building of houses of worship, which had been accelerated by the postwar Baby Boom, began to wane by the 1970s and 1980s along with enrollment in seminaries and convents. Today, religious commissions constitute only a fraction of general construction projects in the United States, though they are increasing in number in countries like Ukraine, where religion was banned under communism.[2] Plus, with few exceptions, religious spaces had never counted for more than a small percentage of the projects executed by high-profile practices in any country. Singular works, such as Frank Lloyd Wright's Unity Temple (1905–08) in Oak Park, Illinois, and Eero Saarinen's Kresge Chapel at MIT (1950–55) in Cambridge, Massachusetts, tend to dominate the popular conception of religious architecture.

Furthermore, most mosques, temples, churches, and religious meeting halls tend to be freestanding structures, distinct from their secular surroundings, no matter how hard they seek to be relevant. The advantage of this condition, not unlike that of a private residence, is that houses of worship often elicit very personal and eloquent architectural responses, the inherent conservatism of the client and the program notwithstanding. For where secular culture would substitute the aesthetic sublime for religious transcendence, the culture of faith views them as interdependent.

Today, a number of forces are converging that encourage a more thoughtful and open-ended examination of the nature of spaces devoted to meditation, to prayer, and to social action. Interfaith initiatives, combined with the effects of globalization, have led to a migration of formal design ideas across the geography of faiths. Excessive displays of material wealth are no longer considered necessary to illustrate the promise of heavenly reward in the afterlife or the dominance of a sect in the here and now. Religious imagery, no longer linked to art as it was in the Middle Ages and the Renaissance, has largely lost its power to convince. Representational elements no longer dominate interiors of churches, which once deemed them essential to the religious education of their then-illiterate congregations. Stained-glass pictorials are being supplanted in churches and synagogues by clear views of nature. If figurative narratives do appear, they are more likely to come from the silhouettes of congregants and celebrants themselves, revealed by translucent materials like alabaster and sanded glass. Light has become the chief spiritual metaphor and architectural determinant. Perhaps most significant is the fact that religious organizations are beginning to realize that vanguard design has a drawing power able to transcend denominational distinctions.

While essential differences in religious beliefs and interpretations persist as do basic symbols of allegiance like the minaret and the crucifix—contemporary interiors are increasingly designed to thwart hierarchy and, outside of the most fundamentalist faiths, mute the barriers of cult. Even the twenty-first-century megachurch—a latter-day "revival tent," with enormous projection screens and theater-style seating—is far less indebted to the pulpits and pews of traditional spaces of worship than it is to the

architecture of entertainment and big-box retailing. Whether designed for mass prayer or for more intimate experiences of faith, religious buildings today draw largely on formalist modes of expression to create the sense of place necessary for collective worship. As in independent structures, today's houses of worship continue to serve as beacons to their communities. However, they enter the new millennium humbled by a history of clerical hubris, and are engaged in a larger debate about the efficacy of the monumental. With a renewed emphasis on the personal, houses of worship are particularly revealing commissions, palimpsests of both architectural and spiritual identities.

Religious spaces today are also increasingly receptive to iconoclasm in design (if not theology), and borrow from a rich history of ecclesiastical architecture without being bound by that history's conventions. Symbolic geometries– from the circular form of the memorial or the rectangular hall of the basilica to the elliptical curves of tents and arks– continue to serve as guiding principles but are subject to new, innovative interpretations. Consequently, the projects that follow are not segregated by articles of faith, but by the abstractions that serve them. The formal properties of design now offer an ecumenism more suitable for their purposes.

Introspective Geometries

In the case of Mario Botta's religious commissions–notably the Cymbalista Synagogue at the University of Tel Aviv (1998) in Israel and the Church of San Giovanni Battista (1998) in Mogno, Switzerland–past and present converge in

Mario Botta Architecture Studio, San Giovanni Battista, Mogno, Switzerland, 1998

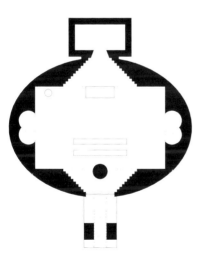

Stanley Saitowitz/Natoma Architects, Temple Beth Sholom,
San Francisco, 2007 (projected completion)

Opposite: Wandel Hoefer Lorch + Hirsch, Dresden Synagogue,
Dresden, 2001

a manipulation of conventional Euclidian geometry to yield
unique solutions. In the Cymbalista Synagogue, two monumental, vessel-like forms begin as squares and end as
circles, echoing the relationship of the finite to infinite, of
human to divine. The towers, each 560 feet (170 meters) in
diameter, sit atop two square rooms linked in a rectangular
plan. Indeed, duality is the leitmotif of the program, which
is designed to serve two communities—one Orthodox and
one liberal. The synagogue's towers are brought into human
scale by ceilings that hover in space, joining the walls at
four points and admitting crescents of natural light in the
spaces between. The controlled presence of sunlight is
reinforced by the warmth of the Tuscan stone used for the
walls and in the light-colored wood seating—mobile chairs
in one hall and permanent seating, flanking the *bimah*, or
dais, in the other. The design's carefully wrought balance,
reflected in its program and its form, mirrors the essential
nature of a synagogue as a place for both worship and
scholarly debate.

In contrast to the equilibrium of the Cymbalista Synagogue,
Botta's Church of San Giovanni Battista depends on
kaleidoscopic rhythms to activate its volumetric forms.
Sheathed in stripes of gray Gneiss stone and white Peccia
granite from local Swiss quarries, the church is a study
in compression, not only of pattern, but also of memory.
Built on the site of a seventeenth-century church, the new
commission both subsumes and extrapolates the remnants
of history. A massive cylinder resembling an oversize
campanile is sliced crosswise to create a circular skylight
for an otherwise windowless interior. Romanesque arches
are carved out of lateral alcoves, revealing the thickness of
the walls. Enormous buttresses support the roof, while the
walls' gray and white stripes pay homage to the medieval
duomos of Orvieto and Siena. So forceful is the effect of the
geometry that these various historical references invigorate,
but never dominate, the form of the church. Here again,
Botta pays his respects to liturgical continuity without
pandering to the past.

Just as the Cymbalista Synagogue and the Church of San
Giovanni Battista are enclosures for reflection, Temple Beth
Sholom (projected completion 2007) offers a place of
contemplation removed from the urban distractions of San
Francisco. Exploring the idea of fortification in a fully

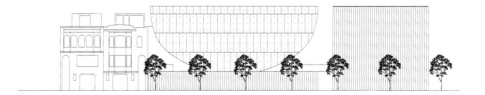

modernist language, Stanley Saitowitz/Natoma Architects designed the temple's concrete-clad sanctuary in the shape of a gigantic ark. The absence of hierarchy is reflected in the synagogue's central plan. In place of a typical plan with the rabbi officiating in front of the congregation, here symmetrical rows of seating descend along the curved walls, allowing congregants to face both each other and the bimah. A narrow skylight bisects the ceiling from east to west; where it meets the top of the east wall, a glowing, red illuminated band, signifying eternal light, flows down the wall to the ark. At night, pinpoint lights interspersed across the dark blue ceiling simulate the cosmos and emphasize the sanctity of the space.

The inviolability of sacred space, breached so egregiously in the desecration of synagogues in Europe during World War II, is poignantly reappraised in the Dresden Synagogue (2001) designed by Wandel Hoefer Lorch + Hirsch. The synagogue's suggestion of monumentality, urban separation, and fortification is a direct response to the history of the site. The new structure replaces the temple designed by Gottfried Semper that was destroyed by SS troops during *Kristallnacht* in 1938.[3] The synagogue is divided into two buildings: a windowless, sky-lit sanctuary and a tautly fenestrated community center separated by a courtyard paved with broken glass to symbolize and commemorate the destruction of original temple. The sanctuary's solemn interior is veiled with a curtain of delicate metallic rings that forms a translucent enclosure around the dark oak of the pews, bimah, and ark. Together with the suspended lighting, the scrim mitigates the defensive quality of the space. Its shimmering verticality, like a shaft of light, reflects the hopefulness of the small but growing Jewish community.

Penetrating Light

Like the new Dresden synagogue, the Catholic Academy (2000) in the former East Berlin owes its existence in large part to German reunification, which brought an end to the enforced atheism of Communist East Germany. For this commission, which would serve as the new headquarters of the German Roman Catholic Church, formerly situated in Bonn, Sarah Hare and Thomas Höger of Höger Architects designed two new structures, one public (the Church of St. Thomas Aquinas) and the other private (the Chapel of St. Bonifatus, which would serve the German Catholic Bishops'

Höger Architects, Chapel of St. Bonifatus, Catholic Academy, Berlin, 2000

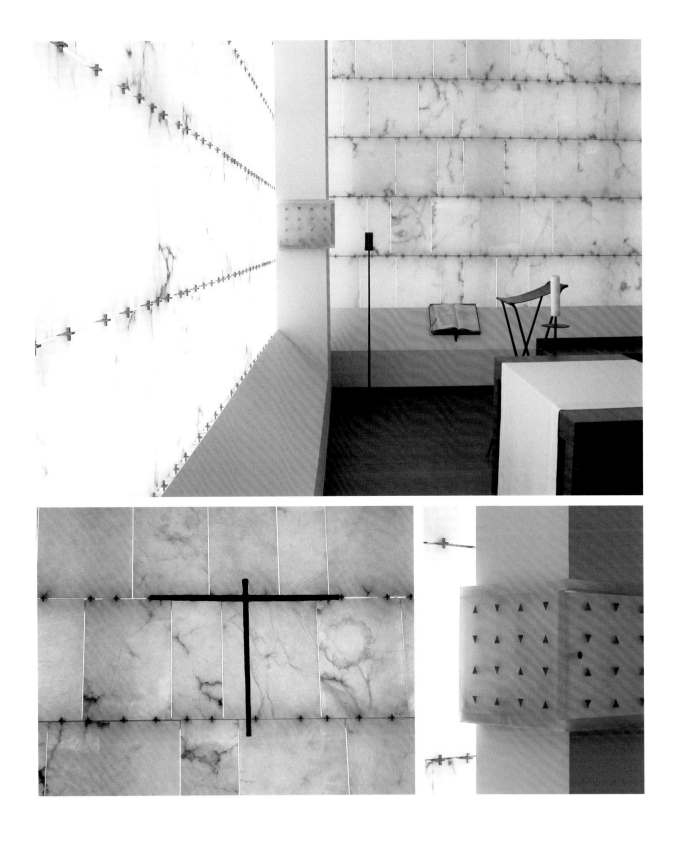

Synod). Both are defined by the twinned notions of interiority and introspection, qualities reinforced by the intimate scale of the spaces. (The church is 505 square feet [47 square meters]; the chapel is half as large; both are housed within a new, 9,388-square-foot [872-square -meter] seven-story building built to host the community of German Catholic bishops for conferences and debates.) Staggered among the thin, horizontal granite slabs forming the walls of the Church of St. Thomas Aquinas are equally thin glass bricks that increase in number as the walls rise. In an allusion to heavenly space, light is gradually released through the glass striations, and the walls appear to lose half their mass at the top. The dematerializing effect is countered by a flat, hovering white ceiling supported by four slim columns—a latter-day baldachin that acts as a canopy not just for the ritual site of the altar but for the congregation as well.

The smaller Chapel of St. Bonifatus similarly alludes to historical sources. Alabaster panels, a surrogate for glass in many medieval churches, line two external walls, producing a luminous, parchment-like effect. The only surface orna-ment in the space is the alabaster's subtle veining and stainless-steel wedges that separate the panels. These double-height alabaster windows also help block out noise and shadows of street traffic. Both the chapel and the church's handsomely crafted furnishings were designed by the artist Norbert Radermacher, in collaboration with Thomas Höger.

The Norwegian firm Jensen & Skodvin Architects is similarly preoccupied with gradations of light in their design for the Mortensrud Church (2002), located on the outskirts of Oslo, where daylight is at a premium during all but the short summer months. In a reversal of the convention that religious light flows from above (simulated in the Chapel of St. Bonifatus), this church is designed to admit illumination at the floor plane, at the level of the congregation. In lieu of traditional windows, broad expanses of glass line the lower portion of the structures and heavy masonry walls appear to hover above its transparent base. Built of unmortared slabs

of slate, the upper portions of the church's walls are flecked with the light that filters through the irregularly spaced stones. The upper reaches of the space grow progressively darker under a roof of corrugated metal. The effect is that of immersion in the dense forest, where light comes through the tree canopy. Capitalizing further on the rocky site, the architects allow boulders to protrude through the floor to demarcate the congregation from the choir, both of whom enjoy sunlight as a consequence of the inverted clerestory.

Heinz Tesar's design for the Christ, Hope of the World Church (2000) in Vienna, deploys the strategy of perforation to more explicitly symbolic ends. Clad in dark, pierced metal plates, the Catholic church's low, square form gives

no hint of the light created inside. Warm birch-plywood walls glow with light from circular cutouts that are all but invisible from the outside. A curved incision in the ceiling creates a large swath of light meant to represent the bleeding heart of Christ. Pews are arranged centripetally around the altar, behind which another circle, etched into the wall, circumscribes a cross to illustrate the intersection of human and divine natures—Christ as a crucified man, who is simultaneously divine.

Theological corollaries of form and space are pursued in an appropriately Jesuitical spirit—intellectually rigorous and visually powerful—in Stephen Holl's Chapel of St. Ignatius (1997), located on the campus of Seattle University in

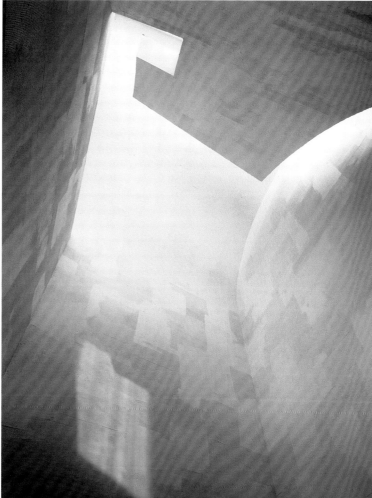

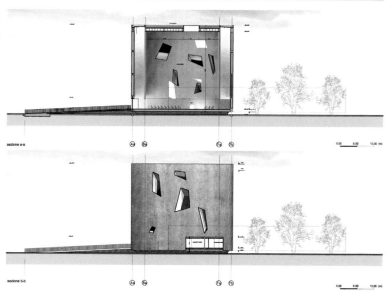

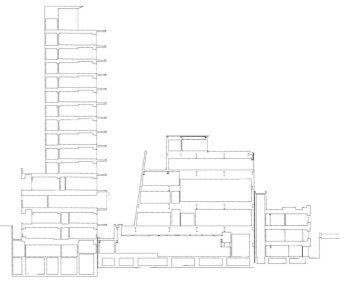

Seattle, Washington. Holl responds to the notion of spiritual growth through the discernment of inner light and darkness, the search for self-knowledge advocated by Ignatius Loyola, founder of the Jesuit order.[4] In response to the Ignatian metaphor, seven spaces, or vessels, of light are situated within a sculpted stone box: a processional corridor, a narthex (for social gathering), a nave (for services), a choir, a bell tower, and two smaller interior chapels. Beginning with the baffled light that focuses attention on various aspects of the liturgy, the chapel's design is an argument for revelation through perception, an important Jesuit tenet. (Since the Counter-Reformation in the sixteenth century, Jesuit churches have relied heavily on the seductive powers of scenography to engage their parishioners.) Here, the stress is on the haptic. Crafted surfaces and custom furnishings—ranging from hand-textured plaster walls, and a carpet designed by Holl that depicts the religious odyssey of St. Ignatius, to the fragrant beeswax finish of the tabernacle chapel walls by artist Linda Beaumont—work in tandem with the architecture to engage the senses during devotional rites.

In a competition-winning proposal for the San Giacomo Parish Complex of Foligno (2005) in Italy, Massimiliano Fuksas went even further to isolate the ray of light as a celestial expression of the divine. Two enormous rectangular concrete volumes containing 10,000 square feet (929 square meters) of space, one nested inside the other 10 feet (3 meters) apart, are joined by an armature that supports the internal box and creates rays, or buttresses, of light. A glow emanates from the three naves, formed by the spaces between the two boxes. Outlined by light, the sheltered sanctuary appears to float weightlessly inside. Within it, verses from the Bible in thin blue neon lighting, a site-specific work by the artist Maurizio Nannucci, rise from the corners behind the altar, providing a singular decorative complement to Fuksas's minimalist iconography.

Striking a balance between the exalted and the everyday, Kengo Kuma's Baiso Buddhist Temple (2003) in Tokyo is a multipurpose community complex that includes a building intended for worship and cultural activities and a separate residential volume. In place of the slanted tiled roof of a conventional Buddhist sanctuary, Kuma offers instead a sloping wall of vertical steel blades that can be seen from the glazed interior. Parodoxically, the strict simplicity of the

facade animates the temple within, casting rhythmic light and shadow on the interior's otherwise plain white walls.

The paradoxical sensations of grandiosity and humility provoked by large-scale ecclesiastical spaces are resolved eloquently in Álvaro Siza's Santa Maria Church and Parochial Center (1997) in Marco de Canavezes, Portugal. Parishioners enter the church through a 33 foot by 10-foot (10-meter by 3-meter) doorway that simultaneously dwarfs and celebrates the ritual of entrance. Deep-set windows without lintels meet the ceiling seamlessly, creating trapezoidal planes of reflected light that draw the eye upward. The warm wood floor creates a center of gravity for the rituals that occur within the church's soaring nave. In its conflation of the ethereal Gothic and grounded Romanesque, the church's design expresses both the authoritative and communitarian nature of religion.

If an interior can participate in a theological discussion (and it can), then the interior of the Singapore-based architecture firm WOHA's Church of St. Mary of the Angels (2003) places its emphasis on the mortality of the Christ figure. Here, no gilt-robed, heavenly deity reigns over the altar; instead, the tortured body of Jesus levitates over the congregation, arms outspread on an invisible cross. The emphasis on the humanity of the messiah carries an implicit message of compassion for all people that is reflected in the democratic arrangement of pews around the altar, instead of behind it. Furthermore, a glazed facade offers views of the rituals conducted inside, again, with the intent of rendering religion more human and less mysterious. A public forecourt links the church's various buildings, creating a civic space that both participates in the everyday life of Singapore and complements the egalitarian philosophy of the Franciscan friars who commissioned the complex.

Rafael Moneo's Cathedral of Our Lady of the Angels (2002) in Los Angeles speaks to the ongoing debate between stasis and change in the Roman Catholic Church, underscored by the Church's recent history of conservative leadership.[5] Moneo brings new currency to the archetypal Latin-cross plan with asymmetries and skewed axes that emphasize active participation and movement during the services rather than passive observation. Entry and egress are via two ambulatories punctuated by side chapels that, atypically,

are open only to the long, softly lit processional spaces and not to the nave. By reversing the traditional orientation of the side chapels, Moneo preserves the purity and power of the vast sanctuary, which seats 2,600 around a central altar platform. Daylight enters the space through windows made of veined Spanish alabaster shingles, subtly ornamenting a geometry of deeply incised volumes and scored surfaces. The pink-toned concrete walls create a warm field for the lines of the window mullions and the slatted wood ceiling. The two predominant features of the space are a cherrywood pipe organ 85 feet (26 meters) high, and a great projecting

cross, placed slightly off-center. In its multiple focal points,
Moneo's design places the cathedral's prestige in the service
of a local community and gives form to the church's more
progressive ideals.

Searches for relevance and transcendence converge with
elegant precision in Tadao Ando's Church of the Light (1989)
in the Osaka suburb of Ibaraki, Japan. In this seminal work,
a simple concrete box articulates both presence and absence
through its use of positive and negative space. (When Ando
was awarded the Pritzker Architecture Prize in 1995,
Kenneth Frampton described the church as "an exemplary
exercise in modesty and discretion."[6] Behind the altar, four
square, concrete planes form the wall, leaving a cruciform
void of natural light that projects into the darkness of the
church. This spare gesture illuminates the edges of the concrete, making a humble material appear to glow. The economy of the design extends to the furnishings, made from
scaffolding salvaged from the church's construction. The
simply constructed floor and benches are finished with a
black oil stain and complement the austere tranquility of
the space.

The Live Oak Friends Meeting House (2000) in Houston
gives form to the Quaker conviction that the seed of divine
"inner light" resides in every person. Houston-based Leslie
K. Elkins Architecture designed a modest shed for the
Friend that frames a quiet interior illuminated by an awe-
provoking skylight installation by the artist James Turrell,
himself a Quaker. The 12-foot-square (1-meter-square) skylight, cut into a gently curved ceiling, produces a view of
the sky that changes throughout the day and night, creating

Tadao Ando Architect & Associates, Church of the Light, Ibaraki-shi, Osaka Prefecture, Japan, 1989

Leslie K. Elkins Architecture with James Turrell, Live Oak Friendly Meeting House, Houston, Texas, 2000

Maki and Associates, Tokyo Church of Christ, Shibuya, Tokyo, 1995

fields of deeply saturated color above the worshippers. A band of artificial light set in the soffit between the ceiling and the walls can be manipulated to further alter the perception of color. Rows of white-oak pews, also designed by Turrell, are arranged in a circular formation to face the center of the room.

Celestial Volumes

Half a millennium after the Copernican revolution, the idea of the universe as a vaulted ceiling over the earth permeated

by divine presence continues to be a remarkably potent metaphor in contemporary religious architecture. Where previous generations relied on frescoed ceilings and literal images of heaven, contemporary designers utilize the abstractions of broad forms that hover seemingly unsupported over a space. Japanese architect Fumihiko Maki references this conceit by placing a broadly arching roof, dotted with constellations of hanging lamps, over the congregation to define the sanctuary of the Tokyo Church of Christ (1995). This subtle invocation of the heavens is countered by an

overtly modernist treatment of the space below. The apse is flattened into a glass-and-steel wall covered in layers of fabric that veil the church from its dense urban context. Apart from a single cross woven into the cloth scrim, iconography is reduced to the shadows created by the trusswork, a play of light that changes constantly over the course of the day.

The most literal invocation of the heavens is the dome, a form that reinforces the intrinsic interiority characteristic of both secular and religious buildings in Islamic cultures. And while a dome is not essential to a mosque—a building whose essence is the *qibla*, the horizontal axis terminating in Mecca[7] —it continues to be a vital and expressive feature of mosque design. A classical but contemporary example is the Corniche Mosque (1988) In Jeddah, Saudi Arabia, designed by Abdel Wahed El-Wakil, which won the Aga Khan Award for Architecture in 1989. In traditional mosques, dense latticework and intricately patterned surfaces give the illusion of infinite space. In this case, the architect used the opposite approach to achieve a similar effect. In the prayer hall, calligraphic decoration is replaced by concentric pointed arches that echo the outline of the indented alcove of the *mihrab*.[8]

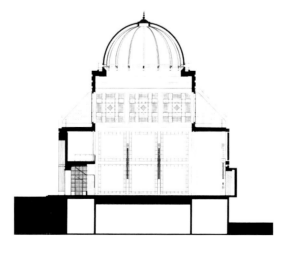

Legorreta + Legorreta, Metropolitan Cathedral of Managua, Managua,
Nicaragua, 1993

Sculpted white plaster walls give way to exposed brick creating a scalloped edge between dark and light. Painted a deep bronze, the cool upper recesses of the dome elicit both a cave-like sense of enclosure and a sense of infinity.

In contrast to the mosque in Jeddah, which appears to float on the surface of the Red Sea, SOM/Skidmore, Owings & Merrill's monumental Islamic Cultural Center (1991) in Manhattan holds squarely to its urban site with a deep center of gravity. Oriented toward Mecca, and thus at a conspicuous angle to the street grid, the building echoes its urban context with a palette of stone, bronze, and glass. The design reflects the architects' commitment to fuse the geometries of modernism with Islamic abstraction. Its monumental proportions signify the center's prestige as the first mosque to be designed and built for New York's Muslim community. The prayer hall is a square capped by a circle that outlines the base of the

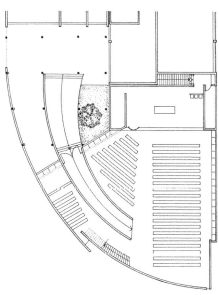

Abramson Teiger Architects, First Presbyterian Church of Encino, Encino, California, 2002

dome. The hall's stone walls, composed of nine square
sections, give way to large glazed panels with geometric-
patterned ceramic decoration in the Islamic tradition. The
daylight that filters through these ceramic patterns is augmented by a ring of suspended lights that traces the circumference of the dome. The dome itself is scored by sixteen
radii, built on a numerological system that references
Islamic tradition.[9]

So compelling and ecumenical is the form of the dome that
it bridges Eastern and Western religions. Mexican architect
Ricardo Legorreta designed no less than sixty-three domes
atop the Metropolitan Cathedral of Managua (1993) in the
capital city of Nicaragua. Responding to the ideal of dispersed authority within contemporary Catholic culture,
Legorreta located the highest dome over the congregation,
instead of over the priest and altar. This central dome
becomes a canopy by virtue of its saturated cadmium-yellow
surface that extends to the floor through the interior niches
of four massive cruciform columns. The stark strength of the
concrete interior is balanced by these intense passages of
color and by wells of natural light in each of the sixty-three
domes. Handmade, colored-concrete tiles cover the floor,
and the pews and doors are made of native wood. A separate
rounded chapel for the locally venerated image, "Sangre de
Cristo," has saturated red walls studded with small circular
apertures that transform the space into an illuminated vault
alluding to the stars. While paying tribute to the culture of
Nicaragua, the design of the cathedral transcends its locality
and shares in the timelessness at the core of religious belief.

The Modern Baroque

The material expression of timelessness—of the infinity
of the spirit—is never immune to temporality, of course.
Today, parochial orthodoxy, embodied in the dome and in
the idea of a unified cosmology, is being challenged by
fractured curves and multiple vistas that reflect the sometimes contradictory realities of global communities of faith.
What may seem to be a new strain of architectural doctrine,
however, can be better understood as a recessive gene
of the baroque that has emerged periodically from the sixteenth century on, from the ecstatic spirals of Francesco
Borromini's Church of St. Ivo alla Sapienza (c. 1650) in
Rome to the voluptuous swells of Le Corbusier's Chapel
at Ronchamp (1955) in France. The baroque gene is

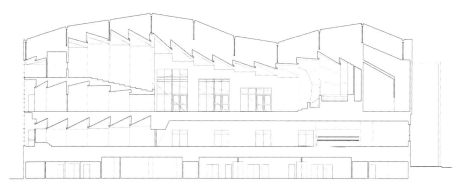

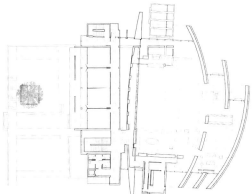

manifesting itself once again, but today digital engineering
is allowing an unprecedented reduction of mass, and, with
it, a soaring lightness.

Fittingly, Enrique Browne's first drawings for the Chapel
of the Villa Maria School (1992) in Santiago, Chile, were of
clouds–not the ecstatic, pink-hued clouds of Tiepolo, but
sheer white clouds pierced by light. Working within the
complex of a Catholic girls' school, Browne made an event
of the interior passage to the chapel by creating a *promenade architecturale.* Students and teachers enter the chapel
via a ramp that gradually rises to sanctuary, where two
asymptotic curves appear overhead. Here, the bands of the
sculptural ceiling unfurl, parting to admit a stream of white
light over the congregation. The wave of the ceiling stops
at the altar, allowing golden light to wash over the white
wall behind it. The walls' rough concrete surfaces appear
to hover between glowing reveals that outline the floor
and the ceiling. For all its figurative qualities, however,
Browne's cloud-like chapel is less about promoting a child-
like image of heaven than it is about creating the overall
sensation of being suspended in space in an atmosphere
of contemplation.

The general absence of representational images, which were
once so dominant in sacred spaces, has given added impetus
to the more expressive, personal designs emerging from
the late modernisms of the twentieth century. In Abrams
on Teiger Architects' renovation of the First Presbyterian
Church of Encino (2002) in California, the original, modest
A-frame exterior was retained, but augmented by a new
interior of cubist volumes and intersecting planes. Inspired
by medieval depictions of hands cupped in prayer, the
space's canted walls become a surrogate for traditional
iconography. The only graphic symbols are three crosses:
a 16-foot-tall (5-meter-tall) white plaster cross cantilevered
over the altar, an oak cross of similar dimensions saved
from the original church and placed at the back of the nave,
and a cross carved into the communion table. The chief
source of animation is the light and shadow emanating
from the church's fourteen new skylights. White-oak pews
were custom-designed with oblique angles that counter
the rectangular plan inherited from the original structure.
Symbiotic in form and program, the church privileges
social interaction over private worship.

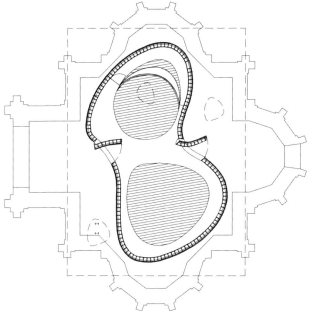

The architects of the Korean Presbyterian Church of New York (1999) in Queens went beyond merely reinvigorating form to interrogating the typology of religious space by housing it in a secular context. Greg Lynn, Douglas Garofalo, and Michael McInturf (working in Los Angeles, Chicago, and Cincinnati, respectively) transformed an 88,000-square-foot (8175-square-meter) former industrial laundry facility into a church whose formal aesthetic of folding planes was determined by the complex calculus of computer algorithms. Critic Joseph Giovannini describes the church as "an environmental origami."[10] Collaborating long-distance via a digital network—a novelty at the time—the architects turned the factory into a campus of sacred and educational spaces that includes a cafeteria and wedding chapel. The 2,500-seat sanctuary sanctuary is on the top floor, approached by staircases housed in the building's signature flanges. Inside, lines of the building's new structural ribcage are repeated graphically in the ceiling and floor, their regular rhythms offset by the asymmetrical placement of the altar, choir, and pulpit. The design is especially noteworthy as a harbinger of the explosion of digital design at the end of the twentieth century.

In the years following the first millennium, Europe was said to have donned a "white robe of churches,"[11] and the turn of the second millennium seems to be an equally auspicious time for religious expression. At the close of the twentieth century, the Vatican commissioned fifty new churches for the city of Rome alone. From that initiative came what may be architect Richard Meier's most satisfying and original work, the Jubilee Church (2003) in the Roman suburb of Tor Tre Teste. Meier succeeded in creating a structure that keeps faith with Cartesian geometry and simultaneously implodes it. The three arcing walls that describe the nave, side chapel, and baptistery are derived from circles of equal size, but the walls' unequal height and improbably bending mass yield a potent asymmetry of frozen movement. Similarly, the irregularly shaped glass between the shells offers a counterpoint to the windows' rational gridded mullions.

Meier designed the elegant travertine liturgical furnishings with their subtle, sculpted curves, as well as the simple beechwood pews. Soaring white walls of plaster and concrete are grounded by a screen of hemlock slats that separates the sanctuary from the social and administrative spaces. The warm wood tones suggest human presence in a space that aspires to ideals of perfection, both tectonic and spiritual. Tempering his geometries without compromising his rationalist faith, Meier offers a meditation on the Church as a gathering place that keeps the domestic ritual of breaking bread at the heart of its liturgy. In the process, he gives Tor Tre Teste—a neighborhood of undistinctive 1970s highrise apartments—a true social center and offers a tribute to the baroque city of Rome.

John Pawson, Novy Dvur Monastery, Novy Dvur, Czech Republic, 2004

If the turn of the century finds itself preoccupied with the angles and passages of the baroque, it is less a reaction to a sense of modernism's stylistic dessication than it is a transfusion of vitality into modernism's ethos of invention. In the case of Mecanoo's Chapel of St. Mary of the Angels (2001) in Rotterdam, The Netherlands, elements of the baroque—its narrative, its processional plans, its concave and convex rhythms, even its gilded ornament—subtly infuse a dignified, calm space befitting the nature of a cemetery church. In fact, the Italian baroque church of Santa Maria Assunta in Venice is among the historical churches Francine Houben of Mecanoo visited as part of her research for the commission.[12] Houben might also have cited the Roman funerary temple as a precedent for the chapel's skewed figure-eight plan. (The use of the circle to suggest the continuity of life after death is now so much a part of Christian culture that its ancient and pagan origins are often overlooked.) Here, two round spaces open onto each other: a sanctuary for the funeral rite and a vestibule where the coffin rests during the service. The chapel's shimmering, copper-clad, tin-plated walls are painted a saturated blue—a subtle but certain reference to the enveloping cloak of the Virgin Mary. This cerulean ribbon, anchored between two clerestories, floats below a golden ceiling that is pierced to project a beam of daylight onto the funeral bier. Together, these intense concentrations of color and light respectfully celebrate the ultimate ritual of passage and make beauty an integral aspect of consolation.

While Klein Dytham's Leaf Chapel (2004) in Yamanashi Prefecture, Japan, has an organic grace similar to that of Mecanoo's chapel, it was built to celebrate another of life's major rites of passage: marriage. Situated on the grounds of a resort popular with newlyweds and surrounded by natural vistas, the Leaf Chapel is so called because it is constructed of one glass and one steel leaf-shaped form that enclose the couple, officiator, and guests during the ceremony. Once the ceremony is over, the steel leaf opens—a moment likened to a bride's veil being lifted for the kiss—to reveal the natural surroundings. The steel leaf is perforated with thousands of holes in a floral lace pattern that produces playful shadows while it is closed during the daytime, and glows from within during evening ceremonies.

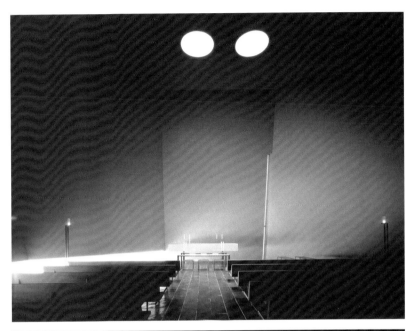

Spiritual Retreats

While many contemporary houses of worship put an accent on inclusiveness and connectedness, certain religious commissions call for spiritual isolation. The architecture of John Pawson's Novy Dvur Monastery (2004) in the Czech Republic, parallels lives lived within the shadows. Designed for the cloistered monks of the Cistercian order, who have historically used architecture to reflect their creed of simplicity, the monastery includes a chapel that is also used by lay visitors. The chapel, a simple rectangular nave and semicircular apse with lime-rendered walls, is distinguished by indirect light that filters down into the space through overhanging screens. The striated patterns of light give the church a processional quality, reinforced by the placement of the pews. The monks sit together along the sides of the nave, in pews situated at right angles to those behind them. To insure visibility for the visitors, the floor level of the altar is raised within the apse, where narrow stripes of light create the illusion that this, the most sacred space of the church, is floating in a haze of luminescence.

Sanaksenaho Architects, St. Henry's Ecumenical Art Chapel, Turku,
Finland, 2005

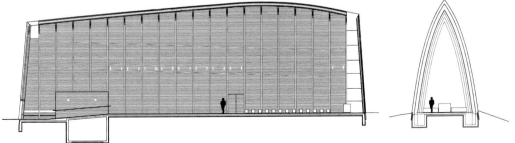

The introspective nature of mourning defines Fumihiko Maki's design for the Kaze-no-Oka Crematorium (1997) outside Nakatsu, Japan. Named for the adjacent ancient burial site, Hill of the Winds, the low-profile complex consists of a funeral hall, crematorium, and waiting area, all embedded in the grass to connote the primordial relationship between life and death. In the octagonal funeral hall, with black slate floors and simple plaster walls, darkness is pierced by light entering from two round skylights, a thin ribbon of glass along the floor, and a vertical slit at the front of the room. Attention is drawn inward and focused on the pulpit, where rituals are conducted. Apart from candles, there is no artificial light to compromise the profoundly stark illumination. The rooms where the bereaved gather between ceremonies are characterized by broad expanses of glass that afford views of the landscape and admit generous amounts of light. These rooms feature a warmer brown palette, with wood and COR-TEN steel elements. Outside, an open-air courtyard filled with water mirrors the sky, as if to mitigate the closure of death. While each aspect of the complex has a distinct character befitting its purpose, its three distinct spaces work in concert to create a narrative of the passage from the here-and-now to the unknown.

In contrast to Maki's sepulchral space, Juan Felipe Uribe De Bedout and associates Mauricio Gaviria and Hector Mejia designed a Cremation Unit and Ashes Temple (1998) in Medellín, Colombia, that is flooded with light, thanks to a massive skylight cut into the room of the first building and a ceiling of oxidized steel and glazing in the second. Dramatically situated in the city's Campos de Paz cemetery, the dual-volume complex features exteriors and interiors of limestone, granite, and sandstone, lending a sense of solidity and permanence in the face of life's evanescence. The double-height temple holds a multiplicity of storage banks for ashes that follow the line of the terrain in a gentle slope emphasizing the departeds' proximity to earth.

In Turku, Finland, Sanaksenaho Architects created a lone object in the woods, St. Henry's Ecumenical Art Chapel (2005), which is as much a piece of sculpture as it is functional space. Clad entirely in copper, the exterior is designed to patinate in harmony with its setting in the forest. The Nordic chapel functions as both gallery and church. Inside its wood-ribbed cavity (the ribs are a conscious

E. Fay Jones, Mildred B. Cooper Memorial Chapel, Bella Vista,
Arkansas, 1987

Daniel Bonilla Architects, Porciúncula de la Milagrosa Chapel, La Calera,
Colombia, 2002

Tadao Ando Architect & Associates, Komyo-ji-saijo Temple, Ehime, Japan, 2000

evocation of the stomach of a fish), massive wood benches, sculpted by the artist Kain Tapper, can be moved to accommodate special exhibitions or augmented with additional seating for larger religious gatherings. Under normal conditions, however, exhibitions are viewed in the back of the space and services are held at the front, so that one type of contemplation need not cancel out the other. The equanimity of the program is echoed in the chapel's symmetry: Light enters from both ends of the space–through the rectangle of the entrance and through the pointed arch of the glass wall behind the altar–illuminating the secular and the sacred equally.

Acts of Communion

The late American architect Fay Jones (1921–2004) interpreted ecclesiastical space as an act of communion with nature. In his well-known chapels in Arkansas, Jones built structures so well integrated into their sites that they are, at first, almost indistinguishable from the surrounding woodlands. Two of his most important commissions, Thorncrown Chapel (1980) in Eureka Springs and the Mildred B. Cooper Memorial Chapel (1987) in Bella Vista, are defined by enfilades of vertical piers set within clear-glass walls–forests within forests. Yet, both chapels retain vestiges of formal ecclesiastical language–the basilica

Axel Schultes and Charlotte Frank, Baumschulenweg Crematorium,
Berlin-Treptow, 1998

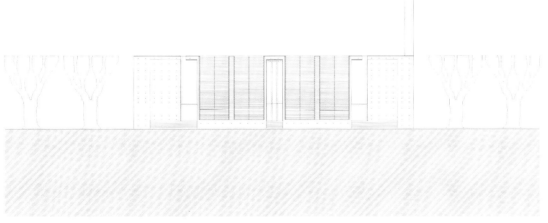

(in the case of Thorncrown's shed) and the Gothic cathedral (in the case of the Cooper chapel's pointed arches). In both projects, Jones stripped the church down to its most elemental components, as if to humble it in the face of nature. Only the rafters overhead emphasize the material role of the church in providing shelter and refuge to those who see it.

The interplay of shadow and light, fissure and volume, also acts as a metaphor for the relation of the human to the divine in Daniel Bonilla's design of the modest Porciúncula de la Milagrosa Chapel in La Calera, Colombia. Through Bonilla's inclusion of a massive sliding wall constructed of glass and irregularly placed vertical wooden slats, this intimate thirty-seat chapel transforms to accommodate large public functions and open-air services in the gently sloping landscape. When closed, the interwoven design of the glass-and-wood walls admit a play of light into the otherwise meditative interior.

The strategy of filtering light cinematically through a lattice is enjoying renewed popularity, particularly in residential architecture, as a means of collapsing distinctions between positive and negative space, between inside and out. In the Komyo-ji-saijo Temple (2000) in Ehime Prefecture, Japan, however, Tadao Ando used the tactic to establish boundaries rather than eliminate them, creating a spiritual place apart from the world for the Pure Land Buddhist sect. Here, the

shadows cast by the vertical bands of the temple's slender piers become as substantial as the wood structure itself, which envelopes the visitor in a complex optical weave created by exquisite Japanese joinery. Rather than melding into the landscape, the temple remains a discrete object rooted to the land only through its reflection in the surrounding pool.

Architecturalized Nature

Where Jones honors the forest, Ando derives potency from the essence of wood itself, and Bonilla celebrates the landscape, Axel Schultes uses the architectural column to create a concrete grove at the heart of the Baumschulenweg Crematorium (1998) in Berlin-Treptow, Germany. Mourners pass through either of two symmetrically opposed forecourts under a slender span of sky that is visible through a cut in the ceiling. They then meet in the condolence hall, where massive piers seem to be scattered at random. Each concrete pylon is capped by a skylight, which allows sunlight to filter through the columns. A basin of water set into the floor produces bubbling sounds that complete the woodland metaphor. The presence of these architectural elements is intended to remind mourners of the continuity of life, and the architectural prominence accorded to the condolence hall suggests that the shared act of grieving is the most essential of the last rites. By contrast, the chapels at opposite ends of the hall are strictly symmetrical, with gridded concrete walls, and are minimally furnished with simple, modern benches.

The columns of Paolo Portoghesi's Mosque of Rome (1984) can also be read as trees—a species of flowering trees. Arranged around the periphery of the prayer room is a series of piers, each composed of four columns. These columns pull away from each other in separate strands at the top and, instead of giving way to capitals, weave a fantastical pattern of arabesques under the concentric circles of the central dome. Though articulated in contemporary gray concrete, the tracery evokes the intricate patterns that cover the sculpted niches of traditional Islamic domes. Color is used to define the congregants' space: The traditional prayer rug is a carpet of deep turquoise striped in gold; the same tones are echoed in the stained-glass windows of the *qibla* wall and in the lustrous mosaics on the lower part of the columns and in the balconies of the women's galleries. Circular brass chandeliers seem to swirl above the space and introduce yet another layer of ornament. In concert with the columns, they give scale to the vast, open room. Though it is virtually empty of furnishings, except for the liturgical fixtures along the wall, the mosque is filled with allusions to nature, creating an abstracted Garden of Paradise that transcends the limits of the mosque's urban locality.

In his design for the synagogue of Congregation B'Nai Yisrael (1999) in Armonk, New York, Lee Skolnick took a canonically modern stance in his approach to nature and narrative. An abstracted canopy, meant to recall the tent of the first Tabernacle and the nomadic lives of the Israelites, rests lightly over a sanctuary with a view onto the landscape through a glass curtain wall. Within this floor-to-ceiling window, a thin armature of maple creates a pattern of acute angles that provides a visual counterpoint to the gridded mullions. The effect recalls stained glass, though here the panes are clear. Despite the formal allusions, the essence of the design is its unequivocally social program. In addition to providing rooms for meetings, study, and research, Skolnick designed the perimeter wall so that it can be folded away, allowing the temple to increase its capacity from 240 to 910 persons for special occasions. This gesture opens the sanctuary to nature and the world outside, symbolizing the link between religious observances and the activities of daily life.

In the Mosque of the Turkish Grand National Assembly (1989) in the capital city of Ankara, Behruz and Can Çinici used nature to evoke another kind of continuum—that between the earthly present and the afterlife. The paradisiacal tree, the Islamic symbol of heaven, appears here in the form of an actual garden. Not without controversy, the architects reversed the architectural conventions of the mosque in an effort to bring the structure closer to the essence of Islam. Instead of facing a traditional opaque *mihrab*, worshippers address their prayers toward a glass wall that opens onto a terraced courtyard and pool containing fountains, trees, and

Cultural

Museums, concert halls, theaters, galleries, and exhibition halls are not just spaces in which cultural activities take place but also indices of culture, reflecting both the state and the status of architecture and design. Buildings that were once all but the private preserve of the upper echelons of society and the cultural cognoscenti are now vying for competition as public palaces, driven by forces both from within and from outside the arts themselves. Until the advent of "blockbuster" exhibitions, art museums, in particular, rarely gauged the success of their endeavors in terms of attendance figures. This shift of focus was both populist and self-serving on the part of the institutions. It ushered a new era of corporate sponsorships and the idea of quid-pro-quo patronage. The conditions for granting donations became inextricable from meeting commercial marketing objectives.

The other side of the coin was that arts institutions became instruments of democratization, fulfilling their stated but often overlooked missions to cultivate new audiences. The same blockbuster exhibitions, ancillary educational programs, and often purely social events brought younger and more diverse audiences to dance, music, theater, and the visual arts. The resounding success of these new strategies has led to an unprecedented boom in the construction of cultural facilities all over the world.[1]

At the same time, some artists and their institutional patrons have retreated from this mass market approach, going through episodes of hermetic withdrawal and searching for an antidote to officially sanctioned culture and what they perceive as an overly self-conscious populism. Institutional efforts to make art completely transparent and nonthreatening often contradict the very nature of art, which can be a transgressive and unsettling enterprise. As a consequence, all but the most heavily endowed arts institutions now often vacillate between accommodation and confrontation to attract audiences and funding while retaining their credibility.

Museums of contemporary art in particular have had to contend with the challenge of serving the broadest possible audience while presenting work that disrupts the status quo. Whether the program is opera, orchestral music, or modern dance, performance spaces, too, share the dual burden of satisfying the ambitions of the artist and embracing the audience. These conflicting ambitions have led to two extremes in philosophy and design: On one end of the spectrum are cultural institutions that have adopted the model of the shopping mall, convinced that their visitors are comfortable with a consumerist ethos; on the other are those institutions that have rejected spectacle for immersion, endeavoring to create environments that bridge life and art.

Broadly speaking, over the last two decades cultural spaces can be divided into three types, based on the philosophy of the institution and the formal predisposition of the designer. The first aspires to be neutral, a recessive background for the works the space presents; the second aspires to be integral to the experience of art, occupying a middle ground of mutual engagement; and the third aspires to be separate but equal, as much in the foreground as the art itself. Each of these three broad approaches suggests a bias toward the nature of art itself, reflecting different perspectives on its status and its relationship to the audience. Interiors that aspire to be in the background privilege the identities of art and artists over the identities of institutions, complementing an art-for-art's sake institutional philosophy. Those spaces that take on the quality described here as the middle ground suggest that art needs to be put into perspective and given a context to be understood; these spaces are often the product of commissions by arts organizations that see education as their raison d'être. Spaces that claim the foreground provide a strong aesthetic counterpoint of their own; they most likely to be a reflection of an arts organization's belief that the experience of its spaces is equal to the experience of the art it displays, be it paintings or performances. But regardless of how aggressive or recessive all of these spaces are, they nonetheless function as performances or exhibitions in their own right and influence public perception of art today.

Background: The Recessive Space

The first model, of course, while aspiring to be neutral, is anything but. The classical modernist interior, often mistakenly understood as an unarticulated blank box, is as much a period room as is its historicist counterpart. Its abstracted spaces evolved in tandem with an aesthetic credo that views art as autonomous. Paradoxically, however, the architecture of the white box also aspires to merge with its context, its physical site. Interiors are marked less by traditional mullioned apertures than by erasures, as walls become windows and windows become walls filled with views. The modernist cul-

tural institution is thus often the product of the conflicting desire to both eliminate distractions and offer connections to the building's environment, in keeping with the modernist dictum to bring the outside in. The problem in the context of a museum becomes one of controlling exposure to light while adhering to a tradition based on celebrating its benefits.

In the Beyeler Foundation Museum (1997) in Riehen/Basel, Switzerland, Renzo Piano resolved this dilemma with an elongated rectangular box that opens on each end to the landscape. What's more, he conflates architecture, art, and site within one remarkable gallery on the south side of the building. Here a pond meets the building like an extension of the floor, casting reflections that flicker across the wall, on which a Monet water lily painting hangs. Long white sofas invite contemplation and give the room a residential quality distinct from the spaces where exhibitions are staged. These latter galleries are contained within three long corridors that run the length of the museum, each approximately 395 feet (120 meters) long, variously segmented with lateral walls to create spaces for discrete exhibitions and for expressing curatorial concepts.[2] Here, the museum's glass roof compensates for the absence of windows. A mechanical ceiling, engineered by Ove Arup and Partners, filters potentially harmful natural rays through a series of angled steel shades, painted white. Visitors enjoy fugitive glimpses of the sky and experience art under the natural fluctuations of sunlight on all but the darkest of days, when artificial sources are added. The exhibition spaces glow with evenly dispersed illumination, in contrast to the patterns of shadows that animate the galleries at either end. A museum book-ended with vistas, the Beyeler offers the experience of a contemplative stroll through an art-filled space that begins and ends in a park.

German architect Stephan Braunfels's design for the Pinakothek der Moderne (2002) in Munich, is a paragon of lucidity and rationalism. Rectangular galleries are grouped symmetrically around a rotunda that rises through all three floors like a pristine panopticon. Two dramatic stairways on either side of the central atrium create a diagonal axis up through the museum, making the layout of the galleries even more legible. Such consideration for the visitor's orientation in no way compromises the primacy of the art. The floors are uniformly terrazzo, and the white-plaster walls are so brilliant

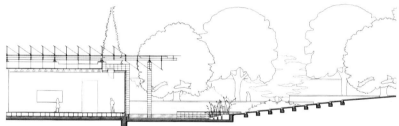

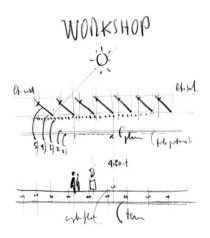

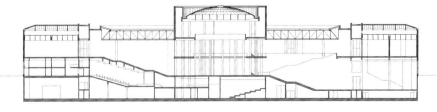

that they all but disappear behind the paintings. The museum is lit evenly by a computer-controlled system of artificial and natural light that makes adjustments for color and intensity according to the time of day. In its quest for perfection, the Pinakothek's interior circumscribes a place of Apollonian rationalism,[3] exposing the classical roots of the modernist ideal.

In the 21st Century Museum of Contemporary Art (2004) in Kanazawa, Japan, architects Kazuyo Sejima and Ryue Nishizawa of SANAA balance a younger generation of architects' penchant for complexity with stark formal simplicity by inserting a labyrinth of galleries within one all-embracing circular volume. Possessing neither front nor back, the museum's interior is implicitly nonhierarchical. At the same time, since the galleries are framed as squares and rectangles, the architects eliminate the notorious installation challenges of rotundas, like that of the Guggenheim New York. Exhibition areas range in proportion and lighting—some brightly lit with glazed ceilings, others devoid of natural light—according to use and conservation requirements. Galleries are connected by corridors that run maze-like through the building, offering surprising glimpses through the entire building. A glassed-in hallway circumnavigates the perimeter, connecting with the lounges and seating areas, giving visitors 360-degree views onto the surrounding landscape, while a series of glazed courtyards bring light into the heart of the complex.

One of the paradoxes of minimalist museum architecture is that it needs to be self-important and self-effacing at the same time. Yoshio Taniguchi's expansion of New York's Museum of Modern Art (2004) satisfies both requirements. MoMA's institutional stature conferred a level of prestige on the project even before it was built, a fact that allowed Taniguchi to play to his strength as a minimalist and bring his humbly aggressive modernism to a commission that affected the original building (by Philip L. Goodwin and Edward Durell Stone, 1939) and three subsequent additions (two by Philip Johnson, 1951 and 1964; one by Cesar Pelli, 1984).

It is revealing that Taniguchi emerged as the winner in a competitive selection process that included vanguard architects such as Rem Koolhaas, Herzog & de Meuron, and Bernard Tschumi. The museum directors did not want an

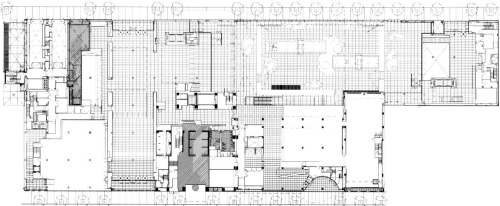

architect that would compete with its collections, and they
knew they could rely on Taniguchi to stay within not only
Cartesian coordinates, but Cartesian logic. Taniguchi separated what he characterizes as the "dual missions of the
Museum in the twenty-first century—exhibition of the collection and education of the public"[4]—into two separate structures
facing each other across the museum's Abby Aldrich
Rockefeller Sculpture Garden. Furthermore, he segregated the
commercial spaces (restaurants and a shop) along Fifty-third
Street and placed the cultural spaces on the Fifty-fourth
Street side, linking the two zones with a massive entrance
corridor that cuts all the way through the building. This
unabashedly functional entry reverberates with the proletarian spirit of Goodwin and Stone's revolving doors and signals
the Modern's ambitions to be fully a part of its surroundings
and open to the public.[5] The antithesis of a grand entrance—in
form and function It has a slightly oppressive quality—the
ticket sales corridor reveals only a glimpse of the building's
four-story atrium, which must be reached by stairs on the
east side of the space.

Any suggestion of a stultifying symmetry at the entrance is
countered by luminous interiors with a series of apertures
that offer views of both the internal city of museum-goers and
the external cityscape of midtown Manhattan. (The exterior
fretted-glass windows create a particularly elegant veil
between the city and the museum.) The galleries arrayed
around this central fulcrum are reached either by elevator or
escalator (another reference, borrowed from the department
store, to the classless aspirations of the old, and new, Modern)
and then, more spectacularly, through a series of bridge spans
that offer vertiginous views of Barnett Newman's *Broken
Obelisque* below. Apart from the angles of the escalators and
stairs, the only diagonals in the entire building are the invisible
sight lines that crisscross the atrium as visitors catch sight of
each other on floors above and below. The atrium is truly the
beating heart of the building, pulsing with an urban energy
that is separate from the serenity of the galleries beyond.

Taniguchi has frequently attributed the success of the
galleries to their invisibility, their determined deference to
the art that they hold. So pristine are the spaces, so planar
their configuration, that the artworks themselves become
wayfinding landmarks in a sea of uniformity and a convoluted
system of circulation. The reveals, air vents, track lighting,
and even the hardware of the service doors stand out almost
distractingly as the only design details in sight. The insistent
neutrality not only grants immediate access to the art, it also

suggests a limitless potential to expand—one of the museum's stated ambitions for the coming years. Taniguchi's design essentially creates an elegant vacuum of space to be filled by an unmediated experience of art: unmediated either by design or extensive exhibition didactics or over-elaborated installation designs.

In his design for the expansion of the Morgan Library (2006), also in New York, Renzo Piano was faced with the similar problem of how to extend the museum's identity and programmatic capabilities into the future without running roughshod over the past—in this case the original McKim, Mead & White library and two mansions that once housed members of the Morgan family. Piano's response was to connect the disparate buildings with a light-filled piazza covered with a "flying carpet" glazed roof and triple-height glass wall. While the connective tissue is exquisitely realized, the interstitial volume tends to dwarf the now dispersed galleries, clearly reflecting the priority that contemporary cultural institutions place on spaces for performance and dining, once considered ancillary. Piano, however, provides compensation for the reorientation (and spatial disorientation) with the addition of welcome new exhibition spaces tiered above the café.

Where both the Museum of Modern Art and the Morgan Library wrap themselves in and around their earlier incarnations and have to insinuate themselves in a dense urban context, the Modern Art Museum of Fort Worth (2002) in Texas is at liberty to stand alone. It is more like a cathedral than an extrapolated streetscape, in spite of the fact that it sits opposite the Kimbell Art Museum (1972), designed by Louis I. Kahn, and near the Amon Carter Museum (1961), designed by Philip Johnson. In Tadao Ando's design, grandeur becomes largesse, as much a function of the sprawling Texan landscape as it is part of this museum's curatorial agenda. Fifty-three thousand square feet (some 4,925 square meters) of galleries are tailored to give viewers the luxury of encountering sculpture and painting in ample space, minimizing any feeling of restrictive enclosure. Majestic double-height sculpture galleries of sensual concrete are characterized by Y-shaped columns that effectively give the galleries a sense of scale. A protective moat accentuates an exhilarating sensation of retreat from the quotidian; the large exterior reflecting pond also creates dappled light that is reflected on the grand foyer's soft-gray walls.

A grand processional stairway under a luminous vault makes an event of arrival to the galleries, but doesn't overpower the experience of the museum, which continues in intimate white-walled, oak-floored exhibition spaces spread over two floors. In these galleries, diversions are reduced to the slender seams of reveals and the grace note of Ando's custom seating—benches split down the middle in an echo of the museum's signature cantilevered roof lines. Warmed by natural light from a continuous linear skylight and clerestory windows, the exhibition spaces evince purity but not sterility. Paul Goldberger, architecture critic for *The New Yorker*, calls them "gracious, clear, generous, and varied ... never overwhelming," even when two stories high.[6]

Under similar climatic conditions, in the Spanish town of León, the architecture firm Mansilla + Tuñón alternately punctured and closed the modern box to yield a concert hall that is itself a kind of shadow play. The heart of the Auditorio Ciudad de León complex (2001), the concert hall, is completely sealed off and enveloped in darkness, while the peripheral foyer and exhibition hall are studded by a mosaic of light, the interior counterpart to the facade's cubist symmetry. Paneled in wengé wood, the hall has a womblike quality that is accentuated by the fact that the stage is cradled between two opposing tiers of seating, themselves upholstered in deep blue and purple fabric. Instead of traditional overhanging balconies, square loges

Tadao Ando Architect & Associates, Modern Art Museum of Fort Worth, Fort
Worth, Texas, 2002

are carved into the walls, creating window-like apertures that echo the deeply incised exterior. With dramatic juxtapositions of dark and light, Mansilla + Tuñón have managed to invigorate the neutrality of the modernist canon while adhering to its reductivist score.

In the glass box of the Fondation Cartier (1994) in Paris, Jean Nouvel struck a single, crystal-clear note. On the ground level of the new nine-story building (the Fondation's head office for France), Nouvel created a double-height exhibition space that is completely glazed, using a minimum of steel framing. Because the gallery walls are also doors, the entire space can to be opened to the surrounding garden. The building was constructed around the famous Tree of Liberty, a Lebanese cedar said to have been planted by the writer Chateaubriand during the French Revolution (1789–99). Ephemeral and urbane, the design demonstrates a commitment to transparency and public participation that belongs to the ideology of utopian modernism. Not only are the Fondation Cartier's exhibitions fully visible, but so is the city and its *citoyens*.

With its power to collapse and expand space and to create vistas and ethereal reflections, glass has been a beacon of modernity since 1851, when the Crystal Palace designed by Joseph Paxton opened in London for the Great Exhibition of 1851. Glass became a signature aspect of twentieth-century modern design largely through the influence of Mies van der Rohe. More recently, the presence of I.M. Pei's famous glass pyramids at the Grand Louvre (1989) in Paris changed forever

the character and perception of a globally famous destination. Pei's pyramids are as much a sculptural gesture as they are his design solution for illuminating the 550,000-square-foot (51,000-square-meter) underground expansion of the museum. While the Louvre's pyramids can aptly be described as merely the tip of the iceberg in a massive reorganization and renovation continued by Pei Cobb Freed & Partners (1993), Pei's controversial intervention is most interesting as a harbinger of other large-scale projects in which institutional prestige and civic pride require grand spectacle. Similarly, the Los Angeles Museum of Contemporary Art (1986) by Arata Isozaki was the first component in that city's plan for a downtown cultural center that is just now, at the beginning of the new century, becoming viable with the completion of such landmarks as Frank Gehry's Walt Disney Concert Hall (2003) (see Cultural, p. 313) and Rafael Moneo's Cathedral of Our Lady of the Angels (2002) (see Religious, p. 240).

A decade after Pei's pyramids, Norman Foster also chose the solution of a glazed canopy as entrance and connective membrane to the British Museum's galleries, but to completely different effect. In the Great Court (2000), Foster + Partners made an interior with the scale of an urban street that incorporates the museum's original nineteenth-century facades and central reading room. The diagonal lines of the lattice overhead appear, but the effect is softened by the slight opacity of the solar-filtered glass and by its curvature, which gives the steel framework the decorative quality of netted lace. The delicacy of the pattern and the shadows it casts serve as a foil to the overwhelming monumentality of the 20,000-square-foot (1,858-square-meter) space, although with its filtered daylight, The Great Court creates a strangely artificial atmosphere that subtly undermines the symmetry of its design. As much as both the Louvre and British Museum additions are meant to provide neutral containers for the more celebrated contents of their respective institutions, they inevitably and intentionally call attention to themselves.

Urban Backdrops

The city in the park is the setting for New York-based Richard Gluckman's Mori Art Museum (2003) in Tokyo. The cultural centerpiece of the Roppongi Hills development, the museum has an eclectic program of temporary exhibitions and sits atop a fifty-four-story tower. In a departure from his usual

strict white minimalism, Gluckman situated the classically
modern museum within a framework of unexpected color
and subtle references to traditional Japanese motifs that
make it distinctive. Visitors enter the museum at the base
of the skyscraper via a cone clad in glass shingles that
becomes a lantern by night and a sort of thatched hut by
day. From there, a high-speed elevator takes visitors to the
fifty-first-floor atrium, where the latent vernacular seen in
the building entrance appears again in large tiles of rough
pink sandstone. From the atrium, an escalator leads visitors
to the galleries on the fifty-second and fifty-third floors.
White rectilinear exhibition spaces are arranged around the
core on both levels and divided into four quadrants by diagonal corridors. On the fifty-second and fifty-fourth floors,
the corridors lead to an observation deck that circles the
museum. The interior circumference of this circular corridor
glows with the color of back-painted glass wall panels, while
the exterior circumference is filled by breathtaking views of
the city below. Thus, the uninflected spaces of the museum
sit in lively counterpart to the complex panorama of Tokyo.

Four years earlier, Gluckman had been engaged with a
radically different juxtaposition of vistas when he collaborated

on Rem Koolhaas's design for the Second Stage Theater (1999) in New York. Ordinarily, scenery other than that of the stage set itself is extraneous in any theatrical context, but here the architects broke with the protocol of the black box. Koolhaas, who has made a career out of reconnecting cultural institutions to their urban surroundings, retained the three enormous windows on the south facade of the four-story building, formerly a bank. Expansive views of Forty-third Street fill the wall to stage right, allowing the city to entertain the audience until the lights go up. At showtime, a mammoth, grommeted gold velour drape, designed by Petra Blaisse, is drawn over the window to announce that the performance is about to start.

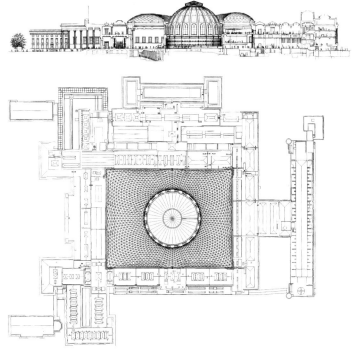

Like the Second Stage Theater, New York's Jazz at Lincoln Center (2004) does not reside in a stand-alone building, and it is even more strongly conditioned by its context. The organization's new home, which constitutes the world's first performing arts center designed especially for jazz, is not on the campus of Lincoln Center but rather a few blocks away in

Gluckman Mayner Architects, Mori Art Museum, Tokyo, 2003

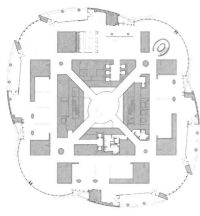

the towering AOL Time Warner Center at Columbus Circle (2004), designed by SOM/Skidmore, Owings & Merrill. For the prestigious jazz organization, headed by Wynton Marsalis, Rafael Viñoly designed two formal performance spaces, as well as a jazz club and a hall of fame, all of which are accessed from the same sprawling interior foyer. In the Rose Theater, the larger of the two halls, 1,220 seats are arrayed around the performers, insuring that no one in the audience is more than eighty feet from the stage. Movable seating towers give the space an unusual degree of flexibility, allowing the hall to accommodate opera, dance, and drama as

well as jazz. The 140-seat club is flanked by undulating wood walls with irregular curves that offer a quiet metaphor for the nonlinear rhythms of jazz. Visitors to the club or either of the two concert halls can stop into the Ertegun Jazz Hall of Fame, a room open to the public that features an installation by the Rockwell Group: a twenty-four-foot-long video wall, flanked by glass panels bearing the names of individual inductees. By far the most compelling space, however, is the smaller performance space, the 600-seat Allen Room. Though smaller than the Rose Theater, it is infinitely grander. Seating is arranged amphitheater-style around a half-moon stage behind

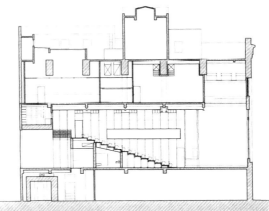

which unfolds a visual spectacle: a floor-to-ceiling glass wall
that overlooks Central Park and, beyond that, the twinkling
lights of Manhattan's East Side.

It is no small irony that the museum that comes closest to an
urban paradigm is the Getty Center (1997), with its galleries
housed in a complex of buildings connected by a streetscape
of plazas and passages. Pointedly sited in Santa Monica,
twelve miles from downtown Los Angeles, the center is a
suburban city-on-the-hill whose contradictions are paralleled
in the museum's interiors. Richard Meier's scheme of carefully

sequenced galleries paced around central atriums and flanked
by light-filled corridors is uncomfortably interrupted in galleries devoted to the decorative arts. The majority of the Getty
holdings, however, enjoy the spatial freedoms that are the
hard-won legacy of modernism, a legacy that can be credited
in part to Meier himself.

The designers of the new Ondaatje Wing (2000) and East
Wing (2004) of the National Portrait Gallery in London did
not have the advantage of working from a tabula rasa, though
they did have to contend with the re-presentation of history.

Instead of giving in to anxiety and generating a faux contextualism, Jeremy Dixon and Edward Jones catapulted the venerable nineteenth-century museum into the present with extreme economy and a distinctly gracious minimalism. The dark existing entrance hall now gives onto a tall, rectangular space lit at the top by a continuous clerestory window. Visitors begin their tour of the faces of British history after gliding to the second floor on a long escalator that, in effect, cuts diagonally through time by traversing multiple floors exhibiting seven centuries of portraiture. A new hall for the Tudor Gallery is painted a warm dark gray; on the level below it, a white corridor flanked by galleries houses the most recent portraits. A new rooftop restaurant unites the museum and its city with generous views of the London skyline.

With its sensuous curves, Steven Holl's Kiasma Museum of Contemporary Art (1998) in Helsinki exudes a serene yet confident presence in its urban context. Holl is a master of the effects of light in space, and he designed the museum to take advantage of the horizontal rays of the northern sun. Each floor is quietly energized by natural light admitted by a special system of baffles. The museum's asymmetrical curved sequences aim to provide a sense of "mystery and surprise," according to Holl.[7] Galleries are varied in scale to accommodate artworks of various sizes and, in no small measure, to save the museum from constructing costly temporary walls that would disturb the equilibrium of the rooms' proportions. Every doorknob, every lamp, every detail was designed to provide a consistent environment for the art. Walls are white sand-finished plaster, hand-troweled for texture, and the concrete floors have been blackened. As a counterpoint to the controlled, ascetic beauty of the interior, Holl brings the city into the museum through the west wall. Alternating planes of frosted and clear glass open up the atrium by day and turn it into a glowing beacon when seen from outside at night.

The Rose Center for Earth and Space at the American Museum of Natural History (2000) in New York, designed by Polshek Partners, is as much a science museum as it is a breathtaking new urban lantern, particularly at night. The center boasts the largest suspended glass curtain wall in the United States, which creates an enormous glass cube that contains the spherical Hayden Planetarium and Cullman Hall of the Universe, a permanent exhibition hall housing models of planets and celestial bodies. Rose Center straddles the

divide between the modernist rationalism of the twentieth century and, with its 360-degree ramps and undulating gallery fixtures, the twenty-first century's reprise of the organic. In the end, however, the spirit of this building flows from the reasoned history of the Enlightenment. Echoing the fantastic geometries of the eighteenth-century visionary Étienne-Louis Boullée, the stunning interior space embodies the center's narrative of cosmic spheres and spirals.

Jacques Herzog and Pierre de Meuron use the strategy of the light box to make the Laban Centre for Contemporary Dance (2003) a pulsing cultural beacon in the neglected London suburb of Deptford. Instead of transparency, however, translucency and color define the dynamics of the space, which houses Europe's leading institution for contemporary-dance training, while still keeping faith with the notion of the building as backdrop to the art it contains. Here the activity in the interior is integral to the nature of the facade. A double layer of vertical tongue-and-groove polycarbonate strips (once a typical greenhouse cladding) allows passersby to see shadow images of dancers performing inside—a sort of continuous open rehearsal for the citizens of Deptford. The thirteen individual dance studios in the two-story structure are distinguished by the color of the polycarbonate strips; the energy-efficient and virtually un-breakable polycarbonate also shields dancers from sun glare without denying them daylight during long hours of practice.

Here, as in the IKMZ library in Cottbus, Germany (see Civic, p. 206), Herzog & de Meuron use two massive spiral staircases to organize the circulation routes. Made of black rough-finished concrete, the stairways provide sculptural transitions between floors. The interior is an urban landscape in micro-cosm, negotiated by corridors and courtyards that revolve around a 300-seat theater. Undulating hand railings made of a new type of manipulated hardwood called Bendywood line the corridors, stairs, and dance studios, adding a slender grace note to the free-floating volumes of the building. The studios' vinyl floors, designed to absorb impact and return energy, contribute yet another level of color and texture to a composition that radically reinterprets the classical glass box. Instead of favoring modernist nudity, the architects seduce with colored veils. For their achievement, Herzog & de Meuron were awarded the 2003 Royal Institute of British Architects Stirling Prize.

The Loft

Another variant of cultural space that is intended to show-case its contents first, and foremost, is the loft. So familiar is the genre–from the Geffen Contemporary (Frank Gehry, 1983) at the Los Angeles Museum of Contemporary Art to the Chelsea Art Museum in New York (CMA Design Studio, 2002)–that it is worth remembering that lofts first gained favor in the 1960s for practical reasons of economy, and most of all, scale, for a generation of artists whose work required enormous spaces to be made and seen.

Much of the art of the postwar years no longer fit on an easel, and many performances no longer fit on a convention-al stage. Functional and minimally domesticated, early loft spaces were in a sense "found" boxes for art, the rough-hewn cousins of the modernist boxes purpose-made for exhibition. In one important way, however, the loft is anti-thetical to the notion of modernist self-effacement: that is, in its implicit engagement with the city and its explicit engagement with the culture of making art. Indeed, the institutional loft–be it a museum gallery or theater–owes as much to the domesticated nature of artists' live/work lofts as it does to their raw state as abandoned shells.

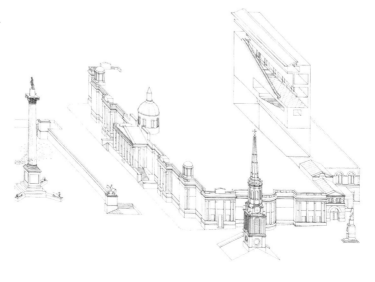

Founded in 1976 in an abandoned public schoolhouse in Queens, New York, as an alternative venue for contemporary

Steven Holl Architects, Kiasma Museum of Contemporary Art, Helsinki, 1998

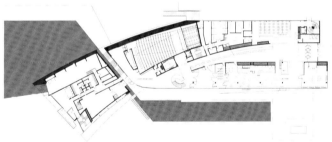

art, PS 1 operated entirely within the structural framework of its former institutional shell for the first two decades of its existence. The abandoned site was used for artists' site-specific interventions and as a space for changing exhibitions. Though located outside Manhattan, across the East River, PS 1 became a highly trafficked venue for alternative art; it has since been absorbed by the Museum of Modern Art as a satellite branch. The 1997 renovation by Los Angeles-based architect Frederick Fisher preserves the ad hoc nature of the space while introducing the codified aesthetic of the "white shoebox," a term attributed to the Italian collector Giuseppe Panza.[8] Larger galleries were created by removing non-loadbearing walls; existing classroom galleries in the loadbearing masonry wing were retained, with special care to preserve historical elements such as windows, hardware, and architectural detailing, including the painted brick surfaces of

the original walls. A new wing features a full-floor gallery into
which daylight enters from two sides; a nearby generator
room is used as a cabaret. All of the six original stairways are
in use, sustaining the multiple circulation patterns that have
always contributed to the carnivalesque nature of PS 1's
program of installation, exhibition, and performance. Fisher's
renovation selectively introduces discrete aspects of the
modern museum into the messy patchwork of the urban fringe.

Richard Gluckman's approach to the New York loft as exhibition space in his design for the Dia Center for the Arts (1987),
had a different genesis. One of the first warehouse conversions in the Chelsea gallery district, the center had an ambience of refined rawness (it is now closed and relocating to
a new space). By sheathing almost the entire facade in glass,
Gluckman encased four flours of exhibition space in an architectural vitrine, making the loft itself into an artifact. The
spaces felt stripped, but in fact they were sealed—the brick
walls and cement columns and beams were painted white,
the radiators silver. Gluckman's taut aesthetic was an ideal
match for Dia's exhibition program, which generally devotes
an entire floor to a single artist, who may choose to manipu-
late a system of movable walls or alter the entire space as the

installation requires. Less concerned with evoking the loft's industrial past, Gluckman's design highlighted the voids that industry leaves behind.

This industrial legacy operates on a wholly different scale in the vast former munitions plant in Karlsruhe, Germany, that now houses–or, more accurately, warehouses–the Zentrum für Kunst und Medientechnologie (Center for Art and Media Technology, 1997), or ZKM. The building's past is unsettling–it was constructed in 1918 and, under Nazi rule during World War II, was operated by slave labor.[9] Today the rambling three-story factory, adapted by the Hamburg-based architectural firm ASP Schweger, houses two museums, a technology center, and a municipal gallery dedicated to new media and the arts. The plant's reinforced-concrete skeleton has largely been left exposed, but skylights were added to ten courtyards (originally designed for the benefit of the plant's employees) to create enormous light wells that punctuate the mammoth building and provide welcome pauses between the dark environments of the media-arts spaces that dominate the center. Along the length of the building, a 700-foot-long (213-meter-long) corridor becomes a boulevard that links galleries, libraries, and theaters. A suspended catwalk runs through this spine, a reference to surveillance and to the conveyor belts that at one time carried the machinery of war. Schweger + Partner neither created an entirely new interior nor faithfully restored the old; rather, their hybrid renovation allows memories of the past to become a subliminal, if disquieting, part of the visitors' perception of contemporary art.

Herzog & de Meuron faced a similar challenge in converting the storied Bankside Power Station in London into the Tate Modern (2000). The architects drew on the latent energy of their site: the defunct power station that was famously portrayed in a World War II propaganda poster by Edward McKnight Kauffer that showed a muscled black arm transmitting electricity from the plant.[10] Pointedly, Herzog & de Meuron likened their approach to aikido, a martial arts strategy in which the opponent's energy is used to one's own advantage.[11] In their first British commission, the architects co-opted the power plant's art deco mannerisms and its brute structure to create a "super-modernism" for a mega-museum.

The plant's awesome turbine hall was converted into an entrance hall used for large-scale installations that are commissioned specifically for the site. Above the stream of visitors pouring into the cavernous entrance are gangways that traverse the space laterally and which are used to transport artworks from display areas to storage and vice-versa. A new two-story glass roof structure inserted over the hall creates a filtered band of light that runs the length of the enormous rectangular volume.

This daunting interior/exterior has brought a completely new scale to the convention of the sculpture court. Herzog & de

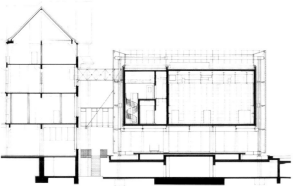

Meuron retain the sobriety of the hall but they effectively prevent any facile interpretation of the space as an industrial theme park. Even the soft blue-green, windowed glass volumes that project into the space do little to leaven the weight of the great hall; likewise, the ground floor bookstore and rooftop café, while both handsome and expansive, give the appearance of slender bands sandwiched into the vast enterprise. By comparison, the room-sized exhibition spaces that occupy the north side of the Turbine Hall, with windows that look out onto the Thames River, are decidedly intimate, countering the overwhelming scale of the entrance. Painted a warm shade of white, the galleries offer a welcom contrast to

the industrial gray stone walls of the Hall. Criticisms have been raised about the apparent aimlessness of the galleries' organization, but those comments would seem to be directed less at the architects' spatial configurations and more at a postmodern curatorial perspective that questions traditional art historical hierarchies.[12] Though the meandering arrangement of the galleries complements current museological thinking, by virtue of their confinement to the perimeter of the building, their sequencing is never disorienting.

One appeal of using industrial spaces for the exhibition of art is that these sites resonate with the act of making, of produc-

tion, and as such they are an analogue of the artist's studio. If one contemporary gallery owes its success to this analogy, it is Dia:Beacon (2003) in Beacon, New York. Fittingly, the conversion of a former Nabisco box factory was the product of a collaboration between artist and architect, between American minimalist Robert Irwin and New York-based OpenOffice.[13] With its stripped-back structure, clerestory windows, ceiling trusses, and sawtooth skylights salvaged from the original building, Beacon firmly remains a work of industrial architecture, particularly in the raw brick-and-concrete basement of the building that houses the lower galleries. All of the spaces are pristinely stripped, and new walls were stealthfully inserted, but only where necessary to accommodate specific works of art. There is a tensile beauty to the space that suits the rigor of a collection dominated by conceptual art and sculpture that dates largely from the 1960s and 1970s. Here OpenOffice demonstrates an acute understanding of the dual nature of the loft—a spartan space, indelibly associated with the permissiveness of the counterculture that pioneered its possibilities. They deftly rendered Dia:Beacon's exhibition space as both passive envelope and permissive environment for some of the most intellectually challenging art of the twentieth century.

Middle Ground: The Engaged Space

The loft, which straddled the realm of the modernist box and that of the artist's studio, was just one facet of a growing movement to make the experience of art more visceral, to escape the rarified air of pure formalism. As the loft matured, a growing number of museum and gallery directors sought to commission spaces that more directly engaged their audiences, and whose interiors participated in the narrative of the art they contained. Contemporaneous with the social movements of the 1960s, museums began to embrace their educational missions, striving for more inclusivity and adopting a more populist philosophy in an effort to meet their goals. A pivotal work in this new effort to engage the public was Gae Aulenti's design for the Musée d'Orsay (1986), which occupies the Gare d'Orsay train station in Paris, designed by Victor Lalou and built as part of the International Exposition of 1900. In repurposing the obsolete station, Aulenti chose to look back to the nineteenth century through the revisionist lens of postmodernism. In spite of the mixed critical reception of its design, the public embraced the Musée D'Orsay; its building (and its collection of Impressionist paintings) has made it a key Parisian tourist destination. In that light, Aulenti succeeded in meeting the populist mandate growing among museums,

but she did so at the expense of two design idioms, compromising the integrity of Lalou's Beaux-Arts architecture and reducing her own hybrid postmodernism to the equivalent of an architectural cartoon, dwarfed by the vastness of the former train station's vaulted space.

As museums look for ways to be more relevant and more accessible to their audiences, new designs often draw on references to familiar forms from other building types and interiors. With his design for the Contemporary Art Museum (1991) in Monterrey, Mexico, Ricardo Legorreta introduced a domestic sensibility into the ostensibly neutral zone of the modern cultural institution. As in a traditional Mexican house, entry is via an interior courtyard, here animated by a palette of yellows and pinks, surrounded by a columned loggia, and paved with a circular pattern of marble tile. Notably, Legorreta did not confine these domestic references to the museum's convivial social spaces but extended them into the galleries. Openings are cut through thick walls to yield views inside and out; two tones of wood were used on the floors to create grids of rectangles and squares. Modern white walls continue to foreground the art, a collection of contemporary works by Latin American artists, but the exhibitions are set within a framework that encourages connections with the world the art came from.

Mario Botta's design for the San Francisco Museum of Modern Art (1995) is a hybrid of another sort, both formally and programmatically. Well known for his religious commissions, Botta reintroduced the archetype of the museum as a temple. Reversing expectations, however, the public lobby, not the hushed galleries, is the consecrated space. Here a three-story staircase rises through a 135-foot (41-meter) cylinder, with balconies on each level that have been likened to pulpits.[14] Though unquestionably a reference to medieval cathedrals, the highly polished black-and-gray granite structure supporting the stairs conveys a slickness and sophistication associated more with high-end retail establishments and corporate lobbies than with religious structures. By contrast, the enfiladed second-floor galleries are unremittingly spartan. Instead of conflating the sacred space of art and the profane realities of revenue and attendance, Botta compartmentalized contemplation and socializing. In over-dramatizing their distinction, he creates a strong formal dissonance between them.

In contrast, harmony is the overriding metaphor for Kengo Kuma's Museum of Hiroshige Ando (2000) in the Japanese town of Bato. The museum is defined by a tautly synthetic relationship between the singular contents of the Museum—the *ukiyo-e* work of the featured artist—and the signature style of its architect. Inspired by the way in which the nineteenth-century master of woodblock landscapes depicted rain, Kuma has created a building defined by glass and irregularly spaced cedar poles that replicate the vertical flow of storm showers. His otherwise simply constructed steel shed becomes a shrine not only to Ando but to nature itself, which can be seen peeking through the scrim depending on the varying density of the wooden poles.

Similarly created to house traditional Japanese painting, the O Museum (1999) in Nagano also features vertical visual interruptions. In this instance they take the form of a network of delicate lines silkscreen printed into the building's long, sinuous curtain walls; the museum's front affords a clear view onto a near-lying traditional structure, while the lines in the back wall serve to control the light depending on how fragile or delicate the object being shown. Another museum designed by the innovative Tokyo firm SANAA, the narrow, gently curving building is elevated from the ground by steel columns wrapped in glass, enhancing the sense that the

museum and its contents are floating above the surrounding wooded landscape.

Context is less a matter of site than culture in Jean Nouvel's acclaimed Institut du Monde Arabe (1987)–a center for Arab culture in Paris comprised of a museum, changing exhibition spaces, a theater, restaurant, auditorium, and offices. The institute unites ornament and architecture in a way that uncannily prefigures the crafted, articulated surfaces characteristic of early-twenty-first-century design. Beyond their obvious reference to Islamic ornament, the famous ocular motifs of the south facade, with their technological lace, play an important role within the galleries. Light-responsive, motorized diaphragms were built into the polygonal patterns of the glass curtain wall, opening and closing in response to sunlight. The shifting pattern of the resulting shadows provides a cinematic counterpoint to the institute's interior, reinforced by glass-walled elevators that give the visitor glimpses of the activities ongoing throughout the ten-story structure. (Nouvel frequently cites the ephemeral nature of film, of moving light and images, as a critical reference for his work.) The museum's vitrines, seating, and display furniture, all designed by Nouvel, contribute to the formal dialogue between reflection and transparency, interior and exterior. Objects sit on bases clad in reflective tiles and encased by glass vitrines that allow their contents to be viewed against the background of the Seine or the complex geometry of the building's optical irises. In some cases, the vitrines rest directly on the floor plane, without an intervening base, creating a refreshing immediacy.

Mario Botta Architecture Studio, San Francisco Museum of Modern Art,
San Francisco, 1995

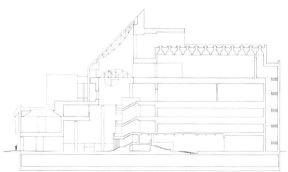

By using a combination of technology and natural light, Nouvel revisits on an ornamental tradition with centuries-old roots, at the same time he reanimates the modern glass box.

A similar precedent, the first built work in Europe by Frank Gehry, the Vitra Design Museum (1989) in Weil am Rhein, Germany, both extrudes and implodes the self-same box, though here it remains canonically white. In keeping with the reflexive nature of a building designed to house exhibits on design (in some ways as parallel to its contents as Nouvel's institute), the viewer is offered a complex interior landscape of stepped planes and sky-lit vaults. Unexpectedly, it is the pronounced curves and angles of the walls that make the space lucid, creating discrete zones of focus on a surprisingly intimate scale appropriate to the furniture and architectural models on view. Curatorial narratives are enhanced by partial views across galleries and by beams of natural light extending down through the galleries and alluding to what is ahead. The building itself becomes a silent guide, guiding the visitors' sight with the rhythms of its architecture.

The interiors of the Groninger Museum (1994) in Groningen, The Netherlands, designed by Milan–based architect Alessandro Mendini, are unapologetically interpretative, taking on a curatorial function typically associated with exhibition design. Bridging two sections of the city, the museum is dispersed across three islets in the canal that runs through Groningen. The museum consists of four discrete galleries, each devoted to a different aspect of the collection and connected by bridges, with the entire complex connected by a surreal checkered entrance. In response to Director Frans Haks's desire to dispense with the conventions of the monumental museum, Mendini put together a team of designers and set out to create a different design language for each pavilion. For the Old Masters gallery, Coop Himmelb(l)au created an intricate maze of stairs and platforms. In an overtly sympathetic approach to the domestic contents of the decorative arts galleries, Philippe Starck substituted his trademark sheer white curtains for actual walls. Michele de Lucchi used dark red interiors for the archaeology and history galleries. And Mendini and his brother Francesco developed a range of saturated colors for the contemporary-art pavilion, also distinguished by trapezoidal portals. Each room is an event, with each designer acting

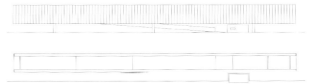

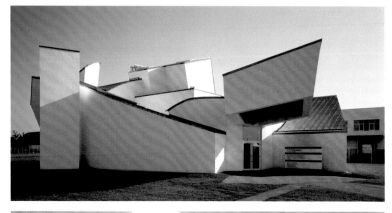 

as a tour guide, reminding visitors that art and design are processes of translation.

In his design for the Jawahar Kala Kendra (1992), a museum in Jaipur, India, dedicated to Jawaharlal Nehru, India's first Prime Minister, and to the preservation and revival of Indian arts, Mumbai-based architect Charles Correa also chose a segmented, interpretive approach, but his system is less concerned with layers of style than layers of history. An ancient metaphysical unity governs the museum's modern grid: It consists of nine 1,000-square-foot (93-square-meter) pavilions, each of which contains a different configuration of indoor galleries and outdoor courtyards. One is placed off-axis to mirror Jaipur's city plan, which resembles a broken mandala; together they represent the planets. Accordingly, each space has been given a different interior treatment.

A domed ceiling decorated with a painting of the cosmos shelters the center for administration, and distinct color palettes are used to signify the nature of the museum's activities and holdings: red and brown for crafts, gray for arms and armor, yellow for the library, and so on. Each square is connected to the next by a series of enfiladed doorways that define a circular path through the labyrinthine complex, suggesting the orbit of the planets. However, as Correa has pointed out, this museum is not only based on Jaipur's oldest myths (the mandala of the nine planets) but on the newest ones as well: the myths of science and rationality.[15]

Processional spaces that reveal themselves only when visitors are in motion have a behavioral aspect to their design. This is especially true in the theater, where the audience arrives anticipating a story to unfold, but also plays a role of its own.

In its design for the New Luxor Theater (2001) in Rotterdam, the Netherlands, Bolles + Wilson play on the sense of occasion surrounding arrival, intermission, and departure. Their deftly orchestrated composition begins in a foyer animated by skewed structural piers. Theatergoers ascend to the auditorium via staircases that rise to a broad ramp that serves both as an observation deck to view the comings and goings in the entry below, and a promenade to the double-height bar and restaurant above. Between acts, the ramp takes the place of traditionally tiered balconies, becoming a fluid stage for the audience. The stage is wedged into the heart of the building, one story above the foyer. Furnished with festive red seating designed by the architects, the auditorium boasts one unusual dramatic element in the otherwise symmetrical space: a huge domino-shaped light that is lifted away when the performance starts. With its emphasis on the spaces devoted to the audience and on intermission, the design of the Luxor reflects the service orientation of contemporary culture. Indeed, it is hard to imagine any comparable space existing a century ago, when the focus and the drama would not have been directed toward the performance space itself.

Buried underneath Arauco Park in Santiago, Chile, Felipe Assadi's Park Theater (2004) engages patrons in a dramatic processional that brings them deep below the ground. There they find themselves ensconced in a 250-seat auditorium, lined in thin strips of Bolivian cedar that form folds on the ceiling and horizontal lines on the walls. The angled wooden envelope not only produces excellent acoustics, its rich brown tone also lends a warmth to the subterranean space, which is further enhanced by vivid red upholstery. However, what truly distinguishes this essentially proscenium theater space is the counterpoint created by a deliberately erratic pattern of fluorescent tubes that ornament the ceiling and the walls.

Museums frequently state that they want to promote interactivity to dispel any vestiges of intimidating stateliness, but few actually create physical environments that truly encourage an energetic engagement with art. Tod Williams and Billie Tsien's American Folk Art Museum (2001) in New York does precisely that by making the staircases as important as the galleries. In fact, the stairways are galleries of a sort, lined with recessed display cases holding pieces from the collection that capture visitors' attention as they pass through what would normally be a forgotten in-between space. The

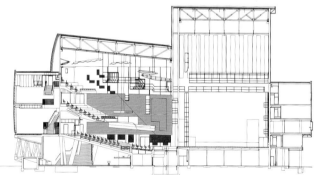

staircases eloquently make the point that looking is a constant experience, not a compartmentalized action cued by exhibition signage. The designers also used the stairs (they even included a redundant set) to offer as much variety as possible within the museum's extremely narrow confines–the five-story-tall building is only 40 feet (12 meters) wide. Apart from creating an intimate scale, the most masterful aspect of the design's relation to its program is the intentionally ad hoc quality of the materials used. An eclectic combination of corrugated green fiberglass, rough and smooth stone, plaster, wood, and steel complements but in no way imitates the folk art on display. What makes the collage-like mix of materials cohere is the one element that's immaterial: light. A sky-lit well descends through the core, subtly unifying the space and drawing attention simultaneously upward and downward.

Hans Hollein's Vulcania (2002) in Auvergne, France–a science museum dedicated to the study of geology and volcanoes–also creates a potent system of vertical movement, though here the designer's intention is more explicit. Hollein created an *architecture parlante* that leads visitors on an imaginary journey to the center of the earth. This largely underground museum, built with local volcanic rock and red Jura stone, is announced by a 1,220-foot-high (372-meter-high) bifurcated entry cone lined with embossed, gold-tinted, titanium-clad stainless steel. Visitors progress through spaces cut into the sloping site as they make their Dante-esque descent into a massive manmade crater that is 100 feet deep and wide (30 meters deep and wide). This rough-hewn grotto, studded with structural bolts and rivets, bears the scars of the drilling and blasting that formed it and the labyrinth of Piranesian galleries below. The rawness of the walls is further accentuated by the presence of pristine stone columns and state-of-the-art exhibitions. By literally excavating the museum's interior from bedrock, Hollein speaks to both the reality and the metaphysics of a subterranean passage.

The notion of geological passage also defines Will Bruder's design for the Nevada Museum of Art (2002) in Reno. Here the journey is concentrated in the core of a four-story atrium, in which the dominant feature is a dark metal staircase. Under the black ceiling around the skylight, the vertiginous risers suggest a hike through Nevada's Black Rock Desert,

Foreground: The Pro-Active Space

When a designer provokes a confrontation in a cultural context, it is to insure the autonomy of two enterprises–architecture and art–instead of subordinating one to the other. What may appear to be radical tactics today, in fact, are often part of a long tradition. One can look as far back as 1942, when Frederick Kiesler curved the walls of Peggy Guggenheim's Art of this Century Gallery to release the artworks from what he considered to be their bourgeois ballast, the passive flat surfaces of a mere container. Frank Lloyd Wright famously followed suit seventeen years later when his Solomon R. Guggenheim Museum opened on Fifth Avenue. These were designs as propositions, arguments for a new relationship between objects and events in space. Today, similarly risky design is enjoying unprecedented levels of patronage as communities look for ways to differentiate themselves within the monotony of globalism and its interchangeable architectures. What was once considered visionary and marginal has now moved to center stage.

In 1987, Rem Koolhaas made his professional debut with a design for the Netherlands Dance Theatre that could quite literally be considered an act of internal rebellion. Part of the Spui Complex in the center of The Hague, the theater shares a common foyer with an adjacent concert hall but adamantly refuses to be absorbed by it. An intense red wall stakes out the territory of the theater like a warning flare. A balcony boomerangs over the lobby, its mass supported by columns, painted in De Stijl colors, that appear to float under their load. Suspended above the balcony, as though balanced on a trapeze, is the oval disk of the refreshment bar. As extroverted as the theater's public spaces are, its auditorium is relatively tame; its warped corrugated-steel roof and gold-rubbed wood acoustic wall panels give just a hint of the design idea that would come to fruition almost two decades later in Portugal in Koolhaas's Casa da Música.

Set in the small city of Oporto, the Casa da Música (2005) is the work of a mature architect. Like the Netherlands Dance Theatre, Casa da Música accords the deepest respect for the central stage, but here the experience of reaching the stage

Below and opposite: OMA/Office for Metropolitan Architecture,
Casa da Música, Oporto, Portugal, 2005

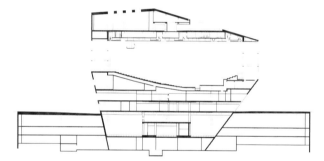

Wonder gives way to unambiguous joy in Frank Gehry's design for the Guggenheim Museum Bilbao (1997) in Spain, which has entered the pantheon of the world's great buildings. As both an organic structure and a marker of place, the building operates on a wholly new scale, more akin to the Gothic cathedral than to any twentieth-century model of a contemporary museum. So successful was Gehry's creation in improving the city's reputation and economy that cities around the world now commission new museums with the openly declared goal of replicating the "Bilbao effect." Half of the design's genius lies in the synthetic relationship among the building's disparate elements, and half lies in their very disparity. Gehry's design offers tremendous variety of spaces for the different functions of the museum while, at the same time, giving it an unforgettably coherent image.

The museum's 180-foot-high (55-meter high) atrium, cinched with a corset of swerving columns and a giant fretwork of window mullions, is an ideal space for artworks of an architectural scale. Another long horizontal gallery—often likened to a boat because of the curving buttresses under its ceiling—extrudes the exhibition space laterally along its 450-foot (137-meter) length. Some of the galleries are irregularly shaped and appear to be carved out of solid volumes, while others possess a more normative form and have square skylights in their floor to insure that natural light reaches the level below. Bilbao articulates a new set of possibilities for the experience of art, matching and enhancing the art's emotional charge with a dynamism that questions the very gravity of the space. Gehry successfully thwarted the innate tendency of museums stifle that emotional dynamism by mummifying their contents. Instead, he created an environment equal to contemporary art's ambitions to provoke and unsettle, inspire and instigate. It is also an environment hospitable to hosting the Guggenheim's program of traveling exhibitions that do not adhere to a singular historical framework.

Because of the stasis of its program—seated audience and stationary musicians—the interior of the concert hall has been far more resistant to innovation than that of the museum, though it is no less a beacon of civic identity. Housed in three beetle-shaped shells, Renzo Piano's Parco della Musica (2002) in Rome holds out the promise of such a breakthrough but denies it with interiors composed of handsome but staid boxes containing its theaters. Only in the Sala di Santa Cecilia, the

Eisenman Architects, Wexner Center for the Visual Arts and Fine Arts Library, Ohio State
University, Columbus, Ohio, 1989

Architecture Studio Herman Hertzberger, Theater Markant, Uden, The Netherlands, 1996

largest of the three halls, with its ceiling of adjustable cherry-wood "sails," does the interior design match the muscularity of Piano's lead-clad exterior. (Though it could be argued that these ceiling elements are too glossy and polished to fulfill the organic metaphor of the complex and come closer to feeling like sculpted pillows.) The most exceptional feature of the three halls is invisible: The acoustics—which some would argue is a concert hall's only truly important interior feature—are enhanced by the concert hall's distinctive cladding. Held aloft by galvanized-steel beams whose tension is regulated by suspension cables, the lead shells become tuning instruments for each hall's acoustics.

It is in Los Angeles, not Rome, that the concert hall broke free from the box, in the radical virtuosity of Frank Gehry's Walt Disney Concert Hall (2003). Ironically, Gehry's design was inspired by the legacy of renaissance Rome. Gehry made studies of drapery in the works of Michelangelo and Leonardo da Vinci, creating pliable wax molds that would inform the ultimate design of the hall.[19] Indeed, its interior spaces—in particular, the Founders Room—are best described in terms of a fabric's folds and creases. And while this aspect of the design represents only a single facet of a long and complex process, it is an index of how these interiors play with tradition by recasting the curtain in a new role.

In the main performance space, audience and orchestra sit beneath tent-like billows of bent Douglas fir. Walls of the same wood stop short of the ceiling, revealing another layer of light-washed plaster walls behind them and making it seem as though the concert hall is floating within its skin. At the back of the hall, an eruption of skewed timbers houses an organ custom-designed by the architect. The upholstery—an abstracted floral pattern that Gehry designed in tribute to the late Lillian Disney—adds yet another layer to the room. Despite its originality, Disney Hall has been frequently likened to Hans Scharoun's seminal Berlin Philharmonie. But such comparisons tend to obscure the fact that Gehry has taken the essence of Scharoun's idea (the central stage surrounded by nonhierarchical seating) and given it a voluptuous nature, part sinew and part drape, that has never been seen before. He has gone to extraordinary lengths to meet the conductor and his ephemeral art on equal footing and to envelop the audience in the experience of music.

Studio Daniel Libeskind, Jewish Museum Berlin, Berlin, 1999

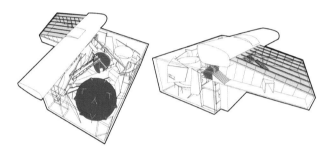

In the Lois and Richard Rosenthal Center for Contemporary Art (2003) in Cincinnati, Zaha Hadid shows an equal regard for the audience by pulling the sidewalk right into the lobby in an overt gesture of welcome. Beginning on the ground floor, with its black slash of a staircase, Hadid has made a museum of streets and rooms—replete with broad vistas, tight corners, and dead ends—that demand the same navigating skills, and offer the same exhilarating rewards, as does the experience of exploring a foreign city. Though it doesn't work on the inner ear like the Vitra firehouse (1994) she designed in Weil am Rhein, Germany, where the adjacencies of complex curves actually disturb the body's sense of equilibrium, the Cincinnati museum does encourage visitors to get lost amid the art. These are spaces that never obsequiously retreat from the aesthetic experience but instead fold themselves into it. Only one of the galleries has walls that meet at right angles. Critic Ann Wilson Lloyd notes, "[T]he interior's angularity and constantly varying ceiling heights offer fitted, cloistered spaces" that are suited to "chattering" video works and other iconoclastic installations.[20] Nonetheless, the building is demanding in its spatial complexities: visitors must negotiate contorted spaces and curators are challenged with newfound opportunities to make relationships between artworks, not only from wall to wall but also from floor to floor.

In Peter Cooke and Colin Fournier's outrageous design for the Kunsthaus Graz (2003) on the banks of the Mur River in Graz, Austria, the designers have bred a new species of exhibition hall that mixes twenty-first-century technology with parts left over from the 1960s experiments of Archigram, the British architectural collaborative that explored the possibilities of mobility through technology. The ceiling of the fully glazed ground-level courtyard is actually the underbelly of the blue-skinned, amoeba-shaped building. Visitors are propelled into the spaces of this multidisciplinary venue for contemporary art exhibitions, video installations, and events via what the architects call the Travelator. Part conveyance and part amusement park ride, the Travelator is a moving ramp that shuttles visitors up to two floors of amorphously shaped concrete exhibition areas. Visitors arriving at the top discover that the underside of the Kunsthaus's horny nozzles turn out to be functional skylights filled with spiral fluorescent lamps. Discretely positioned windows afford views outside, and visitors can enjoy panoramic views of the Old Town of Graz. Like

the vanguard work the Kunsthaus champions, the building is nothing less than a goad to art that settles for categorization.

"The building is not the museum, it's an activity, a group of activities" is how Lars Nittve, director of the Moderna Museet in Stockholm, characterized the twenty-first century museum.[21] His succinct summary aptly describes Herzog & de Meuron's 2005 addition to the Walker Art Center in Minneapolis. For an institution in an active state of self-education for the benefit of its patrons and its art, Herzog & de Meuron's design integrates the art center's multifaceted program of galleries, theaters, and media labs and embodies the Walker's commitment to a socially active museum model. The interior's intimate niches and active transitions parallel the Walker's concerted efforts to privilege "journeys over destinations," in the words of Andrew Blauvelt, the Walker's design director and curator—to encourage pauses, conversations, and interruptions in spaces where silence has traditionally reigned.[22]

The programmatic synthesis Herzog & de Meuron were entrusted to achieve was rendered even more complex by the fact that the design had to encompass Edward Larrabee Barnes's original hermetic brick building from 1971. This was handled through a variety of connection points and continuities, including the use of brick (as flooring) and modernist furnishings, which are a staple of the original Walker.

As skillful and diplomatic as the addition is, it is also assertive and iconoclastic. The designers introduced several key elements that erase any doubt about whether the

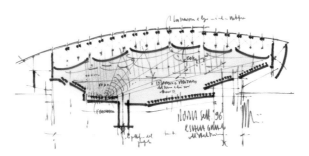

Gehry Partners, Walt Disney Concert Hall, Los Angeles, 2003

museum has entered a new era of permissiveness. Not only does the building seem to bend back on itself, it also fleetingly glances back in time, using overblown textile motifs and using them as surfaces for ceilings and doors. These postmodern reveries of decoration have a practical function as well. Stylized acanthus filigrees serve as air returns, and the alcoves they delineate function as transitional spaces between the brighter illumination of the lounges and the lower light levels of the galleries. The same pattern is also cut into the rolling door that closes off the galleries at night; its perforations allow evening theater-goers a glimpse of the exhibitions. The floral motif also appears in the black metal mesh of the walls of the theater itself.

Another unexpected pairing of sensibilities appears in the perimeter lounges that are scattered throughout the building: They are furnished with minimalist seating that complements the angled geometries of the building but are illuminated by lush chandeliers made of irregular chunks of raw glass encased in wire netting. The attention accorded to these in-between spaces is yet another indication of the premium the architects and the art center itself placed on informal encounters. Indeed, the Walker's director and curators have used the metaphor of the town square as shorthand for the convivial spaces they want to create and nurture but avoid controlling.

Zaha Hadid Architects, Lois & Richard Rosenthal Center for Contemporary
Art, Cincinnati, Ohio, 2003

Spacelab Cook-Fournier, Kunsthaus Graz, Graz, Austria, 2003

Designers like Koolhaas, Gehry, and Herzog & de Meuron are effectively making the case for cultural spaces as social spaces, trading the monastic language of modernism for judiciously fabricated collages that are unabashedly textured. There is a generosity to these spaces that claim the foreground, and such generosity is directed toward those who use them. They perform the invaluable service of priming the visitor, of heightening expectations. Rather than distract from the culture they contain, they charge it with a welcome and reciprocal energy.

Retail

AB Rogers Design, Comme des Garçons, Paris, 2001

The shop is a chameleon. With as many guises as there are garments and goods, its only constant is the tidal rhythm of merchandise. A hardy species, the shop depends on its ability to change its appearance without altering its basic retail anatomy. Its interior must be both stable and flexible by design. When potential customers identify with its spaces, displays, and goods, the store becomes more than a container for ephemera and commercial transactions. No longer simply a place to make purchases, the store, in its familiarity, becomes an extension of ourselves. By holding out the promise of the unexpected, the shop goes beyond the reassurance of predictability, appealing to desires customers never knew they had, and implicitly negotiates those transactions by intentionally diverting attention from any singular sense of purpose.

The balance that designers and their merchant clients strike between reassurance and risk varies depending on the cultural climate and on the demographics of their clientele. In the nineteenth century, the department store both rationalized and celebrated the bewildering profusion of goods from around the world that had become available to average citizens. The combination of mass production, colonial largess, widening international trade, and technological inventions—from the elevator to electric lighting—led to the development of a whole new architecture for shopping. It is telling that the earliest incarnations of this new retail culture appeared in France, a country whose economy has always had a strong base in luxury goods and is known for elevating fashion to an art form. The first department store, Le Bon Marché, which opened in Paris in 1872, was a super-structure of iron and glass designed by M.A. Laplanche.[1] In comparable style, Le Printemps and La Samaritaine followed in 1865 and 1869 respectively, launching a boom in department stores around the world. (New York's Macy's [1858] and Chicago's Marshall Fields [1868] were also forerunners of the department store boom, but these early stores occupied much humbler spaces. It wasn't until 1899, the year Louis Sullivan's Carson, Pirie Scott store opened in Chicago, that American retail culture could boast an architectural icon.)

In an era when stores were still tinged with the lower-class status accorded to merchants, these blatant monuments to trade were legitimatized and integrated into the urban fabric with elaborate historicist facades designed to arouse excitement and dispel the threat of new enterprise. Since the primary patrons of these grandiose bazaars were women, however, any intimations of wanton excess expressed in the stores' design needed to be tempered in their programs. Social respectability came in the form of amenities such as tearooms, art galleries, salons, theaters, and libraries. Going to market—which had always been an informal social pastime, an opportunity to meet, to gossip, and to bargain—took on a new self-consciousness. These were not shops for impromptu errands, but destinations for planned, time-consuming excursions, with interiors that took their cues from other realms, in particular the home—the primordial site of intimate relations.[2] Not only were there places to sit and eat, but there were now retail displays that simulated the parlor and the boudoir. The advent of the department store represented a seismic shift in consumer culture (which until this point could hardly have been considered a culture at all): The merchant psychology of servitude evolved into an attitude of authority and control. Store design became an enterprise, with its own science and its own artistic culture producing venues where the aristocracy and the middle class would meet on common ground.

Unlike Denise, the overwhelmed heroine of Emile Zola's 1883 novel *Au Bonheur des Dames* who fairly swoons at the "series of perspectives … and the plate glass windows"[3] of Le Bon Marché, today's consumers are hard to impress. No longer awed by the seductions of the retail environment, they became complicit with its flirtations. Indeed, the department store's century-long dominance began to wane in the 1960s when vanguard shoppers abandoned them for the boutiques of London's Carnaby Street and Abingdon Road. Designers like Mary Quant and Barbara Hulanicki of Biba opened shops that were both intimate and adventurous, and that responded to a new marketing niche: teens and young women who defined themselves by their musical tastes and distanced themselves from the mainstream by the way they dressed and where they shopped. These boutiques brought the middle classes what haute couture had always offered the upper classes: the security of membership in a subculture and the frisson of distinction and deviance.

A decade later, with the rise of punk, Vivienne Westwood's
London shops raised the stakes on risk with a dystopic
alternative to the flower children's hippie bazaars. In 1982
Westwood opened Nostalgia of Mud, her first store in
central London, where customers were required to walk
down a scaffolding from street level to a muddy excavation
site (complete with a bubbling pool of fake lava) and a shop
that occupied the remains of a Georgian house. Here, the
circus-like spectacle of the grand emporium was wedged
into the boutique and given an apocalyptic edge for a jaded
and fundamentally cynical clientele. This was the shop as
event, informed by the cult of rock star celebrity–a singular
instance of the power of design to create viable subcultures
and contest the powerful economics of the normative.
Indeed, throughout the 1980s, the boutique provided a
fertile incubator for the shop as persona. Architects such
as Eva Jiricna, Shigeru Uchida, and Nigel Coates formalized
this niche-market approach with shops for, respectively,
Joseph, Miss Akita, and Jigsaw–spaces that ultimately
influenced the flagship stores of today.

Today, the personality-driven boutique has been subsumed
into the identity of the brand, and design has become the
pressure valve for the release of a store's experience, be it
one that is insistently coherent or deliberately chaotic.
A store's interior is now equivalent to its logo, all but replacing the need for a street sign. In its quest for legibility, the
postmodern shop interior takes on the language and rituals
of other typologies–the museum, gallery, theater, and theme
park–in guises that are infinitely mutable. In articulating
the protocols of dissimulation, designers are exercising
ever-more subtle strategies to ensure the survival of the
fittest in the hyper-competitive arena of retail.

The Store as Museum
Given that the process of selling and buying has always
involved the art of guile–from the ritualized bargaining
of the bazaar to the enticements of seasonal sales and
discounts–there is an insecurity that underlies the culture
of the store. Deep-rooted anxieties, stemming from the
inevitable exaggerations and prevarications involved in
selling, are often countered by the suggestion of virtue.
Hence the frequency with which the shop looks to the
model of the museum, with all its references to the integrity,
rarity, and refinement associated with art.

So respectfully restrained is John Pawson's design for the
Calvin Klein flagship store (1995) in New York that it
elevates the store's wares to the level of art objects. Not
only did Pawson confer an aura of uniqueness by isolating
garments against fields of white—a strategy not unfamiliar
to the cyclical world of fashion—but he also went further
in evoking the monumentality of the traditional museum.
Twenty thousand square feet (1,858 square meters) of space,
twenty-foot (six-meter) ceilings, and three-story panels of
glass lend an almost unassailable stature to Calvin Klein's
collections. The first floor and second-level mezzanine
open onto each other with a spatial grandeur that was
unprecedented at the time. This is a scale more familiar in
the context of banking, and indeed, the Calvin Klein store
benefits from the subliminal advantage of occupying the
former J.P. Morgan Bank. (The connotations of financial
security and museological authenticity are not quite the
mixed metaphor they might seem in this case, given
Morgan's historic role in the museum culture of New
York.) Here, as in Calvin Klein's flagship stores in Seoul
(1996) and Paris (2002), Pawson astutely merged the art

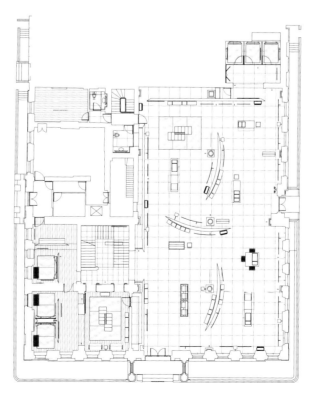

gallery's radically minimal white walls and stone floors into the store with an aristocratic confidence of scale and proportion and a classicism intended to transcend the particulars of place.

One of the interesting ironies of the minimalist retail envi ronment is that draws its credibility from an art movement shaped by an anti-consumerist asceticism and discipline. In the 1960s and '70s, artists ambivalent about the commodi fication of their work began to create site-specific pieces that stressed public experience over that of the static, privately owned object. When they did create such objects, they attempted to neutralize their preciousness by using serial production and self-deprecating surfaces. Architects found the minimalist artists' emphasis on space, proportion, and light particularly sympathetic at a time when the principles of modernism were suffering from dilution and disparagement. Minimalism and post-minimalism brought a new integrity to an International Style architecture that had become a formulaic aesthetic.

In the case of Richard Gluckman, who had friendships with the artists Donald Judd and Dan Flavin, the influence of sculptural minimalism was profound and led to a career distinguished for its museum and gallery commissions. Gluckman's embrace of the ascetic also drew clients from the fashion world such as Helmut Lang. By 1997, the year when he designed Lang's SoHo boutique in New York, Gluckman had to contend with the fact that minimalism had gone well beyond being a rigorous ethos to becoming a familiar style. So Gluckman approached the boutique as an exercise in reverse psychology. Instead of proclaiming its presence up front, the architect placed the merchandise toward the rear of the store, hidden in a series of dark, monolithic boxes that on closer examination prove to be illuminated clothing cabinets. Not content to simply allow the shop's white walls, indigenous columns, and painted tin ceiling to serve as a reference to the art gallery loft, Gluckman brought the gallery into the shop by inserting a work by Jenny Holzer amid the designer's understated collection. The presence of Holzer's work—a vertical LED installation that flashes cryptic, cautionary messages—was

both undermining and validating; but, in the end, buyers were given to understand the aphorisms less as a critique of the act of shopping than as a compliment to their own aesthetic discrimination, and that of the designer.

While uncertainty continues to color the discussion of art's relationship to fashion—does art lose its identity in the context of the store or is it simply reaching a broader audience?—designers who limit their borrowings to the language of art avoid this dilemma altogether. Charged to make the mundane events of daily life more meaningful, designers like Michael Gabellini and Johnson Chou have no qualms about repurposing the aesthetic of art, counting on subliminal memories of "the original" to lend prestige to their interpretations.

Among Michael Gabellini's many retail commissions, perhaps the best known is his design for the Jil Sanders stores, all of which assume the aspect of the modern museum—a considerable feat given that many of the stores, notably those in Paris (1993), Hamburg (1996), and London (2002), are

housed within ornate historic structures. In each case, Gabellini used the gravitas of the historic fabric to his advantage. Frozen in an opaque mask of brilliant white paint, their original architectural ornament provides a distinguished foil to Gabellini-designed fixtures in nickel silver and macassar ebony. (In fact, many European art museums take similar liberties with historic interiors, unlike American counterparts that take a strict preservationist approach.) Reflecting the casual modernity of the Jil Sanders line, Gabellini uses the ghostly outlines of architectural ornament to temper the severity of his minimalist sensibility.

In the London store, Gabellini brings mercantile and cultural environments even closer together. Within the eighteenth-century fabric of a building that formerly housed a branch of the Bank of Scotland, he incised the space with tilted walls that lean and curve in an ethereal homage to the weighty sculpture of Richard Serra. No doubt, some will see in Gabellini's departure from a strictly orthogonal language the influence of Frank Gehry, who himself drew inspiration

from contemporary sculpture, including Serra's. Here, the presence of computer-generated parabolas not only sequences the store's merchandise in a series of galleries within a metaphorical museum, they also function more obviously as a surrogate for the art that inspired it.

In contrast to the bravura of the work of sculptors like Serra, Johnson Chou's TNT Woman clothing store (2001) in Toronto more readily invokes the installations of minimalists like Robert Irwin, who sought to dematerialize the art object. A series of floor-to-ceiling walls creates L-shaped alcoves for clothing displays. Translucent and only partially volumetric, the interior architecture reveals only the ghosts of garments before showing themselves completely in three dimensions inside the L-shaped displays. Continuing the effect, pivoting reflective planes hinged to glass piers serve alternately as display tables and mirrors. These simple devices suggest both the illusive pleasures and real satisfactions of acquisition in an environment that tempts the prospective buyer with silhouettes before revealing them as possessable, wearable pieces of clothing.

The design store Moss (1994/1999) in New York's SoHo is best described as overt in its ambitions; there is not an ounce of coyness in its posture. The result of a collaboration between interior and industrial designer Harry Allen and the store's founder, owner, and de-facto curator, Murray Moss, the space is straightforward in its appropriation of the museum model, both as a site of collection and edification.[4] Objects are sealed under glass or kept out of reach as if they were one-of-a-kind museum pieces; each one is accompanied by a label that looks more like an accession document than a price tag, complete with product description and history, designer biography, and scholarly quotes. The reality, of course, is that most of these objects are mass-produced or at least issued in limited editions.

What Moss and Allen have created is a retail strategy, to be sure, but they have also contrived an environment that reconsiders the status of objects in culture, and the status of design as a cultural activity—the space, in essence, is rhetorical. Housing objects made for use, collected by museums, and sold on the street (as well as in museum raw-sheet-metal shelving configured in rectangles weaves through the interior and also projects out between the steel columns supporting the shop's facade. In all three venues, Lazzarini Pickering achieves a careful balance between the assertiveness of their graphic lines and airy weightlessness that comes from the pattern of voids they create.

Armatures of Display

The idea of exhibiting merchandise on bands that wend and wrap their way through the store is an increasingly familiar trope that owes its existence almost entirely to the digital revolution. Beyond giving designers new capabilities to draw freely in space, advanced computer software gave rise to its own aesthetic language of folded, malleable forms. We see this language in microcosm in Yasuo Kondo's design for Yohji Yamamoto's boutique (1998) in Kobe, Japan. The first of several commissions for Kondo from Yamamoto, the store is defined by a display system made of rippling steel ribbons. Painted white on the underside, they appear as light and thin as a pen stroke. Kondo, who received the prestigious Mainichi Design Award in 2000 for his renovation of the Tokyo Stock Exchange, says he "sees interior design as a mathematical equation," resulting here in a field of waves.[6] In a witty riposte to Kondo's futuristic forms, Yamamoto inserted a freestanding antique door–a relic from the pre-digital era of store design that works as a provocative foil to the warping strips of steel. For Y's Store (2003) in Tokyo, London-based designer Ron Arad transformed an otherwise nondescript white space into a kinetic sculptural installation with gently rotating aluminum armatures that serve as clothing displays for Yamamoto's seasonal offerings.

Computer-generated calligraphy is also the leitmotif for Massimiliano and Dorianna Fuksas's design for the Giorgio Armani Charter House (2002) in Hong Kong, where the curve takes on a functional and symbolic role, giving scale and semantic richness to the tired form of the shopping-mall franchise. Beginning at the metro exit (the store can be entered directly from the subway), a thick, scarlet fiberglass ribbon scrolls and loops through the street-level shops (Armani's bookstore, a florist, a cosmetics area), leading visitors into the emporium itself. Like a drawing in lipstick, the fiberglass band works as a map, as a sign, and–in the café, where it touches down to become a bar–as a piece of

furniture. Both spatial and graphic, its curves find a subtle echo in two incised glass walls that frame an exhibition space on the opposite side of the store and appear again on the facade, whose whiplash neon lines abstract the energy of a Chinese dragon.

Where the Rome-based Fuksas Studio use the ribbon to suggest a map of a retail universe, and Lazzarini Pickering, Yasuo Kondo, and Ron Arad bend it to form a venue of display, others reduce its width to play games of illusion. In Wendela van Dijk's fashion boutique (2003) in Rotterdam, The Netherlands, Eva Pfannes of OOZE Architects wove a tubular railing through walls of silk chiffon so that the railing's whimsical protrusions appear to be floating in space. The effect is enhanced by the Volcano display table Pfannes designed from sheets of clear polyester resin, each indented with craters of various sizes that form funnel-shaped supports and niches for showcasing small items. The shop's design thrives on the marriage of hard and soft, of industrial chic and sensual glamour–offering yet another confirmation that the twentieth-century's curtain wars are finally over. Long considered inimical to the modernist agenda, curtains were seen as superfluous decor and as an impediment to open vistas. In the realm of retail, however, maintaining open vistas is, if anything, counter to the agenda of keeping visitors' attention firmly directed inside, not out.

This new minimalist sensuality finds an even more succinct expression in the young Croatian firm Sadar Vuga Architects' scheme for the Mura Image shops (2003) in Split, Croatia, and Moscow. The humble garment rack is transformed into a sinuous, self-contained architecture of its own and is the only three-dimensional design element in the stores' spare interiors. Clad with beige artificial leather and studded on the underside with eye hooks, parallel bands of curving steel pipes form a series of discrete environments that fold around the garments they hold and then bend out in different directions to extend each display area. The undulating flesh-colored bands, only intermittently attached to the light blue shell of the ceiling, walls, and ceramic floor, loop through the space in a series of soft waves. Creating a series of directional currents and cross-currents, the armatures echo the peripatetic rhythms of shopping and browsing.

Ronan and Erwan Bouroullec, the designers of Issey Miyake's A-POC store (2000) in Paris, take the concept of armature-as-architecture further, adapting it to create an interchangeable kit-of-parts, a hallmark of their award-winning practice. The Bouroullec brothers, whose work has been widely exhibited, most notably at the Los Angeles Museum of Contemporary Art in 2004, go beyond isolated acts of furniture design to create what they call "micro architectures." The Miyake store is a prime example. Its design comprises a mutable network of bright green plastic bars—three of them hung across the space at different heights, plus a web of them that crisscrosses the ceiling. A series of accessories can be attached to this system, including vertical metal planks to which clothes are attached with magnets, as well as horizontal planes on which clothes can be laid flat. Dressing rooms are curtained with strips of wool, foam, and rubber. In contrast to Sadar Vuga's design for Mura, the Bouroullecs' use of line is ultimately less sensual than playful, closer in spirit to industrial design and in keeping with the do-it-yourself spirit of Issey Miyake's own micro-architectures of clothing, designed to be variously cut out from a roll of fabric with no sewing required.

The Surrogate Gallery

Because Miyake's designs evolve from questions of use (how will the garment be stored? how can it adapt to different body types or different ages?), the designer is particularly attuned to the architectural program of his stores. Though it has since been altered, Toshiko Mori's design for Miyake's Pleats Please store (1998) in New York had an especially symbiotic relationship to the clothing line for which the store is named. Mori treated the SoHo storefront not as a void or a passive looking glass, but as an interactive surface that would tell the story of Miyake's innovative textile technology. Designed with moving pedestrians in mind, film-coated glass windows revealed animated glimpses of the garments inside, with alternately expanding and contracting vistas that mimicked the behavior of the designer's patented pleats. The shifting veil was intended to stimulate curiosity just as traditional window displays used to do, teasing potential customers with its now-you-see-it, now-you-don't glass scrim. Mori's design appeared at a moment when the downtown art world was shifting to Chelsea and shops became stand-ins for the disappearing galleries. The shift was all the more subtle in this case

considering that Miyake's work can be found almost as readily in museum collections as in retail shops.

Four years later, the trope of the visually equivocal facade appeared on a grand scale in Jun Aoki's design for the Louis Vuitton store (2002) in Tokyo, now removed from the context of the art world and absorbed as a conceit of retail design. (Even at that, the Tokyo store is in large measure a refinement of Peter Marino's interior design of the 1990s, which became the template for all of the three hundred Louis Vuitton shops around the world.) Here, Aoki wraps the two-story flagship store in a shimmering mesh made of four types of metal. Handsome as it is, the scrim bears no relation to the Vuitton product line and is merely a tasteful tease, echoed in the store's display niches, filled with

holographic images layered over the real shoes and handbags behind them.

The relationship between fashion and art has become so intimate in recent years that it is common to see stores and boutiques treated as veritable exhibition galleries. And just as exhibitions have evolved from straightforward catalogued displays into overtly didactic narratives, the store shows signs of embracing an editorial role. Not content simply to borrow from the behaviors and display tactics of the museum, or to cordon off a separate "gallery area" as they would a café, a growing number of entrepreneurs see their stores as platforms for their politics and philosophies as well as their merchandise.

The young Tokyo-based firm Klein Dytham Architecture gave form to client Kosuke Tsumura's critique of the harsher realities of city-living in its design for his Final Home shops (2002–2003) in the Ikebukuro, Harajuku, and Shibuya districts of Tokyo. A disciple of Miyake, Tsumura designs clothing for seasoned urban nomads who–at least in theory and style–want to be prepared for discomfort and disaster (garments come with ID labels that include a line for the wearer's blood type). In the spirit of Tsumura's street fashion–he designed a jacket that can be stuffed with newspaper for insulation against the cold–Astrid Klein and Mark Dytham conceived of the Final Home stores as temporary encampments. Freestanding, zippable fabric wardrobes are placed in the space as installations, and the building shells they inhabit remain untouched.

Konstanin Grcic's design for Turkish fashion designer Ayzit Bostan's Berlin shop and showroom (2001) also raises the specter of uncertainty and transience. With only a short-term lease, Bostan was unwilling to commit to a permanent interior architecture; she also felt that a fully resolved space didn't fit her idea of a retail environment for a city seemingly under constant construction.[7] Grcic, best known for his clean-lined minimalist furniture, answered the design brief with an interior landscape of cardboard mountains and plateaus whose taped seams do double duty joining edges and graphically calling attention to the merchandise displayed on the sculptural forms. For this temporary installation, Grcic dispensed with the display case entirely. The crate became the pedestal, in an elegant comment on the ephemeral nature of fashion and its venues, while

OOZE Architects, Vandijk Fashion Store, Rotterdam, 2003

Sadar Vuga Architects, Mura Image Store, Split, Croatia, 2003

quietly raising uncomfortable connotations of homelessness in the context of luxury.

Fashion designer Rei Kawakubo goes beyond the politesse of metaphor and inference that inform Final Home and Ayzit Bostan's store, setting up jarring, intentionally confrontational installations in her shops. In defiance of conventional brand conformity, each of her Comme des Garçons stores assumes a unique architectural identity as part of her determination to inject a measure of unpredictability and thoughtfulness into the otherwise familiar rituals of shopping. Her Kyoto boutique (2002), to cite just one particularly poignant venue, is all but subsumed by the San Francisco-based photographer Catherine Wagner's ghostly photographs of a genetic storage container.

In response to Kawakubo's preoccupation with "obscure entries leading into a place of exploration and invigoration"[8] (witness Future Systems' cave-like entrance to the Comme des Garçons store in the Chelsea neighborhood of New York, which opened in 1999), architect Takao Kawasaki conceals the Kyoto store—and the cautionary story told within it—behind an anonymous facade of black granite. Inside, walls, dressing rooms, counters, and drawers are covered with Wagner's disquieting images of freezers containing research archives of areas of crisis in human health, such as alcoholism, Alzheimer's, breast cancer, and AIDS. The images effectively turn the store into a black refrigerator, giving the impression that the garments on view have been pulled from the frost-covered drawers and boxes. Despite its dystopic intimations, the environment may be less alienating than might be assumed, for the tactic implies an empathic relationship between the concerns of the consumer and those of the designer, albeit in the designer's famously chilly, distant manner. Kawakubo places her goods in the context of a cultural conversation—a polemic—about the health and survival of those who would buy them. In her newest venture, the "guerrilla stores" that began appearing in cities such as Reykjavik and Warsaw in 2004, she offers a meditation on the mortality of the store itself. Installed in raw spaces, in out-of-the-way neighborhoods, with no intervention by architects or designers, these shops have an explicit mandate to close within one year. Such social commentary, when paired with the commercial imperatives of the consumer market—the guerrilla stores, it should be noted, were

wildly successful[9]—reminds us that shopping is an act of the present that, if only briefly, distracts us temporarily from what the future holds.

The Theater

In contrast to the shop as a temple of connoisseurship and—in the case of Kawakubo—sometimes sobering knowledge, there is the shop as stage set. These retail environments are explicitly designed to distract consumers from the cares and routines of daily life. While it is true that the cultural realms of the museum and the entertainment industry seem to be moving ever closer together—both are equally fluent in the language of audience and sales—the projects discussed here all draw heavily on the consumer's willingness to suspend disbelief and temporarily become actors in the theater of retail.

As anthropologist Arjun Appadurai observes in *Modernity at Large: Cultural Dimensions of Globalization*, "modern consumption seeks to replace the aesthetics of duration with the aesthetics of ephemerality."[10] We no longer buy goods to last; we purchase fleeting fictions, susceptible to the rapid

cycles of taste and fashion. The theatrical retail environment has developed a host of strategies to assuage the anxiety of being out-of-season and to offer assurances that their offerings are au courant.

In Tsao and McKown's Joyce Boutiques (1994) in Bangkok and Taipei, the designers deploy a variety of decorative motifs to suggest possible scenarios for aspiring shoppers, like their signature shoe trellises intended to convey the upward mobility of women. A "virtual ballroom" suggests a different kind of social ascent by showcasing gowns under an antique French crystal chandelier, surrounded by walls clad in silver leaf and settees covered in soft velvet. Throughout both stores, Tsao and McKown endeavor to re-present objects to imply their potential for personal change. Clothes are grouped by attitude and type—"intellectual," "classical," or "sensual"—a strategy of display meant to transform commodities into fables of transformed lives.

In the case of the 750-square foot (70-square-meter) store in Milan created for the iconoclastic Dutch fashion duo Viktor & Rolf (2005), the design narrative goes well beyond self-transformation to sophisticated disorientation. Crossing the threshold of the shop, visitors find themselves in an Alice-and-Wonderland version of an eighteenth-century neoclassical interior, turned totally upside down. Italian architect Siebe Tettero, in collaboration with the Dutch firm SZI Design, designed every aspect of the diminutive interior right side up—its parquet flooring, white ceilings, and tiled fireplaces, as well as the architectural details of its arches, pilasters, and cornices. They then had the two-room store constructed invertedly. The dizzying result calls attention to Viktor & Rolf's trademark cheek and their talent for taking staid and classical elements and sending them up in a clever way. A case in point: as visitors enter the designers' lair, they are greeted by a welcome mat bearing the fashion house logo—on the ceiling.

The high-end luggage company Mandarina Duck capitalizes on two kinds of retail fantasies by situating product stories (more than suitcases, they sell dreams of escape) within surreal interiors intended to stimulate their patrons' imaginings. Instead of conventional travel paraphernalia, their stores offer unexpected encounters—the essence of

travel itself and the forte of Droog Design, the Amsterdam-based design network, founded by Gijs Bakker and Renny Ramakers, who serve as producers and art directors. At Mandarina Duck in Paris (2001), NL-Architects opt for an episodic approach like an amusement arcade, employing a series of incongruous fixtures that lure customers from one display to another and, pointedly, from one floor to another. Accessories are strapped to the walls in stripes of elastic colored bands and nest among the protruding metal rods of the indented "pin wall." At every turn visitors are tempted to pull, prod, and otherwise handle not just the products but also the store itself. Even the changing rooms, concealed by forests of bending rods of fiberglass that customers must part to enter, are unusually tactile; they are also partially transparent. The clothing itself is concealed in a steel-clad spaceship-like booth that beckons shoppers inside. In Mandarina Duck's London shop (2002), Droog confederate Marcel Wanders breathes life into a tightly constrained two-story space with a giant yellow mannequin implanted with audio speakers that rises through both levels of the narrow store. Forty smaller, humanoid robots, programmed to exhale periodically, are positioned throughout the store, animating it with mechanical sighs.

The capsule, with its evocations of space travel, has become one of the most romantic objects of twentieth-century nostalgia. It is also an excellent design strategy for severing the shopper's bonds with any sense of earthbound practicality—offering a more imaginative (and considerably more elaborate) alternative to the old ploy of banning the clock from the store. The two-man Dutch studio Meyer and Van Schooten exploited the fantasy of gravity-free (in retail terms, consequence-free) shopping in its design for Shoebaloo (2003) in Amsterdam. At 861 square feet (80 square meters), the narrow volume was a perfect receptacle for the fuselage the two partners created with prefab plastic units, which make up a system of interlocking display "cassettes" that serve to seal the shoe store off from any other reality. Shoebaloo is a completely realized stage set with mirrors that create a sense of infinite space and cartoon-like fins that serve both as seating and also as countertops.

For the worldwide chain Miss Sixty, the Florence-based
Studio 63 updated the same edgeless, organic aesthetic
using materials that would have been alien to any real
starship but right at home in the polyester-and-velour
1970s. (Miss Seventy, in fact, had been the chain's proposed
name, but it was already taken, and the owners realized the
exact decade was of little consequence to a generation of
shoppers who had never experienced those eras.[11]) In the
New York store (2002), and with minor variations in the
chain's other sixty stores around the world, the designers
contrasted a hard, glossy white interior architecture with
overtly sumptuous surfaces, like velvet drapes and shaggy
carpets. Accented in girlish reds and pinks and defined by
the stores' signature wasp-waist columns, Miss Sixty's fran-
chised hedonism is ultimately more Barbie than Barbarella.

Where others allude to science fiction, AZB, the partnership
of brothers Etto Francisco Ohashi and Takamaro Kouji
Ayano, indulge in role-playing games in its design for two
menswear boutiques in the provincial Japanese city of
Akita. Sited 990 feet (about 300 meters) apart, the stores—
whose names are derived from Transformers, the popular
shape-shifting toys of the 1980s—are treated as archetypes
from Japanese culture. The first, called α-Compiler (1999),
is like a futuristic character out of a Japanese manga comic
book; the second, called α-Assembler (1999), looks like an
ancient samurai warrior. Clad in a shiny off-white shell,
α-Compiler's inward-slanting doors slide open to reveal a
smooth space filled with rounded stainless-steel fixtures,
honeycombed shelves, and discrete glowing portals, including a second-floor window that doubles as a projection screen.
By contrast, visitors access α-Assembler by passing through
fabric panels and walking over a tamped-down earth floor.
Only after this ritualistic passage do visitors encounter
another iteration of stainless-steel fixtures—in this case in
a blood-red inner sanctum, where the Japanese word for
danger is spelled out on the wall, reflecting the architects'
view of the samurai as a paragon of ego and greed.[12] Apart
from their paean to action figures, the stores' opposing
personalities signal the difference between α-Compiler's
urban clothing and α-Assembler's sportswear.

London's Oki-Ni (2001)—"thank you" in the dialect of Osaka—is
not so much a performance as it is the digital-age equivalent
of a backstage dressing room, essentially nothing more than

Rei Kawakubo, Comme des Garçons "Guerilla Stores," in (clockwise from top left) Glasgow, Reykjavik, Singapore, and Warsaw, 2004–2006

Tsao & McKown Architects, Joyce Boutique, Taipei, 1994

Tsao & McKown Architects, Joyce Boutique, Bangkok, 1994

Siebe Tettero with SZI Design, Viktor & Rolf, Milan, 2005

a portal to a virtual clothing store. Customers come to the store to try on samples of the limited-edition clothing line; they then place their order online and wait for delivery. The experience is not so different from the customized tailoring boutiques common to Savile Row, where Oki-Ni is located, but the store is decidedly more playhouse than club. Designed by Tom Emerson, Steph Macdonald, and Lee Marsden of 6a architects, Oki-Ni is essentially an oak tray inserted into the raw white walls of an existing structure. Sample clothing is displayed on hangers that are casually hooked over the top of the walls, and in the back of the store are small dressing rooms with walls that are screen-printed with a ghost image of wood grain. Those visitors who are just browsing, or waiting for friends trying on clothes, make themselves comfortable on stacks of natural felt (by the Munich-based designer Johanna Daimer) that also function as display platforms. Every insertion into this bare-bones retail environment is exquisitely and sensitively detailed.

There is a new attention to surface and materials that has arisen in tandem with the emergence of digital technology, whether mitigating the coolness of virtual shopping, as

at oki-ni, or more generally, softening the consumer experience with craft. Hella Jongerius's embroidered pots, Tord Boontje's lacy cutouts, and Gaetano Pesce's poured furniture are all symptomatic of the new appetite for the irregular. There are signs that the less predictable, cruder qualities of the handmade are finding new compatibility in architecture and design, where these qualities were once anathema.

In architect Isay Weinfeld's interiors for Forum boutiques in São Paulo (2000) and Rio de Janeiro (2004), the shops incorporate fixtures and furnishings made with the construction techniques and materials of the Brazilian countryside. On the São Paulo site, the juxtaposition of a *taipa*-fiber wall and a colored-glass-mosaic staircase at the heart of the store creates a particularly strong decorative foil for the stark white interior. In Rio, rough-hewn chairs and striped woven rugs surrounded by lush drapes present a bold contrast of romanticized poverty and extreme luxury, with an unsettling effect. Had the furnishings been more fully integrated into the total environment, they would feel less like crass souvenirs and more like the tribute they were intended to be.

Craft in the twenty-first century needn't be limited to an organic repertoire of wood, metal, and fiber. The New York–based firm Slade Architecture swath Martine Sitbon's boutique (2001) in Seoul in a mask of synthetics that the architects liken to a Botox injection. The space becomes a metaphor for the re-crafted human body. Unique fixtures, like the resilient silicone sales counter and the bizarre overhead beam wrapped in synthetic hair, seem to grow organically out of a surreal interior membrane. Covered in creamy polyester paint, the walls bend around the edges of the space, making the room look as though it were cast from a single mold. The shopper's sense of scale is deliberately distorted, not only by the architects' uncanny application of materials but also by the site conditions. Beginning at the front of the store, the ceiling height shifts from 13 feet to 20 feet to 6 feet (4 meters to 6 meters to 2 meters). Within the slippery, ethereal space, the only stable markers are the

store's mannequins and furniture—notably, a low-slung, black-lacquered fiberglass pod that serves as a display-cum-seating unit and two incongruous Barcelona chairs by Mies van der Rohe.

In contrast to the intimate, haptic nature of the Sitbon boutique, Asymptote's design for the Carlos Miele flagship store (2003) in the meatpacking district of Manhattan draws on the more formal, ritualized theater of the baroque. Here, architects Hani Rashid and Lise Anne Couture update an architectural language rooted in the sixteenth century—a language that rejected the holistic order of the Renaissance for spaces animated by columns, processional paths, and fractured scenic vistas. With the additional dimensional permutations afforded by the computer, the baroque takes a new turn in Miele's shop. Dominating the space is a meandering form that begins as a low wall and coils up to

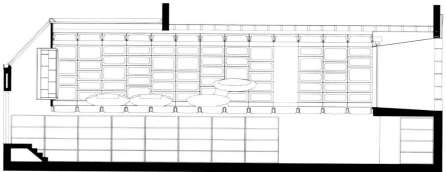

the ceiling, concealing support columns in the embrace of its complex curves. (The sculptural form is made of MDF, the ceiling is covered in a membrane of PVC, and the floor is coated in glossy epoxy resin.) The designers refer to the store as a "piazza," a gathering place for Chelsea's chic denizens, but it is more like a stage set framed (and flattened) by the proscenium of the store's glass facade. The interior is a contrapuntal composition in a rectangular volume, which provides a framework less flamboyant than courtly for the Brazilian fashion designer's elegantly embroidered, beaded, and brocaded fashion.

In contrast to Slade and Asymptote (firms that craft highly plastic spaces out of synthetically derived materials), Milan-based Fabio Novembre creates pulsating interiors with the ancient medium of the mosaic. He fearlessly embraces the ornamental possibilities of the tessera and injects new life into this traditional medium with surprising plays of scale and contemporary reinterpretations of classical forms and images. Art director for the Italian glass-tile manufacturer Bisazza since 2000, Novembre won kudos in 2002 for his design of the company's ground-floor showroom in Milan, which includes a vibrant heated-tile pool room sunk into

the basement and a rich series of decorative interludes–
from artist Sandro Cucchi's mosaic mural of Adam and Eve
to a tiled staircase designed by Novembre as an homage to
Capri's famous Casa Malaparte.

Novembre's design for Bisazza's New York showroom (2003)
in SoHo is equally operatic, but the libretto is necessarily
shorter, given the narrow footprint of the space. Visitors are
pulled into the space by an upwardly curving ceiling and
are immediately enveloped by an undulating mosaic of black
arabesques starkly silhouetted against a field of white and
blue. Three chandeliers with alternating cascades of blue
and white crystals hang between black Corinthian columns
that ascend to a sky-lit rear wall made of glass and screened
with cast iron grillwork painted white. With tongue-in-cheek
grandiosity and an attention to history and rhetoric that is
particularly Italian, Novembre describes his distinct intentions in verse, arguing that his showroom is a rebuttal of
Palladio's rationalism "in a world where the laws of chaos
have triumphed."[13]

Of course, the *signore* of spatial contortion is Frank Gehry.
His life's work has been dedicated to formulating a new
aesthetic of disorder in a host of public spaces, from the
Guggenheim Museum Bilbao (see Cultural, p. 311) to the
Walt Disney Concert Hall (see Cultural, p. 313) to the Ray
and Maria Stata Center at MIT (see Civic, p. 185). While
scale is a critical factor in Gehry's work, his folded forms
also create a series of microclimates within their larger
atmospheres. So it follows that he also thrives on the
small stage.

Gehry's concept for the Issey Miyake boutique (2001) in
Manhattan's Tribeca neighborhood is not that of a
free-standing building but, rather, an insertion within
three floors of loft space. On the relatively diminutive scale
of 15,000 square feet (about 1,400 square meters), Gehry's
giant aviary wingspans are translated into spliced ribbons
and twisted remnants–an ideal complement to Miyake's
fragmented and folded planes of cloth. The leitmotif
established, Gordon Kipping of G TECTS was brought in
by Gehry to design the store itself. The opposite of the
intimidatingly spartan boutique, the shop is a welcoming
vortex. The customer is swept into the store's kinesthesia,
activated by Kipping's steel stairs and transparent glass

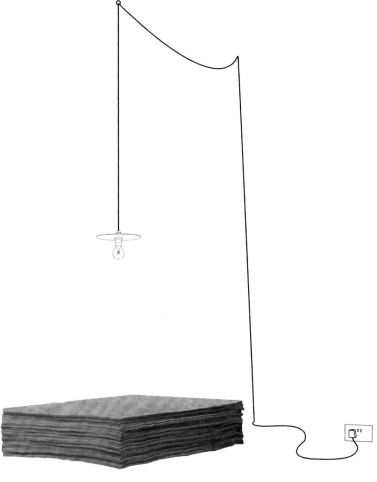

paths, Gehry's titanium "tempest," and the computer-manipulated anime illustrations by Alejandro Gehry, the architect's son—all in perfect synch with Miyake's mutable garments.

A defining feature of baroque space is that it can never be taken in at a single glance, that it exists simultaneously in front of and behind center stage. (This characteristic is expressed equally in baroque operas, such as Jean-Philippe Rameau's *Platée*, where characters float down from the sky and slither and dance across the stage, and in baroque paintings like Velázquez's *Las Meninas*, where figures reflected in mirrors stand both inside and outside of the picture plane.) In the current age of simultaneity, with its ubiquitous hyperlinks, TV news "crawls," and instant messages, these antecedents are particularly compelling for designers looking for ways to shape culture out of the randomness of the everyday.

In the case of the Galeries Lafayette department store (1995) in Berlin, Jean Nouvel further accelerates the already dizzying momentum of everyday life by employing the G-forces of a centrifuge. The store's screen-printed glass facade gives no hint of the stunning conical void suspended within the interior's core; nor do the selling floors' fairly ordinary accoutrements and fixtures, determined by Walker Group/CNI of New York. But once past the obligatory fragrance counters, visitors find themselves on the rim of a void, looking up and down into a vertigo-inducing funnel of space that glints with layered reflections and projections, like the inside of a futuristic Fabergé egg. The seamless panorama reveals five floors of retail space and shoppers in unceasing circular promenade (surely a metaphor for the cycles of capital exchange). Their orbits are separated by bands of mirrored panels, streaked with colored light, that the architect describes as a "scenographical tool … a motor for seduction."[14]

Isay Weinfeld, Forum São Paulo, São Paulo, 2000

Isay Weinfeld, Forum Rio, Rio de Janeiro, 2004

In all his work, Nouvel uses flickering light to convey the contemporary condition of restlessness; his buildings, inspired by the voyeurism of cinema, create indoor boulevards for the urban flâneur. By contrast, the young British firm AB Rogers Design draws shoppers into its interiors with tricks and illusions that have more in common with carnival showmanship. Tapping into the ageless fascination with robots, partners Shona Kitchen and Abe Rogers incorporate motors into their designs, quite literally animating fixtures and mannequins, in Kitchen's words, "to take the edge off exclusive shopping."[15] In the Paris-based Comme des Garçons flagship store (2001), motorized red cubes slowly oscillate within an inner sanctum coated in the same intense, lipstick-red fiberglass. For Al-Ostoura (2003), a luxury department store in Kuwait, Kitchen and Rogers mobilized both the merchandise and its display furniture, putting on a show that intentionally upstages the store's otherwise undistinguished container. A series of suspended "mechanoids," designed in collaboration with D.A. Studio and Dominic Robson, jump through the void of the store's three-floor atrium. Animatronic arms and legs rise and fall, skirts gently swing, and four pale pink fiberglass cubes dance in counterpoint to the mannequins' bizarre ballet.

Where other designers draw selectively from the DNA of either the theater or the museum, Rem Koolhaas splices genes from both pools. In his design for Prada's high-profile New York Epicenter (2001), the peripatetic Dutch architect—who validated fashion's fickleness as integrally postmodern and scrutinized the culture of shopping in his work at Harvard's Graduate School of Design—puts Prada on both a pedestal and a stage. The interior of the store, which occupies the space that was once the SoHo annex of the Guggenheim Museum, is defined by a rolling wave of an amphitheater. In the center of the bi-level store, a series of steps descends to the lower level, then seamlessly dissolves into an upward swell that flattens out into the plane of the main floor. Designed by Koolhaas's firm OMA/ Office for Metropolitan Architecture, and a host of collaborators, the Prada store was conceived as a vehicle for alternating exhibitions of commerce and culture.[16] Though Koolhaas's provision for after-hours performances and parties may not have been originally intended as a Trojan horse for the realities of business, the store's design follows a now-familiar pattern. Just as many contemporary museums are

announced by their shops—including the former SoHo
Guggenheim—commercial emporiums increasingly feel com-
pelled to declare their art-world bona fides. Herein lies the
real genetic mutation of the millennium: the hybrid cultural
circus. In this reversal of old realities, shopping feels almost
virtuous and museums feel almost like shopping.

At the SoHo Prada store, the street-level atrium is a virtual
barker's call, from the changing mural-cum-marquee,
designed by the graphics firm 2x4, that fills the entire north
wall, to the display cages hung from the ceiling that entice
like 1960s go-go girls. Lured by the wave-like curvature of
the floor, shoppers are drawn down to a sub-grade floor
and into a labyrinth of retail displays and dressing rooms
famously equipped with video screens displaying filmic
vignettes. What in other hands would have been vapid
hucksterism became, under Koolhaas's direction, intelligent
seduction; each element of the design—the wallpaper, the
cages, the curved floor—triggers something akin to lust.
The store is transformed into a series of object-events,
entertainments in their own right.

In the Prada store in Beverly Hills (2004, also designed by
OMA), customers are plied with new and old. Surprisingly,
there is no door, only the kiss of an air curtain, but inside
there is the familiar, socially active staircase. The walls of
the second level are lined with an otherworldly looking
coral-like substance (a synthetic material called Sponge,
invented by Koolhaas), while downstairs a gallery under
the stairs, with fixtures and flooring in the style of the first
store in Milan, is meant to recall the Old World. In contrast
to his integrated treatment of the New York location,
Koolhaas—once briefly a screenwriter—treats the LA store
as a series of discrete episodes witnessed by the sharp
changes in surface and color that distinguish each region
of the store. In part, this was a result of site constraints,
but it also parallels the difference between the stage
culture of New York and the screen culture of Los Angeles.

For the Prada store in Tokyo (2003), architects Jacques
Herzog and Pierre de Meuron had the advantage of designing
a freestanding building from the ground up. Housed within
diagonally faceted walls whose pattern is animated by
concave and convex glass, the store comes closest to Miucci
Prada's ideal of an "epicenter" as a flexible architectural

OMA/Office for Metropolitan Architecture, Prada New York Epicenter,
New York, 2001

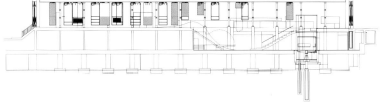

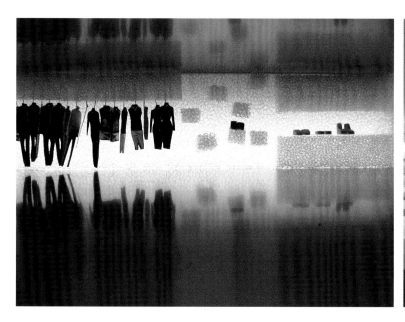

container specific to place. Herzog & de Meuron create a
distinctly utopian environment for the Italian brand in Japan
with features straight out of science fiction: touch-screen
"snorkels," fiberglass tables laced with glowing optic fibers,
pulsing projections of biological imagery, and "sound showers" orchestrated by music producer Frederic Sanchez
designed to draw people into the building's three diamond-
shaped, intestine-like tubes. The building itself owes a debt
to the visionary tradition of glass architecture, in particular
to the work of Bruno Taut, whose prototypical crystalline
architectural proposals made a virtue of transparency in the
years after World War I. Created in the context of a lingering
economic recession in Japan, the Prada facade is emphatically optimistic. It reveals an interior so integrally resolved–
from the narrative of its materials and fixtures to the
orchestration of its channels of vertical and horizontal
space–that it becomes a viable, virtual organism.

Architectural patronage, pioneered in the luxury market by
Prada and Comme des Garçons, officially became a mass-
market strategy when Selfridges invited Future Systems
to design its Birmingham store (2003). And while Future
Systems' previous retail projects had, in fact, included
vanguard boutiques for Commes des Garçons in New York
and Tokyo, Selfridges posed an entirely different problem.
In this case, the retailer was urgently searching for ways
to reinvigorate the department store's staid environment.
Ironically, the newly reborn Selfridges in Birmingham looks

backward in time. Future System's metallic disk facade,
inspired by Paco Rabanne's famous mini-dress, recalls not
only the space-age glamour of the 1960s but also harnesses
a strategy used by the very first department stores–
employing adventurous architecture as a critical sales tool.
Now, instead of acculturating shoppers to the emporium,
the task was to lure them back inside the venerable umbrella
of the bazaar. Future Systems' solution is romantically
futuristic, after a fashion that twenty-first century citizen-
shoppers recognize, not as a brave new world, but as a
perennial and hopeful sign of change. Seen from the outside,
the Birmingham store is a digital amoeboid that seems to
have oozed out of the computer screen onto the streets–not
to destroy the city, but to save it and its retail archetype.
This is the department store on steroids, revitalized for
the new millennium, with super-sized escalators and two
atriums instead of one. The building's brilliance is in its
smooth white lines, and light-filled cores that compensate
for otherwise windowless stores. But make no mistake, this
is not the unified department store of old, but a box of sepa-
rately branded boutiques gathered under Selfridges' skirt.
Here, the store itself, not the mannequins, wears the finery.

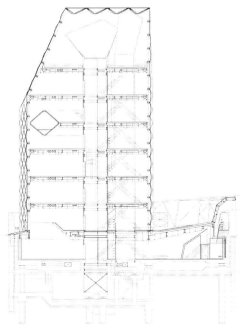

Restaurants and Bars

There is a popular myth that the birth of the restaurant was an invention of democracy, a legacy of the French Revolution. Purportedly, in the years after 1789, after the storming of the Bastille and the ensuing Reign of Terror, there was a glut of chefs who, having lost their aristocratic employers to the guillotine, turned to the public realm to exercise their culinary talents. While it is indisputably true that the restaurant is a French invention, the timing and circumstances of its appearance are quite a different story. The first restaurant was not a place but, in fact, a bouillon–an intensely reduced meat broth thought to have "restorative" powers. (Indeed, the French word *restaurant* was derived from a verb meaning to repair or recuperate.[1]) As Rebecca Spang documents in *The Invention of the Restaurant*, it was an appetite for health, not food, that led to a new type of eating establishment: public rooms where people of delicate constitutions went "*not* to eat but to sit and weakly sip their restaurant."[2]

The first of these establishments actually appeared before the Revolution, in 1766–the brainchild of the now all but forgotten entrepreneur Mathurin Roze de Chantoiseau. The curative consommé, and the places that served it, were the catalyst for a completely new type of public environment and an entirely new set of social behaviors. It took only twenty years for the word to denote a place instead of a soothing palliative. In the process, two intertwined preoccupations of Enlightenment-era Parisians–culinary refinement and physical well-being–were imprinted on the collective unconscious of the restaurant.

And what of the notion of democracy, of the restaurant's role in modern urban life? In fact, the restaurants gave rise to a sort of consumer's bill of rights. Instead of enduring the noisy and messy communal arrangements of inns and taverns, restaurant patrons were entitled to the right to a private table, the right to dine at any time, the right to receive individual service, the right to choose from a specialized menu, and the right to be given a list of prices. Contrary to the republican version of the restaurant's creation myth, these rights were actually threatened, rather than enshrined, during the Revolution. The Jacobins viewed the public eating establishment as a threat to the ideals of *égalité* and *fraternité*, as well as to the family values they believed should be inculcated in the home.[3] (Moreover, public

socializing, of any kind, could lead to public dissent.) But such was the appeal of acting privately in public, so exciting was the frisson of seeing and being seen (early observers found it unsettling that diners at different tables did not converse with each other), that the restaurant endured and thrived, first as a peculiarly Parisian institution and then, by the nineteenth century, as an international phenomenon.

Much of the iconography of the restaurant as we know it today was born in these early Parisian establishments. Mirrors and banquettes (the tête-à-tête arrangement would follow later) were quickly deemed essential devices for patrons who enjoyed watching each other discreetly. Curtained rooms were provided for romantic liaisons or business transactions. Wallpaper, chandeliers, and other appurtenances of the home quickly followed, and were the first props in the evolution of the restaurant as theater. And while clocks and thermometers–the accessories meant to reinforce the science of health in the earliest restaurants– have dropped away, what does remain is the promise of gustatory well-being.

From its inception, the restaurant has operated on the basis of two fundamental but very different principles, one practical and the other sybaritic: that of providing pure nourishment and that of offering an aesthetic performance. These values, however, are not rooted in the eighteenth century, but date back to the rites of the ancients. The Greeks, who gave definition to the epicurean, argued that the senses are heightened by abstemious consumption, while the Romans famously found power and pleasure in extravagant debauchery. These two disparate, competing attitudes continue to define the way we dine today, and the way architects and designers choose to conceive of the restaurant. In his book *The Last Days of Haute Cuisine*, chef and author Patric Kuh outlines some of the milestones in the history of the restaurant in the United States over the past several decades. Taking a look at just a few of these–and, more specifically, at the various languages used in their design–offers a case study in the pendulum shifts underlying how and where we choose to eat.[4]

In 1959, the ne plus ultra of big-city dining was New York's Four Seasons. Philip Johnson's power-lunch modernism was a radical rebuff to the red plush archetype of "fine"

European restaurants of the day; with its beaded curtains and indoor pool, however, it was still unquestionably glamorous. In the 1960s, Joe Baum of Restaurant Associates invited Alexander Girard to design La Fonda del Sol. Girard dispensed with the checkered tablecloths of ethnic restaurants and replaced them with the playful vernacular of Pop. In the 1970s, a new dining standard was set at Alice Waters' Chez Panisse, where rustic Arts and Crafts architecture was used to symbolize the healthful virtues of Californian cuisine and organically grown foods. In the 1980s, as the restaurant world began to mirror the franchise nation the US had become, Wolfgang Puck opened Spago in West Hollywood.[5] Here, Puck and his business partner and wife Barbara Lazaroff virtually invented the exhibitionist kitchen by putting chefs on display in a room decorated with a contrived conviviality–stenciled vine patterns and hanging copper pots–that set the tone for themed chain restaurants to come.[6] Just as significantly, in tandem with making the kitchen part of the spectacle, Puck helped to expand the role of the chef as a critical collaborator in contemporary restaurant design.

The 1990s witnessed the increasing popularity of celebrity chefs on television. In Britain, they ran the gamut from Gordon Ramsay to Jamie Oliver, who each in their own way contributed to the rise of the New British Cuisine, shaking off the country's stodgy "fish and chips" image. At the same time, restaurants like St. John (1994) in London, made a point of preserving and updating country cooking; in this case, inside a former smokehouse whose brick interior was painted white to give it an industrial-modern patina. At the turn of the century, with globalization all but a *fait accompli*, restaurants took on hybrid identities to complement the fashion for the fusion cuisine that grew out of French *nouvelle* cooking. And in the new millennium, restaurants show signs of going even further to satisfy the tastes of their peripatetic diners.

Even in this highly condensed outline of late-twentieth- and early-twenty-first-century flashpoints, it is possible to detect patterns of dining established in antiquity and crystallized in the first notion of the restaurant in eighteenth-century Paris. On the one hand, there is the tendency toward architectural sobriety and culinary seriousness. On the other, there is the natural affinity between decorative

fantasy and social and gastronomic extroversion. Still running strong, these two currents–straightforward sustenance and sybaritic theater–offer a useful framework for understanding the complexity of the contemporary restaurant interior.

Cool Modernism

Coming of age at a time when overweening nationalism was the cause of major world wars, the exponents of utopian modernism sought to develop a universal aesthetic that, in theory, was not German or Japanese, Italian or American. The story of modernism's transition from a utopian mandate to a stylistic option is by now well-known. Yet, even after a century of refutations and refinements, the broad ideal of political neutrality by design retains its potency. The fact that modernism is unquestionably stylistic in no way reduces its value. Form may no longer equal function, but it still equals meaning. Clearly this was something that restaurateur Lawrence Leung understood when he commissioned Rick Mather, an American architect practicing in London, to banish the stereotype of the Chinese restaurant from a series of five restaurants Leung opened in London, Hong Kong, and Montreal. Says Leung, "I wanted a … restaurant that served Chinese food, not a Chinese restaurant."[7]

While each of these establishments (opened between 1984 and 1991) shares characteristics with the others, they were not conceived as a chain by their owner or their designer. What they do have in common stems from the three basic requirements in Leung's brief: First, each interior must have the audible presence of running water (a symbol of prosperity–literally running money–in Chinese tradition); second, the presence of the color red (to connote good luck); and third, patrons had to feel they were part of one room no matter how many levels there were in the space.[8] Now & Zen (1991) in London, the last in the quintet, is especially interesting for the ways in which Mather integrated cultural cues into his essentially minimalist design language. Within the oval well that visually links diners on all three floors, water flows through a cascade of shallow glass vessels hung from stainless-steel rods. Not only does the handsome chandelier-cum-fountain supply the soothing and symbolic sound of running water, but it also alludes to traditional Chinese lanterns without resorting to cliché. Mather's delicate, custom stainless-steel barstools and curved leather seating create their own form of calligraphy against the white expanse of the walls, which is judiciously interrupted by planes of red, yellow, and purple to lend depth to the space. Mather doesn't banish culture, he sublimates it so that, folklore aside, Now & Zen ultimately prospers from a light touch.

The work of rigorous minimalists is often more interesting in spaces or in contexts where it isn't expected. David Chipperfield's Circus Restaurant (1997) in Soho, London, was formerly a television studio. Furthermore, in contrast to the garishness of real-life circuses, color is held to a whisper here. Exposed cookery, à la Spago, would have interrupted the ethereal atmosphere of the firm's trademark partitions (pastel voiles sandwiched between planes of glass) and its custom-designed taupe suede chairs. The beauty of the muted palette against the restaurant's dark wengé timber floors, imparts a distinct sense of calm to the space. In the Enlightenment model of the "healthful" restaurant from which this Circus descends, any note of surprise would be unsettling to digestion.

There is nothing to unsettle diners at Jean-Georges Vongerichten's restaurant Perry St. (2005), located on the western-most edge of New York's Greenwich Village. Ensconced in the ground floor of Richard Meier's Perry Street Towers, the restaurant was designed by Thomas Juul-Hansen. That the interior complements the master architect's sensibility with its own studied (though warmer) understatement is perhaps not surprising, given that Juul-Hansen served his apprenticeship in Meier's office. Juul-Hansen joins a palette of beiges and muted browns with Meier's signature white, introducing a staccato pattern of lighting fixtures whose black armatures are the only overtly expressive elements in the space.

Claudio Silvestrin, by contrast, had the opportunity to test his minimalist mettle against the stark vernacular of a sixteenth-century stable in Graz, Austria. There is no denying the romantic advantage that the original building's romanesque columns and groin vaulting confer on his design for Johan Restaurant (1997), but Silvestrin was savvy enough to use them as both historic foil and formal complement. He dispelled any possibility of mawkish sentiment with the simplicity of his layout. Tables are lined up in two straight rows on one side of the stone piers; on the other, he extended a cocktail bar along the length of the room. Heating and cooling elements are concealed in the floor, so there are no distracting cords or vents to interfere

with the monastic setting. Silvestrin's biggest achievement, however, is the way in which he bathed the vaults with light in order to leaven their mass and delineate their graceful arcs as the signature of the space.

In the case of Bar 89 (1995), in New York's SoHo neighborhood, architects Kathryn Ogawa and Gilles Depardon and interior designer Janis Leonard acknowledged the potency of a faceted ceiling in a thoroughly contemporary way. The space never fails to startle, as much for the dramatic incision in the roof as for the extreme contrast the discrete steel-and-glass box offers to the nineteenth-century context of the neighborhood. Flanked by two six-story landmark buildings, this overtly modern restaurant/bar feels pleasantly alien, as if it fell into its niche from outer space. Inside, the dissonance between past and present is reinforced by the view through the glazed facade, which offers vignettes of the brick-and-cast-iron building across the street. Except for an abbreviated balcony seating area against the rear wall, the space rises up two stories, its minimalist view sharpened by the wedge-shaped skylight and the curve of the glowing bar.

Perhaps the least likely venue for an ascetic design sensibility would be a global hamburger chain. Yet that is just what CKR/Claesson Koivisto Rune brought to the McDonald's flagship restaurant (1998) in Stockholm. The Scandinavian modern interior projects a wholesomeness that counters the negative perception of fast food restaurants. The stainless-steel counters, meticulous matched-grain pinewood walls,

and Noa pine chairs establish a setting for the "golden arches" far more refined than the typical interiors of a production line restaurant. Here, design provides the healthy environment and also frankly participates in a strategy of corporate regionalism. (McDonald's restaurants vary in décor from country to country, but the Stockholm franchise is exceptional in its recognition of modern design as a cultural signifier.) The architects who lead the practice–Mårten Claesson, Eero Koivisto, and Ola Rune–see no reason that even the most casual and populist dining experience should have to occur in garish interiors with hostile lighting.

CKR's design for a Japanese restaurant called One Happy Cloud (1997), also in Stockholm, makes an even stronger case for the practice of what they call "emotional modernism." Austere, acid-etched glass partitions are contrasted with warm bentwood NXT chairs and stools designed by Peter Karpf. A chalkboard mural, with illustrations that change every two months, runs the length of the restaurant behind the bar. By merging cues from the two sympathetic design traditions–cool Japanese restraint and Scandinavian simplicity–CKR has brought an unpretentious sociability to self-effacing minimalism.

Among those designer who, like CKR, have made it their mission to defrost the "white box" without entirely relinquishing its modernist aspirations is Seth Stein, a young British architect whose work is characterized by disciplined contrasts. His design for Baltic (2002), a restaurant and bar in Southwark, London, built within a

Georgian townhouse and a nineteenth-century barn, eschews the sentimentality of self-conscious architectural conversions. Stein retained a minimal set of original elements (an exposed brick wall and massive timber rafters), and inserted dramatic skylights over ivory white walls. In the informal dining area between the bar and the central space a fiber-optic chandelier offers an unexpected note of ornament. The chandelier's honey-colored amber beads, obtained from the Baltic coast, also appear in the bar itself, embedded in panels that glow in the darkness. Stein's elegant interventions ease the transition from an intimate entry space to the open volume of the main room.

Pragmatic functionalism and visionary speculation, two often contradictory strains of modern design, come together with particular urgency in restaurant commissions where the space is problematic—when the dining room is below street level, for example, or when structural considerations prohibit tall ceilings and grand views. Restaurant patrons, in particular, must be persuaded that underground spaces are not dank or unhealthy. To compensate for constricted conditions, designers need to supply alternate vistas and soothing décor. Such was the brief given to Karen Marble and Scott Fairbanks of Marble Fairbanks, the New York firm asked to transform the basement of the Hotel Giraffe on Park Avenue South into an open and light dining space for the restaurant Sciuscia (2002). To counter the absence of windows or skylights, the architects clad the room's ceiling and walls in laser-perforated panels of powder-coated white aluminum; the panels' dot patterns became the defining feature of the space. Crafted by computer, the pierced panels constitute a kind of techno Op Art for the twenty-first century, minus the visual disorientation. On the rear wall, the perforations are backlit for emphasis and create an illusion of receding space. The screens also have the inestimable benefit of being sound absorbent. So, in addition to the visual interest they supply, the patterns on the ceiling and wall panels help create separate acoustical zones. These zones can also be cordoned by series of diaphanous curtain sheers suspended from ceiling tracks, transforming the open spaces into semiprivate dining areas with their own atmospheres of enclosure.

In its equal attention to the aural and the visual, Marble Fairbanks' design recognizes that since its incarnation, the

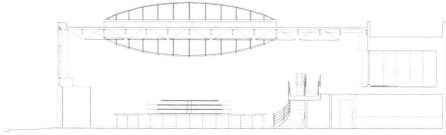

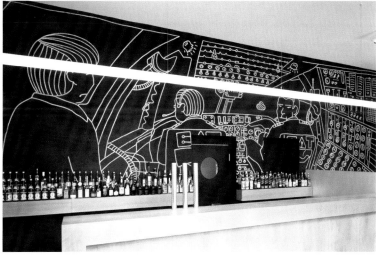

Prast Hooft Architects, Brasserie Harkema, Amsterdam, 2003

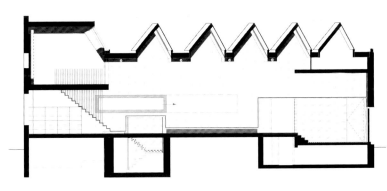

vitality of the restaurant depends as much on the exchange of conversation as it does on the exchange of glances. As Sciuscia illustrates, sound is the designer's invisible material, and a catalyst for material invention. In Amsterdam's Brasserie Harkema (2003), Dutch architect Herman Prast took the counterintuitive tack of muting the din of dining by installing acoustical wood panels that vibrate with colorful vertical stripes painted in one hundred hues—a gesture that succeeds in converting this former tobacco warehouse into a lively, sophisticated, and distinctly contemporary room. New structural elements break up the vast open space, offering a variety of unusual vantage points from which diners can observe each other's comings and goings. A steel chain curtain acts as a seductive separation between the bar and the restaurant, which has sky boxes for small groups suspended over the main hall. Along one side of the dining hall a steel-covered wooden structure blends together several functions: wall, floor, steps, balustrade. The stepped configuration serves as platform for one set of diners and roof for others before it narrows into a five-millimeter-thin steel stairway to the mezzanine. Tables and benches by Prast Hoof and TOM chairs by Lente accentuate the forward-looking spirit of the restaurant, while original elements like the wood floor, the sawtooth roof (which admits abundant northern light), and cast-iron radiators quietly preserve the industrial character of the building.

Textured Modernism

While restaurants like Sciuscia and Brasserie Harkema are recognizable descendants of classical modernism—in the sense that they are ahistorical, open, and give due attention to such functional issues as acoustics—they also follow another tangent of modernism: an emphasis on craft (be it in perforated metal or painted acoustical board) that evolved out of the Bauhaus dictum "truth to materials." That exhortation, intended to eradicate the "deceit" of ornament, encouraged designers to explore in greater depth the possibilities of materials. In fact, the Bauhaus (along with other early-twentieth-century design communities) actively promoted experiments—the most famous of which may be Marcel Breuer's adaptation of the steel tubing of his Adler bicycle into the Wassily chair—that transcended the mere veneration of materials and historic styles that characterized the nineteenth-century Arts and Crafts movement. The goal was to open up new languages for the

handmade and new contexts for the machine-made. Thus, just as the groundwork was being laid for a uniform International Style, another strain of modernism was incubating. The search for a textured modernism, in which craft is integral to invention, has since taken on a genera-tional pattern—beginning in the 1920s with Anni Albers' textile experiments using materials like cellophane, then reemerging in the modern craft movement of the 1950s, and again in the 1960s with a newfound interest in folk art, and, most recently, picking up new momentum at the turn of the millennium in postmodern contractions of past and present. In the case of the restaurant, materials are being exploited as an alternate kind of scenography.

Among those who understand the hedonistic appeal of sheer physicality are Paul Lewis, Marc Tsurumaki, and David J. Lewis of the New York firm LTL/Lewis Tsurumaki Lewis. The firm's first venture in what the trades call hospi-tality design was the short-lived Lozoo (2002) on the edge of SoHo in New York. Faced with a series of fragmented spaces combined from three different properties on Houston Street—some of which had decidedly inhospitable proportions—LTL unified the restaurant by establishing a continuous wainscoting made of felt, handsomely striated in four shades of gray flecked with white. Diners, whether at the banquette in the bar area or under the skylight in the open dining room, were cosseted by the warm panels, which transcended their functional value as sound absorbers and provided an unusual level of visual interest to the otherwise awkward layout.

If the use of materials in Lozoo offered a partial (if unexpectedly sensual) solution to space constraints, LTL's approach for Fluff (2004), a small bakery-café in Midtown Manhattan, was a full-fledged immersion. Here, the walls and ceiling form a continuous arc made of alternating felt and stained-wood bands that create an irregular pattern of striations. Darker at the base and lighter at the ceiling, the narrow bands of neutral colors are sandwiched and sequenced so that they appear to hurtle through the space creating a horizontal vertigo. The distinctly urban sensation of frenetic speed is compounded by the firm's custom chandelier, made of forty separate incandescent lamps. In this modest café, the maximal aesthetic has a practical side, making more out of less by mitigating the constraints

with optical illusion and material sensation. LTL brought
a similar strategy to another project in New York, a small
Chinese restaurant in Lower Manhattan called Tides (2005),
where 80,000 bamboo skewers are embedded in a back-lit
acoustical ceiling, evoking the image of sea grasses waving
overhead. Here, the restaurant's tables, booths, and seating
offers a case study of the possibilities of a single material.

In Shanghai, indigenous materials take center stage in a
martini bar designed by the Shanghai-based architect
Benjamin Wood (formerly of Wood and Zapata in Boston).
Ceramic roofing tiles, sliced one inch thick and stacked in
bands, create a wave-like wall that runs the length of DR
Bar (2002), which is situated in the newly fashionable
district of Xintiandi. The bar itself is made of local black
inkstone and is topped with a taut fabric of silver threads
woven by two women in Guangzhou. The evidence of handi-
work takes on a particular poignancy as the new China
displaces the old. (DR Bar, it should be noted, replaced a
former Communist Party headquarters.) Here, designers
used fragments of an older vernacular that has become
increasingly discredited as traditional buildings–*lilong*–are
torn down to make way for more lucrative new construction
projects in the breakneck race toward modernization.

The increasing interest in craft and in more personalized
environments is not confined to the small scale or quirky
spaces of the examples just discussed; it has also made its
mark in the temples of haute cuisine. Today, such extremes
of customization can be seen as a reaction to the corporate
nature of public life. The almost ubiquitous presence of
advertising in public space and exchange of personal
experience for branded events is also felt in the restaurant
landscape, where values of service and culinary distinction
are often eclipsed by signature logos and signature designs,
repeated with only minor variations in global chains.
Today, the premium on idiosyncratic design can be seen
as a reprise of early restaurateurs' attentiveness to the
individual patron. The case of Chez Panisse, with its
architecture and graphics of the Arts and Crafts movement,
is a prime example. In the first years of the millennium,
a like-minded restaurant opened in New York under the
unabashedly straightforward name Craft (2001), designed
by the Long Island–based firm Bentel & Bentel. While the
design evokes comparisons with the California Mission

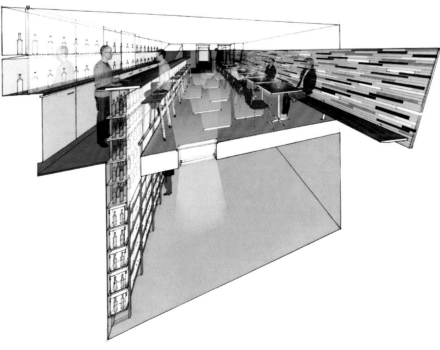

Opposite: LTL Architects/Lewis Tsuramaki Lewis, Fluff Bakery,
New York, 2004

LTL Architects/Lewis Tsuramaki Lewis, Tides, New York, 2005

style, and chef Tom Colicchio comparisons with Alice Waters, something new was gained in the East Coast translation. At the restaurant, Colicchio encourages diners to "craft" their own meals from shared plates of seasonal fresh ingredients, and Bentel & Bentel took a similarly liberated approach in drawing from the well of design history. Here, curved walnut walls clad in leather panels reinterpret the American Shingle Style architecture of the late nineteenth century. A luminous steel-and-bronze wine vault threaded with 512 fiber-optic cables contrasts with rustic exposed terra cotta columns and plainspoken cherry tables. Phalanxes of bare, amber-hued Tesla bulbs hanging by plain cords from the ceiling usurp the role that might have been filled by Tiffany chandeliers in a more traditional Arts and Crafts settings. In each of these elements the architects have wrought a deft synthesis of the artisanal and the tectonic, one that allows them to illustrate the character of the restaurant without sacrificing their own narrative.

One of the ways that George Yabu and Glenn Pushelberg of Yabu Pushelberg, a Toronto- and New York–based partnership, distinguish their interior-design practice (and commissions for such major corporate clients as Starwood Hotels and Resorts) is through collaborations with artisans who straddle the worlds of art and craft. By inserting one-of-a-kind pieces within an essentially modernist framework, the designers create highly recognizable environments that retain their independence and ensure a welcome open-endedness. In this regard, perhaps their most successful hospitality commission is the seafood restaurant Bluefin (2001) in the W Hotel in New York's Times Square (other Yabu Pushelberg projects, like the New York restaurant Dos Caminos, have hewed more tightly to theme). They make an event of the two-story configuration with a floating sculpture by the Japanese artist Hirotoshi Sawada; the graphic silhouette of the black polycarbonate mobile suggests a migrating school of fish or a spiraling flock of seagulls. The sculpture begins its journey against the restaurant's signature wavy plaster wall on the first floor and rises along the stairs to the upper level, where backlit glass walls divide private dining rooms. Classically modern chairs and tables are offset by wood-slat screens that introduce discrete levels of pattern. Their handcrafted quality is echoed in another custom element, an oval light fixture designed by Yabu Pushelberg's Marcia MacDonald, made of hemp twined

around a metal frame. More overtly modern and open dining ambience can be had on the first floor, where low, beige banquettes are arrayed along a glass wall incised with a vertical pattern of reveals that hide fluorescent lights.

Sometimes even the most normal setting gets a reprieve from its ordinariness with a singular iconoclastic voice. Such was the case when Brazilian architect Arthur Casas used a series of sculptural bronze tables made by São Paulo artisans who once worked with Diego Giacometti as the leitmotif for the World Bar (2003) in the Trump World Tower in Manhattan. The soft lines of the upholstered banquettes and chairs and the rich tones of the oak walls and ceiling are curiously complemented by the coagulated bronze stems and legs of the Giacometti-influenced tables. Here, a sculptural sensibility based on the aesthetics of the crude provides an erotic current to the understated luxury of the

room. Casas manages a similar cultural sleight of hand with his interior for the São Paulo–based restaurant Kosushi (2001), where he tempers and textures a Japanese-modern aesthetic with traditional Brazilian materials and orange acrylic Eames chairs. Of course, such stylistic syncretism has its place in the Brazilian city, where South American, European, and Asian cultures meet.

The Narrative Restaurant

Inherent in the evolution of the modern restaurant is the notion of a respite, of being transported to another place— if only for the briefest of lunch breaks. In the contemporary restaurant, the line between the suggestive and the explicit nature of that escape can be fine indeed. The line was irrevocably crossed with the advent of the "experience" restaurant, which asks its patrons to suspend their disbelief and to participate in its theater. What in the 1950s would

have been identified as ethnic or novelty restaurants have evolved into highly refined and engineered environments epitomized by such chains as the Hard Rock Café, which opened in London in 1971 and expanded globally in 1982. In America, the impact of Walt Disney World in Orlando, Florida, after its opening in 1971 and through its subsequent expansions has been enormous. It heralded the transition from singular themed interiors to more thoroughly integrated environments with features such as the simulated urban boulevard called Downtown Disney. As historian Karal Ann Marling has observed, "Disney's distinctive approach to re-presenting the past, the present, and the future in concrete form has helped to transform our responses to architecture and the city."[9] Today, the Disney influence is apparent in a host of themed stores, hotels, sports facilities, residential communities, and, of course, restaurants–environments already engaged in the magician's art of misdirection. It is an evolution that in many ways parallels the transformation of the old-fashioned amusement park, with its separate, unrelated attractions, into the theme park, which ties its attractions together in time and space.

Compounding the rise of entertainment as an increasingly critical dimension of the business of culture were the effects of stylistic postmodernism in the 1980s and its reprise of historical idioms. However facile it now appears, the architecture of overblown columns and capitals legitimized the use of a wider, richer range of design references–both vernacular and classical–leading to the sampling and appropriation that are hallmarks of contemporary

culture. Already permissive by nature, environments like restaurants and clubs became even more eclectic and promiscuous in their design. Today, stylistic post-modernism—which exaggerated or copied historical styles of the past—has given way to a concept of postmodernism that is more synthetic in nature, integrating elements from the past by juxtaposing and collaging design languages. The postmodern examples that follow thus mark a departure from more tightly themed restaurants with a singular, forced frame of reference.

One of the figures who harnessed the chaos and confusion of the late 1980s into an aesthetic of layers is Nigel Coates, head of the Architecture and Interiors Department of the Royal College of Art and founder of the London firm Branson Coates. Coates's hybridized narratives hold a mirror to the increasingly familiar sensation of multiple realities operating within many cultures. Of his many restaurants, perhaps the most instructive is an early project he designed in Istanbul called Taxim Nightpark (1991). Set within the shell of an old dye works, the restaurant/discotheque surrounds its patrons with decorative motifs derived from Turkish tradition while referencing a jet-set disco. In its

time-warp décor, Taxim Nightpark presciently looked to the current condition of globalization. New windows, set into the largely unadulterated structure, were sandblasted with an oversize textile pattern that establishes the club's Turkish locale without aping the local taverna. Conceived as an elegant, if slightly decadent, bazaar, the restaurant is sheltered under canopies of red and orange canvas. It boasts the largest leather couch and the longest beaded curtain in the world, the latter strung by hand by Turkish craftswomen in a pattern of huge eyes. Downstairs, the disco takes the form of an airport runway, complete with footlights and tarmac markings; luggage containers from Turkish Airlines double as video booths and a scissor lift supports the club's lighting console.

This is the realm of "the psycho-geographical"—design in the service of an adult game of make-believe, played with a wink and a nod. Two names that have become almost synonymous with refining the art of the theme are New York-based designers David Rockwell and Adam Tihany. While their port-folios are so extensive and varied that their work inevitably chafes at such categorization, there is little question that the-ater is the strong suit of both architects. Rockwell, as is often

Contrary to what one would expect in a typical Mexican restaurant, these interiors are more formal, less folkloric; there are no sombreros or pattered blankets. Instead, folk art, fine art, and architecture meet each other on equal terms. (Rockwell lived in Mexico for seven years as a child, and cites this experience as highly influential to his work.) In Rosa Mexicano Lincoln Center (2000), booths, curtains, and carpet are vividly striped, and mosaics proliferate. They appear in a context of strong color and rectilinear planes influenced by the work of Mexican modernist Luis Barragán. Both of the restaurants rely on a strong sculptural focal point: a vertical fountain. For the Washington, DC, location, artist David Hughes was commissioned to mount 400 small butterfly figurines on a wall of cascading water to represent the yearly migration of monarch butterflies to Mexico; in New York, Guido and Francesca Zwicker pinned 200 diving plaster figures to a perpetually wet blue tiled wall, a reference to the cliff divers of Acapulco.

Though Adam Tihany's practice is based in New York, this designer is a decidedly European sybarite. Born in Romania and raised in Israel, he is, like so many New Yorkers, a transplant. The designer of the restaurants Remi (New York), Pignoli (Boston), and La Coupole (Paris) is enamored of luxury, fascinated by the immediacy of color, and drawn to the power of bold graphic form. To the faint of heart, his work can seem excessive and, at times, almost vulgar in a way that unabashedly celebrates the trappings of wealth.[11] Nowhere is his Midas touch more visible than at Le Cirque 2000 (1997, closed 2006) located in New York's landmark Villard House, which was designed by McKim, Mead & White in 1882 and now the New York Palace Hotel. Le Cirque's design succeeded not because Tihany's touch was light—diners are saturated in spectacle—but because it was lighthearted. Here, the circus meets Beaux-Arts opulence in a send-up of fin-de-siècle pretensions. But Tihany never forgets that he is designing the equivalent of a masquerade ball—particularly here, where the landmarked walls, floors, and ceilings could not be altered, and his options were confined to décor. One of these options, as critic Paul Goldberger observed, would have been simply to "clean up the elaborate American Renaissance interiors, fill them with flowers and period furniture and the job presumably would be done. And then everyone, after muttering appropriate words of praise, would fall asleep."[12] Instead, Tihany decided

reported, came from a family of performers, and his personal experience left him with a belief in the power of the ephemeral. "The things that have the most lasting effect," Rockwell once said, "are also the most fleeting."[10] This Proustian perspective is translated into décor that is equal parts travel journal and culinary portrait. Of all the Rockwell restaurants in New York—among them Vong, Ruby Foo, and Monkey Bar—perhaps none reflects the architect's signature style more than Nobu (1994) in Lower Manhattan. Rockwell's design for the Japanese restaurant was a radical departure from the austerity of shoji-screen modernism that had traditionally marked the genre. Tree sculptures made of birch, solid ash, and rusted steel offer an urbane yet rustic, fluently nuanced evocation of a Japanese landscape. Cherry blossoms fallen from invisible branches are stenciled on the wooden floor, and smooth black river rocks come out of their bed to surface a wall. So successful was the venture that it inspired an adjacent annex called Nobu Next Door (1998). Unfortunately, the smaller space offered less room for invention, and its design is more tightly themed, with tatami mats hanging on the wall and suspended fishing baskets serving as light fixtures. The other face of the Rockwell persona appears in his Rosa Mexicano restaurants in Manhattan and Washington, DC.

to mount a Renaissance fair for sophisticated Manhattanites. He unfurled banners, put clown buttons on the back of chairs, inserted stained-glass circus balls in an etched-glass screen, put a clock on a high wire, and built striped towers and giant torchères, to set the stage for a decadent feast.

An entirely different flight of fancy, this time in Israel, takes form in Ayala Serfaty's Red Sea Star (1999), an underwater restaurant on the Bay of Eilat. Though it is as tightly conceived as any Disney production and staged in three steel underwater tanks, the Red Sea Star suffers from none of the claustrophobia or predictability of calculated theming. Sculpted blue plaster walls frame four-inch-thick acrylic windows, transforming them into wavy psychedelic portals that frame the aquatic flora and fauna beyond, while barstools, lamps, and screens take in the forms of sea creatures bringing the underwater world inside. Serfaty's signature curvaceous fabric lanterns wrap columns; silk lanterns in the shape of starfish and sea anemones hover beneath the ceiling; and barstools with jellyfish-like legs seem to float above the glossy resin-coated sand floor. Iron railings, laser cut in the lacy patterns of sea anemones, form decorative silhouettes against the warm, reflective surfaces of the fantastic shell, where gravity itself seems to be an abstract idea.

Narratives of Spectacle and Critique

The ambition to design spaces that defy the laws of physics has a long architectural pedigree, from the soaring vaults of Gothic cathedrals to the skewed planes of early-twentieth-century Constructivism. Today, we are witnessing another period in which architects are drawn to the attractions of disequilibrium with formal strategies that mirror the most frenetic aspects of contemporary life. Consider, for example, Zaha Hadid's Vitra Fire Station in Weil am Rhein, Germany (1994). With its tilted walls and dizzying perspectives, it may be one of the most acutely disorienting spaces ever built as a functional entity. (It has since been converted to a conference center.)

In the years before she won the Pritzker Prize in 2004 and realized the award-winning Rosenthal Center for Contemporary Art in 2003 (see Cultural, p. 314), Hadid, one of the principle exponents of the short-lived deconstructivist movement, was known largely for her "paper" architecture:

unbuilt projects that lived in the form of beautifully complex computer renderings. In the late 1980s, a commission for a restaurant and cocktail lounge in Sapporo, Japan, presented her with one of her earliest opportunities to explore the effects of compression and movement within real space. That Monsoon (1990) was an interior commission, and not a stand-alone building, suited those purposes ideally.

Monsoon's interior is an abstracted narrative of frozen compression and volcanic explosion, minus the literal images of lava and ice that might accompany a more explicit interpretation. The ground floor is articulated in the cool grays of glass and metal. Angular tables, like slivers of ice, are scattered across a raised floor that the architect likens to an ice floe. But the real action—the baroque, after all, is about action and movement—occurs overhead. Here, a tightly wound elliptical spiral form emerges above the bar and rips through the ceiling into the upper dome, where it breaks into a firestorm of red, orange, and yellow fragments. Nesting among the shards are sleek sofas with movable trays and plug-in sofa backs that permit an infinite number of seating configurations. Monsoon may appear edgy but its flexible furnishings make for convivial dining and lounging.

Though it is equally embedded in the language of the architectural vanguard, Diller + Scofidio's Brasserie (2000), situated in the base of Mies van der Rohe's Seagram Building on Park Avenue in New York, comes even closer to the spirit of the earliest public dining rooms. Both were designed for the flâneur. Indeed, as early as 1769, these lines of admonishment to an early restaurateur appear in the play *Harlequin Restaurateur*: "Oh you wanted to econo- mize! If that's the case, you shouldn't be in the restaurant business. The ladies, the dandy young men, the handsome lawyers, and the prissy abbés, what will they do here if there aren't any mirrors?"[13]

More than two centuries later, Elizabeth Diller and Ricardo Scofidio have given us video monitors instead of mirrors. At the front door of Brasserie, a camera aimed at the street records images that are continuously displayed on a screen in the foyer—surveillance reframed as entertainment for guests waiting to be seated. Everyone enters via a long glass staircase that brings them right to the center of the main dining area, providing a suitably dramatic analogue to the virtual entry. Here, along a warm, pearwood wall, a row of arcing booths clad in tufted green leather frames its occupants while carving out discrete spaces for tête-à-tête dining. In the smaller rear room, a wall of light conceals the silhouettes of diners who become legible only when viewed at an angle. All of these conceits are subtle; they never encourage guests to break the taboo on staring. The sense of being watched is countered by the distinct pleasure of simply watching in an environment that glows. The more sinister aspects of surveillance—a well-known preoccupation of the architects—is tempered and leavened. In the context of the restaurant, Diller and Scofidio understand that, as Harlequin was reminded, spying has always been a socially acceptable game.

Las Vegas, the theme capital of America, might seem the most unlikely place to find the work of Thom Mayne and his office, Morphosis—a firm known for its intellectual rigor and sophisticated programs. Yet the city's tricks of illusion and its fascination with simulacra find fellowship with Morphosis's own preoccupations with spatial disorientation. Mayne has designed two restaurants in the desert play- ground: Tsunami Asian Grill (1999), where the performance is sheer bravura, and Lutèce (1999), which is a feat of disciplined chaos. With Tsunami, Mayne took the restaurant to the level of extreme sport with a bilevel space of folded planes pierced at skewed angles by massive beams. Tsunami's restless geometry is further—and literally—ani- mated by film projections: floating across and between the fractured ceilings and walls is graphic designer Rebecca Mendez's film of a Japanese woman who dissolves and disappears underwater in waves of imagery. The momentum set up by the film is compounded by black concrete floors whose high polish suggests the lure of the deep. Indeed, the reflections of chair legs on the floor's sleek red surface seem to reach down like tentacles into the sea.

In contrast to the suggestion of shifting plate tectonics at Tsunami, Mayne's second Las Vegas project—Lutèce at the Venetian Hotel—is an oasis of quiet, an off-center foil to the rigidly controlled spaces of the adjoining casino. At Lutèce, a swath of bronze bands forms a conical ellipse that cuts through the restaurant's white walls and ultimately coils into a massive chandelier over the main dining room. Reversing the dynamic of the Herculean myth, Mayne rests

this restaurant's world not on the shoulders of one god but on 19,000 human figures cast in PVC and imbedded by hand in a translucent resin base. The miniature men in this sculptural insertion hint at the invisible labors of workers behind the scenes, whose toils are not fabled but certainly real.

If Mayne's critique of the workplace was necessarily subtle to the point of self-effacement, Damien Hirst's social observations, in his design for the London restaurant-cum-art-installation Pharmacy (1998), was so overt that it quickly spilled over into spectacle. With its pill-shaped barstools, periodic-table plates, stainless-steel medicine cabinets, and surgical gowns and lab coats (worn by the wait staff), Pharmacy was both a comment on the rise of the psycho-pharmaceutical industry in the 1990s and an unblushing celebration of Hirst's own self-advertised addictive personality. Few mainstream restaurateurs would select a motif so closely associated with pain or illness; however, Pharmacy's trendy clientele understood that Hirst was punning on the idea (and fact) of recreational and mood-altering drugs like Prozac and Zoloft. (One story has it that genuinely ill people would wander unaware into the restaurant only to have Hirst tell them that drugs were not sold there.) Like the earliest Parisian restaurants that catered to a fashion for frailty, Pharmacy was designed to assuage the illness *du jour*: depression and all its variants. Ironically, the only "medicine" actually consumed at Pharmacy was French cuisine; the restaurant counted on its medicinal décor and celebrity clientele to lighten the mood. The unmitigated cheek of Pharmacy notwithstanding, Hirst's experiment can also be seen in the light of the resurgence of installation art in the 1990s (Pharmacy was inspired by Hirst's 1992 installation of the same name, now in the collection of the Tate Modern in London) and of the perennial utopianism of the gesamtkunstwerk, the total work of art that wants to live in the world and not merely in the museum. Ironically, however, when the restaurant closed in 2003 its museum-object status was sealed: the restaurant's famed fixtures sold at auction in 2004 for £11.1 million (approximately $20 million).

The Sensualists

In truth, the Hirst venture was less about the behavior of its clientele than that of its creator. Patrons of Pharmacy inhabited Damien Hirst's world. By contrast, when Condé Nast decided that it needed a communal cafeteria for its employees and their guests, the company realized that the concept of a statically themed interior would contradict the rapid business cycles and ever-changing sensitivities of the fashion world. In addition to a more open-ended design language, the publishing giant needed a more open-ended program, one that would offer elegant private and semi-private spaces and also display industry power brokers (and pawns) to their best advantage. (In fact, the cafeteria is open to all Condé Nast employees.)

The choice of Frank Gehry for the Condé Nast cafeteria (2000) not only assured the requisite design imprimatur, but also brought genuine excitement to the normally forgettable environment of the company refectory. In the 10,800-square-foot (930-square-meter) space, Gehry realized his signature tectonic folds in overlapping panels of glass. So fluid as to seem hand-blow, the undulating glass walls appear to shape-shift around the private dining areas they enfold. The voluptuous lines of the walls recur in the semi-opaque sandblasted glass panels that create the partitions between a cellular system of bays furnished with Naugahyde banquettes—virtually the only material remnant of the traditional cafe. Gehry's trademark titanium, here tinted blue, lines the peripheral walls and the ceiling, suspended from which is a series of curved soffits whose contrasting outlines echo the choreography of the tables below.

Paris-based architects Domenica Jakob and Brendan MacFarlane were awarded the competition commission to design the restaurant Georges (2000) on the sixth floor of the Centre Pompidou. Like Gehry, they were faced with a featureless blank box as their tabula rasa, and they chose to populate it with discrete biomorphic spaces spawned from the computer. Unlike Gehry, however, their objective was less a flirty transparency than a system of caves. Patrons prone to claustrophobia have the alternative of dining al fresco and enjoying the Pompidou's renowned views of the city. The play on indoors and outdoors throughout the restaurant has a particular charm in a city known for its sidewalk cafés; it also honors the context of Renzo Piano and Richard Rogers's famously inside-out museum that wears its mechanical systems on its facade in a labyrinth of exposed duct work. But it is the architectural conflation of Georges' booths and the private rooms of the earliest restaurants, which maintained boudoir-like spaces for romantic assignations, that is the most resonant feature. In lieu of the draped alcoves and upholstered love seats favored in the eighteenth century, Jakob and MacFarlane offer diners discretion in the form of aluminum-covered pods lined in colorful natural rubber, each a different saturated hue. There is nothing retiring or coy about the vivid halos of red, orange, gray, and pale green that emanate from the pods wavy portals and reflect off the aluminum floor. Nor are the mound-like structures simply conceits of architectural fashion, though they do invoke inevitable comparisons to Gehry, whom Jakob and MacFarlane admire. Each pod works as a self-sufficient machine, equipped with its own air, water, electricity, and communication networks. They are the rigorous, albeit anti-rational, products of the architects' preoccupation with the possibilities of digital rendering and their parallel work in product design. In fact, all the furnishings were designed by the pair—from the minimalist glass tables to the foam chairs.

While it is increasingly common for architects like Jakob and MacFarlane to reach into the toolbox of industrial design, it is still a relative oddity for an industrial designer to move into the realm of interiors, despite the fact that such pioneers as Donald Deskey, Henry Dreyfuss, Charles and Ray Eames, and Russel Wright designed environments as well as products. By the end of the twentieth century, a higher degree of specialization—the inevitable consequence of professionalization—meant that most industrial designers had to limit their practice to the realm of such artifacts as cars, appliances, electronic devices, and furniture. Thus it was considered something of a coup when Karim Rashid was asked to design the namesake restaurant of Masaharu Morimoto (2001), the former executive chef of Nobu and the

popular star of the television show *Iron Chef*, in Philadelphia, Pennsylvania. Rashid saw the project as a continuation of his already renowned New York-based practice, which was founded on transforming everyday housewares into objects of desire. For Rashid, this commission was different merely in scale and the number of details—including his own black fiberglass sculpture at the door, white leather banquettes, yellow glass side chairs, and "flame" lights on every table.

Never one to shy away from the explicit, Rashid's original proposal for the entrance included a wall-sized lenticular image of a naked woman rolling over in bed, but that was ruled out as too racy. Instead, guests are greeted by a large wall-mounted video screen showing a woman blowing kisses. Thereafter, the entire space vibrates a sublimated sexuality—from the wavy bamboo ceiling, which crests at a height of 20 feet (6 meters), to the slow pulse of the frosted-glass partitions, whose color slowly shifts from lilac to cyan to magenta to green. Finally, glowing deep at the farthest end of the room is the glass sushi bar over which Morimoto himself presides. By using color and light to draw patrons deeper inside, Rashid makes a virtue of the narrow space and, in the process, supplies a soft pulsing counterpoint to the tight rectilinear sequenced rows of tables.

In contrast to the mutating color palette of Morimoto, Restaurant Les Cols (2003) is emphatically monochrome, though such a description is far too flat to accurately describe the solidly gold-hued interior created by RCR Architects in their home city of Olot, Spain. Designed as a narrow steel and glass insertion adjacent to a traditional stone farmhouse, the restaurant features a long, attenuated dining room with gold-toned floors, ceilings, table, and chairs, as well as window treatments comprised of vertically suspended strips of gold cloth. Tellingly, however, the designers' Midas touch does not extend to service areas, which are kept pristine with stainless steel fixtures and glass dividers veiled from the outdoors by artfully trellised plants.

New York-based architect David Ling also deploys the drama of a singular color scheme to give added dimension to a restaurant with a similarly narrow footprint. At the Manhattan sushi bar ED (2002), however, the designer had the additional challenge of working with a windowless space that was totally underground. Ling compensated for these

AFSO Andre Fu, Zenzibar, Shanghai, 2004

Starck Network, Restaurant Theatron, Mexico City, 1985

as the "poor man's silver," and the chandelier was wrapped in stainless-steel gauze, to play down its dominance. Pride of place was accorded to a 32-inch-tall (81-centimeter-tall) minimalist orange clock, which was centered on the ornately carved mantelpiece; the period portraits that had flanked it were replaced with two ethereal contemporary paintings by artist Thomas Duval.

Shortly after completing his work at the Plaza Athénée restaurant, Jouin was asked to rescue another venerable room in the hotel, the Bar du Plaza (2001), which, despite having been damaged in a fire, was similarly restricted by its historic-landmark status; the carved-wood walls had to be restored to their original condition. Once again, Jouin had to make a new room without touching the bones of the old. Furthermore, he had to enliven it for a younger, more mixed clientele. To meet his mandate, Jouin opened his work up to collaboration with artisans and designers, a decision that introduced welcome moments of surprise. The bar itself is the contribution of master craftsman Patrick Desserme: a block of frosted glass that resembles carved ice and glows when touched. (Fittingly, its cambered form harks back to the cabinetry of Louis XIV's reign.) Classic Louis XV chairs with attenuated legs serve as barstools; above them hang Murano-glass chandeliers that have been scaled down to half their normal size. The most sought-after seats in the Bar du Plaza are to be found in niches constructed as giant frames for French photographer Philippe David's photo-

graphic reinterpretations of seventeenth-century paintings by Claude Lorrain. In the lounge, updated club chairs sit under a gargantuan fiberglass lamp that drenches the room in cool colors in the early evening, progressing to hotter hues during the night. Opting to reinvigorate the Parisian landmark rather than recreate it with reproductions, Jouin makes liberal appropriations that not only serve history well, but also guarantee it a future.

Across the English Channel just a year later, another architectural legacy—a dignified 1779 London townhouse on Conduit Street by Georgian architect James Wyatt—also received new life, with an infusion of hyperbolic decorative interventions. Sketch (2002) is the brainchild of the French-Algerian restaurateur Mourad Mazouz. This layercake complex of two restaurants, two bars, and a patisserie was realized by Mazouz and a roster of high-profile designers, including Gabhan O'Keefe, Marc Newson, Ron Arad, Jurgen Bey, and a young Frenchman named Noé Duchaufour-Lawrance, who is a veteran of Mazouz's previous ventures and was his chief contributor on this project. Mazouz and Duchaufour-Lawrance retained the house's eighteenth-century mosaic floors, delicate moldings, and domed skylight, as well as the original room designations—Parlour, Lecture Room, Library, Gallery—as foil and focus for the interventions they invited. Then their collaborations proceeded to fill the four-story townhouse with stylistic samplings that ricochet through the history of design.

Designed to offer its patrons a menu of options—including afternoon tea, evening dinner, late-night drinks—under one roof, Sketch neatly encapsulates the restaurant's history as both sedative and stimulant. In the tea room Jurgen Bey corseted Victorian lampshades in acrylic and covered tables and walls with gentile silhouettes of eighteenth-century figures juxtaposed to create a Rorschach pattern in gray and white; stairs covered in "melted chocolate" resin (courtesy of Droog Design) lead up to two restaurants, the Gallery and the Lecture Room, designed by Gabhan O'Keefe. In the Gallery, a projection screen runs around the upper section of the walls to allow the space to serve as a video-viewing space by day and a dining room by night. Here, the large white leatherette-padded room, with its Regency chairs, custom banquettes, and Marc Newson food-service chariots, bring to mind scenes from *2001: A Space Odyssey*, the classic late 1960s Stanley Kubrick film. By contrast, O'Keefe conceived the Lecture Room—a melange of art déco, art nouveau, and neoclassical quotations, with velvet armchairs and buttoned-leather walls setting the tone—as "a large drawing room and dining room in a private house."[15] In this particular "private house," however, the bathrooms are either bejeweled in Swarovski crystals or housed in opalescent fiberglass eggs—Duchaufour-Lawrance's surreal homage to the 1960s. These delirious, show-stopping moments of disorientation banish any reference to time, to say nothing of historical chronology.

Of course, the site of historical restorations serve as the most important reference for any design, and more often than not the more industrial the original use the freer the brief. In Lisbon, Portuguese design and nightlife impresario Manuel Reis and American actor John Malkovich hired architects Fernando Sanchez Salvador and Margarida Grácio Nunes to renovate a series of old warehouses along the city's Targus river with a view to expressing the spirit of the newly hip and prosperous city. Bica do Sapato (1999), the partners' spacious riverfront restaurant, bears few traces of its rough docklands past, though it takes advantage of the buildings' loft-like interior to showcase several different types of dining experiences, including a sushi bar and cafeteria in addition to the main restaurant area. None of these areas speak a particularly indigenous design language; rather, the architects have chosen a mix of mid-century modern furnishings and lighting fixtures with vibrant wall treatments—in some areas painted in bright monochromes, in others covered with contemporary murals.

The Bacchanalia

In contrast to the restaurant, where dining is the essential part of a larger social matrix, the nightclub drops the pretense of nourishment altogether in favor of hedonism. One element of the classical restaurant does survive in the club, however: the idea of the public living room. In fact, the Anteeksi Allstars—a specially convened design group made up of the Finnish firm M41LH2 and a host of collaborators[16]—

popular star of the television show *Iron Chef*, in Philadelphia, Pennsylvania. Rashid saw the project as a continuation of his already renowned New York-based practice, which was founded on transforming everyday housewares into objects of desire. For Rashid, this commission was different merely in scale and the number of details–including his own black fiberglass sculpture at the door, white leather banquettes, yellow glass side chairs, and "flame" lights on every table.

Never one to shy away from the explicit, Rashid's original proposal for the entrance included a wall-sized lenticular image of a naked woman rolling over in bed, but that was ruled out as too racy. Instead, guests are greeted by a large wall-mounted video screen showing a woman blowing kisses. Thereafter, the entire space vibrates a sublimated sexuality–from the wavy bamboo ceiling, which crests at a height of 20 feet (6 meters), to the slow pulse of the frosted-glass partitions, whose color slowly shifts from lilac to cyan to magenta to green. Finally, glowing deep at the farthest end of the room is the glass sushi bar over which Morimoto himself presides. By using color and light to draw patrons deeper inside, Rashid makes a virtue of the narrow space and, in the process, supplies a soft pulsing counterpoint to the tight rectilinear sequenced rows of tables.

In contrast to the mutating color palette of Morimoto, Restaurant Les Cols (2003) is emphatically monochrome, though such a description is far too flat to accurately describe the solidly gold-hued interior created by RCR Architects in their home city of Olot, Spain. Designed as a narrow steel and glass insertion adjacent to a traditional stone farmhouse, the restaurant features a long, attenuated dining room with gold-toned floors, ceilings, table, and chairs, as well as window treatments comprised of vertically suspended strips of gold cloth. Tellingly, however, the designers' Midas touch does not extend to service areas, which are kept pristine with stainless steel fixtures and glass dividers veiled from the outdoors by artfully trellised plants.

New York-based architect David Ling also deploys the drama of a singular color scheme to give added dimension to a restaurant with a similarly narrow footprint. At the Manhattan sushi bar ED (2002), however, the designer had the additional challenge of working with a windowless space that was totally underground. Ling compensated for these

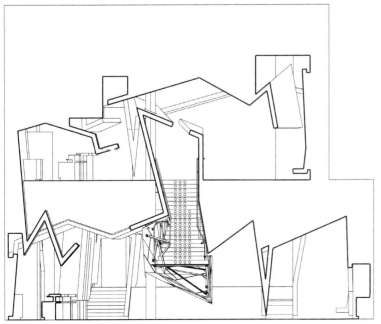

potential shortcomings by creating an environment so simple and complete that it effectively dispels any sense of lack. Serene and super-heated at the same time, the dining room is tented in translucent white fabric and illuminated with violet-hued light. Together they make the space feel both coherent and open at the same time. The furnishings– translucent acrylic chairs, black tables, and black latex banquettes– were kept neutral to sustain the serenity of the ambience. A waterfall glides down a mirrored wall behind the sushi bar providing a soothing but dramatic focal point and the illusion of additional space.

Lebanese architect Bernard Khoury designed the Beirut music club B018 (1998) below ground in response to a variety of conditions that were very different from that of urban congestion. Located in the Quarantaine section of Beirut that once housed an infamous refugee camp decimated in a 1976

militia attack, the club could not be highly visible for fear that it would become an unintentional monument, or worse, a crass intrusion onto a tragic site. Khoury responded to these difficult sociopolitical concerns by respectfully sinking the space beneath a circular concrete disc that is raised only slightly off the ground. Located within the disc is a black metal structure that hydraulically opens at night to expose the social space to open air.

Whereas Ling achieves intimacy with singular focus and Khoury with a sadly necessary bunker mentality, Andre Fu of the Hong Kong firm AFSO relies on the double entendre. The design parlance of Zenzibar (2004), a lounge/restaurant in the newly fashionable Xintiandi district of Shanghai, is recognizably both Chinese and European, updating this city's cosmopolitan history for a new generation. (From the mid-nineteenth century through the 1930s, Shanghai

was host to British, American, Belgian, Dutch, Japanese, Russian, and French trade and banking enclaves; it is now in the process of selectively reintegrating that history into its profile as an international tourist destination.) Fu designed Zenzibar to reflect the optimism of a city with a glamorous past on the rise; to wit, he describes the interior of the 12,540-square-foot (1,115-square-meter) restaurant as a venue where "Courrèges meets Vivian Tam, where Space Age mod meets China."[14] Entry is via the bar, where there is a dreamlike randomness to the mix of cultural cues. French velvet-imprinted and taffeta-upholstered chairs mingle with more subdued oak and leather seating. A curvaceous table of white Corian leads the eye to a fantastical bronze-mirrored column crowned with a luminous, egg-shaped capital; custom-designed hexagonal tiles form a floral motif across the wall above a low-lying mauve leather banquette.

Zenzibar's Sino-Gallic luxury takes on an aura of mystery in a dramatic corridor that peels off from the lounge/bar area. One of the walls is backlit with an amber glow behind a lattice-like wood frame; the other is made up of undulating, horizontal oak slats. At the end of the corridor, four private dining rooms inspired by Shanghai tea salons are variously decorated with ornate wallpaper in traditional patterns, over-scale Chinese latticework, and walls of jade slate. For all its invention, however, Zenzibar's mutant exoticism is hardly foreign. Although designed with equal measures of wit and decorum, it speaks the lingua franca of many contemporary restaurants, a patois of kitsch fantasy and mixed cultural memories.

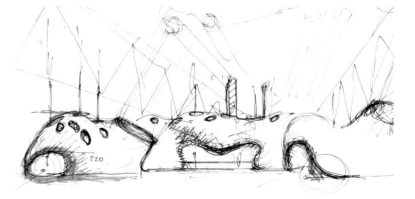

Rococo Redux

Given that the cultural memory of the restaurant is intertwined with culinary fashion, perhaps it is fitting that the
emergence of fusion cuisine–in which cultures blend and
recombine in the kitchen–coincided with the outburst of
eclecticism and appropriation in design where styles from
the past find new life in recombinant form. Where an earlier
generation of designers looked to the authority of classicism
in their historical borrowings, the turn-of-the-millennium
generation is drawn to the asymmetries of the baroque and
unembarrassed by the florid mannerisms of the rococo.
These designers playfully choreograph rooms that are
calculated to entertain the mind and the eye with their
hybrid vocabularies.

Much of the credit for opening this Pandora's box of stylistic
pleasures belongs to design impresario Philippe Starck,
whose restaurant Theatron (1985) in Mexico City was the
first in a long series of restaurant commissions that include
the Peninsula (1994) in Hong Kong and Bon (2000), his first
restaurant in Paris. Here are the first instances of what
would become hallmarks of Starck's language: Swiftian
games of scale, overtly feminine curtains, the presence of
portraits, and furnishings with the curving lines favored by
the *ancien régime*.

It is no small irony that a former Starck protégé would
undertake the resuscitation of one of Paris's most famous
grandes dames, the restaurant at the Plaza Athénée hotel
(2000). The hotel opened its doors on the fashionable
avenue Montaigne in 1913, and was famed for a celebrity
clientele that included such notables as Josephine Baker,
Grace Kelly, and Jacqueline Onassis. This was the first
interior commission for the French industrial designer
Patrick Jouin–and the first of several collaborations with
renowned chef Alain Ducasse–and it came with enormous
constraints. Since the 1911 interior was listed as an historic
landmark, the original gilt-and-ivory walls could not be
touched. As dowdy as the walls appeared in the light of the
new millennium, Jouin was savvy enough to respond to their
recherché charm and astute enough to bend their aristocratic
aesthetic to his own purposes. To make the room feel less
formidable, he used a limited palette of industrial materials,
exercising commendable prudence. Regency chairs were
upholstered in felt and coated in pewter, once thought of

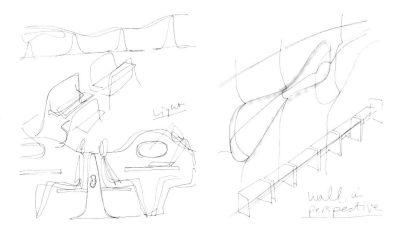

say they brought an urban renewal design approach to their refurbishment of the Helsinki Club (2003), a thirty-year-old nightclub and casino in the Finnish capital. Each part of the complex was conceived as a distinct neighborhood. Champions of city life, the designers even included their own version of a subway car, in a rest area they call "Tunnel and Train." But the heart of the club is a lounge and a dance hall, spaces that are treated less as rooms than as mammoth pieces of furniture carpeted in a hallucinatory pattern of arabesques. Lighting is the only clue to where walls give way to floors and seating rises up from the floor; color is the key to way-finding in the sprawling complex–hot orange on the dance floor, dark blues in the lounge.

The British industrial designer Michael Young, now based in Reykjavik, uses a sensualist vocabulary to give soft definition to the Astro Bar (2001) in Iceland's capital. Because of the protected status of the bar's ninety-year-old building, Young set off the interior within a resin-coated shell. The sleek, almost slippery, surface of the walls and floors is further blurred by a lighting scheme developed by

British light artist Jeremy Lord. Upstairs, in the private Red Room, Lord mimics the effects of sunlight on skin with thermally sensitive walls whose lights go from pink to red in response to increased body movement. Downstairs, Young continues to offer teasing suggestions of summer by bringing an outdoor motif inside with a picnic table and a "pool" filled with red Cappellini cushions set within a saturated field of green. Throughout the club's four bars and two dance floors, suites of Young's chairs and couches provide respites for conversation in the luminous haze.

At this uncertain, self-conscious moment in contemporary culture, there is a tendency to vacillate between the hot and cool currents of design–between biomorphic rococo and minimalist modernism. Both can deliver the eroticism required for nightlife, and designers tend to be drawn to one or the other. The exceptions tend to be in establishments like Sketch, where multiple design entities are at work. The juxtaposition of different design sensibilities is less usual in projects executed by a single firm, but clearly it was the strength of the young German firm 3deluxe when it conceived the design of the Frankfurt based Cocoon Club (2004). The designers found that alternating form languages offered a useful strategy for distinguishing dancing and dining activities. Diners at the Cocoon Club enjoy their meals amid a field of luminous silk strings (14,500 in all) that rain down between them in straight lines; some of the strings are sewn into curtains controlled by mechanized rollers that divide the space into protective enclaves (the cocoons of the bar's name) for guests enjoying the quieter part of the evening. Later, when the DJ warms up, films are projected onto the linear fields gathering their lines into illusions of three-dimensional waves. The vocabulary shifts entirely upon entering the dance floor, which is surrounded by a sponge-like perforated wall that contains oblong pods for lounging in a latter-day *rocaille*—the rocky outcropping that gave rococo its name. But the truly sybaritic feature of the Cocoon Club is the Silk Room, with its gauze curtains and bed-like sofas.

As its name implies, the J-Pop Café (2002) outside Tokyo does feature a restaurant, but the establishment's true raison d'être is entertainment. Tokyo-based architect Katsunori Suzuki designed J-Pop Odaiba primarily as a vehicle to showcase promotional Japanese pop videos, with Japanese cuisine serving as a mere subtext. Located in Odaiba within Sega's Joy Polis, a massive indoor amusement park that has become a popular escape from nearby downtown Tokyo, J-Pop is a streamlined version of a carnival funhouse. Suzuki and his associates at Fantastic Design evoked the brave new world of biotech, today's equivalent to the spaceship and the lunar cavern that are forever synonymous with the futuristic archetypes of the 1960s. The complex is divided into two main zones: the Bio Forest, which contains a DJ booth, a stage, and café tables equipped with DVD players and screens that swell out from the fabric of the wall, and the Bio Cave, where twenty-five white Verner Panton chairs line a curving Decola counter that runs the length of the space, with views over Tokyo Bay. The two regions of J-Pop's anatomy are linked by white curving walls that are surreally shaped like auricles or earlobes—an appropriate metaphor for this twenty-first-century jukebox. There are no posters, costumes, or souvenirs in sight in this music emporium; instead, Suzuki hews to a smooth abstraction that speaks to more current preoccupations with surface and skin.

Today, the bedroom-cum-dining room has evolved into a new genre unto itself, turning up in Amsterdam, Bangkok, and, perhaps not surprisingly, Rome, among other cities.[17] It remains to be seen whether the novelty will become a staple of dining as we slouch into the twenty-first century in a state of perplexed jet lag, but there is no small irony in the fact that the restaurant, an institution originally intended to keep its patrons healthy and on their feet, is now offering the comforts of bed. More plausibly, restaurants like Bangkok's Bed Supperclub (2002), designed by the Bangkok division of Orbit Design Studio, will become yet another narrow niche in the theater of dining, albeit one especially suited to the current obsession with security that pervades affluent societies around the world.

Just as eighteenth-century Parisian restaurants sought to calm their patrons' anxieties about proper social behavior and personal health in the midst of social and political change–the rise of public urban life and the incipient end of monarchy–these sybaritic dining environments can be seen as a design response to the upheavals and complexities of globalization. Whether their interiors are filled with comfortable bedding or updated banquettes and boudoirs, these restaurants offer soothing, secluded spaces to relax the nerves of the citizens of the new twenty-first century.

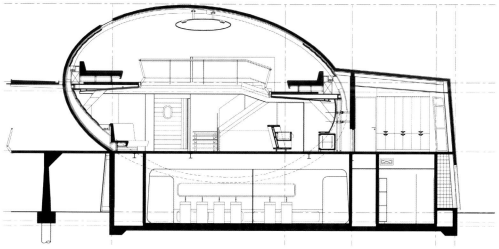

Hotels

Home. Apartment. Loft. Office. Cultural Center. Shop. Restaurant. Spa. Religious retreat. At one time or another, in one place or another, the hotel has played host to each. So well has it absorbed their signs and symbols, their programs and their amenities, that the hotel has become the *ur*-model of interiors, mimicked by hospitals and penthouses alike in their attempts to bring the aura of endless vacation to more quotidian spaces. With its brief injections of service and luxury into everyday life, the hotel meets the traveler's conflicted desires for anonymity and celebrity: it is the safe house where public and private meet.

In today's post-industrial society, the hotel holds a mirror to the increasingly mobile lives of its affluent citizens. Temporary homes to global hybrids who possess an unprecedented ability to imagine themselves in multiple settings in multiple guises (thanks to television and the World Wide Web), hotels must be distinct—even exotic—yet familiar in order to survive. In this highly competitive market, design has become critical to the contemporary hotel's hyper-annuated hospitality. Once a refuge from the dangers of strange terrain and the unmitigated darkness of night, the hotel now offers a different kind of protection to its guests; it has become largely a psychological escape from the less tangible pressures of contemporary life. Whether it appears in the guise of a chalet, museum, or nature preserve, the shape-shifting hotel of today owes its legacy to the roadside inn of antiquity.

Some of the earliest hostelries were way stations for Roman soldiers on extended tours of duty across the Roman empire. While they were hardly more than barracks, these *mansioni*, as they were called, hold within their name-the Latin root for "mansion"–the very notions of luxury and security at the heart of contemporary hotel culture. These early shelters, it's important to note, were not the sole prerogative of the military; they were shared with traveling merchants as well-business accommodations in their most protean form. The role of inns and hostels in commercial life had evolved even further by the thirteenth century. The legendary explorer and raconteur Marco Polo described bedding down, along with fellow travelers and traders on the Silk Road, in way stations built for the Mongolian postal service.[1] Religion played its role in the evolution of the hotel, as regular pilgrimages to Mecca and the Holy Lands contributed to the development of seasonal lodgings. Difficult topographies and weather conditions, like those in the Swiss Alps, also shaped the nature of the hotel, contributing to its romance as a reward at the end of a challenging journey. (Perhaps the most famous of the Alpine shelters is the hostel in the Great St. Bernard Pass linking Italy and Switzerland; it is still operated today by a community of Augustinian monks.[2]) By the seventeenth century, the hotel had taken on yet another role as an extension of the healthful retreat; well-heeled guests in search of various cures arrived at seaside resorts and mountain spas in litters and carriages to bask in the restorative atmosphere of these clinical accommodations and their natural surroundings.

Still, without such essential motivations—war, exploration, commerce, religion, or physical well-being—few people elected to endure the privations of travel, no matter how grand or sacred the destination, until the nineteenth century. However, with the advent of the Industrial Revolution and the rise of a new bourgeoisie, the concept of leisure-time travel became viable as an activity in and of itself; hotels literally rose to the occasion, following the new paths charted by expanding rail routes. Indeed, some hotels were directly supported by the railroads–including, perhaps most famously, Yellowstone National Park's Old Faithful Inn, which was financed by the Northern Pacific Railroad.[3] By the end of the nineteenth century, the status and purview of the hotel had expanded exponentially. Once little more than roadside watering holes for the hardiest travelers, hotels had now evolved into sprawling gateways to natural wonders and status symbols for growing cities. Valets, hairdressers, manicurists, shops, galleries, restaurants, room service, tour guides, scheduled leisure activities–all these things had become commonplace in hotels. It was not enough to attend to the needs of guests, it was also becoming increasingly important to entertain them—within, of course, the limits of social propriety. It was important, after all, to distinguish the hotel from its slatternly cousin, the common bordello.

By the early twentieth century, these new palaces became desirable not only as destinations for wealthy travelers, but also as surrogate homes for rich urbanites. (These early residential hotels, with their respectable tenants, also helped legitimize the apartment building, which had yet to

lose the stigma of tenement housing.) With their domestic
comforts and retinues of staff who filled the function of
maids and butlers, these establishments set the precedent
for the hotel as pied-à-terre or alternative residence for an
extremely prosperous demographic. Ironically, they also
anticipated less savory institutions such as the infamous
Single Residential Occupancy hotels used to warehouse
the indigent.

Naturally, the hotel would not have survived into the twenty-
first century had it served only one segment of society.
Another tribe of transients who, to paraphrase Tennessee
Williams, depend on the kindness of strangers, is that of the
business traveler. By the nineteenth century, the itinerant
traders who followed military encampments and pursued
opportunity at local bazaars had evolved into suited traveling
salesmen. Along with the captains of industry they served,
these salesmen required lodgings commensurate with their
reputations as merchants. In *New Hotels for Global Nomads*,
architectural historian Donald Albrecht notes that, "As
early as the 1830s the public rooms of hotels had become
not only places of social interaction and dining but also
modern day agoras where men conducted business."[4]
From these informal gatherings grew the ballrooms and
conference rooms that would become standard features in

many hotels by the 1920s. Much of the credit for this new iteration of the hotel belongs to Ellsworth Milton Statler, who founded the first chain of hotels designed to serve the needs of corporate commerce, and who understood that these hotels would increasingly depend on communication facilities. By the time Hilton had acquired Statler Hotels in 1954, air travel had begun to extend the reach and appeal of the chain hotel beyond national borders.[5] Furthermore, increased air travel would ultimately raise the demand for hotels—whether for business or pleasure—to the benefit of smaller establishments as well as international chains.

To offset the novelty and disorientation that accompanied the speed of an airplane flight, mid-century hotels offered a measure of predictability and familiarity. Among the few notable exceptions to the ubiquitous International Style hotel towers, which at the time carried a reassuring authority, were the Miami Beach high-rises of Morris Lapidus. The Fontainebleau and Eden Roc Hotels (1954 and 1955) were neither wholly fantastical, like the tightly themed environments of Las Vegas, nor were they, by any stretch of the imagination, remotely abstract. Lapidus's glamorous rococo-modern interiors were more like the stylized stage sets of early-1960s television shows, eclectically scripted and presciently tongue-in-cheek in their décor.

Today, with the playing field leveled by postmodern pluralism, the question is not whether the hotel should be a theater, but, rather, what kind of theater it should be. Hotels have discovered that today's business travelers welcome a new setting as they open their briefcases and laptops in yet another unfamiliar city or town. Once it was reassuring to know that a hotel in Bangkok would be a clone of another in Chicago or Paris, but the increasing banality of air travel today has all but eradicated the homesickness that bred look-alike lobbies and guest rooms. The same generation that domesticated the office (see Offices, pp. 122–167) is in the process of re-grooming the hotel, not only so it will reflect new tastes and a new sense of entitlement, but also so it will update the corporate images they represent.

In a globalized society, difference is now prized as a rare commodity; in a hyper-capitalist environment, consumers expect and demand choice. Hotels have responded accordingly, often offering guests wholly different accommodations within a single establishment, and certainly distinguishing commonly owned venues from one city to another. Among what could appear to be an infinite number of variations, a few broad categories emerge. Considered in this chapter are six basic archetypes: the hotel as refuge, the hotel as playground, the boutique hotel, the fashion hotel, the fictional hotel, the contemporary "grand" hotel, and—a relatively new phenomenon—the postmodern hotel with many authors.

The Refuge

Since the days of the earliest roadside inns, one of the basic functions of the hotel has been to provide shelter in remote or potentially inhospitable places. Despite the fact that advances in insulation, heating, and air-conditioning have turned once threatening environments into little more than scenery, it is still possible to detect a residue of a defensive posture in the contemporary hotel, particularly when located in landscapes of extreme contrasts.

Set within view of Mount Sharidake in the eastern part of Hokkaido, Japan's northernmost major island, Toyo Ito's Hotel P (1992) offers a stark contrast to the wheat fields in which its two volumes sit. The highly abstracted spaces that give the hotel its name—a long, rectangular block of rooms that pierces a large, elliptical lobby—are intentionally antithetical to their surroundings. On one side of the attenuated two-story guest-room volume is a common hallway sheathed in glass block; on the other side is a sequence of twenty-six simple white rooms faced in glass. Designed as neutral backdrops for the stunning views they face, the rooms' Western-style furnishings are purposefully minimal. Within the curved walls of the lobby, glass screens filter natural light and landscape vistas, offering the same alternation of clear and muted views that characterizes the experience of the guest quarters. What at first seems to be a defiant disregard for context is, in fact, a clear recognition of the contemporary condition of artifice, in which no aspect of nature is immune to human intervention. At Hotel P, design and landscape are locked in a state of wary mutual respect.

A more synthetic but no less rigorous modernist, Geoffrey Bawa (who died in 2003), brought a profound respect for the terrain and traditions of Sri Lanka to the design of the Kandalama Hotel (1994) in the Sri Lankan city of Dambulla.[6] Extraordinary in its siting and conscientious in its construction, the breathtaking Kandalama is also an exemplary case of environmentally sustainable design. (With its own sewage and disposal plant, rainwater collection system, and other energy-saving features, the Kandalama Hotel holds a bronze Leadership in Energy and Environmental Design award from the US Green Building Council.)

The 160-bed hotel, whose flat rooftops double as tropical gardens, wraps around two sides of a rocky cliff that overlooks a famous royal citadel in nearby Sigiriya. Entry to the hotel is through the mouth of a cave that cuts through the hillside to connect the entrance to the reception area. Here in the main lobby, rough outcroppings of the terrain reassert themselves again amid specially commissioned sculptures of giant elephants and owls. To reach their rooms, guests traverse open-sided corridors that offer vertiginous views of the landscape.[7] Throughout, austere anodized-aluminum window frames offer a contemporary counterpoint for rattan chairs, old writing desks, and long white curtains. However, both the formal geometry and informal furnishings retire in the face of the hotel's true focal point—the lush jungle landscape itself. The sinuous geometry of the complex ensures that, instead of looking aloofly outward, guests are literally embedded in the spectacular vista without impinging on the region's nearby archaeological sites.

Inside the boundaries of national parks, hotels are often run by private concerns that are granted concessions on government property but do not actually own the land they occupy. In South Africa's Kruger National Park, for example, laws specify that land must be returned to its natural state when leases expire. Apart from the ecological thinking behind this law, the practice of leasing is an implicit reminder that private property is a legal invention, not a condition of nature, and that our very existence is finite. It was with these real and implicit caveats in mind that Boyd Ferguson, principal of the Durban-based firm Cécile and Boyd, approached the design of the Singita Lebombo Lodge (2003). Reconciling the hotel's intrinsic emphemerality with the robustness of its setting, where wildlife all but mingles with guests, Ferguson mixed the language of modernism with a local patois. He framed the compound's fifteen guest cottages in steel and wrapped them in glass walls sheltered under canopies made of strips of saligna gum. The complex is a collage of the industrial and the natural, the imported and the indigenous. The lounge's African carved stools are painted white; mosquito curtains are fitted with oversize zippers and Velcro closures; and the Murano-glass floor "chandeliers" (Ferguson's invention) are inspired by a succulent plant native to the region. With a design that goes further than merely framing the view, Ferguson takes the risk of interpreting the culture of a place as well as its landscape.

In contrast to Singita Lebombo, which will close when its lease finally expires, a ski resort in Les Cerniers, Switzerland, called Whitepod (2004) literally folds up and disappears at the end of every season. Here, in the hands of the Swiss designer Sofia de Meyer, Buckminster Fuller's geodesic domes have found yet another virtuous application. They provide both structure and interior ornament for the guest rooms of Meyer's uniquely eco-sensitive resort. Even without plumbing and electricity, the tent-pods are a far cry from the extreme sport of winter camping. The womb-like sleeping quarters feature the latest insulation technology and are furnished with wood stoves and kerosene lamps as well as an eclectic assortment of armchairs, vanities, and bedding of organic materials. Removed from urban civilization but not entirely off the grid, guests take their meals in a restored nineteenth-century farmhouse that has a solar shower and, for a few hours each day, generator-powered electricity. Any whiff of self-righteous piety, however, is effectively countered by the space-age chic of the domes, which are kitted out with iPods and elliptical portals that bring the monumentality of the Alps into the rooms' intimate confines. Close observers will see firsthand the effects of climate change around them—even here in the Alps the snowline is receding. Allied with the "green skiing" movement, which, among other things, seeks to reduce dependence on artificial snow, this alternative ski resort also encourages environmentally sustainable activities like snowshoeing. Whitepod has already attracted an enthusiastic clientele willing to hike in and spend well for treading lightly on the land.

No less extreme a landscape than the mountains, the megacity presents its own unique environmental challenges. In Mexico City, intense street congestion, traffic noise, and less-than-picturesque vistas were the elements that Enrique Norten of TEN Architects/Taller Enrique Norten had to contend with when he received the commission to convert a dilapidated apartment building into a thirty-six-room hotel. Like all of the other projects discussed so far, Hotel Habita (2000) does not attempt to immerse guests in illusionary mirages or escapist fantasies. In all likelihood, visitors who enter the pristine perimeter of this hotel are less interested in taking leave of their senses then they are in restoring them. The hotel's compact bedrooms feature only a bed and a cantilevered plane of glass that serves as both desk and table. Even the views are carefully edited. To insulate the hotel from the hectic street life below, Norten encased the original building in a box of translucent green-blue sand-blasted glass. Interspersed across the sandblasted glazing are narrow clear panes that afford guests fragmented glimpses of the city. This feature, which creates a random pattern on the building's facade, functions as a veil of privacy that affords both hotel guests and passersby unobtrusive glimpses of each other, tacitly observing the strict urban protocols of eye contact.

The Playground

Discretion may be the better part of valor, but to those with more sybaritic tastes, the discipline of minimalism is contradictory to the uninhibited pursuit of pleasure. Few places on earth can compete with the excesses of Las Vegas, a city that promotes discretion of a different sort: The city's official tag line is "What happens here, stays here."⁹ Las Vegas is like nowhere else and everywhere else at the same time. The hotels themselves are twenty-four-hour urban floor shows, decked out in costumes ranging from the pseudo-classical garb of Caesar's Palace to the pirate-ship vernacular of Treasure Island at the Mirage to the ersatz urbanity of the New York, New York Hotel and Casino.

Among the most bizarre and complete in its fantasy is the Venetian Resort Hotel Casino (1999). In keeping with the scale and ambition of the project, the Venetian's roster of architects and designers reads like the production credits of a Hollywood blockbuster. Wimberly Allison Tong & Goo, in collaboration with the Stubbins Associates, produced the building's architecture; Dallas-based Wilson & Associates provided interior design services for the public areas and guest rooms; and Terry Dougall of Dougall Designs in Pasadena, California, designed the casino.

While the guest rooms are generously furnished and lavishly decorated, with sunken living rooms and weighty swags of drapery, they cannot compete with the complex's shopping "canals" and cafés. Nor are they meant to. Gondolas glide from Banana Republic to Mikimoto on indoor waterways covered by trompe l'oeil skies meant to recall the paintings

of Tiepolo. Despite the obvious artificiality of the hotel's conceits, the effect is truly uncanny, in large measure due to lighting that mimics the gradations of day to night. So skillfully condensed is this stage set–built with American steel, wood, and plaster, and ornamented with Venetian marble, glass, and stone–that the suspension of disbelief is nearly complete.

In the Venetian's casino, the necessary accoutrements of gambling interrupt the carefully crafted simulacrum: blinking lights, slot machines, and commercially produced gaming tables. Surrounded by coffered ceilings, obsessively dentiled woodwork, profusely patterned carpets, and a distinctly eighteenth-century pastel color palette, the casino is a reminder of how far the current generation in Las Vegas has gone to distance itself from its Rat Pack parentage.¹⁰ The designers of the Venetian have fabricated an atmosphere that is deliberately more naive than the wise-guy aura of The Sands, the 1952 casino the Venetian replaced. The per-ception of danger inherent in Vegas's mob-related history that was mirrored in the brassy interiors of the earlier casinos has been upholstered over to make the old gambling strip into a family destination–a sanitized European vacation, minus the passports and unfamiliar food.

As for the real Venice, the great Italian port city continues, against the odds, to maintain the status of a jaded sophisticate, rejecting facile illusion for the disillusionment of the worldly. La Serenissima has never been an unadulterated city, no matter how much the world wishes to freeze-frame her in the past.¹¹ Facing a surfeit of history, newcomers may have difficulty distinguishing the city's layers, but the stratifications are clear to the practiced eye. So when asked to design a hotel in the building that housed Venice's first public casino, the Publico Ridotto, Piero Lissoni didn't consider creating an ensemble that would be historically compatible with the structure. In converting the *piano nobile* of the old casino into the public spaces of the Hotel Monaco & Grand Canal (2002), the Milanese designer opted, instead, to gamble with both the clichés and the canons of design. The main salon may be lined with terrazzo, frescoes, and *faux bois* from the eighteenth century, but it is completed by contribu-tions from the nineteenth and twentieth centuries. Reproductions of J.M.W. Turner's watercolors of Venice decorate a screen that partitions off an ecumenical suite of

furniture that includes Ludwig Mies van der Rohe's daybed, Le Corbusier's LC3 lounge chairs, Eero Saarinen's Tulip table, reproduction Chinese export chairs, custom Louis XV bergères, and Lissoni's own Box sofas.

The artful quotations are even more cleverly integrated in the interstitial spaces of the hotel. Canaletto's scenes of the Grand Canal, reproduced on film, were applied to the glass walls of the elevator lobby, and the elevator doors were mirrored to compound the effect of being surrounded by images of water. While the elevator places guests in the eighteenth century, those who choose the stairs find themselves firmly in the twenty-first: A modernist staircase of Istrian stone, also designed by Lissoni, ascends four stories, flanked only by sheer panes of glass. Here, and wherever interventions were possible—the glazed courtyard, the new bar, and bookshop—the architect exploited the strategy of reduction to provide a cautionary foil to the romanticism that has seduced so many in Venice over the centuries.

Unencumbered by a historic urban context—or, for that matter, any urban context—the Burj Al Arab hotel (1999) sits on an island off the shore of Dubai. Floating mysteriously on the horizon, this conspicuous desert confection unabashedly plays on the myth of the oasis with a faux glamour worthy of Cecil B. DeMille. Part *Arabian Nights* fairytale, part high-tech world wonder, the sail-shaped hotel, designed by the London-based engineering and architecture firm W.S. Atkins, is (at this writing) the tallest dedicated hotel in the world.[12] Throughout the interiors, pattern is piled on pattern like carpets in a souk. Elaborate mosaics create kaleidoscopic effects underfoot, while gargantuan gold-leafed columns attest to the luxury of the guest rooms, which are furnished with canopied beds and are serviced by private butlers. Special effects like the dining room's giant aquarium and the atrium's 100-foot geyser were designed to insure that the hotel's spectacle never flags.

The Boutique

For those who find such unrelenting grandiosity exhausting, or simply not credible, but still crave the occasional visual confection, there is the boutique hotel. This burgeoning niche, catering to more modest budgets but equally finicky tastes, came into its own under the aegis of nightclub impresario-turned-hotelier Ian Schrager. Schrager's alliances with high-profile designers—from Andrée Putman

Below and opposite: TEN Architects/Taller Enrique Norten, Hotel Habita,
Mexico City, 2000

Below and opposite: TEN Architects/Taller Enrique Norten, Hotel Habita,
Mexico City, 2000

to Philippe Starck–have since been emulated by countless other entrepreneurs. Most notable among these new undertakings are designer David Rockwell's work with the Starwood group, and the various ventures launched by hotelier André Balazs, whose taste in designers is both versatile and highly strategic. All of these boutique projects are distinguished by a double identity–that of the hotel group or owner and that of the designer.

This particular entrepreneurial model made its debut when Schrager invited Andrée Putman to design the interiors of the old Executive Hotel in New York, and rechristened it as the Morgans in 1984. Putman's bold synthesis of French moderne furnishings and Wiener Werkstätte patterns quickly established the hotel as the quarters-of-choice for the perpetually mobile design community and for Schrager's natural constituency, the celebrity-nightlife crowd. (Schrager was the co-creator, with the late Steve Rubell, of Manhattan's legendary Studio 54.) Putman's reinterpretation of Viennese black-and-white checks and her rehabilitation of Eileen Gray's furniture were two of the more intelligent responses to the then full-blown infatuation with the repressed aspects of early modernism. Putman was, however, more of a curator than an auteur. For the latter sensibility, Schrager turned to Philippe Starck, forming a creative partnership that still thrives today. (Schrager did honor his collaboration with Putman, however, by naming his budding hotel enterprise the Morgans Hotel Group.)

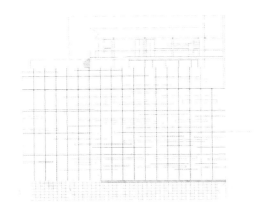

Starck's acumen in fashion, architecture, interior design, and product design was ideally suited to the hotel. Both he and Schrager saw the hotel as a place to vamp and exhibit their connoisseurship of the cool. And, of course, the key to cool is not taking oneself too seriously. Utterly secure in his role as genial host, Starck could afford to parody the luxury hotel, as he did in London's high-baroque Sanderson (2000), or to play Lilliputian games of scale, as he did at the Delano (1995) in Miami Beach, using oversize curtains, lampshades, and flower pots. With his collaborator, Anda Andrei (Starck's president of design), Starck has now completed nine hotel projects for Schrager, each strongly identified with its city. In addition to the Sanderson and the Delano, there is the Royalton (New York, 1988), the Mondrian in Los Angeles (1996) and Scottsdale, Arizona (2007), the St. Martins (London, 1999), the Hudson (New York, 2000), and the Clift (San Francisco, 2001).[13] With the Royalton, Starck's first hotel commission, Schrager and Starck set the priorities that would govern all the projects that followed: Public areas would be lavished with the largest gestures and the most space, and private rooms would have quietly disarming features, like the guardian-angel figurines in the Mondrian or the bedside lamps with allegorical images by Francesco Clemente in the Hudson. In fact, the guest rooms themselves were intentionally kept small.[14] Schrager has realized that his hotels' reputation rests on what happens in and who comes to his restaurants, bars, and lobbies. Starck has obliged him with spaces that work like urban magnets.

In the case of The Omnia (2006) in Zermatt, Switzerland–one of a much smaller line of boutique hostelries–Turkish-born, New York-based architect Ali Tayar created a sophisticated mountain aerie. Teaming with the Swiss modular furniture company USM (the hotel's owner) Tayar avoided the typical Swiss-Alp clichés by using a neutral palette of colors and materials, modernist furnishings and finely wrought details. The hotel, which is reached by an elevator wedged into a mountainside, draws interesting relationships between past and present by juxtaposing classical pieces by Ludwig Mies van der Rohe, Eero Saarinen, and Raymond Loewy, with sympathetic contemporary work, from lighting by David Weeks to customized pieces created by Tayar himself. Although Tayar largely limits his materials to white oak, gray granite, and white walls, their understatement is offset by customized features like the pinhole wooden drop

ceilings milled with decorative cutouts that filter light and sound in public spaces.

Starwood Hotels & Resorts Worldwide, whose properties include the St. Regis Hotels and Resorts, as well as the Sheraton and Westin chains, is also the corporate umbrella for the W Hotels, which in New York are synonymous with David Rockwell and his firm The Rockwell Group.[15] That the designer's name is instantly associated with the W Hotels is a result not only of the power of Rockwell's now-signature theatricality, but also of Starwood's conscious understanding that design is not simply another "value-added" component of its offerings, but also a crucial competitive tool in the current climate of the hotel business. In fact, the strategy has proved so successful that Starwood is launching a line of budget-conscious hotels–called Project XYZ and slated to launch in 2007–that takes its cues from the design-forward brand strategies of companies like Jet Blue and Target, while also emulating the group's own design model, the W Hotels.

The New York W's–three in Midtown and one in Union Square–are meant to appeal to young, affluent business travelers and fashion-conscious locals. While Starck and Schrager were heirs to the aggressive intensity of the

post-punk 1980s and used that sensibility to shape their establishments, Rockwell drew inspiration from the hyperactivity–and the millennial anxiety–of the late 1990s. Bringing his experience as a Broadway stage designer to the hotel, he constructed an assemblage of palpably organic materials that reconciles the W clientele's desire for glamour with their preoccupation with health and comfort. The hotel's curving towers of topiary and planters of wheat grass are designed to signal its therapeutic virtues as an urban retreat. Rockwell's design for the original W New York in Midtown (1998) is based on the elements of the natural world–wind, water, earth, and fire–otherwise generally absent from the urban canyon of Park Avenue. As with its counterpart in Union Square (2000), there is an obviousness to the design details–collages of seed pods and vegetables, tree-stump backgammon tables, trellis headboards–that must be embraced with a wink and a nod. Otherwise, they verge on the disingenuous, more stage set than salve for urban stress. For all their sensitivity to the zeitgeist of the current wellness culture–signified in the spices, grasses, and stones–these highly collaged interiors are closer in spirit to the themed spaces of mid-century designers like Alexander Girard, known for the famed New York restaurant La Fonda del Sol.

Another New York hotel by the Rockwell Group—one not designed in conjunction with Starwood—also bears mentioning. Perhaps because it is a one-off venture and not a template for a chain, the Chambers Hotel (2000) is less self-conscious in its efforts to soothe. For his clients—the developers Ira Drucker, Richard Born, and Steve Caspi (who also have hotel properties in Miami Beach and who commissioned Richard Meier's 165 Charles Street condominiums [see Apartments, p. 75])—Rockwell achieved an urbane sense of comfort, which is immediately felt inside the two-story lobby, with its monumental fireplace, ebony-and-parchment reception desk, leather-wrapped columns, and soft velvet couches and chairs. The subtle shades and textures of the furnishings continue in guest rooms that are notably devoid of theme. Even the 500-plus works of art, including full-scale corridor installations, are not forced to perform as a chorus or as a mnemonic device for a corporate image, but rest comfortably in their residential milieu.

Whereas the Starck hotels are the design equivalent of the dandy, full of dependably literate witticisms, and the Rockwell hotels are like hosts who are gracious to a fault, the designers commissioned to create André Balazs's hotels must resist performing to type. Despite his persona as companion to the stars, first acquired when he resuscitated Los Angeles's fabled Chateau Marmont (1990), Balazs has not translated that identity into a single, overarching style. As if to preempt the perennial ennui of his world-weary guests, his hotels refuse to repeat themselves, notwithstanding the fact that his fastest-growing hotel line is named the Standard. (To date, there are distinct Standards in downtown Los Angeles, Hollywood, and Miami.) As a business strategy, this approach offers flexibility and range; as a design strategy, it requires fluency in multiple languages.

In a Balazs hotel, interiors are especially critical. Like their most famous guests, all his hotels, when seen on the street, are usually incognito. With the exception of his first ground-up hotel, planned for New York's meatpacking district, they often appear in disguise, whether inhabiting a modern office building, as with the Standard in downtown LA, or emerging from the chrysalis of an older hotel, as with the Raleigh in Miami's South Beach. In New York's SoHo district, instead of building new (like most of his competitors in the hotel-challenged neighborhood), Balazs had the savvy and

patience to convert a nineteenth-century manufacturing
building into the Mercer Hotel (1998). He commissioned
the Parisian interior designer Christian Liaigre to tame the
structure's rougher features and at the same time retain a
sense of the neighborhood's character. Liaigre's trademark
wengé furnishings, with their distant echoes of French
1940s modernism and their evocation of Brazilian pop style,
straddle past and present in a fashion that is entirely compatible with the hybrid loft-hotel. With a lobby that houses
a lending library for guests and guest rooms with tubs for
two, Liaigre has made the Mercer a haven for understated
sybarites. While the bones of the industrial loft appear in
the original massive windows, exposed brick walls and
wood floors, and floor-to-ceiling iron columns, Liaigre
softens their edges for the neighborhood's new population
of transients. With soft white drapes and handsome upholstered furnishings, he creates an atmosphere of genteel
bourgeois comfort that would surely have been alien to the
neighborhood's first artist denizens, as would the very idea
of a luxury hotel in their midst.

In contrast to the Mercer, Balazs's Standard hotels are overtly
tongue-in-cheek. In his vision of the future-as-past, irony
rules the day: At the Hollywood Standard (1999), a nude
performance artist slumbers behind the check-in desk, and
a "gardener" mows the Astro-Turf lawn surrounding the
pool. Along with the DJ booth and the tattoo parlor, these
actors' live performances turn the hotel into a kind of theater
in the round, updated with a hint of the prurient voyeurism
of reality TV. Former film production designer Shawn
Hausman carried the role-playing fantasies throughout
the spaces of this Sunset Boulevard hotel (whose facelift
was the work of the Miami-based firm Arquitectonica): He
carpeted the lobby lounge–floor, walls, and ceiling–in white
shag and furnished the guest rooms with Andy Warhol–
patterned curtains, silver-lamé beanbag chairs, and Ultra
Suede floor pillows.

Libidinous attractions such as oversize bathtubs and showers,
complimentary condoms, and thermostat settings that read
"Blow," "Hard," "Harder," and "Stop"–the hallmarks of a
Balazs hotel–are sublimated in retro-corporate chic and
fantasies of illicit office romances in the Downtown Los
Angeles Standard (2002). The hotel occupies the former
headquarters of the Superior Oil Company (1952). Originally

designed by Claud Beelman in classic International Style, and still redolent of the testosterone of mid-century corporate capitalism, the twelve-story marble-clad office tower was converted by the LA-based KEA/Koning Eizenberg Architecture. The firm's artful cosmetic surgery, together with Shawn Hausman's innate sense of theater, elevated the building's intrinsic virility to a new level of bachelor chic. The architects retained the lobby's terrazzo floor, left the escalator completely exposed, and saved such evocative details as a clock that covers fifteen time zones and a frieze intended to illustrate Superior Oil's global reach. Once a reminder that commerce never sleeps, the clock now seems intended to reinstill glamour in world travel for the hotel's youthful, peripatetic business clientele.

Designed for a new generation of entrepreneurs who identify with the aggressive optimism of the post-World War II business boom, the hotel makes prodigious use of wallpaper and super-graphics to change the scenery from room to room. Highly keyed and monochrome color fields define the social areas—announcing them as vacuums waiting to be filled. The restaurant is drenched in yellow, while the lounge is sheathed in hot pink and contains a color-coordinated Vladimir Kagan Omnibus sofa, which measures a languorous 150 feet (45 meters) long.

Balazs's QT Hotel (2005) in Midtown Manhattan, in contrast, eschews camp for an environment that comes closer to actual camping. Here, architect Lindy Roy deploys the modernist "less is more" dictum to create a taut design for those on tight budgets. This is not a monastic minimalism, however, but a witty compression of space and time that revolves around features like bunkbeds, raised platform beds, and ATM-style kiosks for check-in and check-out. The one place Balazs refuses to skimp is in the spa-like amenities. The QT has a pool with underwater music, a gym with steam room and sauna, and the now-obligatory DJ bar in the lobby. In addition to enlivening a frugal business traveler's workday, these recreational features also solve a perennial problem for the business hotel: filling rooms during the weekend.

Fashion Hotels

In a recent *New York Times* interview, Donald Albrecht compared André Balazs to innovators like César Ritz, who founded the first of his eponymous hotels in London in 1906. "In a world … where there's no aristocratic class," said Albrecht, "the tastemaker sitting at your side, telling you 'Yes, do that. No, not that way,' can be a very powerful person."[16] Today, in the absence of a rigid class system to model the etiquette of appearance and chart its social maneuvers, society looks elsewhere for models. With no codified protocols to follow, we embrace what the cultural historian Zygmunt Bauman calls "Tempting alternative offers of authority—notoriety instead of normative regulation, ephemeral celebrities and idols-for-the-day."[17] Perhaps foremost among Bauman's "mobile signposts" are fashion designers, several of whom have recently taken on the additional mantle of hotelier. While designers such as Donatella Versace, Anouska Hempel, Christian Lacroix, and Todd Oldham might be considered *arrivistes* in the hotel business, they bring to the industry the undeniable leverage of their reputations as tastemakers. With their own set of "dos and don'ts," fashion designers are highly skilled at contriving social distinctions in the ever-widening democracy of wealth. They are also well-practiced in the art of creating alternative worlds within their own particular aesthetic universe. With their forays into hotels, fashion designers can expand their brands into places where the imaginary lifestyles behind their clothing can be experienced in three dimensions.

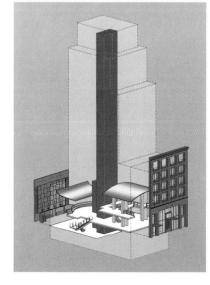

In creating the Blakes Hotel (1981) in London, actress-turned-fashion designer Anouska Hempel accomplished a dual feat: She not only made one of the earliest leaps from the fashion industry to the hotel business, but also created London's first boutique hotel. Foreshadowing the business world's "bundling" strategies–the practice of grouping different enterprises under one corporate umbrella–that led to the rash of mergers and acquisitions of the 1990s, Hempel saw the hotel as a logical way of expanding her services to her clientele. Accordingly, the Blakes' opulent rooms are, as journalist Amanda Morison observed in *The Guardian*, "swathed in the same rich silks she dressed her society girls in."[18] Two decades later, with the Hempel Hotel (2000) in West London, the designer/entrepreneur took a radically different turn, creating an environment that speaks less to the physical trappings of fashion than to the foibles of fashion culture. Lean to the point of anorexic and determined to transcend the trivial, the Hempel offers sunken tatami spaces for meditation and a choice of beds on the floor, on platforms, or simple four-posters. Antique Chinese and Indonesian rattan furnishings serve as a counterpoint to the minimalist sleeping accommodations. To complete the aura of health and well-being, each room comes with a private supply of oxygen, as if to underscore the rarified atmosphere of fashion.

In contrast to the Hempel Hotel, which is almost defensively austere, Todd Oldham's The Hotel (1999) in Miami Beach manages to sustain an unstudied casualness. In his redesign of what had been the Tiffany Hotel, Oldham replaced the art deco pastels of Miami Beach with the patterns of psychedelia, swapping one form of nostalgic indulgence for another with an abundance of tie-dyed fabrics. The hallucinatory affect begins in the lobby with a wall of gold crushed-velvet drapery and continues poolside, with tie-dyed blue-and-white canvas curtains on the cabanas. Wavy-patterned tiles in the guest room showers, airbrushed in glazes of blue and purple, exude a laid-back euphoria. Picture frames bulging with gilded mosaics, hand-printed bathroom tile, and large "portholes" frosted to appear partially submerged, complete a decor that would have been at home in the Beatles' Yellow Submarine. (In fact, novelist Matthew Stadler has likened the hotel to "a drug, a second pill–valerian root and mushrooms."[19]) Blanketing the hotel's furnishings in velours, ribbons, and cotton twills, Oldham extends a tacit invitation

to try on—if not to take home—his particular style of patch-work. Any sense of self-promotion by Oldham operates sub-liminally, staying clear of awkward commercial clashes with the hippie counter-culture he draws on.

By contrast, fashion diva Donatella Versace is as forthright in her empire-building ambitions as she is brazen in her fashion sense. The creation of Palazzo Versace (2000) on the Gold Coast of Queensland, Australia, is no exception. To emphasize the grandeur of the undertaking—her first hotel—Versace shipped river stones, marble, and all manner of materials from her native country to realize her brand of Italy-down-under. Like the Venetian in Las Vegas, Palazzo Versace is a re-creation, but the verisimilitude it seeks is not that of a city but that of a designer showroom. Guests are openly invited to replicate the hotel experience at home with purchases from its on-site Versace boutique. Predictably furnished with pieces from the label's Home Collection, the hotel's public and private spaces are stultifying in their sumptuousness. Oddly missing is the libertine character of the hotel's namesake, the late Gianni Versace.

Though Palazzo Versace is unexceptional in its excess, it is nonetheless noteworthy as a harbinger of more explicitly fashion-branded hotels to come. Most notably, Giorgio Armani—in partnership with EMAAR Properties, the biggest developer in the Middle East—has four resorts and ten hotels on the drawingboards slated to open over the next seven years. The first to open will be in Dubai, complete with an Armani boutique; it is reported to be followed by similar projects in Milan, London, Paris, New York, and Tokyo.

In the meantime, couture designer Christian Lacroix offers a different model, one explicitly tailored to the flesh and bones of a 300-year-old building on the edge of the Marais district of Paris. The Hotel du Petit Moulin (2005) is the first of four hotels that Lacroix will design for owners Nadia Murano and Denis Nourry.[20] The seventeen-room boutique hotel is a veritable map of the designer's psyche; it represents both a compression and an implosion of the flamboyant postmodern pastiche that Lacroix has been nurturing since 1987, when he founded his signature label. With its intimate scale and labyrinthine structure, the building, which used to house a bakery, proved to be an ideal vehicle for the designer's penchant for layering. In narrow corridors lead-

KEA/Koning Eizenberg Architecture, Downtown Los Angeles Standard Hotel,
Los Angeles, 2002

ing from the lobby to the rooms, polka dots collide with dominos on the carpeting underfoot. Each of the guest rooms is dramatically different from the next; some are intoxicating in their hyper-ornamentation, others soothing, with Zen-like fields of green. Even within the rooms there is a marked tendency toward stylistic schizophrenia. In one room, two utterly opposite but equally iconic 1960s pop motifs occupy the bedroom and bathroom—black-and-white Marimekko in the former and hot pink rococo in the latter. In another room, a wall-size mural of the designer's elaborate fashion sketches are offset by sleek Eero Saarinen Tulip chairs.

The Lacroix hotels represent something of an anomaly. They are not financed and owned by the designer's label, and they are not a direct extension of a larger corporate vision. While Hotel du Petit Moulin offers each guest the illusion of the couturier at work, the Versace and future Armani hotels are for those who want to get closer to the label itself. The brand-fueled hotel strategy, not surprisingly, is now being adopted by businesses that are less driven by personal mythology. They are eager to prove that the allure of a product line alone can be equal to the power of a persona. Two companies pioneering this strategy are Bulgari and Camper.

In Milan's Bulgari Hotel (2004), Milanese designer Antonio Citterio created a symbiotic relationship between the culture of the city and that of the renowned jewelry firm. Modernism found a special expression in Milan after World War II as the city rebuilt itself with a fusion of International Style architecture and traditional materials. Just as it is not unusual to see teak on a mid-twentieth-century modernist facade in Milan, it was not surprising to see Citterio bring Burmese hardwood into this twenty-first-century hotel, along with black Zimbabwe marble, Navona travertine, Turkish Aphyon stone, and durmast oak. Though curated with an eye toward a luxury commensurate with Bulgari's reputation, the materials convey the opposite of ostentation and the epitome of deferential grace. Guest rooms are furnished with details and furniture by Citterio, who subtly complicated the otherwise purist spaces with bronze net curtains to create unexpected transparencies between bed and bath. But perhaps the greatest extravagance is the rooms' sheer spaciousness. With ceilings almost 15 feet high (4.5 meters high), every guest room is an orchestrated

suite of spaces with views of a courtyard garden, which, like the social life of this aristocratic city, is largely hidden from public view.

Where Bulgari sells refinement and exclusivity, Camper, the Spanish footwear company, actively promotes transience and youthful informality. In Casa Camper (2005), a new hotel off Barcelona's famed Ramblas, designers Fernando Amat and Jordi Tió created an on-the-road aesthetic that greets guests even before they've had a chance to unpack their bags. Bicycles hang from the ceiling in the lobby, and a backlit wall reveals silhouettes of luggage behind a screen of frosted glass. Mobility is encouraged everywhere. Guest rooms are bisected by a public corridor, which guests have to cross in order to get from their bedroom to their private lounge or vice versa. The added foot traffic might suggest a perpetual party, but according to Amat, the separated quarters were really designed to offer respite, particularly for those traveling together who occasionally need the luxury of a little distance from each other before moving on.

For the Hotel Vittoria (2003) in Florence, Milanese designer Fabio Novembre put a unique twist on the hotel-as-commercial billboard, using a strategy akin to product placement, a specialty of the movie industry. Here, the product is the mosaic, and the company Bisazza, for whom Novembre is the de facto designer-in-residence. At Hotel Vittoria, Novembre lifts the customary entry carpet off the floor and turns it into a mosaic-clad spiral that wends its way through the lobby, merging with the reception desk and the wall behind it. The ribbon is no superfluous computer-generated special effect; its exuberant floral pattern is as confidently decorative as it is spatial. This opulent welcoming gesture also functions as a unique co-signature of designer and manufacturer. The same seductive handwriting can be read in the restaurant, where the walls are broken by convex surfaces that curl up from the floor and are similarly sheathed in Bisazza mosaics.

As much as these miniature tiles function as advertisements for Bisazza, they are by now equally identified with Novembre himself, who is well known in his own right as a furniture designer and interior architect. His treatment of the upper floors of the Hotel Vittoria makes it clear that the tiles are only one of his many rendering tools. Here, the monotony of a long, narrow corridor is banished by the presence of an unusual group of guests: Each guest room door doubles as a gilt-framed, full-length portrait of a different historic citizen of Florence, all reproduced with the permission of the museums that house them. The rooms, too, are long and narrow (21 by 10 1/2 feet, or 6.5 by 3 meters). To give the illusion of more space, Novembre created discrete volumes in each: platform beds are built into miniature rooms within a room, with ceilings pierced by points of fiber-optic lighting. Another rectangular volume, faced with a Florentine lily design in green laminate, serves as a partition for the bathroom. Closets become distinct environments, lined with murals of shoes and hanging clothes. Compared to the gregarious public spaces, the private spaces are deliberately hermetic–almost medieval in their emphasis on compartmentalization. They are firmly linked to the twenty-first century, however, with wireless Internet connections and flat-screen televisions.

Unlike Bisazza or Camper, 10 Corso Como is not a brand name. It is a complex of shops, galleries, and a new hotel called 3 Rooms that has become a Milanese pilgrim site for the fashion and design cognoscenti. Instead of sharing a common logo, the hotel, shops, restaurant, outdoor café, and art gallery offer the prized imprimatur of the establishment's founder, Carla Sozzani, the former editor of Italian *Vogue* and *Elle* magazines. A tastemaker, not a designer, Sozzani recognizes the weakness of branded homogeneity, particularly in her newest venture, which caters to a cosmopolitan clientele weary of institutional hotels and averse to the very notion of checking-in–even at the most stylish of boutiques.

Sozzani, who spends inordinate amounts of time away from home herself scouting, sampling, and buying, reasoned that the only solution for hotel fatigue was the "nonhotel hotel," which is the concept for 3 Rooms (2003) at 10 Corso Como. With the exception of the fact that they have to be booked in advance, the three individually furnished apartments, each with a separate entrance, scrupulously keep their distance from the traditional hotel. The suites (each with a sitting room, bedroom, and bathroom) were styled by Sozzani in collaboration with her partner, the American artist Kris Ruhs, in a melange of mid-century modern and custom design furniture, art, and craft that constitutes Sozzani's idea of a home away from home. (The paintings and raku-

fired tiles are by Ruhs.) Her guests enjoy the ultimate in privacy, while knowing they will be in the reassuringly familiar company of Arne Jacobsen, Charles and Ray Eames, Isamu Noguchi, Pierre Paulin, and Bang & Olufsen. In fact, 3 Rooms may be the only hotel in the world that uses furniture checklists on its website to advertise its rooms. The museum-like cataloguing of each room's design objects–a not-so-subtle test of prospective hotel guests' design literacy–insures a self-selecting group of travelers who can be counted on to patronize the boutiques of 10 Corso Como. Sozzani's innovation is in selling design (and design history) as a commodity in and of itself. Furthermore, the discrete residences of 3 Rooms eliminate the often awkward conditions of other ultra-small occupancy establishments–specifically the forced conviviality of the traditional bed and breakfast.

The Apartment Hotel

Among the more distinctive descendants of the 3 Rooms model is Azzedine Alaïa's 5 rue de Moussy (2005) in Paris. Alaïa in fact collaborated with Sozzani in shaping his version of this new genre, which Leonardo Ferragamo, scion of the famed Italian shoe and apparel company, calls "extreme retailing"[21] for its conflation of lodging and shopping. Like 3

Rooms, 5 rue de Moussy, which occupies the same address as Alaïa's studio and boutique, rests somewhere between a guest house and a three-room bed and breakfast. In contrast to the colorful exuberance of Sozzani's guest rooms in Milan, Alaïa's pieds-à-terre reinterpret the elegant reserve of Paris, with high-modernist pieces from his private museum-quality furniture collection, which includes work by Jean Prouvé, Marc Newson, Charlotte Perriand, Jean Nouvel, Harry Bertoia, and Serge Mouille. The interiors are frequently rearranged by the designer himself. Alaïa sees his hotel-residence not as a static response to the condition of constantly moving, but rather as a medium that is itself constantly malleable.

The concept of the hotel as an intimate and wholly private residence is showing signs of increased popularity and is taking form in a diverse range of styles. Aficionados of minimalist chic can take refuge in one of three neutrally contemporary apartments in the Miauw Suites (2005) in Antwerp, the brainchild of Belgian fashion designer Analik. Those more comfortable surrounded by the accoutrements of Old World culture can find sympathetic accommodations in the ultra-exclusive Residenza Napoleone in Rome (2003), where Princess Letzia Ruspoli has opened two rooms of her home, the Palazzo Ruspoli, to paying guests. Likewise, they will find the same degree of privacy in Madrid, where

aristocrat and art historian Marta Medina presides over Casa de Madrid (2003), a renovated eighteenth-century palace, with seven apartments that function as private, temporary residences. Both the Roman and Spanish establishments (affiliates of the London group Chic Retreats) follow Sozzani's lead, as does the Miauw Suites in Antwerp. All signs and symbols of the conventional hotel are banished to give lodgers the illusion of ownership.

Where the previous examples offer the panache of their interiors and prestige of their hosts as their chief attractions, a hostelry in The Netherlands adds another ingredient to the apartment hotel. Like Sozzani's enterprise in Milan and Alaïa's in Paris, the Lute Suites (2005), located on the outskirts of Amsterdam, evolved as an ancillary commercial enterprise. Instead of fashion, however, the allure is food. Restaurateurs Peter and Marieke Lute conceived of the Suites as an appendage to their two year old restaurant, feeling it would be better served if its guests could spend the night. As well-regarded for their patronage of design as for their culinary instincts, the couple hired Marcel Wanders to create a series of guest apartments out of the dilapidated eighteenth-century row houses that shared the restaurant's site. Unlike another recent interior design project by Wanders–New York's Hotel on Rivington (2005), where the designer was confined to the public spaces–the Lute Suites

Antonio Citterio and Partners, Bulgari Hotel, Milan, 2004

presented him with an opportunity to play on, and with, the domestic arena.

Each of the six luxury apartments that comprise the Lute Suites has a separate entrance and each is distinct from the other, furnished with pieces by Joep van Lieshout, Jurgen Bey, Konstantin Grcic, and Wanders himself, among others. With what seems to be a uniquely Dutch gift for subverting and revitalizing the past with consummate good humor and grace, Wanders submits each room to a lavishly iconoclastic décor. Oversized floral patterns—woven into rugs, transferred to Bisazza tile, painted onto wardrobes, and imprinted on wallpaper—intermingle promiscuously with eclectic contemporary furnishings and exposed wooden joists. The restaurant-hotel annex also includes two modest conference rooms, furnished as idiosyncratically as the suites themselves, with Maarten Baas's bizarrely charred Smoke Chairs (providing a subversive but witty commentary on the fate of transactions conducted in these rooms). With its culinary focal point and its design's embrace of the strange and peculiar, Lute Suites brings the hotel-as-private apartment full circle to its roots in the ancient roadside inn.

The Fictional Hotel

Still another iteration of the hotel as alter ego surfaces in New York's Soho House (2003) designed by Ilse Crawford for the British hotelier Nick Jones. A public hotel that doubles as a private club, Soho House encourages its nonmember guests to sample the members-only deluxe facilities. Crawford took up the theme of seduction implicit in this arrangement by giving provocative names to the different classes of rooms—Playpen, Playroom, Playhouse, and Playground—which range from 325 square feet (30 square meters) to a sprawling 950 square feet (88 square meters). Crafted with a studied nonchalance tailored to its high-profile film and media patrons, Soho House is designed to bring the credibility of the loft to a new generation of self-conscious aesthetes. Vintage pieces mingle comfortably with modern furnishings by Cappellini and B&B Italia and the glitter of Swarovski chandeliers. One guest room appears as a work in progress, its walls marked with long daubs of paint in different colors, like samples waiting to be chosen. In another room, a free-standing tub in the bedroom recalls a makeshift bohemian garret. In the exclusive sixth-floor restaurant, pressed-tin ceilings and salvaged pine

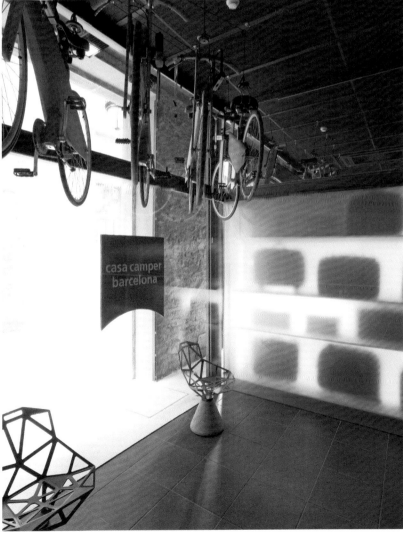

Opposite: Fabio Novembre, UNA Hotel Vittoria, Florence, 2003

Azzedine Alaïa, 5 rue de Moussy, Paris, 2005

Carla Sozanni, 3 Rooms, 10 Corso Como, Milan, 2003

floors serve as reminders of the proletarian history of the
meatpacking district where Soho House resides. With her
preference for collage, Crawford rejects the straitjacket of
the period environment. Nonetheless, for a hotel that
attracts the entertainment industry, she creates a series of
convincing set pieces with unforced artfulness.

At a time when digital technology has made everything susceptible to imitation, the premium placed on individuality
has risen exponentially. Hotels must go to ever-greater
lengths to set themselves apart and, concomitantly, to cater
to a clientele absorbed in a perpetual exercise of personal
reinvention. With brutal and erotic honesty, Jean Nouvel
exposes this narcissism with his cinematically driven
design for The Hotel (2000) in Lucerne, Switzerland. Here,
guests find their idealized doppelgängers floating on the
ceilings of their bedrooms. Enormous prints of still images
from the films of Buñuel, Bertolucci, Almodóvar, Fellini,
Fassbinder, Lynch, and Greenaway strike poses that, according to Donald Albrecht, guests "would hope to see if they
were in a honeymoon suite with a mirrored ceiling."[22]

Like private theaters, the rooms are all but blacked out to heighten the effect of these latter-day frescos. (Visible from the street when the curtains are open, these movie portraits also have the effect of transforming the entire hotel into a peep show at night.) The guest room furnishings, made of matte stainless steel and Brazilian cherry, were designed by Nouvel to pick up glancing reflections while remaining unobtrusive. The only other obvious light source in the bedrooms are sconces—that is, until the eye adjusts and discerns the specially tinted walls, created by Nouvel and artist Alain Bouy to suggest the glow of projected film. (In this dreamy context, the obligatory desk and desk lamp seem almost superfluous.) But the optical games do more than supply a back story for the hotel. Nouvel has brokered a bargain between the rational and the irrational. By situat-ing his own modernist tendencies among the mythologies of the cinema, the architect acknowledges the ephemeral nature of both.

Another strategy for closing the gap between the polarities that constrained twentieth-century thought—the modern isolated from history, the organic from the Cartesian, and the fixed from the transitory—emerged in the vernacular of "blobitecture." (The ungainly name refers to the biomorphic smoothness made possible by the complex rendering capa-bilities of the computer.) Pioneered in the mid-1990s—and with formal antecedents in art nouveau and Surrealism—these spaces are still unorthodox, symbolic of an organic ideal but still never quite free from the sense of novelty.

The Berlin- and Los Angeles–based architecture firm
GRAFT saw the hotel as an ideal vehicle to exploit both the
serious and frivolous dimensions of the style. Located off the
fashionable Kurfürstendamm in Berlin, Hotel Q! (2004) has
a lobby covered in deep-red linoleum that could double as a
skateboard park; guest rooms are reminiscent of boat cabins
with baths directly adjacent to beds and built-in furnishings
clad in imitation white ostrich leather; and the bar is a
three dimensional puzzle with furnishings nestled into
walls that swell from the space of the lobby. The overall
design is an updated version of streamlining that dismisses
the interior's usual spatial dissections arbitrary. Here,
GRAFT employs tectonics instead of images to suggest the
romance of bodies eliding. (Though the architects did pay a
subtle, if unintended, homage to Nouvel in the guest rooms,

where a photograph of a woman is lightly screened onto the
curved ceiling.)

While GRAFT views the guests of Hotel Q! as participants
in an experimental landscape of furniture and architecture,
French designer Matali Crasset takes the notion of interactivity further in her design for the Hi Hotel (2003) in Nice,
France. Not only does she offer guests nine different
fictions in nine different room types, but she also re-casts
the furniture, subverting each piece's traditional function
to a new one. Best known for her modular product design–
children's building blocks that make up a couch, trays that
work equally as tables and shelves, sleeping mats that
double as stools–Crasset has spent most of her career illuminating the functional. Her infatuation with multitasking is

adamantly low-tech; instead of relying on digital acrobatics, she offers a potent but modest thoughtfulness.

With the Hi Hotel, Crasset is more fully able to exploit the poetry of the unexpected by creating the context as well as the content. In the White & White room, for example, her Lit-table is both a bed and a washstand with two marble sinks; the hygienic hybrid beckons to workaholics who fantasize about guilt-free vacations in hospitals. Those unwilling to leave the trappings of work can opt to stay in the blue Digitale room, which has walls painted to resemble giant pixels and a table that cuts through a dividing wall to serve two spaces. Wardrobes that look like clothing bags with pitched roofs are small works of felt architecture, while a hedge of greenery doubles as a shower curtain. Crasset is adept at wresting the maximum efficiency out of the nature of objects–a skill in evidence in the hotel's public spaces: The Happy Bar, loosely circumscribed by a handsome slatted-wood hull, is capable of functioning as breakfast room, dining room, cinema, or performance space.

Tokyo's first boutique hotel, the Claska (2003), located in a neighborhood known for its furniture and design shops, is a another kind of design composite. With spaces designed by Intentionalities, an interior design firm, and Torafu Architects (both based in Tokyo), the Claska occupies an eight-story structure renovated by Urban Design System. A hybrid in program as well as design, the "apart-hotel" has only nine guest rooms but offers twenty-three residential rooms for stays of six months or longer–all atop a restaurant, café, dog-grooming salon, gallery, and cooperative workspace for art, design, and fashion companies. Intentionalities was responsible for the overall interior design of the public spaces and the first suite of guest rooms that opened in 2003. Abstract wall reliefs, handmade furniture brought in from Bali and Thailand, and original pieces by the designers create a handsome, if familiar, East-meets-West modernism

The hotel's most original spaces–three rooms, each no more than 194 square feet (18 square meters)–were specially designed by Torafu Architects in 2004 for guests booking weekly or monthly stays. Where Matali Crasset uses the methodology of product design, Torafu uses its iconography. Mahogany-veneered walls were laser-cut with the silhouettes of common objects–hair dryers, chairs, suitcases, coffee

cups, waste baskets, and other accoutrements—and the objects themselves are, in turn, compactly stored within their own outlines. The back-lit niches not only cleverly enshrine the talismans of daily life, they sometimes transform the object altogether, rendering them merely as two-dimensional abstractions, as with the lamp and the picture frame. Fold-down tables, partially stored chairs, and a Sony Aibo robot dog complete the cast of characters.

The Grand Hotel

In the 1932 Oscar-winning movie *Grand Hotel*, the character of Dr. Otternschlag (played by Lewis Stone) answers the rhetorical question "What do you do in a grand hotel?" by saying:

> Eat. Sleep. Loaf around. Flirt a little. Dance a little.
> A hundred doors leading to one hall, and no one
> knows anything about the person next to them. And
> when you leave, someone occupies your room, lies in
> your bed, and that's the end.

The archetypal grand hotel—the rambling seaside resort or the urbane art deco tower that once served the upper echelons of a stratified society, a place where stays could last as long as a season—has long since been drafted into the world of work, along with the aristocrats themselves. Since the advent of the skyscraper, the monumentality that was once the prerogative of class has been co-opted by capital. In the process, whatever romance once attended business travel has all but disappeared, weighed down by too many frequent-flyer miles and expense receipts. Today, the conventions of corporate travel are more likely to be the subject of parody in hotels like the Downtown Los Angeles Standard, or repressed altogether in boutique hotels like the Sanderson in London.

Even with the rise of boutique lodging and residential-style specialty hotels, not all business travelers feel comfortable with unmarked entrances and apartment-like quarters. To many. the "domesticated" hotel conveys an uncomfortable intimacy, a femininity, and a suggestion of extravagance contradictory to the circumspect realm of financial transactions. Yet total anonymity is equally suspect; a hotel is still an index of status and prestige. The full-service grand hotel of the past has been drafted to serve that role. This is not the family retreat, populated with prams and nannies, but the adult version, complete with all the amenities required by

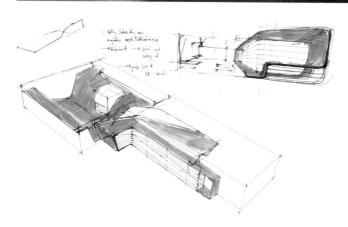

business travelers and those who treat travel as a serious business in and of itself. Three contrasting responses to the contemporary business hotel can be found in the Brazilian city of São Paulo.

The least risk-averse of the three is the Unique (2002). With distinguished progenitors in the oeuvre of Le Corbusier and Oscar Niemeyer, Ruy Ohtake's wedge-shaped form announces itself confidently in a city all but devoid of architectural landmarks. Yet for all its external bravado, this hotel is a prudent balancing act between Ohtake's unremitting modernism and the more flexible styling of João Armentano, who designed the interiors. Much has been made of hotel developer Jonas Siaulys's decision to pair such odd bedfellows. In his bid to meet the often conflicting requirements of the business market, Siaulys was anxious to insinuate the cachet of the boutique hotel inside the monumental building's portholed weathered-copper facade. Nonetheless, the hotel's most gestural features flow from Ohtake's architecture, not from Armentano's interior treatments, which are handsome and deferential.

In the guest rooms along the periphery, the floors climb up the wall, tracing the outline of the building itself; the slope, here, is not a conceit but a structural imperative. Armentano merely exaggerates the glamour of the effects by placing a flat-screen television on the curve itself. Special effects of light, visible throughout the hotel, are also attributable to the building's structural fabric, from the operable porthole windows to the upstairs refracting pool that filters light to each floor through a shaft. Ohtake also created a cloud-like ceiling for the events room, creating the same Arp-like surrealism that governs the inverted arc of the hotel. Admittedly, it is Armentano, the curator, who keeps Ohtake's design from turning the hotel into a museum. Decisions like appointing the bar with baroque angels by the eighteenth-century Brazilian sculptor Aleijadinho and using furniture of local design in the guest rooms. Notably, he included chairs made of circular pressed-paper tubes—Armentano's way of honoring both Brazil and Ohtake himself, one of the country's most revered living architects.

Arthur Casas's 57-room Hotel Emiliano (2001), in the upscale Jardim section of São Paulo, offers the business traveler a commodious, sybaritic conservatism: a sleek, sophisticated interior of limestone, wood, and leather, punctuated by the exuberant lines Humberto and Fernando Campana's string chairs. Despite the hotel's relatively modest size, the architect is able to play with scale in its soaring 30-foot (9-meter) lobby, where clusters of low-slung armchairs are offset by Casas's custom-designed brobdingnagian floor lamps. The hotel's entirely glazed top floor offers guests a spa that overlooks the panorama of the city and—the pièce de resistance for hurried travelers—the luxury of a helipad.

In the same city, Isay Weinfeld and Márcio Kogan's twenty-five-story Fasano Hotel (2003) takes an even more synthetic approach to the business hotel, welcoming guests with familiar antique club chairs and leather couches while introducing them to modernist masters like Thonet and Eames. There is nothing self-conscious or overtly didactic about Weinfeld and Kogan's furniture tutorial, however, or the hotel's decidedly modern spaces. Here the ground floor is truly opened up by the ingenious strategy of making it a plinth for the hotel's guest rooms above. By extending the footprint of the tower's base, the architects were able to create a perimeter skylight that illuminates the lobby, lounges, and restaurant. In the private spaces, the designers engendered a comfortable sense of sophistication, using the same mix of furnishings seen in the lobby, set on warm wood floors and brightly striped area rugs. Elegantly appointed work spaces are made to feel even more commodious with mirrors and frosted glass.

Though owner Rogério Fasano is clear about the clientele he serves—a well-traveled international business community—it is worth noting that he is a newcomer to the industry. The scion of São Paulo's most celebrated restaurant dynasty, Fasano joins the growing ranks of restaurateurs who have opened hotels, including the aforementioned Dutch entrepreneurs Peter and Marieke Lute as well as Alain Ducasse, who opened the Hotel Ostape (2004) in Biarritz, France, and New Yorker Steve Hanson, who opened the James Hotel (2004) in Scottsdale, Arizona. Ostape's interior takes its cues from the traditional lodge, while the intensely colorful James, designed by Deborah Burke, reflects Hanson's ambitions to attract a younger, design-savvy clientele. Following the lead of fashion luminaries, these culinary entrepreneurs bring a new dimension of taste to the ever-changing hotel.

Like most things Roman, the Es Hotel (2003) cannot escape its history—it is only the latest layer of an urban environment that is twenty-seven centuries old—but unlike most things Roman, this new hotel gives no outward sign of its provenance. The only exception is a small cache of ruins discovered during the hotel's construction, now encased in protective glass in the lobby. Situated parallel to Rome's sprawling central train station, the 253-room hotel meets the criteria of the contemporary grand hotel without sacrificing its sleek, low profile. The Rome-based architects Jeremy King and Riccardo Roselli take the position that the hotel is anything but a home away from home; they see it as a port of call. Far from the luxury hotels near the Piazza di Spagna, the Es is both a convenient meeting place for business travelers and a remarkably glamorous piece of an official urban renewal program in the gritty Esquiline neighborhood, from which the hotel takes its name.

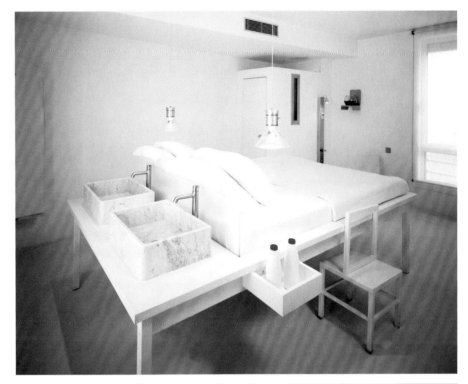

Though the hotel is thoroughly contemporary in form, its program harks back to the days before air travel, to the modes of transportation that gave rise to the hotel as we know it: the train, the car, and the boat. The regular comings and goings of rail cars can be seen through the hotel's windows, which were designed to glow in a random pattern of color visible inside and out at night, and the west wing of the hotel is a scrim-curtained seven-story parking structure (an underground garage was out of the question because of the archaeological treasures that lie beneath the hotel). But, by far, the dominant source of inspiration for the interior is the boat. White leather and polished mahogany furnishings, wooden decks that serve as patios, springy foam-backed PVC floors indoors, even the back-lit, pontoon-like reception desk that snakes through the lobby—all these elements draw on the romance of the yacht. But even more interesting are King and Roselli's nautical economies of form. Just as any seafaring vessel must be rigged efficiently, the Es is an elegant exercise in functionality. To the voguish combination of platform bed and bath they have added a third function: When the demand for conference space becomes overwhelming, the sleeping raft is fitted with a matching lid to become a conference table. As if to underscore the intention to create an entirely new mise-en-scène for the traveler, every piece of hardware in the hotel—sensor lights, mirrors, hooks, handles, baggage trolleys—was designed by the architects themselves. Even the terrazzo floor of the lobby is custom-

crafted; its oversize egg-shaped pattern was made by slicing specially made columns of stone. Here, the grand hotel is like an ocean liner landlocked in the center of Rome.

Where the Es Hotel contends with a nondescript site in a world-class city, the Gran Hotel Domine Bilbao (2002), with its telegraphic name, faces the opposite context. Across the street from Frank Gehry's monumental Guggenheim Bilbao (see Cultural, p. 401) in the medium-sized industrial city in northern Spain, the 145-room hotel achieves its own stature as a kind of domesticated museum of design, with a collection of carefully framed views of Gehry's building. Working with interior designer Fernando Salas, famed Spanish artist/designer Javier Mariscal drew his own history of twentieth-century design on the walls of the hotel. The hotel's owner, Silken Hotels, gave Mariscal wide latitude to exercise his connoisseurship, and the result is a stimulating venue for the city's newfound culture pilgrims and for the steady flow of curators, artists, and administrators who come to Bilbao to conduct the business of art. References begin in the lobby atrium that is an homage to Frank Lloyd Wright's Guggenheim New York and the site of Mariscal's *Fossil Cypress*, a massive "trunk" of stones caged in mesh. Guest rooms are incised by planar geometries reminiscent

of Russian constructivism, and the café evokes the Bauhaus and the design of the 1920s, with reproductions of furnishings by Gropius, Mies van der Rohe, Breuer, and Le Corbusier. The cocktail lounge offers a trip into 1960s pop, and the reading room is a relaxing sanctuary furnished with organic pieces by Aalto, Eames, Mollino, Jacobsen, Bertoia, Noguchi, and other design icons of the 1950s. Mariscal insured that the gallery effect is never airless or stilted by also including his own lively work and that of contemporary designers like Ron Arad and Philippe Starck (whose bathtub, in full view from the bed, appears as if it is on display in a museum vitrine). As for the incipient history of twenty-first-century travel, the success of the Gran Hotel Domine Bilbao suggests that the grand hotel has found new purpose as an adjunct to architectural icons in out-of-the-way locales.

The Postmodern Hotel

Mariscal's design for the Gran Hotel Domine Bilbao has often been characterized as a total work of art,[23] yet another incarnation of the gesamtkunstwerk that ushered in the twentieth century—first in the Arts and Crafts Movement, then in the Bauhaus. In fact, in its self-conscious accounting of modern design movements, Mariscal's approach is more in line with the newest model for hotel design, in which a

developer gathers a group of high-profile architects and designers under one roof, not as a collaborative but as a collection. The strategy goes beyond mere differentiation, affording patrons a rare opportunity to experience (if only for a few short days) the spatial and material languages of a highly particularized design sensibility. At the same time, beyond the confines of their signature guest rooms, guests can immerse themselves in a variety of public spaces equally distinguished by their celebrated authors. Taken as a whole, the postmodern hotel is deliberately discontinuous. Here the hotel itself is deconstructed—the names of its parts are greater than its name as a whole. With the nearly concurrent openings of the Lloyd Hotel & Cultural Embassy (2004) in The Netherlands, the Hotel Castell (2004) in Switzerland, and the Hotel Puerta America (2005) in Spain, the phenomenon might seem to be the birthright of the new millennium. In truth, however, the hotel of multiple personalities was foreshadowed in the late 1980s by a singular venture: the Hotel Il Palazzo (1989)in Fukuoka, Japan, a project that was postmodern both in style and in philosophy.

When plans began for the hotel, Shigeru Uchida, who held the title of art director on the project, persuaded the client that extraordinary measures were needed to "create cultural

meaning and visual attraction with the architecture when introducing services to such an unprepossessing site."[24] The Italian architect Aldo Rossi (who died in 1997) had designed a monumental, colonnaded building that provided a dramatic counterpoint to the local architecture, and the interior public spaces called for a sympathetic but equally strong response. Uchida decided on not one response, but six: his own and that of Alfredo Arribas, Ettore Sottsass, Gaetano Pesce, Shiro Kuramata (who died in 1991), and Rossi himself.

Echoing the vertical rhythms of the facade, Uchida planted an allée of terrazzo columns in the lobby and the restaurant; the Spanish architect Arribas, known for his structural pyrotechnics, caged a dance floor in glass and steel. One bar each was accorded to Sottsass, Pesce, Kuramata, and Rossi. Sottsass crowned his Zibibbo Bar with a dark blue ceiling of gold stars; Kuramata opted for slender vertical light poles in the Russian Bar; Pesce created secluded spots for conversation with his I Feltri chairs in the El Liston Bar; and Rossi (with Morris Adjani) created a magisterial space for the El Dorado Bar, introducing a gold-leafed model of the hotel's facade over the bar itself. In contrast to the highly articulate social spaces, the guest rooms are oddly muted. Designed in conventional Western and Eastern styles by Ikuyo Mitsuhashi, the private quarters of the hotel were considered incidental to the story, a not uncommon trait in hotels of the late 1980s. Today, however, no room is overlooked as a design opportunity.

In the short years since the Hotel Il Palazzo opened there has been a sea change in the public perception of design. What was once viewed as a service or a rarified symbol of luxury has become a commodity in and of itself. Information that was interesting only to a tiny coterie of connoisseurs—specifically, the names and roles of a hotel's architects and designers—has now taken on considerable marketing value as a sign of quality and innovation. The public now follows the latest ventures of famous design-savvy developers in the mainstream press: Schrager, Balazs, Sozzani, Starwood, Silken, and others.

Set in the heart of a city, such collaborative projects have their cultural equivalent in the art gallery. But the paradigm changes in more remote locations, especially in the moun-

Isay Weinfeld, Fasano Hotel, São Paulo, 2003.

tains where a blizzard can transform a hotel stay into a snowbound refuge. Located in the Swiss Alps and owned by Swiss collector and educator Ruedi Bechtler, the Hotel Castell is actually part art colony and part social community. Meditative by design, the Castell grants its guests a slower sense of time in every sense. No grand narrative prevails, however, only provocative adjacencies, amenable both to those who come to ski and to those who come for Bechtler's Art Weekend performances.

The Amsterdam-based firm UN Studio was responsible for most of the renovation of the original 1912 Castell Hotel and designed sixteen of its twenty-five guest rooms. (The other nine, with modest pine furnishings, are credited to Swiss architect Hans-Jörg Ruch.) Painted in low-key hues of red and green that are offset by expanses of brilliant white, the guest rooms by UN Studio's Ben van Berkel and Caroline Bos are contemplative environments, wholly appropriate to the art, whether Lawrence Weiner's conceptualist koans screened on the hotel facade or the video installation by Swiss video artist Pipilotti Rist in the Red Bar.[26] Not least among the hotel's aesthetic highlights is the spectacular

view of St. Moritz that can be enjoyed from the terrace designed by artist Tadashi Kawamata. Van Berkel and Bos exhibit the more expressive side of their practice inside the hotel's Turkish bath. The intimate confines of the 860-square-foot (80-square-meter) *hamam* are saturated with vibrating color: the entire room is tiled in vivid red and partitioned by curved-glass dressing rooms whose walls change color with the light.

While collaborations between private hoteliers and high-profile designers have become a veritable commonplace, it is patently rare to find a government agency entering into such partnerships. One exception to this rule, not surprisingly, can be found in The Netherlands, a country where official support for design is enviably robust. Indeed, the decision to turn a hotel into a showcase for Dutch design is a logical extension of government policy: it is a living advertisement for one of the country's most influential exports.

The Lloyd Hotel & Cultural Embassy in Amsterdam is a joint venture between four young developers,[25] the Dutch government, and a housing foundation, which provided the startup money to renovate the 1917 building that houses the hotel. Seven years in the making, the Lloyd was motivated as much by national pride as it was by business instincts, though the latter have been clearly vindicated. Leaving the brick facade intact, the Rotterdam architecture firm MVRDV gutted the interior to create a six-story atrium for a restaurant and a satellite office of the Dutch cultural ministry; in the process, it increased the hotel's capacity to 120 rooms by inserting new floors in the wings. The firm also designed several inventive guest rooms, including one with a hinged wall that, when set in one position, increases the footprint of the room (while cleverly framing the sink) and, when set in another configuration, creates a private room for showering.

The balance of the Lloyd's guest rooms and interstitial spaces were assigned to a consortium of designers and artists who give the hotel its raison d'être. The roster, not strictly Dutch, includes Hella Jongerius, Joep van Lieshout, Peter Lakenvelder, Gerald van der Kaap, Damien Hirst, Suchan Kinoshita, Jasper Morrison, Tejo Remy, Wiel Arets, and Christoph Seyferth. Their work fills guest rooms and hallways alike. Atelier van Lieshout created a sound-insulated space called the Music Room, with an eight-person bed that is big enough for a band and a few groupies. At the opposite end of the scale, Seyferth makes a traditional Dutch cupboard bed in a defunct elevator shaft. The dispersion of design continues throughout the hotel, but never devolves to theming, in large part due to the conceptual nature of Dutch design. Each artifact and environment at the Lloyd tells a short story but they never add up to a single narrative point of view.

The hotel-as-art-gallery takes on the proportions of a blockbuster exhibition in the fourteen-floor Hotel Puerta America in Madrid—the remarkable result of the Silken group's effort to brand itself by collecting the best-known specimens of architecture and design from around the world. An enormous cabinet of contemporary curiosities, the Madrid venture brought together an extraordinary roster of nineteen internationally known architects and designers (this number does not include their collaborators), including Ron Arad, Eva Castro and Holger Kehne, David Chipperfield, Kathryn Findlay, Norman Foster, Richard Gluckman, Zaha Hadid, Arata Isozaki, Marc Newson, Christian Liaigre, Javier Mariscal and Fernando Salas, Jean Nouvel, John Pawson,

Teresa Sapey, and Victorio & Lucchino. Each floor of guest rooms (including the corridors and their lobbies) was governed by a single architect, as was each of the public spaces—restaurants, bars, main lobby, even the parking area. Getting off the elevator is the equivalent of meeting a new designer on his or her own terms.

The thrill of travel may have dissipated in the post-jet age, but the 342-room Hotel Puerta America offers its own form of disorientation to replace the frisson of the unfamiliar that travel once held. Zaha Hadid, for example, decided to greet guests in the lobby with her double-helix Vortexx chandelier and then, in the guest rooms, envelop them in curved white walls (except for three rooms that are entirely black). The language of the organic appears again on the seventh floor, in rooms by Ron Arad, who custom-

designed circular beds to echo the wave of the walls. On the eighth floor, Kathryn Findlay of Ushida Findlay sculpted surrealist spaces with cantilevered beds and baths. (In her lobby, Jason Bruges's interactive lighting installation *Memory Wall* takes on the colors of guests' clothes.) The youngest of the designers, Eva Castro and Holger Kehne of London's Plasma Studio, were awarded the fourth floor by competition—the only firm so commissioned. The pair created crystalline geometries of steel and glass that fracture reflections the way memory distorts the actual experience of travel.

Not all the floors of the Hotel Puerta America attempt to explode the Cartesian plane. On the second floor, Norman Foster paid tribute to the late Basque artist Eduardo Chillida (a personal friend of Foster) with glass drums that link each

Hotel il Palazzo, Fukuoka, Japan, 1989, with interiors by (clockwise from top right) Aldo Rossi, Ettore Sottsass, and Shiro Kuramata

MVRDV, Lloyd Hotel and Cultural Embassy, Amsterdam, 2004, with interiors by Atelier van Lieshout (top) and Christoph Seyferth (bottom)

room to the corridor and create sensuous partitions in the rooms themselves, which are clad in white leather. On the third floor, David Chipperfield offered a neutral haven, with hand-made floors, upholstered walls, and white marble. Arata Isozaki took a similarly minimalist approach on the tenth floor, but reversed the palette to black, masking superfluous details in shadow. In the bar, Marc Newson created a black marble bar 26 feet (8 meters) long set in a wall of aluminum blades. In the restaurant, Christian Liaigre extended a gracious hand to Spain itself, using materials drawn from Galicia, Catalonia, and Andalusia. At the heart of the hotel, John Pawson's minimalist reception areas broker the peace between the restless and the serene, without compromising the tensions that make the experiment a success.

At the beginning of the twenty-first century, the Hotel Puerta America's promiscuous, eclectic design stands in stark contrast to the universalizing ambitions of the earliest moderns. It is tempting to view this exercise as an expression of an ideal put forward by the Italian philosopher Gianni Vattimo—the ideal of heterotopia, of many visions coexisting in one framework, here in the micro-universe of the hotel—the opposite of the monolithic utopian dreams and designs of the twentieth century.[27] Certainly, there is something to be said for the hotel—be it the Hotel Puerta America or a boutique chain like the Morgans Group—as a mirror of the non sequiturs of an Internet culture whose citizens leap from world to world with a single click of the mouse.

But in truth, for all its efforts to embrace diversity, the hotel is not likely to breed new social networks across cultures and class; it attracts a self-selecting community of global hybrids already accultured to the notion of endless change. The risk of embracing such a fractured, postmodern worldview is the risk of designing a tower of Babel with no way out, and worse, with no common bonds among those inside it. It may seem absurd to lay the burden of this societal dilemma at the foot of the hotel, an institution largely designed to induce a temporary amnesia from everyday cares. Yet, as the hotel moves away from its essence as temporary shelter to embrace the vagaries of fashion, the products of consumption, and fictions of film in its design, surely it is at least symptomatic of, if not fully participatory in, the larger forces that keep the citizens of affluence in a perpetual state of impermanence. The hope for the hotel lies in the lacunae in time that it offers to people always on the move. Playtime and leisure, imagination and fantasy are as much its opportunities as its liabilities for a society determined to insulate itself from reality.

Hotel Puerta America, Madrid, 2005, with interiors by John Pawson (top) and
Norman Foster (bottom)

Below and opposite: Hotel Puerta America, Madrid, 2005, with interiors by (clockwise from top left) Marc Newson, Jean Nouvel, Zaha Hadid, and Plasma Studios

Therapeutic

Of all the categories of space considered in this book, none is more squarely situated at the crossroads of science and art—the rationalist science of medicine and the enduring arts of healing, rooted in mysticism and religion—than the genre of the therapeutic space. It has been more than two millennia since Hippocrates argued that illness and good health were not the punishment and reward of the gods, but factors of human physiology. Yet despite centuries of accumulated medical knowledge, the incontrovertible fact of our mortality—and the loss of control over mind and body that attends sick-ness and death—continues to charge the spaces of healthcare with enormous power and significance.

The history of the therapeutic institution is inextricably tied to the evolution of cultural attitudes toward illness, aging, and death. Today's wellness culture owes as much to the ancient Greeks, who advocated natural palliatives (sunlight, water, and exercise), as it does to the medieval monks, whose austere monasteries presaged the contemporary hospital. We may no longer believe that disease is caused by sin or wrongdoing, but the absence of a cure is still perceived as failure. In an era when mortality seems ever distant in affluent societies, debates rage about just how far doctors should go to prolong life, and how much expertise should be accorded to patients and families in the therapeutic environment. The tensions between clinical knowledge and emotional need that operate within the practice and spaces of medicine not only affect life and death decisions but also extend to the entire spectrum of health care. In the process, hospitals are reexamining their missions, and health clubs and spas are repositioning their roles in a culture that prizes longevity.

Modern medicine continues to insist on sterile conditions to ward off infection, to be sure, but there is a growing consensus that an antiseptic environment can retard recovery as much as an infection can. There is skepticism that too much attention has been focused on the technical, and not enough on the less quantifiable aspects of health care—chief among them reassurance. In the past, those who could afford to consulted the sibyls to assuage anxieties about their future well-being; today, the nervous affluent subscribe to boutique medical practices that provide treatment on demand. Instead of making offerings to the gods, they pay special membership fees for the privilege of immediate access and coordinated care.[1]

The social movements of the twentieth century promoted, among other things, the rights of choice and control for all citizens, the healthy as well as the sick. Although the ideals of the 1960s remain largely unfulfilled for much of the world's population, the notion of patient advocacy did lead to the acceptance and rise of new models of care in hospices, birthing rooms, and homeopathic centers. Furthermore, in recent decades, the growth of privatization has brought the ethos of the service economy to a field once solely identified with social welfare and charitable works. As troubling as such a development might seem on the surface, the impetus of competition accelerated the shift from an institutional health care model toward one that takes its cue from the home, the first site of care. The first superficial signs were the introduction of color onto the blank canvas of hospital white, and the appearance of decorative patterns on modesty curtains. These tentative formal gestures, erratically adopted over the course of the late twentieth century, were soon complemented by greater attention to behavior and to the full spectrum of the senses.

In both the public and private sector, health care interiors are also increasingly based on models borrowed directly from the realm of entertainment. Instead of calling attention to medical prowess and the latest technical equipment, these spaces are designed to promote distraction from disease and diversion from depression. Children's hospitals, for example, now frequently borrow from theme parks; adult facilities designed on this model look to resorts and hotels—even the archetypal cherry-paneled office suite.

At the same time that traditional medical institutions are changing their parlance and design models to promote a more convivial atmosphere—"wards" have given way to "suites" and "patients" have become "guests"—spas and private health centers (those that offer elective cosmetic enhancements, for example) are gravitating toward the clinical to bring the aura of legitimate science to their services. As with so many other interior languages, the realm of health care and therapeutic design is experiencing a convergence of public and private, of the communal and the personal, and the value of security is being tested

Below and opposite: Koh Kitayama + Architecture Workshop/Taro Ashihara Architects, Katta Public General Hospital, Shiroishi City, Miyagi Prefecture, Japan, 2003

against that of comfort. But unlike the library that doubles as a living room or the museum that serves as a community center, in this domain, such shifts in program and attitude can quite literally become a matter of life and death.

Regardless of whether treatments—the term of choice for chemotherapy and facials alike—are offered under for-profit or nonprofit auspices, the environments in which these services are provided are now understood to play an active role in their effectiveness. It is no accident that vital medical procedures and revitalizing therapies increasingly share the same vocabulary and vie with each other for claims on the public attention. It is a direct reflection of the social changes occurring as the prosperous Baby Boom generation flattens the peak of the demographic pyramid. Much of the impetus for the research on the curative benefits of natural light, on

the therapeutic role of nature, and on the value of creating homelike environments in medical settings stems from the undeniable fact that, in many parts of the industrialized world, the population is graying. Just as Baby Boomers changed the culture of birth and child care, producing in the process countless varieties of diapers, strollers, and educational toys, they are now confronted with the opportunity to change the culture of aging, driven by the imperative of self-interest, if not solely by altruism. Given the bewildering array of health care options and bureaucratic tangles during times of stress, design culture has an unprecedented opportunity to intervene and serve as advocates for people undergoing stressful times of illness and insecurity.

This chapter will begin by looking at the state of institutional health care spaces—from large metropolitan hospitals to

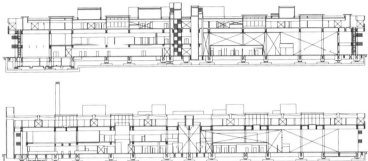

assisted-living centers, from outpatient centers to mobile health units—and will conclude by examining the nature of therapeutic spaces such as cosmetic surgery centers, apothecaries, spas, and health clubs. The ways in which design works to reduce qualms and promote confidence will be seen in light of the larger transition from an authoritarian modernism toward a pluralistic postmodernism, a transition paralleled by the contemporaneous shift from a closed, hierarchical culture of health experts to a more transparent culture of shared knowledge.

The Hospital

In antiquity, apart from shrines where supplicants prayed for health, few institutions existed to minister to the sick outside of the family.[2] One notable exception was the Roman military hospital. The impetus behind it, however, was purely pragmatic: the empire needed healthy soldiers to control its vast territories. The idea that the sick deserved care instead of expulsion from society first arose in the West in the fourth century AD, when Christianity became the official religion of the Roman Empire. Founded on the principles of both divine and human compassion, the church made the care of the elderly, poor, and sick central to its mission. Even though the well-being of the soul was always considered paramount to the needs of the body, over the centuries monasteries evolved into models of ministration and founded the earliest pharmacies. Secular health care institutions did not arise until the Middle Ages.

The earliest hospitals stressed care over cure, and valued prayer over prescriptives. It was not until the nineteenth century, when Louis Pasteur discovered the existence of

Ernst Giselbracht + Partner, Ear, Nose, and Throat Clinic, Graz Regional
Hospital, Graz, Austria, 2000

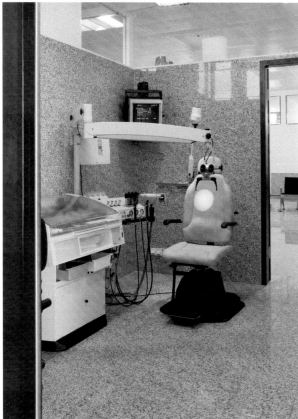

microorganisms, that the balance shifted toward matters of hygiene and medical intervention. It was also during this period that the less technical aspects of care–namely compassion and a healthful environment–were institutionalized in the reforms attributed to Florence Nightingale (1820–1910), who established nursing as an independent profession. Nightingale, horrified by the conditions endured by injured soldiers during the Crimean War, introduced new life-saving efficiencies, most famously the "Nightingale ward" system, which allowed nurses to supervise large numbers of patients. She also adamantly insisted that the less tangible benefits of natural light and personal attention were vital to recovery.

However, by the early twentieth century, as architecture critic Peter Blundell Jones has observed, "the hospital had become a bastion of scientific control, defending its occupants against the invasion and chaos of unreason and diseases … [and the] purity and abstraction of the Modernist architectural language became synonymous with health and hygiene."[3] Le Corbusier's famous Law of Ripolin (*ripolin* is the French word for whitewash), first pronounced in his 1923 book *Towards a New Architecture*, established modernist white not just as a stylistic preference but as a symbol of "inner cleanliness." The formal aesthetic of purity, in tandem with the rise of industrial design, proved an ideal complement to the mechanistic view of medicine and the rapid advances in medical equipment. In ensuing years, a narrow, misguided iteration of modernism became the architecture of choice in an increasingly cost-conscious health care industry. The first modernist principle to be sacrificed was the requirement of expansive views of nature; smaller windows were more energy-efficient, and as hospital wings grew ad hoc the absence of windows altogether was routinely accepted.

Humanistic models like Alvar Aalto's tuberculosis sanatorium (1928–33) in Paimio, Finland, with its patient-centered proportions and custom-designed furnishings, were (and frequently still are) deemed largely beyond the scope of budgetary considerations.[4] Only in recent years has a correlation been made between the quality of a facility's amenities and a patient's recovery time. Data now show that design in the spirit of Aalto–though not necessarily in the style of Aalto–can actually be cost-effective, reducing the length and expense of hospital stays.

Kada Wittfeld Architecture, Regional Hospital Hartberg, Hartberg,
Germany, 1999

By the late twentieth century, modernism had been so discredited (both by patients, who view it as hostile, and by practitioners, who reject its formal singularity) that hospitals, like shopping malls and housing developments, sought relief from its strictures in postmodern pastels and pediments. In the search for properties with the same recuperative properties Le Corbusier ascribed to white, designers embraced superficial signals of domesticity–framed posters and patterned rugs and curtains–that are only now being considered more holistically. Between the extremes of degraded late modernism and hyperbolic postmodernism, two dominant tendencies continue to prevail in thoughtfully designed hospitals–tendencies that are rooted in the conversation begun a century ago between the two camps of modernism: on the one hand, the rational, minimalist sensibility generally attributed to Le Corbusier, and, on the other, the warmer modulations associated with Aalto.

In their definitive book *Healthcare Architecture in an Era of Radical Transformation*, Stephen Verderber and David Fine succinctly outline the shortcomings of the cookie-cutter late-modernist hospital, citing, among other failings, the "adoption of the hermetically sealed building envelope, dependence on artificial lighting … [and the] rejection of courtyards and other green spaces for use by patients."[5] In Shiroishi City, Japan, Koh Kitayama's design for the Katta Public General Hospital (2003) reminds us that this litany of faults is not a reflection of modernism itself but, rather, an aberration of its original agenda. With a ribbon window that affords spectacular views of the mountains nearby and a rooftop garden designed as both a place to recuperate and a source of natural air and light for patient rooms, Kitayama rehabilitated the reputation of classical modernism with clarity and grace. Here are the pilotis, championed by Le Corbusier almost a century ago, rising like birches through the interior between strategically spaced oculi that bring light down to the lowest level. The pristine environment is ornamented only by its environmental signage: bright red characters chromatically telegraph the medical function of the building. Devoid of competing graphic clutter, the signage provides remarkably clear orientation–a necessity in spaces so uniformly white.

A competition to design the new addition to the Ear, Nose, and Throat Clinic (2002) in Graz, Austria, might easily have elicited a purely contextual response given its adjacency to the Regional Hospital of Graz, a historic structure designed between 1903 and 1912 by pupils of the pioneering Viennese architect Otto Wagner.[6] However, in awarding the commission to Ernst Giselbrecht, whose architecture practice is based in Graz, the hospital's administrators clearly opted to announce the new addition as a state-of-the-art resource and teaching facility that can stand alone among equals. The public spaces are a day-patient clinic and an emergency-services area on the ground floor of the three-story structure. Since this floor is fully glazed, the consulting rooms are masked from view by a lipstick-red partition wall, a surprising note of glamour in an otherwise minimal design. Not only do the patients inside the consulting rooms receive light and visual orientation through clerestory windows, but accompanying family and friends also have full views of the surrounding landscape and can enjoy a covered outdoor waiting area in warm weather. This being a teaching facility as well as a clinic, closed-circuit video systems were installed to transmit live images of operations to nearby classrooms. Considerable energy was invested in embedding and concealing the electronic networks to avoid the usual visual chaos of tangled cords and cables. As a result, the operating rooms are remarkably elegant. The visual and spatial clarity not only makes the environment easier for doctors to work in, but it also imparts confidence to patients.

Home to a number of notable contemporary buildings produced by its own architecture community, the town of Graz has become both a magnet and a catalyst for design innovation in health care, of which Giselbrecht's modest new addition to the Ear, Nose, and Throat Clinic is just one example. At the Graz West Regional Hospital (2002), Günther Domenig and Rupert Gruber, of the local firm Architecture Consult, have introduced an unusual dynamism into the genre of the multistory mega-hospital. The innovation is less in the patient rooms, which retain a reassuring equilibrium in their rectangular footprints, than in the circulation corridors. Wayfinding in large hospitals is often the bane of both patients and visitors, who are distracted by the cares of illness and recovery. Domenig addressed the problem with skewed, transparent walls that provide directional cues to the different treatment wings. In the atrium, a bright red sculpture signals the social center of the hospital, replete with the usual amenities of reception desk and cafeteria, as well as shopping facilities and a bank outlet.

Hartberg, a suburb of Graz, is the site of Klaus Kada's Regional Hospital (1999) and offers another example of how the vocabulary of pilotis, boxes, plinths, and planes has been given renewed purpose in the hospital setting. Here, the application of the modernist dictum to "bring the outdoors in" is not merely a formal counterpoint to the austerity of glass and concrete, but a central tenet to the program of healing. Studies have proven that the simple act of giving patients access to views of nature not only shortens postoperative stays, but also reduces the amount of medications they take.[7] In Hartberg, Kada not only provided a convalescence terrace, but also ensured that patients have the best views of the garden. Facing south and west, their rooms are shaded against glare by automatic solar blinds. Details such as the delicate horizontal stripes of the blinds are echoed throughout the building. The central hall is articulated by its slender steel structure, and animated by bridges that cross the four-story atrium. Each floor can also be accessed by a switchback staircase that lends further articulation to the hall. (Elevators, of course, are also available). By keeping the circulation routes so transparent, Kada gave visitors and patients a sense of vertical location that is often lost in a complex of this size.

The Rijnstate Hospital (1995) in Arnhem, The Netherlands, designed by Dutch architect Nijst Idema, provides a useful plot pivot in the narrative of the contemporary hospital. Idema is equally alert to the vital role of light, and to the concept of the central atrium as social hall, but the language he uses—an amalgam of modern abstraction and postmodern decoration—differs from that of the architects discussed above. Idema's is a disciplined synthesis, incorporating disarming touches of whimsy without sacrificing clarity. At the heart of the 750-bed hospital is an immense courtyard that rises eight stories under a glazed roof. Suspended in the light-filled galleria is a confetti-like sculpture that provides an aerial calligraphy above the reception and café spaces. The expanse is so large that a catwalk, paved with a lively graphic pattern, offers a diagonal shortcut across the indoor plaza to the patient areas. The rooms are equally engaging, with bright orange and turquoise furnishings. This is no

timid antidote to the institutional nature of health care, no pale cosmetic mask, but a clear assertion of the visceral effects of scale and color on the senses and the psyche.

As powerful as light, orientation, and sheer volume of space can be, other design factors are equally critical to the hospital experience. In 2002, architect and psychologist Bryan Lawson published in *The Architectural Review* a summary of research he had conducted for the British National Health Service.[8] In this article, he categorized two broad approaches to the design of health care spaces: The first considers the sensory experience of the patient (surface colors and room temperature, for example); the second focuses on relationships between people (that is, the desire for privacy or socializing). His studies at Poole Hospital NHS Trust and South Downs Health NHS Trust in Brighton, England, indicated that while designers care more about the first category, patients' priorities were weighted more toward the second. His conclusion was that designers should pay more attention to affording privacy, views (not just of nature but also of people interacting), and noise control. Visual appearance was not inconsequential, but among the patients Lawson polled, it ranked third after privacy and quiet. Few designers would disagree, and few would see a hospital's form and its program as anything but integral. But a designer's control over such desirables as single rooms and decentralized nursing stations is limited by a hospital's philosophy. Today, there is hardly a medical institution that doesn't advertise itself as patient-centered, but rare are those that employ design as a strategy to increase patient satisfaction.

In an initiative called the Pebble Project, begun in 2000, a small group of American hospitals has been working with the Center for Health Design in California to document the impact of design—spatial, experiential, and visual—on patient recovery, nursing turnover, and medication requirements. As its name suggests, the Pebble Project hopes to create a ripple effect, to encourage others in the industry to respond to and employ what they call evidence-based design.

One participant in the Pebble Project, Bronson Methodist Hospital in Kalamazoo, Michigan, designed by Shepley Bulfinch Richardson and Abbott of Boston in 2000, reports that it has reduced infections that originate or occur in the

hospital by 11 percent through such measures as better placement of sinks, more private rooms, and better airflow.[9] Methodist Hospital/Clarian Health Partners in Indianapolis reported that BSA LifeStructures' decentralized design of its cardiac care unit reduced patient falls by 75 percent by creating better sight lines for observation.[10] In these facilities, it is clear that priority has been given to Lawson's second principle: the social impact of design.

A parallel initiative in the UK called CABE Healthy Hospitals (CABE stands for Commission for Architecture and the Built Environment) has also launched a campaign to improve the quality of hospital care through design. Healthy Hospitals made the shrewd decision to partner with the Royal College of Nursing, knowing that nurses, perhaps even more than doctors, constantly see first-hand how the design of their working environment impacts staff and patients. In November 2003, CABE asked four teams of British architects and designers to propose designs that would challenge conventional thinking about hospital design. McDowell + Benedetti did away with the conventional waiting room and centered its concept around the idea of the town square alive with activity twenty-four hours a day. Fat and DEMOS proposed a loft hospital that included a demonstration kitchen where hospital nutritionists would lead cooking classes. Muf Architecture/Art and Rosetta Life brought a sense of immediacy to their scenario, proposing to offer patients oversize pillows when they check in; the pillows give off an electronic bleep when patients are called for their appointments. Jane

Darbyshire and David Kendall Limited, the most experienced in the health care field of the four teams, introduced an organic language into the genre, envisioning corridors that worked like "meandering streams" and beds set into curved alcoves.

It is undeniably true that, because these were speculative projects, the British designers were freer to pursue their ambitions than their American counterparts in the Pebble Project. They also had the distinct advantage of working within a much more deeply established tradition of subsidized public service, which has naturally created a more fertile environment for lively architecture and design within the health care field and social services generally. In the United States, by contrast, a consumerist model reigns; the more expensive a project, often, the more risk-averse the design. Large hospitals, being among the most costly of buildings, are no exception. Admittedly, hospitals have made advances in projecting a more friendly public face, but systematic analyses of patient experience such as the CABE Healthy Hospitals initiative are rare.

In the US, one of the most interesting contributions to the field has come from IDEO, an international industrial design, engineering, and consulting firm with deep experience in analyzing the social dimension of the products, places, and organizational structures that give shape to daily life. Best known for its work for Palm, Handspring, and Steelcase, IDEO merges first-hand anthropological research with the

design process of evaluation, negotiation, and form analysis to come up with proposals that are truly informed by lived experience. This multidisciplinary approach, coupled with IDEO's reputation for involving both its clients and its clients' clients in their working methodology, won the firm invitations to the Mayo Clinic (Rochester, Minnesota), DePaul Health Center (St. Louis), and Memorial Hospital & Health System (South Bend, Indiana), where they were commissioned to envision new ways of delivering care. In diagnosing the ills of the hospital, the designers of IDEO all but become patients themselves, tracking and analyzing the experience of patients and their families from admission to discharge. As *Metropolis* magazine reported:

> Nearly all of IDEO's suggestions … concentrate on making the patient's journey easier and more understandable; very few addressed medical equipment or architectural space. The proposals include adding monitors to the emergency room so patients can know where they rank on the waiting list; installing whole walls of dry-erase boards … so patients' relatives can turn them into huge get-well cards; keeping information booths staffed at all times … ; adding valet parking at emergency-room entrances; … and giving patients Velcro patches that tell hospital employees which phases of the treatment process they've already been through, in an effort to avoid repeated nerve-racking questions that suggest to patients that they're getting lost in the process.[11]

That IDEO's consulting work remains disconnected from actual interior design and architecture reflects the fact that mainstream American culture, by and large, still takes a puritanical view of aesthetics. Style and form are seen as separate from pragmatic considerations like orientation and safety, when in fact they are interdependent. The true challenge is to combine an understanding of the nuances and rhythms of hospital behaviors (how many times a patient is moved in the course of a stay, for example, or how far nurses have to walk to check on their patients) with design that integrates those concerns into a wholly considered environment. In the pursuit of a more humane aesthetic, however, there is the risk of falling prey to what Blundell Jones calls the "fourth-hand myth of domesticity"–that is, the hospital as a stage set that becomes a poor parody of home.[12]

While it is an axiom of contemporary culture that distinctions between the public and private realms–in this case hospital and home–are blurring, there is an argument to be made for developing a formal design language that doesn't erase the distinctions as much as bridge them. An early example of such an approach is Morphosis's design of the Comprehensive Cancer Center (1988), located within Cedars-Sinai Medical Center in Los Angeles. Light took on a particularly crucial role in the interior, given the center's underground location. The atrium and lobby, set 24 feet (almost 7.5 meters) below grade, are illuminated by a half-barrel skylight, giving visitors the perception of being at ground level. The focal point of the waiting area is a two-

Morphosis, Cedars-Sinai Comprehensive Cancer Center, Los Angeles, 1988

NBBJ, The Heart Center of Greater Cincinnati, Christ Hospital, Cincinnati, Ohio, 2004

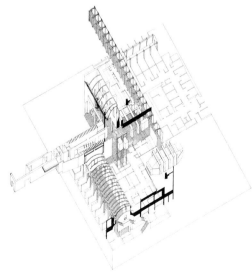

story sculpture out of which grows a living tree—a symbol of the architects' stated intention "to create a design strong enough not to condescend to patients, yet uplifting enough to reflect their courage in struggling to recover from their disease."[13]

In contrast to Morphosis, with its staff of twenty-eight, the sixty-year-old Seattle firm NBBJ is the third largest design practice in the United States and the fifth largest in the world. Often, as firms grow and mature, creativity is sacrificed for longevity, but with NBBJ the reverse is true, particularly in the realm of health care. As will be seen in the projects that follow, NBBJ has brought the same humanism and innovation to hospital design as to large technology companies like Telenor in Norway (see Offices, p. 128).

Despite their quilted bed covers, there is no mistaking the rooms at the Heart Center of Greater Cincinnati (2004) for suites in a hotel or a cozy bed and breakfast; the state-of-the-art hospital beds give the rooms away. Yet, the spacious singles in this new addition to Christ Hospital exude an

unusual degree of calm and graciousness—just one aspect of an overall design intended to reduce stress, a crucial mission in an institution dedicated to cardiac care. Screens and warm wood panels create separate workspaces for caregivers, and minimize the patient's exposure to clinical items like monitors and charts. Couches, writing desks, and Internet-ready computer shelves bring the activities of daily life into an arena where they so often seem suspended. Though these amenities are intended to convey the message that illness is temporary and the patient is still vital, it is nonetheless ironic that the Heart Center's interiors resemble corporate office suites in a context that calls for rest. It is a reflection of the tremendous social value placed on work, even the mere perception of it. Indeed, this ethic has become so codified that a new genre of hospital interiors has emerged: "executive style."[14] The inference of the designation is that the office is, indeed, home to many of these patients.

As important as such visual semantics may be in ameliorating the patients' experience, the factors of time and space are arguably the most critical to safety in the hospital.

Efficiencies in the conduct of procedures and the delivery of patient care are also easier to measure. At Christ Hospital's Heart Center, NBBJ's space planning works in tandem with the décor and amenities to create an overall feeling of tranquility. The distances doctors and patients have to travel between procedures have been shortened by the clustering of the intensive care units and the consolidation of four floors of cardiological and cardiovascular services onto just two levels, significantly reducing the number and length of trips for at-risk patients and their doctors. Ambulatory patients, connected to the staff by monitoring equipment that works outdoors, can enjoy a rooftop garden overlooking the Ohio River.

The regional context for NBBJ's next health care project, the Banner Estrella Medical Center (2005) in Phoenix, Arizona, could not be more different. Banner Estrella was conceived as a healing oasis in the urban desert. The 450,000-square-foot (41,800-square-meter) center's uncomplicated tectonic forms pick up the colors and the light of the landscape, and are textured to capture shadows over the course of the day, to help maintain patients' circadian rhythms. Three critical precepts of forward-thinking hospital practice—private patient rooms, decentralized nursing stations, and coordinated physician services—have been incorporated into the spatial principles that define Banner Estrella. (Every one of the hospital's 172 rooms is single-occupancy.) And because information technology has untethered nurses from their stations, the designers were able to eliminate the traditional hubs and replace them with what they term "a clinical integration suite" that disperses nursing functions, bringing caregivers closer to their patients. By contrast, surgery, cardiology, and imaging services were brought together in a single core, facilitating better communication among staff and yielding better operational results. This "interventional services suite" ensures that coordinated care—so often lacking in large institutions of this nature—is not a luxury but part of every patient's experience.

Much is made of patients' need for daylight, but little is written about the effect of light deprivation on physicians, nurses, and staff, who work notoriously long hours and often have no sense of day or night. Recognizing this deficit and the toll it takes, NBBJ, in collaboration with Rick Keating of Keating/Khang Architecture, designed the Surgery Pavilion of the University of Washington (2003), in Seattle, so that daylight reaches every primary circulation corridor, even those underground, through a system of sloping planes and skylights. Similarly, the circulation corridors themselves, torturous in most facilities, were greatly simplified to reduce fatigue. Finally, as if to emphasize the restorative properties of growth and greenery, a glazed wall leans out toward a newly landscaped glade.

Children's and Maternity Hospitals

When a hospital is identified by the patients it serves—whether women, children, or the elderly—its design inevitably takes on the cultural narratives associated with that population. The selective examples that follow show responses ranging from the abstract to the literal. Both approaches employ strategies to make the hospital less formidable and alienating. And both would argue that just as an injection hurts less if the muscles are relaxed, the entire experience of in-patient care is bound to be less stressful if apprehensions are reduced as soon as the patient walks in the door. Children are especially susceptible to fear of the unknown; they not only have to cope with a less than complete understanding of their medical condition, but also with separation from many of the people and daily routines that make them feel safe. (Though it is now virtually an axiom of pediatric care that parents accompany their children during most of their treatment, including overnight stays, this was not the case until relatively recently.[15]) And while it is true that illness has a regressive effect on virtually every patient, regardless of age, there is no question that society recognizes the vulnerability of the child differently. How best to protect the child's interests—including optimizing treatment and reducing recovery time—becomes the central question for designers.

Rafael Moneo's design for Madrid's Gregorio Marañón Maternity and Pediatric Hospital (2003) clearly signals his belief that infants need not be introduced to the world in an infantilizing environment surrounded by cartoon characters and saccharin colors. Moreover, his design emphasizes that pregnancy is not a disease but a human condition. Here, residential references are subtle and largely tectonic—from the interior courtyard, the defining feature of a traditional Spanish house, to the use of maple louvered shutters in the patient rooms. The primary consideration of both the archi-

tects and the doctors in this remarkable public hospital, however, was to create not a facsimile of the home, but rather a clean and bright space that, according to Moneo, "embodied the logic expected of science by the patients and their families."[16]

Patients' rooms all look out onto the courtyard, but never onto each other. Inside each room, the windows are framed by walls painted in colors that are neither timid nor cheerfully garish, and are offset by bright white adjacent walls and ceiling. The ample, door-size windows are operable and are made of a distinctive pearly glass. This domestically scaled fenestration is subtly insinuated into the five-story facade, and it admits fresh air when desired but also effectively seals out the cold when the temperature drops. Instead of subjecting patients to bland images intended to soothe, Moneo gives them control of their own environment—over light, noise, and privacy, all highly ranked factors in patient-satisfaction studies. At the behest of the client, Moneo also designed seventeen furnishings for the hospital, including the cabinetry, meeting tables, reception seating, a rocking armchair, night tables, and even meal trays—a dramatic expansion of the usual parameters given to designers of hospital environments. With its emphasis on calm and rationality, Moneo's design convoys to mothers and their families the reassuring authority of medical expertise at one of the most vital moments of life—childbirth. The fact that it does so without resorting to distracting artifice, placing its faith in the healing abstractions of light, color, and order, separates the Madrid hospital from the majority of obstetric and pediatric facilities, where a more populist ethos reigns.

In the US, where outright skepticism of authority is all but
institutionalized, growing numbers of hospitals are searching
for ways to promote a sense of active participation among
patients in their own care–even when those patients are
children. Consider, for example, the admissions area at the
University of California San Francisco's Pediatrics Clinic
Ambulatory Care Center (2001), designed by Anshen + Allen:
One check-in desk stands at the customary height, but another
has been designed lower for children, so they, too, can feel
part of the admissions process, the first step of any hospital
visit. The reception area is just one feature of a complete
second-floor renovation in a state-of-the-art outpatient
children's health center designed to serve 50,000 patients
a year. To break the institutional monotony, the designers
eschewed the typical coloring-book-style wall decorations
in favor of variations in surface materials, from wood
paneling to plaster to etched Corian. Instead of mimicking
children's art, the architects created a space for them to
make their own, with floor-to-ceiling blackboards for artists
of all heights.

In contrast to the approaches taken by Anshen + Allen and
Moneo, who both employ a modulated minimalism to calm
and reassure new parents and the youngest of patients, the
New York-based architect David Rockwell entered the field
with a completely different perspective. Rockwell's extroverted style of patient-friendly design flows intuitively
from his personal and professional history as an entertainer.
He grew up in a theatrical family and has made a career
of inventing fictional and fantastical spaces, from Broadway
stage sets to casinos and restaurants. Like the magician who
never fully reveals the secrets to his art, Rockwell entertains
his audiences with fragments and clues to a story that trans-
late into an aesthetic of collage. This idea of discovery–in
both visual surprises and narrative elements–is the leitmotif
of Rockwell's design for the Montefiore Children's Hospital
(2001) in The Bronx, New York. Rockwell took much of his
inspiration for this design from the teachings of the late
astronomer and scientist Carl Sagan, who believed that great
comfort was to be found in finding connections with the
cosmos. In the lobby, which resembles a museum of natural
history more than a hospital, parents and children are greeted
by a domed planetarium, interactive maps, a Milky Way
mural, and a Foucault pendulum designed by Tom Otterness
that tracks the rotation of the earth. Instead of mindless

distractions, these lively elements offer the pleasures of stimulation. What might be overly didactic in other hands is smart and playful in Rockwell's. In the words of Pentagram designer Michael Bierut, "Rockwell Group's work for Montefiore makes a memorable event out of an experience that many of its guests would probably like to forget."[17]

Mental Health Centers

The social stigma once attached to illness is a fading memory at the beginning of the twenty-first century. Medical psychology has brought a gratifying, holistic perspective to the clinical environment at large. Still largely the exception, however, is the psychiatric institution, which continues to be haunted by the image of the Victorian prison-madhouse. The role of design in rehabilitating this genre is still in its nascent stages, but a few noteworthy instances stand as models of change.

The Dutch firm Mecanoo has deployed the strategy of separate houses or domiciles within a single complex in its Emergis Centre for Psychiatric Health Care (2001) in Goes, The Netherlands. The institution includes two units for patients with differing needs: One building houses the Centre for Geriatric Psychiatry and is designed to accommodate twenty-eight in-patients; the other building houses the long-term Residential Care facility, which houses up to forty-two elderly patients. The design of both buildings was inspired by the local vernacular, and was based on a traditional monastic typology. The architects demonstrated their sensitivity to the two different patient populations' unique needs (the in-patients, for instance, are more mobile than the full-time residents, whose conditions tend to be more intractable) by making the plan of the Geriatric Psychiatry building the reverse of the plan for the Residential Care facility. Since the center's permanent

Mecanoo Architects, Emergis Centre for Psychiatric Health Care, Goes,
The Netherlands, 2001

residents have a need for peace and quiet, their communal living areas are oriented toward the inner garden courtyard. And because the Geriatric Psychiatry patients have a greater need for contact with the outside world, their communal living rooms look outward via large glass fronts onto the orchards and gardens of the Zeeland landscape. Both buildings have austere, robust exteriors and warm, intimate interiors with ample color and light shed from skylights and reflected off slanted ceilings.

The Emergis Centre is just one example of the greater level of attention being given to geriatric psychiatry—long thought pointless and a wasteful use of resources—by medical communities around the globe. New knowledge about the biology of the brain, as well as new breakthroughs in psychopharmacology, have reinvigorated the medical study of aging and changed social attitudes in the process. While aging in and of itself is no more a disease than pregnancy, it is now an accepted fact that depression often accompanies the normal decline of the body. Recognizing the interrelated nature of age-related disabilities and their effect on mental health, Our Lady's Hospital in Cashel, Ireland, built a complex of new buildings (2004) on a six-and-a-half-acre site for a range of residential and outpatient facilities for the elderly, mentally ill, and physically disabled. Here, the London-based firm Avanti Architects employed a crisp interior vocabulary with Mondrian-like planes of color announcing the end of a hallway or the beginning of the reception area. The coherence of the design contributes handsomely to an environment intended to mitigate the confusions of its patients. Painted black, otherwise ordinary details like handrails, doorframes, and window mullions impart a self-assured compositional framework to sparkling white corridors, which are punctuated by clerestory windows throughout.

Elder Care

It is only relatively recently that the term "assisted living"—which denotes a private living environment for seniors in a group setting that also offers medical support—entered the parlance of health care. According to the US-based Consumer Consortium on Assisted Living,

> The assisted living industry evolved over the past two decades ... rapidly becoming an attractive alternative to nursing homes. There are approximately 1,000,000 older

adults and individuals with disabilities residing in assisted living nationwide. The average assisted living resident is 83 years old and in need of assistance with at least one activity of daily living. An estimated 50 percent of residents have some form of memory impairment.[18]

What has now become an "industry" in America was actually pioneered in The Netherlands. The country's tradition of progressive social services proved an ideal incubator for the altruistic ambitions of the architect Herman Hertzberger. Hertzberger adheres to a Structuralist philosophy of "spatial possibility" that actively encourages a building's residents to influence its design and, by extension, maintain some semblance of control over their lives.[19] His De Overloop Residence (1984) in Almere-Haven is a landmark in elder care design, both in the humility of its aesthetic and in its integration of multiple social services for an aging population. Situated in the town center, De Overloop is itself a microcosm of urban energy, belying the notion that aging requires constant rest and removal from the daily hustle and bustle of city life. Accordingly, windows look out either onto the city itself or onto the social activities in the courtyard.

Stephen Verderber has observed that Hertzberger's design is a conscious attempt "to avoid both an institutional look and a literally home-like one."[20] It might also be said that, with the use of white concrete block in the interior corridors and common social spaces, he accomplishes that feat by conflating both genres. Even more telling are photographs that document this project; they are always populated with residents and strewn with plants and personal effects. Indeed, the spaces at De Overloop were conceived to incorporate evidence of the residents' individual taste. They were also designed to give nurses closer contact with patients. Both strategies work together to support the core principle of De Overloop's program: the elimination of loneliness.

Two members of a younger generation in Holland took an entirely different approach—one honed in the field of product design—to creating a stimulating environment for elder care. In contrast to Hertzberger, whose aesthetic of the incomplete allowed patients to fill the void of decoration themselves, Hella Jongerius, working in collaboration with Jurgen Bey, opted for interactivity in designing the interior of Het Schild (2002), an institute for blind and visually impaired senior

citizens in Wolfheze, The Netherlands. Working from the understanding that Het Schild is a place for family and staff as well as patients, the designers crafted spaces to capture the attention and interest of the full spectrum of the population: blind and sighted, old and young. Jongerius and Bey, both known for their involvement with the Droog design movement, leveraged wit and emotional intelligence to contradict the stereotypes of deprivation attached to the condition of blindness. The designers not only dispelled anxiety by removing any potentially dangerous physical obstacles from the living and circulation areas, but have also relieved boredom by inserting gentle distractions. An ordinary walk through the halls offers, in the words of Jongerius, "a surprise, something that did not happen the last time or something you haven't noticed earlier."[21] In the lobby, visitors encounter a giant dog made of soft, squeezable artificial clay. Elsewhere, they discover walls embellished with chameleon-like "flowers"—rounded, raised forms—that respond to temperature; when it warms up outside, an icy halo forms around the flowers indoors. When it gets cold outside, infrared lamps warm the chilly hallway. Another passageway features moveable magnetic disks that create pixilated images of tulips. Even the most functional—and indispensable—

elements take on new properties. A handrail, for example, doubles as a radio receiver that serendipitously picks up broadcasts from around the world; at different points along their route, patients can find themselves listening to an opera being performed in Hong Kong or to a sound bite from a CNN reporter at the White House. Such auditory and tactile devices offer reassurance of another order—namely, that the loss of sight is not the end of exploration.

Flora of a more literal sort—those tokens of sentiment ubiquitous in health care environments—also make an unusual appearance at the Dornach-Auhof Center for Senior Citizens (1999) in Linz, Austria. A glamorous wallpaper motif—pink on the second floor, yellow on the third—consisting of giant photographs of roses by artist Rudi Molacek is a refreshingly diplomatic way-finding device for both visitors and those who make the center their home. This gracious graphic gesture is just one mark of architect Helmut Christen's attention to orientation in the new building—a particularly acute concern for residents adjusting to new circumstances. To that end, the architect said he deliberately designed the interiors to create "ambiguous boundaries between care and home."[22] Each room has a living area, oriented toward the communal hall, and a sleeping area, which opens onto a private exterior veranda. The flexible layout allows even bedridden residents the choice of orienting themselves toward the center's public or private spaces–a reflection of Christen's contention that "the capability of secluding is a prerequisite for the willingness to take part in social life."[23] For those who do want company, there is no shortage of places to find it. A library, a hair salon, a chapel, a gymnasium, and a variety of gathering places are aligned along an interior street flooded with light by a glazed sawtooth roof. Beyond providing a generous range of services, the indoor avenue provides an animated exercise route when weather precludes walks in the center's park and garden.

Clinics and Doctors Offices

Just as patients are more likely to receive personalized care in intimate settings, designers tend to have more freedom when operating on a smaller scale. Clinics and specialized institutes may have smaller budgets, but they often offer more latitude for expression. In private clinics, designers are perhaps better able to respond to the patient experience more explicitly. For instance, Brazilian architect Angelo Bucci's firm SPBR Architects designed a psychology clinic (1998) on the outskirts of São Paulo that combines the region's modernist concrete and glass architecture tradition with sensitivity to the patients' desire for privacy. Hybrid indoor-outdoor breezeways leading to the clinic's consultation rooms are shielded from view by a double layer of wooden screening. Jacques Herzog and Pierre de Meuron's design for REHAB Basel, Centre for Spinal Cord and Brain Injuries (2002) in Basel, Switzerland, responds to patient needs on a larger and more complex scale. Their design demonstrates an exquisite sensitivity to the needs of paralyzed and brain-damaged patients, one that also integrates several architectural epiphanies into their treatment.

Two seemingly contradictory design dialects (planar and spherical) and two seemingly incompatible materials (rubber and wood) come together to improve the patient experience. The wood lathe of the brise-soleil gives the first indication that this is a design infused by the mythical, restorative properties of the primal forest–an impression carried through in the planks of the floors and ceilings and the courtyard garden planted with birch trees. Only the slightly foreign note of the Plexiglas dowels in the sun blinds

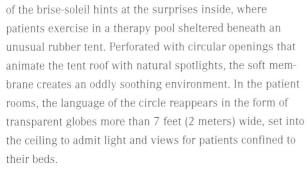

of the brise-soleil hints at the surprises inside, where patients exercise in a therapy pool sheltered beneath an unusual rubber tent. Perforated with circular openings that animate the tent roof with natural spotlights, the soft membrane creates an oddly soothing environment. In the patient rooms, the language of the circle reappears in the form of transparent globes more than 7 feet (2 meters) wide, set into the ceiling to admit light and views for patients confined to their beds.

It may not be surprising to see such considered, sensitive design lavished on residential, long-term care facilities, but it is more unusual to see it in clinics and doctors' offices—the transitory spaces of consultation. Certainly visitors to these places are just as likely to feel the same anxieties and exhibit the same environmental sensitivities as long-term hospital patients. The clinic is the first point of contact with doctors, and often the beginning of a medical odyssey. Guy Greenfield's design for the Hammersmith Bridge Road Surgery (2000) in London, winner of a RIBA (Royal Institute of British Architects) Award in 2001, is that rare doctor's office matching medical acumen with architectural invention—an event all the more remarkable considering the modest government subsidy that underwrote the project. The office's

arcing white walls peel away from each other to admit natural light to the corridors serving the medical rooms. The RIBA judges took special note of this feature, commenting that "corridors, which are so often the most disheartening moments in such buildings … are here genuinely life affirming as they shape the light and allow limited glimpses out."[24] Oddly, they did not note that the office's layered, curved walls also bear an uncanny resemblance to Richard Meier's Jubilee Church in Rome (see Religious, p. 247). If Greenfield did consciously (or unconsciously) use Meier's design as a model, he could not have chosen a better one. For a sense of the spiritual is not at all out of place in the context of care— nor are the ineffable qualities of light and air, here generously supplied to the waiting room and all the consulting rooms by a glazed interior courtyard.

Among clinics, those dedicated to reproductive medicine are perhaps the most freighted with controversy. In societies of affluence, medical advances (such as artificial insemination) and changes in mores (indicated by choices such as the practice of surrogate motherhood) have now all but eliminated infertility as an obstacle to conception. At the same time, in an ethical climate in which women increasingly retain control over their bodies, family planning and abortion have become legitimate, if highly contested, options. Concomitantly, new understandings of the physical and social development of newborns and young children have led to major advances in neonatal and pediatric care. With each of these cultural shifts have come parallel advances in design, leading to new kinds of interior environments that reflect and sometimes advance the values of feminism, education, and social justice.

Buschow Henley's design for the Centre for Reproductive Medicine (2002) in London imparts a distinctly feminine atmosphere to an environment intended to serve women struggling with infertility. Knowing that most patients must make multiple visits during the course of their treatment, principal Simon Henley mitigated the inevitable monotony of the clinical experience by creating a warm ambience. Elegant white drapes filter light from the exterior windows, offering patients privacy not from each other but from the

Below and overleaf: Herzog & de Meuron, REHAB Basel, Centre for Spinal
Cord and Brain Injuries, Basel, Switzerland, 2002

Guy Greenfield Architects, Hammersmith Bridge Road Surgery, London, 2000

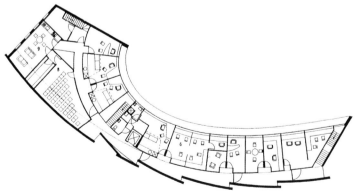

street—and, in the process, reprise the domestic nature
of the patient's modesty curtain. By wrapping the fabric
around structural piers, a gentle curvature is created on
one side of the corridor, offset by a vertically timbered
wall on the other. These considerations are not merely
cosmetic. Like a doctor with a good bedside manner,
Buschow Henley's design purportedly helps to relieve
patients' tensions in this clinic that reports above-average
fertility rates.[25]

When it comes to family planning facilities and clinics
that offer abortions, care providers and designers alike must
often address patient stress of a different order to create
environments in which both visitors and staff can feel not
only relaxed but also physically secure. In 1995, after a rash
of violent incidents at abortion clinics around the US, designer
Anne Fougeron decided to offer her services pro bono
to Planned Parenthood in San Francisco. The organization
availed itself of Fougeron's offer and ultimately commissioned
her to design its Eddy Street office (2001), which would
house Planned Parenthood's administrators and call-center
counselors, who often provide the initial phase of treatment,
namely someone to talk to. Fougeron's first task was to convince the organization that building a fortress was not in its
best interests. Strength and warmth are the leitmotif of the
design, which uses a steel framework to outline office bays
and semi-transparent wood-slat partitions to screen them.
By combining finely detailed craftsmanship with a modernist
sensibility, Fougeron invested an otherwise conventional,
low-ceilinged office floor with a progressive sense of humanity
commensurate with its tenant's mission.

Planned Parenthood was so convinced by the results at the
Eddy Street office that it designated Fougeron the organization's affiliate architect.[26] Three years later, in 2004, the
MacArthur Clinic, also designed by Fougeron, opened in
Oakland, California. To meet continuing security concerns
without conveying a siege mentality, Fougeron integrated
protective measures so seamlessly as to make them invisible.
What stands out instead is the architect's savvy use of light.
In lieu of exterior windows—a security risk—she pulled light
into the clinic from an interior courtyard centered on an
olive tree, symbolic of peace. Skylights flood the interiors
with natural light that, refracted off the building's richly
painted roofs, colors the walls with varying intensity

throughout the day. The clinic's cork floors and rice paper laminate and frosted glass walls are framed by Fougeron's signature steel bands, which orchestrate the entire composition. The sturdy, geometric armatures implicitly declare that no one here, least of all the architect, will stand for being bullied. Just as noteworthy, if not equally righteous, is the fact that an organization providing low-cost women's health care is also able to provide its patients with the highest caliber of design.

Fougeron's work in the field of women's health care also includes the obstetrics floor at the University of California Davis Medical Center (2002). In contrast to the Planned Parenthood project, which presented predictable budgetary constraints, this commission offered Fougeron (working in association with fellow San Franciscans Anshen + Allen) the largess of a well-endowed major institution and the mandate to create a luxurious, discrete haven within it. A polished tone of restrained luxury is announced by eucalyptus veneer and terrazzo floors in the lobby, a tone that is extended to the more workaday spaces of the maternity ward itself. Fougeron surfaced workstations in bronze and marble and included considerate touches like cork floors to soften the steps of overworked staff and expectant hallway pacers. The labor and delivery rooms are especially interesting, as much for what has been edited as for what is present. Instead of the frills and faux-homespun touches that smother so many birthing rooms with well-intentioned sentiment, Fougeron introduced furnishings that recognize mothers as adults. Different color schemes respond to each room's solar orientation: warmer tones in the north-facing rooms, cooler tones in those facing east. The result is a dignified alternative to the claustrophobia of overweening design.

Such knowledge and access to resources cannot be taken for granted in poorer communities, however—a fact recognized by the British government when it launched Sure Start, a health support program for babies and toddlers and those who care for them. Muf Architecture/Art–an all-woman practice specializing in public projects like CABE Healthy Hospitals, discussed earlier in this chapter—was commissioned to design a Sure Start space in the Ocean Estate housing project in the Sussex town of Stepney.

Sure Start on the Ocean (2000) is one space with two functions.
By virtue of a sliding door, a folding tabletop, and a hinged
toy cupboard, a playroom designed for children under four
also becomes a boardroom for Sure Start's administration
and vice-versa, squeezing a dual program into less than
1,000 square feet. It is the softer amenities and the social
intelligence of the project, however, that make it so noteworthy.
Placing cultural literacy over institutional jargon, the architects screened the storefront window with a curtain of gold
lettering in Bengali and English the dominant languages of
the housing project's residents. Inside, a rug with a padded
relief of hills and lakes, sound-absorbent cork floors, and
window seats upholstered in pink corduroy and wired for
telephones and computers are provided for the comfort and
convenience of staff and families who come to the center
to avail themselves of Sure Start's social services. Muf has
made an art of working directly with communities, listening
and proposing solutions, but always with a keen awareness
of the moment when, in the partners' words, "consultation
fatigue sets in and no one wants to be asked their opinions."[27]
Only then do the designers take the lead in shaping the
space, informed intuitively but not prescriptively by their

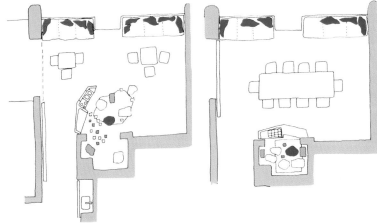

user research. It is this process (which never reduces the designer to the role of focus-group scribe) that accounts for the refreshing directness of Muf's work, allowing the group to integrate popular and decorative references in ways that are light years ahead of the commercialized juvenilia reflexively used in similar settings.

In a similar spirit, the Dutch duo of Marleen Kaptein and Stijn Roodnat designed a children's clinic in Upper Manhattan that is part jungle gym, part funhouse. Pediatrics 2000 (2004) is sweetly eccentric but deeply sophisticated in its playfulness. Its reception desk is made of polyester blocks left over from the SoHo Prada store designed by Rem Koolhaas (see Retail, p. 356). Designed in collaboration with another Dutch designer, Vincent de Rijk, the blocks, when lit from behind, transform themselves into a light wall. Recognizing that waiting is often the worst part of a doctor's visit, particularly for the very young and restless, Kaptein

and Roodnat adapted the two-story storefront facade to create a playhouse. A two-story window offers views of the street and also serves as the armature for a giant climbing net that children can scale and slide down. When finally called, instead of going to a doctor's office, the patient goes to a Dino Room or an Aquarium Room or a Letter Room. These camouflaged examination rooms, named by the New York graffiti artists who painted them, feature murals in screaming bright colors drawn from the immediate neighborhood.

While Muf and Kaptein Roodnat bring a playful spirit to socially conscious health care design, the Dutch firm Atelier van Lieshout is militantly aggressive in its political and social ambitions. Considered a controversial figure for his anarchist design philosophy, Joep van Lieshout runs his art and design practice (founded in 1995) from a studio compound in Rotterdam's harbor district that he has declared

simple, direct design approach would be a genuine asset in soothing patients' fears. She was confident that he would create what she called "a friendly and comfortable space."[28] And, in fact, once the patient is inside the clinic's rough corrugated shell, she finds herself in a crisply delineated white envelope with state-of-the-art equipment and a couch to rest on during recovery.

The Wellness Culture

In the field of health care, the idea that the mind and the body are wholly separate entities requiring separate treatment has long since collapsed under the weight of evidence to the contrary. Over the course of the twentieth century—the century of both Sigmund Freud and Watson and Crick—our understanding of illness was completely redefined, on one hand, by advances in psychology, and on the other, by the unraveling of genetic code. Feeling emotionally and mentally balanced is now understood to be integral to feeling and being physically healthy. This more holistic view of illness and wellness has spawned a host of disparate niche therapies. Medical specialties once at the margin of health care, like plastic surgery, have been given new therapeutic legitimacy in affluent societies in which outward appearance is considered an index of success and looking good is considered essential to feeling good.

a "free state." Working in the context of a busy, international shipping port, van Lieshout was one of the first designers to reclaim the shipping container as a tool of guerrilla architecture, converting one in 1998 into a mobile field hospital to be used in the event of wars or emergencies—the first installment in what he called his A-Portable projects. In 2001, he added another care facility to the series, this time for an activist group called Women on Waves, which operates a shipboard women's clinic that sails to countries where abortion is illegal with the mission of providing women in these countries with safe abortions. The medical facilities themselves are housed in van Lieshout's "A-Portable 2001" converted shipping container, which sits on deck. Dr. Rebecca Gomperts, director of Women on Waves, shares van Lieshout's transgressive instincts; she and her colleagues risk crossing legal, medical, and navigational territories to reach the women they serve. Beyond recognizing their similar political affinities, Gomperts believed that van Lieshout's

Today, plastic surgery is less associated with the correction of birth defects and physical deformities than it is with attempts to reverse or forestall the aging process. Furthermore, there is a new comfort with body alteration not only because advances in medical technology have made organ transplants, skin grafts, and bone reconstruction possible, but also because the same advances offer the implicit assurance that patients can change their minds, whether by removing an unwanted tattoo or reversing a breast enlargement. While resorting to surgery for purely cosmetic reasons might still be considered radically invasive, such exorcisms of mortality are hardly new. They are but latter-day initiations into the ancient cults of youth and beauty. The architects Walter Camagna, Massimiliano Camoletto, and Andrea Marcante, of the Turin firm UdA/Ufficio di Architettura, paid a discreet homage to this historical legacy when they designed the CIEG Medica, Plastic Surgery Centre in Rome (1999). The team tacitly drew upon the architecture of the Eternal City as a foil for its explicitly contemporary interior and the

transformative procedures that take place there. The architects describe their program in just such terms, philosophically stating that their objective is to represent "the new dimension of mankind in the third millennium suspended between ... immateriality and corporeality and coexisting in different parallel worlds: history and the moment ... memory and oblivion."[29]

Located between Piazza di Spagna and Piazza del Populo in the baroque heart of the city, the center's Zen-like spaces, with soothing images of bamboo groves screened on backlit glass walls, are a world away from the tourist-thronged streets around them. The luminous green fronds of the bamboo are just one element in an architectural panorama created by the circular arrangement of introverted spaces. Throughout the space, natural and artificial light bounces off high-gloss white surfaces, opaline glass, and stainless steel, attenuating the shadows of moving figures and subtly underscoring the center's raison d'être—the limitless mutability of the body.

In Taipei, the UK-based designer Michael Young also used the illusion of transparency instead of actual windows to create a sheltered but luminous atmosphere for Dr. James' Cosmetic Surgery Clinic (2005). Backlit wall panels printed with geometric patterns designed by Young's wife, Katrin, create a feminine enclosure, transforming the clinic into a lacy boudoir. The gently pulsing positive and negative silhouettes of the print take on new subtlety when their reflections merge with the delicate pattern of the glass floors. (The floors were printed using a novel technique developed by Young and Dupont Corian that employs film used to tint car windscreens.) Limited-edition chairs, commissioned from Cappellini and Poltrona Frau in white leather and polyurethane, provide svelte lines to complement an environment that prides itself on its high-tech handicraft.

Another dimension of today's wellness culture can be seen in pharmacies that have augmented their services as resources not merely for medications but also as places of education. The De Lairesse Pharmacy (2002) in Amsterdam, a project by the Dutch firm Concrete Architectural Associates, is gregarious in spirit and design. For her shop, which specializes in homeopathic medicine, pharmacist Marjan Terpstra rejected the model of the clinic in favor of

but tightly branded experience in and around them. Visitors to the spa are not mere "bathers," but "guests," as at a full-service hotel. Of course the presence of water in this desert environment is a purely artificial conceit, not a natural phenomenon. A postmodern spa of the imagination, the Bathhouse is perfectly at home among the other fantasy environments around it; it reflects the wholesale inversion of our relationship to nature. No longer a destination (regardless of the semantics of the spa industry), nature is now imported to the client.

Nowhere is this approach more evident than in the urban day spa. At Bliss 57 (1999), designed by Richardson Sadeki, wild turkey feathers float in transparent glass scrims. And at Bliss's flagship SoHo branch (1996), also by Richardson Sadecki, trademark blue furnishings and a soothing ambiance create a sense of refuge. Here, however, one small gesture breaks the new-age spell and reminds patrons of where they really are: The walls of the women's steam shower are tiled like a New York subway station, complete with a sign for Prince Street and Broadway, the location of the spa—a conceit based on the playful presumption that Bliss's more-jaded downtown clients might get a thrill from the idea of walking naked in public.

While privacy was not a real concern at Bliss SoHo, which is safely ensconced on the second floor of a loft building, it was a major determinant in the design of Qiora (2000), a street-level spa on Madison Avenue. Designers Stephen Cassell and Adam Yarinsky of ARO/Architecture Research Office devised a solution to the problem of street exposure that, paradoxically, revolves around light. The defining feature of the flagship store and spa is a soft interior architecture of translucent curtains (designed by the late Mary Bright) that enabled the designers to leave the large windows of the twenty-foot-high space open to receive natural light. Curving "walls" of aquamarine organza hang from the ceiling with no visible supporting elements, seeming to hover above the seamless white epoxy floor. The fabric panels continually reconfigure collages of color and light, while giving clients the pleasant sensation of being inside the folds of an ethereal garment as they move through the space. Where true privacy is required—namely, in the massage cabins and showers—the curtains are lined with Ultrasuede. Fabric is also used to diffuse the fluorescent lighting on the perimeter of the space,

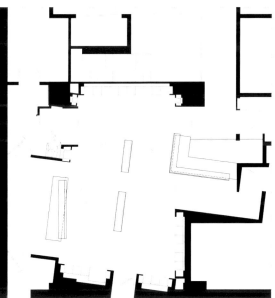

ARO/Architecture Research Office, Qiora Store and Spa, New York, 2000

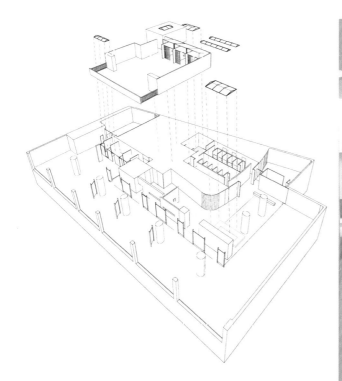

eliminating the need for distracting fixtures. A dimming system modulates the light between warm and cool shades to simulate daylight and maximize skin glow. The luminous minimalism also highlights the display of spa products, which are lit by fiber optics. Illuminated with white light during the day and blue light at night, the displays offer a subliminal reminder of the diurnal cycles that the modern metropolis has all but erased.

Just as the spa has become synonymous with healthful well-being, the gym is in the process of shedding its pugilistic past for a more sybaritic identity. Once a thoroughly male dominion associated with sports like wrestling, fencing, and boxing, the gym has morphed into the co-ed health club, and the health club into the fitness-nutrition center. But for all that the new workout centers are beginning to incorporate spa-like amenities, they fill a completely different function. Most significantly, they are used on a much more frequent basis and by a broader cross-section of the population. (In this respect, today's gym is closer to the ancient Roman baths and *gymnasia* and to traditional Japanese pools, where exercise was, and is, considered integral to daily life.)

Recognizing the particular social life of gyms—equally solitary and communal—was the key to the design of the Lower Manhattan health club Clay (2002), where Brent Capron of the New York office of STUDIOS Architecture struck a balance between the serious and the sensual. Designed to enhance concentration, exercise areas are free of distractions like loud music and bright color; instead they offer views of the treetops outside the second-floor windows. Departing from the conventional chromatic spectrum of black to gray, Capron specified a rubber exercise floor the color of tea leaves, as well as ebonized-cherry towel holders and faux-calfskin upholstery for the weight machines, benches, and Pilates equipment. Even the lockers, made of interlocking wood panels, are treated as a significant visual element. Nothing is lost or unconsidered, not even the transitional spaces. In view of the fact that most conversations in the gym occur between workout activities, Capron situated a sky-lit conversation pit and a synthetic-stone fireplace between the cardio equipment and weight training areas. These gathering places afford the club's members a different kind of stimulation: that of each other's company.

In Japan, where massage remains an intrinsic part of health and fitness culture, the Japanese chain Natural Body has, with an unprecedented level of invention, elevated the massage salon into a viable, independent fitness niche. In his design for the Natural Body salon (1996) in the Hankyu International Hotel in Osaka, Akihito Fumita of Fumita Design Office used a palette of pale yellow to create an other-worldly environment. A curved ceiling wafts above a suite of massage furniture designed by Fumita for three different types of massage: back, foot, and full body. The designer deftly defused any awkwardness occasioned by the physical intimacy of a massage by introducing whimsical futuristic shapes and anthropomorphic features that enhance privacy and comfort. The back-massage table, for example, looks like a cartoon of a foot and the foot-massage chairs have huge "ears" that shield the customer from unwanted glances. With an interior that is reminiscent of a space-age science fiction film set, Natural Body transports its clientele outside the realm of the everyday, if only for the briefest of respites.

These latter-day incarnations of the spa and the gym—along with their clinical counterparts—demonstrate how the distinctions among the spaces of elective indulgence, preventive medicine, and vital treatments are becoming increasingly blurred. They are indicative of significant shifts in contemporary attitudes toward health care. With hospital stays being shortened more and more by private health care management, and with alternative therapies in noninstitutional settings gaining new levels of legitimacy, design plays an increasingly compensatory role, supplying amelioration to the former and credibility to the latter. Operating in a culture of entitlement, in the larger context of healing, designers—whether of hospitals or massage salons—increasingly find themselves cast in the role of mediators for what may well be a new generation of enlightened hypochondriacs.

Acknowledgments

A book of this magnitude would be inconceivable without the support of family, friends, colleagues, even institutions. Indeed, the foundation for this project was laid at the American Academy in Rome during my fellowship there in 2003-04. The Academy provided the space—the remarkable McKim Mead and White villa on the Janiculum, an extraordinary interior in and of itself—and the time and funding to write the crucial first chapters of the book. Most importantly, the Academy offered a congenial scholarly environment, conducive to sharing and testing the ideas of a work in progress. In that regard, I am grateful to all of the Fellows of 2004, particularly Andrea Volpe for his introductions to Italian architects, and to the administration and staff of the Academy, most especially its distinguished President, Adele Chatfield-Taylor.

Well before the actual writing began in Rome, there was a year of preliminary work during which I was fortunate to have invaluable assistance from the Japan National Tourist Organization in New York, which, through the good agency of Mariam Goldberg, supported my research in Japan. During my research in the United States, I was the beneficiary of Barrie Olsen's considerable investigatory talents. She identified many of the South American and Australian projects included in the book and she introduced me to several key photographers' archives. Barrie also provided untold hours of moral support during the years of the book's gestation, for which I owe her a deep debt of gratitude. My dear friend Allison Harberston contributed to the research and created the first data base for the book. I also want to thank Denise Ramzy for serving as a research assistant and generously giving her time as a reader for several chapters on my return to the United States, as did Lindsay Stamm Shapiro, Dr. Martha Greenwood, and Barrie Olsen. I am immensely grateful for their astute comments. Thomas Reynolds deserves special mention, not only for his instrumental contributions to the research on therapeutic spaces, but also for his critical role as the book's photo researcher. A long-time friend and colleague, Thomas brought his deep knowledge of design and exquisite sense of order to the project and for this I am truly thankful.

I owe special gratitude to Karen Stein, Editorial Director of Phaidon Press, New York, for bringing the project to me at such a propitious time in my career and for enabling its success. Few writers are so fortunate as to have two excellent editors, but I was fortunate to work with both Megan McFarland and Andrea Codrington at Phaidon. Ever the gracious diplomat, Megan's advocacy and counsel was invaluable throughout the book's development. Andrea not only provided additional thoughtful commentary in the course of the editing process, she also guided the book through its final critical phases. I am also especially indebted to Mischa Leiner for his extremely insightful design, which has made the text all the more vivid.

Henry Casey, a writer and editor in his own right, would be thanked in any event for bringing so much joy to my life as my son; but, in this case, he also merits formal credit for organizing data and providing deeply appreciated technological assistance. For Michael Casey, my husband, I reserve my deepest thanks, love, and respect for his incomparable sensitivity to the art of prose. I am forever grateful for his quiet and unflagging support.

Bibliography

Design and Architectural History

Abercrombie, Stanley. *A Century of Interior Design 1900-2000: A Timetable of the Design, the Designers, the Products and the Profession*. New York: Rizzoli International Publications, 2003.

Albrecht, Donald; Lupton, Ellen; Skov Holt, Steven with introduction by Yelavich, Susan. *Design Culture Now: National Design Triennial*. New York: Princeton Architectural Press in association with Cooper-Hewitt National Design Museum Smithsonian Institution, 2000.

Albrecht, Donald; Lupton, Ellen; Owens, Mitchell; Yelavich, Susan. *Inside Design Now: National Design Triennial*. New York: Princeton Architectural Press in association with Cooper-Hewitt National Design Museum Smithsonian Institution, 2003.

Banham, Joanna, ed. *The Encyclopedia of Interior Design*. London: Bath Press; Chicago: Fitzroy Dearborn Publishers, 1997.

Bullivant, Lucy. *International Interior Design*. New York: Abbeville, 1991.

Byars, Mel. *The Design Encyclopedia*. New York: John Wiley & Son, 1994.

Frampton, Kenneth. "Toward a Critical Regionalism: Six Points for an Architecture of Resistance," from Foster, Hal, ed., *The Anti-Aesthetic: Essays on Postmodern Culture*. Port Townsend, Washington: Bay Press, 1983.

Jongerius, Hella. *Hella Jongerius*. London, New York: Phaidon Press, 2003.

Holtzman, Joseph, ed. *Every Room Tells a Story: Tales from the Pages of Nest Magazine*. New York: Distributed Art Publishers, 2001.

McQuaid, Matilda. *Shigeru Ban*. New York: Phaidon Press, 2004.

Müller Stahl, Julie, ed. *Dish: International Design for the Home*. New York: Princeton Architectural Press, 2004.

Pile, John F. *History of Interior Design*. New York: John Wiley, 2000.

Praz, Mario. *An Illustrated History of Interior Decoration: From Pompeii to Art Nouveau*. London: Thames and Hudson, 1987.

Raimondi, Giuseppe. *Italian Living Design, Three Decades of Interior Decoration, 1960-1990*. New York: Rizzoli International Publications, 1990.

Ramakers, Renny and Bakker, Gijs. *Droog Design: Spirit of the Nineties*. Rotterdam: 101 Publishers, 1998.

Ramakers, Renny. *Less + More, Droog Design in Context*. Rotterdam: 010 Publishers, 2002.

Rykwert, Joseph. *The Villa: From Ancient to Modern*. New York: Harry N. Abrams, 2000.

Sharp, Dennis. *The Illustrated Encyclopedia of Architects and Architecture*. New York: Quatro Publishing, 1991.

Smith, C. Ray, and Alan Tate. *Interior Design in the 20th Century*. New York: Harper & Row, 1986.

Thornton, Peter. *The Domestic Interior, 1630-1920*. First published in the UK in 1984, by George Weiden & Nicolson; London: Seven Dials, Cassell & Co., 2000.

Trocmé, Suzanne. *Influential Interiors*. New York: Clarkson Potter, 1999.

Venturi, Robert, with Denise Scott-Brown and Steven Izenour. *Learning from Las Vegas*. Cambridge, MA: MIT Press, 1972.

Vidler, Anthony. *The Architectural Uncanny: Essays in the Modern Unhomely*. Cambridge, MA: MIT Press, 1992.

Wharton, Edith and Codman, Ogden, Jr. *The Decoration of Houses*. 1902. Revised and expanded Classical American edition; London and New York: W.W. Norton & Company, Inc., 1997.

Wilton, Sherrill. *Elements of Interior Design and Decoration*. Philadelphia, New York, Toronto: J.B. Lippincott Company, 1951.

Yelavich, Susan. *Design for Life*. New York: Cooper-Hewitt, National Design Museum, Smithsonian Institution and Rizzoli International Publications, 1997.

Houses

Barreneche, Raul. *Modern House 3*. New York: Phaidon Press, 2005.

Cerver, Asensio Francisco. *Houses of the World*. Cologne: Könemann, 2000.

Daguerre, Mercedes. *20 Houses by 20 Architects*. Milan: Electa Architecture, 2005.

Doubilet, Susan and Boles, Daralice. *American House Now*. New York: Universe Publishing, 1997.

Meier, Richard. *Richard Meier: Architect, Volume 3*. New York: Rizzoli International Publications, 1999.

Meier, Richard. *Richard Meier, Architect, Volume 4*. New York: Rizzoli International Publications, 2004.

Melhuish, Clare. *Modern House 2*. London: Phaidon Press, 2000.

Ngo, Dung and Zion, Adi Shamir. *Open House: Unbound Space and the Modern Dwelling* New York: Rizzoli International Publications, 2002.

Owen Moss, Eric. *Eric Owen Moss, Buildings and Projects 2*. New York: Rizzoli International Publications, 1996.

Pollack, Naomi. *Modern Japanese House*. New York: Phaidon Press, 2005.

Riley, Terrence. *The Un-Private House*. New York: The Museum of Modern Art, 1999.

Robson, David. *Geoffrey Bawa: The Complete Works*. London: Thames and Hudson, 2002.

Welsh, John. *Modern House*. London: Phaidon Press, 1995.

Zermani, Paolo. *Identity of Architecture*. Rome: Officina Edizioni, 1995.

Apartments

Hawes, Elizabeth. *New York, New York: How the Apartment House Transformed the Life of the City, 1869–1930*. New York: Alfred A. Knopf, 1993.

Jenkins, David. *Unité d'Habitation Marseilles: Le Corbusier*. London: Phaidon Press, 1993.

Staudenmeyer, Pierre, et al. *Garouste Bonetti*. Paris: Éditions Ds Voir, nd.

Tasma-Anargyros, Sophie. *Andrée Putman*. Woodstock: Overlook Press, 1997.

Lofts

Cassell, Stephen and Yarinsky, Adam. *aro architecture research office*. New York: Princeton Architectural Press, 2002.

Fisher, Frederick, Beaud, Marie-Claude. *Frederick Fisher Buildings and Projects*. New York: Rizzoli International Publications, Inc., 1995.

Krauel, Jacobo, ed. *Lofts: Living, Working and Shopping in a Loft*. Barcelona: Gribaudo, 2003.

Nestares, Marcos. *Studios and Lofts, One Room Living*. New York: Universe Publishing, 2003.

Schwartz, Frederic, ed. *Alan Buchsbaum, Architect & Designer: The Mechanics of Taste*. New York: Monacelli Press, 1996.

Zukin, Sharon. *Loft Living: Culture and Capital in Urban Change*. Baltimore: Johns Hopkins University Press, 1982.

Offices

Antonelli, Paola, ed. *Workspheres: Design and Contemporary Work Styles*. New York: The Museum of Modern Art, 2001.

Bellini, Mario, et al. *Emilio Ambasz: The Poetics of the Pragmatic*. New York: Rizzoli International Publications, 1988.

Blanco, Manuel. *Campo Baeza: Light is More*. Madrid: T.F. Editores, 2003.

Helfand, Margaret. *Margaret Helfand Architects: Essential Architecture*. New York: Monacelli Press, 1999.

Holl, Steven. *Chapel of St. Ignatius*. New York: Princeton Architectural Press, 1999.

Jacques, Michael and Never, Annette. *Steven Holl*. Zurich: Artemis Verlag, 1993.

Workplaces, *AREA 69*, July/August 2003. Milan: Federico Motta Editore.

Civic

Arnold, Hadley, ed. *Work/life: Tod Williams and Billie Tsien and Associates*. New York: Monacelli Press, 2000.

Betsky, Aaron. *Koning Eizenberg: Buildings*. New York: Rizzoli International Publications, 1996.

Blundell Jones, Peter, *Günter Behnisch*. Basel, Boston, Berlin: Birkhäuser, 2000.

Brawne, Michael, et. al. *Library Builders*. London: Academy Editions, 1997.

Dunlop, Beth. *Arquitectonica*. New York: American Institute of Architecture Press, 1991.

Forster, Kurt, W. *Hodgetts & Fung: Scenarios and Spaces*. New York: Rizzoli International Publications, 1995.

Hardingham, Samantha. *London: A Guide to Recent Architecture*. Cologne: Konemann, 1996.

Hertzberger, Herman. *Herman Hertzberger: Articulations*. Munich, New York: Prestel, 2002.

Pizzi, Emilio, ed. *Mario Botta: The Complete Works*. Basel, Boston: Birkhäuser, 1993.

Predock, Antoine. *Antoine Predock: Architect 2*. New York: Rizzoli International Publications, 1998.

Sanin, Francisco. *Münster City Library: Architekurbüro Bolles-Wilson + Partner*. London: Phaidon Press, 1994.

Taniguchi, Yoshio. *The Architecture of Yoshio Taniguchi*. New York: Harry N. Abrams, 1999.

Tzonis, Alexander. *Santiago Calatrava: The Poetics of Movement*. New York: Universe Publishing, 1999.

Ursprung, Philip, ed. *Herzog & de Meuron: Natural History*. Canadian Centre for Architecture: Montreal, and Lars Müller Publishers: Switzerland, 2002.

Wilson, Colin St. John. *The Design and Construction of the British Library*. London: The British Library, 1998.

Religious

Crosbie, Michael, J. *Architecture for the Gods, Book II*. New York: Watson-Guptill Publications, 2003.

Dal Co, Francesco. *Complete Works. Tadao Ando*. London: Phaidon Press, 1995.

Grube, Ernest, J., "What is Islamic Architecture," from Michell, George, ed. *Architecture of the Islamic World: Its History and Social Meaning*. London: Thames & Hudson, 1978.

Hejduk, John. "Cemetery for the Ashes of a Still Life Painter," *Adjusting Foundations*. New York: Monacelli Press, 1995.

Ivy, Robert Adams. *Fay Jones: The Architecture of E. Fay Jones, FAIA*. Washington, DC: American Institute of Architects Press, 1992.

Maki, Fumihiko. *Fumihiko Maki: Buildings and Projects*. New York: Princeton Architectural Press, 1997.

Plattus, Alan, "At the Edge of the Urban Millennium," from Yelavich, Susan, ed., *The Edge of the Millennium: An International Critique of Architecture, Urban Planning, Product and Communication Design*. New York: Whitney Library of Design, 1993.

Safdie, Moshe. *Moshe Safdie*. London: Academy Editions, 1996.

Cultural

Aulenti, Gae. *Gae Aulenti*. New York: Rizzoli International Publications, 1997.

Berdard, Jean-François, ed. *Cities of Artificial Excavation : The Work of Peter Eisenman, 1978–1988*. Montreal: Canadian Centre for Architecture; New York: Rizzoli International Publications, 1994.

Blauvelt, Andrew, "Experiencing the Center," from Blauvelt, Andrew, et. al. *Expanding the Center: Walker Art Center and Herzog & de Meuron*. Minneapolis: Walker Art Center, 2005.

Buchanan, Peter. *Renzo Piano Building Workshop: Complete Works*. London: Phaidon Press, 1993.

Correa, Charles. *Charles Correa*. London: Thames & Hudson, 1996.

Dal Co, Francesco and Kurt W. Forster *Frank O. Gehry: The Complete Works*. Milan: Electa Architecture, 2003.

Henderson, Justin. *Museum Architecture*. Gloucester, MA: Rockport Publishers, 1998.

Isozaki, Arata. *Arata Isozaki: Architecture, 1960–1990*. Los Angeles: Museum of Contemporary Art; New York: Rizzoli International Publications, 1991.

Meier, Richard. *Building the Getty*. New York: Alfred A. Knopf, 1997.

Morgan, Conway Lloyd. *Jean Nouvel, The Elements of Architecture*. New York: Universe Publishers, 1998.

Moneo, Rafael, et. al., *Wexner Center for the Visual Arts, The Ohio State University: A Building*. New York : Rizzoli International Publications, 1989.

Newhouse, Victoria. *Towards a New Museum*. New York: Monacelli Press, 1998

Retail

Barreneche, Raul. *New Retail*. New York: Phaidon Press, 2005.

Bouroullec, Ronan and Bouroullec, Erwan. *Ronan & Erwan Bourellec*. London: Phaidon Press, 2003.

Grunenberg, Christoph and Hollein, Max, eds. *Shopping: A Century of Art and Consumer Culture*. Ostfildern-Ruit: Hatje Cantz Publishers, 2002.

Israel, Lawrence, J. *Store Planning/Design: History, Theory, Process*. New York: John Wiley, 1994.

Ketchum, Jr., Morris. *Shops & Stores, Progressive Architecture Library*. New York: Reinhold Publishing Corporation, 1948.

Miyake, Issey, et al. *A-POC Making, Issey Miyake & Dai Fujiwara*. Berlin: Vitra Design Museum Berlin, 2001.

Sudjic, Deyan. *John Pawson: Works*. London: Phaidon Press, 2000.

van Tilburg, Carolien. *Powershop, New Japanese Retail Design*. Basel, Boston, Berlin: Birkhäuser; Amsterdam: Frame Publishers, 2002.

Restaurants and Bars

Farrelly, Lorraine. *Bar and Restaurant Interior Structures*. West Sussex: Wiley-Academy, 2003.

Hadid, Zaha. *Zaha Hadid: The Complete Buildings and Projects*. New York: Rizzoli International Publications, 1998.

Kuh, Patric. *The Last Days of Haute Cuisine, America's Culinary Revolution*. New York: Viking Penguin, 2001.

Spang, Rebecca L. *The Invention of the Restaurant: Paris and Modern Gastronomic Culture*. Cambridge, MA, and London: Harvard University Press, 2000.

Tihany, Adam D., et al with McCarthy, Nina. New York: Monacelli Press, 1999.

Welsh, John. *Zen Restaurants: Rick Mather*. London: Phaidon Press Ltd, 1992.

Hotels

Albrecht, Donald. *New Hotels for Global Nomads*. London: Merrell in association with Cooper-Hewitt, National Design Museum, 2002.

Heneghan, Tom, *The Colours of Light: Tadao Ando Architecture*. London: Phaidon Press, 1996.

Robson, David. *Modernity and Community: Architecture in the Islamic World*. London: Thames & Hudson, 2001.

Uchida, Shigeru, et al. *Interior Design: Uchida, Mitsuhashi, Nishioka & Studio 80, Vol. II*. Cologne: Taschen, 1991.

Ypma, Herbert; Liagre, Christian. *Christian Liagre*. London: Thames and Hudson, 2004.

Therapeutic

Pleasure: The Art and Design of the Rockwell Group. New York: Universe, London: Troika, 2002.

Hospitals Issue, *The Architectural Review*, London, March 2002.

JA 48, The Japan Architect: Yearbook 2002, Tokyo: Shinkenchiku-Sha Co. Ltd, Winter 2003.

Shonfield, Katherine, Dannatt, Adrian, and Ainley, Rosa. *This Is What We Do, a muf manual*. London: Ellipsis, 2001.

Verderber, Stephen and Fine, David J. *Healthcare Architecture in an Era of Radical Transformation*. New Haven; London: Yale University, 2000.

Zumthor, Peter. *Peter Zumthor, Works: Buildings and Projects, 1979–1997*. Basel, Boston: Birkhäuser, 1999.

Notes

Introduction

1 The two most thoughtful texts on the subject–Mario Praz's *An Illustrated History of Interior Decoration* and Peter Thornton's *Authentic Décor*–cover only up to the early years of the twentieth century. These two resources are unusual for their analytical perspective. Praz is the more poetic of the two authors, attributing metaphysical properties to the interior that the contemporary reader will find unsubstantiated but nonetheless provocative. Thornton brings a more conventional art historical methodology to the subject. See Bibliography.
2 Joel Sanders, "Curtain Wars," *Harvard Design Magazine*, Winter/Spring 2002, p. 14.
3 Kenneth Frampton, "Community Builder," *Design Book Review* 44/45 (Winter/Spring 2001), p. 84.
4 Castiglione was the author of the *Book of the Courtier*, the quintessential Renaissance book of manners. The quote was excerpted from James Cleugh, *The Divine Aretino*. (New York: Stein and Day Publishers, 1966), pp. 200-01.
5 Fred Dust, head of IDEO's Smart Space practice, shared these characterizations, conceived by IDEO for an American housing developer, in his lecture "Tales of the City," Parsons The New School for Design, New York, 20 September 2005.

Houses

1 Mario Praz, *An Illustrated History of the Interior: from Pompeii to Art Nouveau* (London: Thames & Hudson, 1987), p. 50.
2 Rosemary Haag Bletter, "Mies and Dark Transparency," in *Mies in Berlin*, ed. Terence Riley and Barry Bergdoll (New York: The Museum of Modern Art, 2001), p. 352.
3 Frank Lloyd Wright, "A Home in a Prairie Town," *Ladies Home Journal*, February 1901. Reprinted in Terence Riley, *The Un-Private House* (New York: The Museum of Modern Art, 1999), p. 14.
4 Joseph Rykwert, *On Adam's House in Paradise: The Idea of the Primitive Hut in Architectural History*, 2nd ed. (Cambridge, Mass.: The MIT Press, 1981), p. 13.
5 In fact, the complete disappearance of walls was anticipated, but not realized, a century ago. Mies van der Rohe's ideal schemes for at least three houses, including the Tugendhat Villa, apparently included great sheets of glass that could be lowered mechanically into the floor. See Terence Riley, "Wall-less House," *Nest*, Spring 2000.
6 Dana Buntrock, "Designer of the Year: Shigeru Ban," *Interiors*, January 2001, p. 61.
7 Riley, *The Un-Private House*, p. 72.
8 "Light filter: This house, dug into the side of a sand dune in Victoria, elegantly makes the case for a new kind of Australian culture that blends Asian and European strands," *The Architectural Review*, December 2000, pp. 50-53.
9 The Suitcase House, along with the ten other villas that constitute the Commune by the Great Wall, has led a double life as a hotel for the Commune, which was the creation of developers Pan Shiyi and Zhang Xi, of SOHO China. As of 18 August 2005, Kempinski Hotels & Resorts announced that they would assume the management of the complex, suggesting that the developers no longer intend to sell the villas as private houses. Nonetheless, the houses were originally designed as residences, albeit in a speculative sense, both theoretically and economically. See "Hospitality and Travel News," website of 4Hoteliers (www.4hoteliers.com/4hots_nshw.php?mwi=2072).
10 "Atelier Bow-wow," in *Fusion: Architecture + Design in Japan*, exhibition catalogue (Jerusalem: The Israel Museum, 2004).
11 Anthony Vidler, "The Baroque Effect," in *Eric Owen Moss: Buildings and Projects* (New York: Rizzoli International Publications, 1996), pp. 6-11.
12 John Brickerhoff Jackson, *A Sense of Place, a Sense of Time* (New Haven: Yale University Press, 1994), p. 90.
13 Catherine Slessor, "Touching Nature," *The Architectural Review*, July 2001, p. 49.
14 Michael Frank, "New Zealand Idyll," *Architectural Digest*, May 2004, p 143.
15 Julie V. Iovine, "A Beacon on a Path to Fame," *The New York Times*, 26 December 2002, p. F7.
16 Frampton's seminal essay, "Towards a Critical Regionalism: Six Points for an Architecture of Resistance," was first published in *The Anti-Aesthetic: Essays on Postmodern Culture*, ed. Hal Foster (Port Townsend, Wash.: Bay Press, 1983).
17 In her article "Architecture for the Aborigines," which appeared in the July/August 1996 edition of *Architecture Australia*, Kim Dovey, an associate professor of architecture at the University of Melbourne, questions whether Murcutt or any white architect can or should apply modernist Western architecture to their perceptions of indigenous living systems. While admiring Murcutt's dedication and personal sacrifice–he helped finance the project–she questions "the Miesian ideal of the autonomy of architecture from society, the state and the market."
18 Robert Venturi, with Denise Scott-Brown and Steven Izenour, *Learning from Las Vegas* (Cambridge, Mass.: The MIT Press, 1972), p. 87.
19 "Robert Venturi, Pritzker Architecture Prize Laureate 1991," website of the Pritzker Architecture Prize (www.pritzkerprize.com/venturi.htm).

Apartments

1 Vincent Scully, "Modern Architecture: The Architecture of Democracy," in David Jenkins, *Le Corbusier: Unité d'Habitation Marseilles, 1945-52:* (London: Phaidon Press, 1993), p. 11.
2 Elizabeth Hawes, *New York, New York: How the Apartment House Transformed the Life of the City, 1869-1930.* (New York: Alfred A. Knopf, 1993), p. 22.
3 "Architecture in New York: A Field Study," New York University Department of Fine Arts website (http://www.nyu.edu/classes/finearts/nyc/). The site is linked to an undergraduate course of the same title taught by Professor M.G. Broderick.
4 Wendy Goodman, "The Culture Business: The World is Not Enough," *New York*, 20 December 1999.
5 Matthew Stadler, "Four Accommodations," *Nest*, Winter 2002/03, p. 40.
6 Herbert Muschamp, "Blond Ambition on Red Brick," *The New York Times*, 19 June 2003, p. F4.
7 Andrée Putman, "Andrée Putman by Herself," *Nest*, Winter 2000/01, p. 71.
8 Mary Bright (1954-2002) was a New York-based designer who specialized in architectural curtain and fabric treatments. Born in Edinburgh, she moved to New York in 1979 and became one of the unsung pioneers of the re-introduction of custom-crafted textiles into contract design. Notably, she worked on the Museum of Modern Art's 1991 exhibition *Mies in Berlin*, where she created curtains in the spirit of another pioneer, Lilly Reich, a frequent collaborator of Ludwig Mies van der Rohe. She died of cancer in 2002 at the age of 48.
9 Putman, p. 71.
10 Putman, p. 79.
11 Product semantics is the "theory of the symbolic dimensions of industrial products," according to Reinhart Butter, a designer and professor of design at The Ohio State University, and one of the proponents of this theory. See Reinhard Butter, "Putting Theory into Practice: An Application of Product Semantics to Transportation Design," *Design Issues*, Vol. 5, No. 2 (Spring 1989), pp. 51-67.
12 Suzanne Trocmé, *Influential Interiors: Shaping 20th-Century Style Through Key Interior Designers*. (New York: Clarkson Potter, 1999), p. 122.
13 Marta Laudini, "Interior as Narration," *Abitare*, June 2002, p. 88.
14 Hamish Bowles, "Planet Perry," *Vogue*, September 2002, p. 690.
15 Alistair McApline, "Dissolving Horizons," *The World of Interiors*, April 1999, p. 106.
16 Edie Cohen, "Ciao Bello," *Interior Design*, September 2004, p. 126.
17 Ibid., p. 106.
18 Judith Eiblmayer, "solar.dach.wein," trans. Gregory Cowan. Essay provided to the author by Lichtbau Wagner Architects, June 2004.
19 Aric Chen, "Swedish Modern," *Interior Design*, June 2002, p. 139.
20 Aric Chen, "Outside In," *Metropolis*, June 2002, p. 129.
21 Andrea Codrington, "Aura Spaces," *Metropolis*, June 2003, p. 147.

Lofts

1 Raw industrial lofts in New York City are still illegal residences unless they meet standard housing codes. New loft zoning regulations went into effect in the late 1970s that allowed early pioneers who were certified by a special board as "artists-in-residence" to reside in "joint live-work quarters." See Nadine Brozan, "In a Changed SoHo, Legal Pentimento," *The New York Times*, 8 June 2003.
2 Mimi Zeiger, "The Lofting of America," *Dwell*, October 2000, p. 75. Zeiger credits Sharon Zukin's 1982 book *Loft Living: Culture and Capital in Urban Change* (Baltimore: Johns Hopkins University Press, 1982).
3 Though they pioneered many Southern California conversions, Fisher and Partners's practice does not take a purist line on the loft as a converted space. Recognizing the potential of the loft as program and not just as a physical entity, they now specialize in the newly-built loft typology, with projects realized in Venice, California (the 16-unit North Venice Court artist-in-residence complex) and Tokyo, Japan (West Shinjuku Lofts)
4 Frederic Schwartz, ed., *Alan Buchsbaum, Architect & Designer: The Mechanics of Taste* (New York: The Monacelli Press, 1996), p. 160.
5 Today the loft functions solely as Estudio Campana's office/workshop/showroom. However, it did function as Fernando's residence and work space when the business was started in 1994.

6 According to the historian Mario Praz, "The nomadic habits of…feudal lords, who used to stay first in one, then in another of their castles, meant…that their furniture had to be easily transportable. Only the bed stayed in its place. The chests served to contain clothing and crockery during moves, but were also used as seats and storage cupboards." From Mario Praz, *An Illustrated History of Interior Decoration: from Pompeii to Art Nouveau* (London: Thames & Hudson, 1982), p. 79.
7 From a conversation with the author, June 2005.
8 This concept is explored in Anthony Vidler, *The Architectural Uncanny: Essays in the Modern Unhomely* (Cambridge, Mass.: The MIT Press, 1992).
9 Beppe Finessi, "Staccati da Terra: Attilio Stocchi vicino a Bergamo," *Abitare*, vol. 418 (June 2002), p. 120.
10 Lucy Lippard, *Changing: Essays in Art Criticism* (New York: E. P. Dutton, 1971), p. 132.
11 Carly Butler, "Raw Discipline," *The Architectural Review*, March 2002, p. 80.
12 Zukin, *Loft Living: Culture and Capital in Urban Change*, p. 68.
13 Dave Hickey, *The Invisible Dragon: Four Essays on Beauty* (Los Angeles: Art Issues Press, 1993).
14 Gianni Vattimo, *The Transparent Society*, trans. David Webb (Baltimore: The Johns Hopkins University Press, 1992), p. 72.
15 Doris Saatchi, "Josef and his Amazing Technicolor Dream House," *Nest*, Winter 1998/99, p. 135.
16 From correspondence with the author, 11 August 2004.
17 From correspondence with the author, 9 July 2004.

Offices

1 Véronique Vienne, "Sugar and Noise," *Metropolis*, July 2000, p. 97.
2 Christopher Budd, "The Office: 1950 to the Present," in *Workspheres: Design and Contemporary Work Styles*, ed. Paola Antonelli (New York: The Museum of Modern Art/Harry N. Abrams, 2001), pp. 27-28.
3 Ibid., p. 28.
4 See John Seeley Brown and Paul Duguid, *The Social Life of Information* (Cambridge, Mass: Harvard Business School Press, 1997). Among the many publications that have analyzed the social life of the office, this book has been extremely influential.
5 Consistent with Foster's own practice and Germany's legal requirements for sustainable design, every office has a window that employees can open two-thirds of the year, resulting in a significant reduction of energy consumption. (Foster claims the bank uses half the energy of a conventional office tower.) See Foster + Partners website (www.fosterandpartners.com/Projects/0626/Default .aspx).
6 See Manuel Castells, *The Informational City* (Oxford, UK: B. Blackwell, 1989).
7 Not only does Pioneer Chile's landscaping recycle large accumulations of earth from previous construction on the site, but it also insulates the offices.
8 Sheila Kim, "Ready for Takeoff," *Interior Design*, May 2003, p. 240.
9 David Dix, "Virtual Chiat," *Wired*, July 1994, pp. 84-85.

10 Christopher Budd, "The Office: 1950 to the Present," p. 34.

11 The creed has become part of Chiat/Day legend, as has the pirate flag that flew above the company's San Francisco office. See Stevan Alburty, "The Ad Agency to End All Ad Agencies," *Fast Company* (December 1996), p. 116.

12 Sarah Brownlee, "Just Did It," *FX*, March 2003.

13 The Gehry sculpture, colloquially known as the horse head, is identical to the horse-head-shaped sculpture in the Institute for Integrative Genomics at Princeton University, discussed in the Civic chapter. Both forms were fabricated from a computer model for an exhibition of sculpture at the Gagosian Gallery in New York City; the sculpture was then purchased by Peter Lewis, who donated it to Princeton University. The original concept for the horse head was developed in the early 1990s to serve as the entry gallery at Peter Lewis's residence, but it was never built. (From email correspondence between the author and Keith Mendenhall of Gehry Partners, 24 September 2004.)

14 Steven Skov Holt, "Ayse Birsel," in Ellen Lupton, Donald Albrecht, Steven Skov Holt, eds., *Design Culture Now: National Design Triennial* (New York: Princeton Architectural Press, 2000), p. 64.

15 Michael Jacques and Annette Neve, *Steven Holl* (Zurich: Artemis Verlag, 1993).

16 Hazel Clark, "Dish from a Design Theorist," in *Dish: International Design for the Home*, ed. Julie Müller Stahl (New York: Princeton Architectural Press, 2004), p. 158.

17 Ian Phillips, "Creativity on Six: an 1899 department store now houses BETC Euro RSCG, a Paris advertising agency designed by Frederic Jung," *Interior Design*, July 2002, p. 174.

Civic

1 Though there have certainly been efforts to turn back the clock since the events of September 11, 2001, it is telling that authoritarian efforts to circumscribe behavior met with immediate, vocal resistance. The cultural reflex to question authority is now automatic. This was not the case before the late 1960s, when dissent was largely the domain of subcultures of students, artists, and political activists.

2 From project description on the website of Behnisch Architekten (www.behnisch.com/projects/eduction/03/index.html)

3 Peter Blundell Jones, "Kindergarten Chats: Kindergarten Building in Stuttgart, Germany," *The Architectural Review*, September 1996.

4 Justin McGuirk, "DSDHA Architects," *Icon*, June 2004, p. 36.

5 Aaron Betsky, "Skinning the Program," in Aaron Betsky, et al., *Koning Eizenberg: Buildings* (New York: Rizzoli International Publications, 1996), p. 17.

6 From project description on the website of Architectuurstudio Herman Hertzberger (http://www.hertzberger.nl/content2.asp?id=18)

7 Heinz Rudolf of BOORA points out that the building was designed before the existence of the U.S. Department of Energy's establishment of the LEED (Leadership in Energy and Environmental Efficiency Design) awards. It ultimately received a silver award retroactively, two years after the school opened. From an interview with the author, 6 October 2004.

8 Brian Libby, "Light Fantastic," *Metropolis*, March 2003, p. 101.

9 From a description of the Educatorium on the website of the University of Utrecht (link is no longer accessible). See main website of the university (www.uu.nl).

10 See note 13, Offices chapter, above.

11 David Eisen, "Gehry Takes a Village to Create the Stata," *The Boston Herald*, 9 May 2004, p. 39.

12 Paul Roberts, "MIT Looks to Liven Campus with Gehry's Stata Center," IDG News Service, Boston Bureau, 5 July 2004 (www.idg.net).

13 Sara Rimer, "Putting A Smile on Sober Science: Frank Gehry Gives M.I.T. Its Newest Experiment," The New York Times, 13 May 2004, p. E1.

14 Peter Davey, "Bibliotheca Alexandrina," *The Architectural Review*, September 2001, p. 42. I am indebted to this excellent essay, which cites circular antecedents for the library–Sydney Smirk's reading room for the British Library and Erik Gunnar Asplund's Stockholm City Library.

15 Michael Brawne et al., "The National Library of France," *Library Builders* (London: Academy Editions, 1997).

16 Samantha Hardingham, *London: A Guide to Recent Architecture* (Cologne: Könemann, 1997).

17 Colin St. John Wilson, *The Design and Construction of the British Library* (London: The British Library, 1998).

18 Kurt W. Forster, "The Supercalifragilistic Architecture of Hodgetts + Fung," in *Hodgetts + Fung: Scenarios and Spaces* (New York: Rizzoli International Publications, 1997), p. 15.

19 Francisco Sanin, *Münster City Library: Architekurbüro Bolles Wilson + Partner* (London: Phaidon Press, 1994), p. 14.

20 Beppe Finessi, "Invenzione di una biblioteca," *Abitare*, no. 423 (December 2002), pp. 123–29.

21 As of October 2004, the list of architectural and design firms involved included 1100 Architect, Alexander Gorlin Architects, Dean/Wolf Architects, Deborah Burke Architect, Della Valle Bernheimer, Gluckman Mayner Architects, Helfand Myerberg Guggenheimer, Marpillero Pollak Architects, Paul Bennett Architect, Richard H. Lewis Architect, the Rockwell Group, Rogers Marvel Architects, Ronnette Riley Architect, Tod Williams Billie Tsien Architects, Tsao & McKown Architects, Weiss/Manfredi Architects, and Ken Smith Landscape Architect.

22 It is something of a misnomer to use the possessive here (i.e., "Koolhaas's"), as it always is with a project of this scale, but particularly because the architect is an avowed champion of participatory design. Even his own firm, the Office for Metropolitan Architecture, does not bear his name. In this case, as has been widely publicized, the project was catalyzed by Koolhaas's partner Joshua Ramus, a Seattle native, and was collaboratively realized with chief librarian Deborah Jacobs and her staff. It was designed in association with LMN Architects in Seattle. For excellent insights into the design process as a brilliant orchestration of public chorus and architectural aria, see Matthew Stadler, "An Artificial Heart," *Nest*, spring 2004.

23 Herbert Muschamp, "The Library that Puts on Fishnets and Hits the Disco," *The New York Times*, 16 May 2004, p. AR 31.

24 Paul Goldberger, "Architecture View: A Public Work That Enobles As It Serves," *The New York Times*, August 13, 1995.

25 See the website of EMBT Arquitectes Associats (www.mirallestagliabue.com).

26 Ibid.

27 Peter Blundell Jones, *Gunther Behnisch* (Boston: Birkhäuser, 2000), p. 16.

Religious

1 Pope John XXIII convened Vatican Council II in 1962, with the intention of making the Roman Catholic Church more responsive and open to its members, and to the world at large.

2 As of 1 January 2005, there were 2,445 religious buildings under construction in Ukraine, according to the U.S. Department of State's International Religious Freedom Report, 2005 (www.state.gov/g/drl/rls/irf/2005/51588.htm).

3 *Kristallnacht*, the "Night of Broken Glass," occurred on 9 November 1938, when the German authorities carried out a wave of attacks on Jewish houses, synagogues, and businesses. The virtual elimination of Judaism in Germany during World War II was compounded by the ensuing five decades of Communism in the East, where religious observances were banned until reunification in 1989. Even today, security remains enough of an issue in the East to require the presence of armed guards at major synagogues. See David Cohen, "A Complex and Tragic History Informs Wandel Hoefer Lorch + Hirsch's Poetic Design for the New Dresden Synagogue," *Architectural Record*, June 2002, p. 106.

4 In *The Spiritual Exercises*, written in the sixteenth century, St. Ignatius referred to this inner light and darkness as "consolations and desolations." See Gerald T. Cobb's introduction in Steven Holl, *Chapel of St. Ignatius* (New York: Princeton Architectural Press, 1999), p. 9.

5 Since the reforms of the Vatican Council II, the Roman Catholic Church has been involved in transforming a liturgy of observance into one of participation. In recent years, however, Pope John Paul II and his successor, Pope Benedict XVI, have set a more traditionalist course.

6 Kenneth Frampton, "Thoughts on Tadao Ando," *Tadao Ando: Pritzker Architecture Prize Laureate, 1995* (www.pritzkerprize.com/ppg7.htm).

7 Ernst J. Grube, "What Is Islamic Architecture," in *Architecture of the Islamic World: Its History and Social Meaning*, ed. George Michell (London: Thames & Hudson, 1978), p. 33.

8 Grube defines a *mihrab* as an acoustic device, a resonator for the voice, the place where the imam stations himself to lead the congregation in prayer. Concave, and pointed in the direction of Mecca, it is the opposite of an altar. It is not the niche itself that is sacred but the holy place it points to. Grube, p. 33.

9 Reza Sarhangi, "The Sky Within: Mathematical Aesthetics of Persian Dome Interiors," *The Nexus Network Journal*, Vol. 1 (1999), pp. 87–97. In one tradition, sixteen points on a circle create radial arcs that inscribe a rosette on the underside of a dome. In the Islamic Cultural Center, they create a pattern of wedges.

10 Joseph Giovannini, "Computer Worship: New York Presbyterian Church, Long Island, New York, NY," *Architecture*, vol. 88, no.10 (October 1999), pp.87–99.

11 Alan Plattus, "At the Edge of the Urban Millennium," in *The Edge of the Millennium: An International Critique of Architecture, Urban Planning, Product and Communication Design*, ed. Susan Yelavich (New York: Whitney Library of Design, 1993), p. 78.

12 Catherine Slessor, "Precious Palimpsest," *The Architectural Review*, November 2001, p. 41.

13 John Hejduk, "Cemetery for the Ashes of the Still Life Painters," in *Adjusting Foundations*, ed. Kim Shkapich (New York: The Monacelli Press, 1995), p. 48.

14 Gianni Vattimo, *Nihilism and Emancipation* (New York: Columbia University Press, 2003), p. 31.

Cultural

1 According the American Association of Museums, "The last thirty years of the twentieth century saw the birth of more than six hundred art museums in the United States alone, with equal proliferation in much of Europe." From the American Association of Museums' online review of Victoria Newhouse, *Towards a New Museum* (New York: Monacelli Press, 1998). (www.aam-us.org/bookstore/detail.cfm?id=752).

2 Dean Hawkes and Wayne Forster, "Piano's Beyeler Foundation Museum," *Architecture Week*, 5 November 2003.

3 The term Apollonian is derived from the myth of Apollo, the ancient Greek god of the sun, who is associated with light and reason, and, by extension, structural clarity. His virtues are considered synonymous with classical forms because they are orderly and legible. In contrast, Apollo's mythological opposite, Dionysus, the god of drunken ecstasy, inspired the term Dionysian, associated with design that is asymmetrical and spatially complicated.

4 From "Architect's Statement" by Taniguchi, originally published on the website of the Museum of Modern Art (www.moma.org).

5 Nicolai Ouroussoff, "Art Fuses with Urbanity in a Redesign of the Modern," *The New York Times*, 15 November 2004

6 Paul Goldberger, "A Delicate Balance," *The New Yorker*, 23 and 30 December 2002, p. 161.

7 From the website of Steven Holl Architects (www.stevenholl.comPT123-4C.html).

8 Marie-Claude Beaud, *Frederick Fisher Architect* (New York: Rizzoli International Publications, 1995), p. 82.

9 The Industriewerke Karlsruhe-Augsburg factory opened in 1918, shortly after the end of World War I, and continued operation during World War II. Abandoned after the war, the plant was taken over by artists before receiving official civic support. See Layla Dawson, "Mixed Media, Architectural Design of an Art Center in Karlsruhe, Germany," *The Architectural Review*, April 1998.

10 Susan Yelavich, *Design for Life* (New York: Cooper-Hewitt National Design Museum, Smithsonian Institution/Rizzoli International Publications, 1997), p. 168.

11 "Herzog and de Meuron Pritzker Prize," *Architecture Week*, 4 April 2001.

12 Catherine Slessor, "Cauldrons of Culture: London's Tate Modern," *The Architectural Review*, March 2001.

13 OpenOffice disbanded in 2005. Partners Lyn Rice and Galia Solomonoff have established independent practices, respectively named Lyn Rice Architects and Galia Solomonoff Architecture.

14 Newhouse, p. 62.

15 Charles Correa, "Museums: An Alternate Typology," *Daedalus*, Vol. 128, Summer 1999.

16 This quote is taken from Ouroussoff's audio commentary, "Building the 'Casa da Musica,'" 10 April 2005, on the *New York Times* website (www.nytimes.com).

The two other concert halls he considers to be equal to Casa da Musica are Frank Gehry's Walt Disney Concert Hall in Los Angeles and Hans Scharoun's 1960 Berlin PhilharmonieSee also Nicolai Ouroussoff, "Rem Koolhaas Learns Not to Overthink It," *The New York Times*, 10 April 2005.

17 From the website of OMA/Office for Metropolitan Architecture (www.oma.nl).

18 Raymund Ryan, "Stage Play, Local Theater for the Small Town of Uden, Netherlands," *The Architectural Review*, March 1999.

19 Richard Weinstein noted this aspect of the design process in a lecture on the Disney Concert Hall ("The Priming of Frank Gehry: Disney Hall, the Cultural Politics from the Inside Out, 1980–2003") given at the American Academy in Rome on 29 September 2003

20 Ann Wilson Lloyd, "The Art That's Living in the House Hadid Built," *The New York Times*, 8 June 2003, p. AR 29.

21 Steven Henry Madoff, "Going Public," *ArtForum International*, 1 April 2005.

22 The author is indebted to Andrew Blauvelt, design director and curator at the Walker Art Center, for the many insights he shared in a series of e-mails on 16 and 17 August 2005. See also Andrew Blauvelt, "Experiencing the Center," in *Expanding the Center: Walker Art Center and Herzog & de Meuron* (Minneapolis, Minn.: Walker Art Center, 2005) p. 17.

Retail

1 Kenneth Frampton and Yukio Futagawa, *Modern Architecture: 1851-1945* (New York: Rizzoli International Publications, 1983), p. 36.

2 Chantal Béret, "Shed, Cathedral, or Museum," in *Shopping: A Century of Art and Consumer Culture*, ed. Christoph Grunenberg and Max Hollein (Ostfildern-Ruit, Germany: Hatje Cantz, 2002), p. 69.

3 Emile Zola, *The Ladies' Paradise* (1863), trans. Brian Nelson (Oxford, U.K.: Oxford University Press, 1995), p. 4. Cited in fn17 of Béret, p. 70.

4 Interestingly, the artist Haim Steinbach has pointed out that "Moss occupies the space, which [was] … one of the most important end of the century galleries: Metro Pictures." He also notes, "'Appropriation Art' has been associated with many Metro artists." See "Interview: Shop Talk, Amanda Sharp Visits Prada and Moss with Haim Stainbach," *Frieze*, April 2003, p. 51.

5 Stanley Abercrombie, "1100 Architect," *Interior Design*, September 1995

6 Carolien van Tilburg, *Powershop: New Japanese Retail Design* (Basel, Boston, Berlin, Amsterdam: Frame/Birkhäuser, 2002), p. 102.

7 Rob Houst, "Cardboard City," *Frame*, no. 25 (March/April 2002), p. 78.

8 The quotations cited here, attributed to Rei Kawakubo, are from a statement provided to the author by Catherine Wagner, describing her 2002 installation at Comme des Garçons in Kyoto.

9 Amanda Fortini, "The Anti-Concept Store," *The New York Times Magazine*, 12 December 2004, p. 54.

10 Arjun Appadurai, *Modernity at Large: Cultural Dimensions of Globalization*. Public Worlds series, vol. 1 (Minneapolis, Minn.: University of Minnesota Press, 1996), pp. 84–85.

11 Shonquis Moreno, "Young at Heart," *Frame*, no. 32 (May/June 2003), p. 66.

12 I am indebted to Carolien van Tilburg, cited above, for my insights into AZB's design of a-Compiler and a-Assembler. See *Powershop*, pp. 10-14.

13 Fabio Novembre, "Palladio and I," undated press release from Bisazza.

14 From project description of Galeries Lafayette on the website of Ateliers Jean Nouvel (www.jeannouvel.com).

15 Lucy Bullivant, "The Walls Have Gears: How Kitchen Rodgers Design makes Interiors Come Alive," *I.D.*, May 2004, p. 59.

16 Shonquis Moreno, "Rem and the Art of Shopping," *Frame*, no. 25 (March/April 2002), p. 60.

Restaurants and Bars

1 Rebecca Spang, *The Invention of the Restaurant: Paris and Modern Gastronomic Culture* (Cambridge, Mass.: Harvard University Press, 2000). I am indebted to this excellent book.

2 Ibid., p. 115.

3 Ibid., p. 42.

4 Patric Kuh, *The Last Days of Haute Cuisine: America's Culinary Revolution* (New York: Viking Penguin, 2001), p. 3.

5 Ibid.

6 The first Spago restaurant, in West Hollywood (1982), was designed by Puck's (now) former wife and business partner Barbara Lazaroff. Puck's empire has expanded to include, at last count, twelve fine-dining restaurants, eighteen Wolfgang Puck Cafés, books, a television program, a line of packaged foods, and a growing chain of Wolfgang Puck Express fast-casual dining franchises. See Steve Kaufman, "Wolfgang Puck Express: Live, Love, Eat," Visual Store website, an online publication of *Visual Merchandising and Store Design*, 13 May 2004 (www.visualstore.com/index.php/channel/27/id/7551).

7 John Welsh, *Zen Restaurants: Rick Mather* (London: Phaidon Press, 1992), p. 9.

8 Ibid.

9 "The Architecture of Reassurance: Designing the Disney Theme Parks," Press Release for exhibition of the same title, Canadian Centre for Architecture, June 1997.

10 Bill Breen, "David Rockwell Has a Lot of Nerve," *Fast Company*, November 2002, p. 77.

11 Paul Goldberger, "Introduction," in Adam D. Tihany and Nina McCarthy, *Tihany Design* (New York: The Monacelli Press, 1999), p. 10.

12 Ibid.

13 From *Arlequin, Restaurateur*, fol. 56, quoted in Spang, p. 55.

14 From AFSO project description of Zenzibar.

15 Susan Welsh, "The New Xanadu," *Interior Design*, February 2003, p. 116.

16 The partners in M41LH2 are Johanna Hyrkäs, Toimmi Mäkynen, Tuomas Slitonen, and Tuomas Toivonen. They invited Vesa Oiva, Selina Anttinen, and Tumoas Kivinen, as well as members of a design agency called com-pa-ny, to develop the scheme for Helsinki Club. See Asko Ahokas, "Condition Red," *Frame*, November/December 2003.

17 Consider, specifically, the supper clubs in Amsterdam and Rome designed by the Dutch firm Concrete.

Hotels

1 *The New Encyclopedia Brittanica*, 15th ed., Vol. 6, Micropaedia (Chicago: Encyclopedia Brittanica, Inc., 1994), p. 79.

2 Ibid.

3 The Old Faithful Inn was designed by architect Robert Reamer and built between 1903 and 1904. See the website of Yellowstone National Park (www.nps.gov/yell/oldfaith/index.htm).

4 Donald Albrecht, *New Hotels for Global Nomads* (London: Merrell/Cooper-Hewitt National Design Museum, 2002), p. 21.

5 Ibid.

6 Bawa received, among other honors, the highly coveted Chairman's Award, part of the Aga Khan Award for Architecture, in 2001. This was only the third Chairman's Award ever to be given by the Aga Khan Foundation, which honors architecture in countries with a strong Muslim presence.

7 See David Robson, *Modernity and Community: Architecture in the Islamic World* (London: Thames & Hudson, 2001). See also Michael Brawn, "Paradise Found: The Kandalama Hotel in Dambulla, Sri Lanka," *The Architectural Review*, December 1995. I am indebted to these two authors for their descriptive information about the Kandalama hotel.

8 Tom Heneghan, "Architecture and Ethics," in *The Colours of Light: Tadao Ando Architecture* (London: Phaidon, 1996), p. 28.

9 "What happens here, stays here" was the brain-child of advertising copywriter Jeff Candido, who came up with the slogan in 2004 at the behest of the Las Vegas Convention and Visitors Authority, which sought to boost tourism in the wake of the attacks of September 11, 2001.

10 The Venetian stands on the former site of the Sands Hotel (1952). Owned at one time by millionaire Howard Hughes, the Sands was frequented by Frank Sinatra, Sammy Davis Jr., Joey Bishop, Dean Martin, and other celebrities whose reputations became synonymous with Las Vegas.

11 Venice is not immune to the forces of globalization: It now has its own high-end fashion mall, on Calle Larga XXII Marzo.

12 Elizabeth Johnson, "Burj Al-Arab," in Albrecht, *New Hotels for Global Nomads*, p. 127.

13 The Paramount Hotel (1990) in New York City was also designed by Starck for Schrager, but it is not a member of the Morgans Hotel Group. It is a property of Sol Melia, SA.

14 Elizabeth Johnson, "Philippe Starck and Anda Andrei: Clift, Sanderson, St. Martin's Lane," in Albrecht, *New Hotels for Global Nomads*, p. 41.

15 According to Donald Albrecht, the numerous W offshoots use the Rockwell Group's design as a template to achieve a consistency in ambiance in the national chain.

16 Julie Iovine, "Granting Entry to the Land of the Hip," *The New York Times*, 12 December 2004.

17 Zygmunt Bauman, *Liquid Life* (Boston: Polity, 2005), p. 31

18 Amanda Morison, "Couture Clubs," *The Guardian*, 14 February 2004, Travel section.

19 Matthew Stadler, "On the Beach," *Nest*, Summer 1999, p. 62.

20 In 2005, Lacroix's label was sold to a consortium of American investors, the Falic Group. See Chris Scott, "Dressing Room," *Frame*, no. 44 (May/June 2005), p. 97.

21 Michael Gross, "Haute Couture," *Travel + Leisure*, June 2004.

22 Albrecht, p. 151.

23 Patrizia Scarzella, "Human Touch," *Interni*, November 2002, p. 132.

24 Shigeru Uchida, "Hotel Il Palazzo," in Shigeru Uchida et al., *Interior Design: Uchida, Mitsuhashi, Nishioka & Studio 80: Volume II* (Cologne: Taschen, 1991), pp. 110-11.

25 The developers of the Lloyd Hotel are Suzanne Oxenaar, Otto Nan, Gerrit Groen, Liesbeth Mijnlieff. See Tracy Metz, "Dutch All-Star Team," *Metropolis*, March 2005, p. 97.

26 Shonquis Moreno, "The Hills Are Alive," *Frame*, no. 44 (May/June 2005), p. 80. The Rote Bar (Red Bar) was designed by Swiss architect Gabrielle Hächler in 1998, prior to the 2004 renovation of the guest rooms.

27 Gianni Vattimo, *The Transparent Society*, p. 10.

Therapeutic

1 Also called premium or platinum practices, boutique practices limit the number of patients they accept and provide round-the-clock phone access and same-day appointments with no more than a fifteen-minute wait. Perhaps most important, the physician coordinates the full scope of treatment, liaising between patients and their various specialists. Fees can range from $1,500 to $20,000.

2 The history of the hospital should not be confused with the history of the practice of medicine, which is much older and culturally universal. For example, acupuncture is said to have been in use in China as early as 2500 B.C.

3 Peter Blundell Jones, "The Hospital as Building Type," *The Architectural Review*, March 2002.

4 Ibid.

5 Stephen Verderber and David J. Fine, *Healthcare Architecture in an Era of Radical Transformation* (New Haven: Yale University Press, 2000), p. 343.

6 Peter Blundell Jones, "Clinical Precision: An Extension of a Distinguished Ear, Nose and Throat Hospital Department is Both Efficient and Lyrical—Regional Hospital of Graz," *The Architectural Review*, March 2002, p. 44.

7 Verderber and Fine, p. 344.

8 Bryan Lawson, "Healing Architecture," *The Architectural Review*, March 2002, pp. 72-75.

9 Heather Livingston, "Design Matters in Healthcare Facilities, and the Pebble Project Has the Stats to Prove It," *AIArchitect* 9 April 2004.

10 BSA LifeStructures is an architecture, engineering, and interior design firm based in Indianapolis. The statistics on Methodist Hospital were reported by the director of communications for the Center for Health Design. See Sara O. Marberry, "Health Design: A Ripple Turns into a Wave," *ISdesignNET*, online magazine, March 2002 (www.isdesignnet.com).

11 Christopher Hawthorne, "The IDEO Cure," *Metropolis*, October 2002, p. 100.

12 Blundell Jones, "Clinical Precision," p. 48.

13 From architect's statement provided to the author on 30 April 2005.

14 Verderber and Fine, p. 218.

15 According to Cynthia N. Sparer, executive director of the Children's Hospital of New York Presbyterian, it wasn't until the late 1970s that the recovery process began to include parental involvement on a large scale. See Edwin McDowell, "At Children's Hospitals, Friendly Designs," *The New York Times*, 11 November 2002, Section 11, p. 1.

16 From a statement by the architect provided to the author on 19 July 2005.

17 Michael Bierut, "Comfort," in *Pleasure: The Architecture and Design of the Rockwell Group* (New York: Universe Publishing, 2002), p. 112

18 From the website of the Consumer Consortium on Assisted Living (www.ccal.org/history_accomplishments.htm).

19 Dennis Sharp, *The Illustrated Encyclopedia of Architects and Architecture* (New York: Quatro Publishing, 1991), p. 75.

20 Verderber and Fine, p. 244.

21 Hella Jongerius, "Het Schild," from the website of JongeriusLab (www.jongeriuslab.com).

22 "Seniorenzentrum Dornach-Auhof, Linz: Center for Senior Citizens, The Architectural Concept," from the website of Atelier in der Schönbrunnerstraße (www.ats-architekten.at/lda/info.htm).

23 Ibid.

24 Simon Glynn, "Hammersmith Bridge Road Surgery, London," from the Galinsky website (www.galinsky.com/buildings/hammersmith/index.htm)

25 The claim that fertility rates are above average at the Centre for Reproductive Medicine in London is taken from the architect's statement about the project, provided to the author on 11 March 2003.

26 Allison Arieff, "Nice Modernist: Security by Design," *Dwell*, April 2003, p. 60.

27 Katherine Shonfield, "SureStart on the Ocean," in Katherine Shonfield et al., *This Is What We Do: A Muf Manual* (London: Ellipsis, 2001), p. 178.

28 Jennifer Allen, "Up the Organization, Joep van Lieshout, Atelier van Lieshout, Interview," *ArtForum*, April 2001.

29 From promotional materials provided to the author by the architects.

Illustration Credits

Abbreviations: t=top, b=bottom, l=left, r=right

Houses p10: Satoshi Asakawa; pp12-13: Hiroyuki Hirai/Hirai Photo Office Co. Ltd; p14: Rômulo Fialdini; p15: Ross Honeysett; p16: Richard Davies; p17: Russ Widstrand/Widstrand Photography; p18: Jens Markus Lindhe; pp19-20: Earl Carter; p21: Emilio Conti; pp22-23: Satoshi Asakawa; p24: Satoshi Asakawa; p26: Takashi Homa; p27: Christian Richters; p28: Tom Bonner; p29: William Kidow/William Kidow Photography; p30: Shinkenchiku-sha; p31: Takashi Homa; p32: Duccio Malagamba; p33: Philippe Ruault; p34: Timothy Hursley; p35: Eric Sierins/Max Dupain and Associates; p36: Roland Halbe; p37: Richard Barnes (t&bl), Shinkenchiku-sha (r); pp38-39: Paul Warchol; p40: Jeff Goldberg/Esto; p41: Dave Whittaker; pp42-43: Edward Huebner/Arch Photo Inc.; p44: Hans Werlemann; p45: Hisao Suzuki; p46: Shinkenchiku-sha; p47: Sofia Brignone; p48: Earl Carter; p49: Katsuhisa Kida; p50: Mario Davoli; p51: Luis Seixas Ferreira Alves; p52: Matteo Piazza; p53: Lyndon Douglas; p54: Hector Velasco Facio; p55: Wison Thuraweerasuk; p56: Zhan Jin; p57: Christian Richters; p58: Earl Carter (tl&br), Jean-Luc Laloux (tr); p59: Reiner Blunck; p60: Anthony Browell (t&bl), ©Scott Frances/Esto (t&br); p61: ©Scott Frances/ Esto; p62: Paul Czitrom; p63: Reiner Blunck Fotograf; p64: Åke Erikson Lindeman; p65: Timothy Hursley (t&bl), Andreas Pauly (r) **Apartments** p67: Richard Bryant/Arcaid; p68: ©Matuso Photo Atelier (t), Paul Warchol (b); p69: Paul Warchol; p70: Ross Honeysett; p71: Paul Czitrom; p72: Courtesy Starck Network; p73: Courtesy Conran & Partners (l), Roland Halbe (t&br); p74: ©Scott Frances/Esto; p75: Courtesy Richard Meier & Partners Architects/dbox; p76: Deidi von Schaewen; p77: Andreas Pauly; p78: Michael Moran; p79: Richard Bryant/Arcaid; p80: Roberto Bassaglia; p81: Ivan Terestchenko; p82: Peter Aaron/ Esto; p83: Matteu Piazza; p84: Almond Chu; p85: Eric Laignel/courtesy the architect; p86: Richard Barnes; p87: Gionata Xerra; p88: Michael Stepanov; p89: Bruno Klomfar (t&bl), Michael Moran (t&br); p90: Pekka Littow (t&bl), Matteo Piazza (t&br); p91: Mikael Fjellström; p92: Elizabeth Felicella; p93: Paul Warchol; p94: James Morris/Axiom Photo; p95: Hiroyasu Sakaguchi **Lofts** p97: Paul Warchol; p98: Wayn Fuji/©GA Photographers (tl), ©Oberto Gili (tr), Paul Warchol/courtesy the architect (b); p99: Xabier Mendiola; p100: Nio Tatewaki; p101: Andrew Bordwin; pp102-03: Jeff Goldberg/Esto; pp104-05: Andrea Martiradonna; pp106-07: Paul Warchol/courtesy the architect; p108: John Peterson/courtesy the architect; p109: Sara Blee (t&bl), Volker Seding/courtesy the architect (t&br); p110: Hélène Binet; p111: Bruno Helbling; p112: Bruno Helbling (l), Nick Kane/Arcaid ; p113: Mario Carrieri; p114: Luigi Filetici (l), Jan Verlinde (r); p115: Santi Caleca; p116: Michael Moran; p117: Richard Davies; p118: Paul Warchol; p119: Santi Caleca; p120: Thomas Loaf (t&bl), ©Joshua McHugh (t&br); p121: Paul Warchol **Offices** p123: Roland Halbe; p125: Hisao Suzuki; p126: Nigel Young/courtesy Foster + Partners; p127: Anton Grassi/ courtesy the architect; p128: Tim Griffith; p129: Margherita Spiluttini; p130: Roland Halbe (t), Werner Huthmacher (b); p131: Duccio Malagamba; p132: Guy Welbourne/courtesy the architect; p133: Gregory Goode (l), Brad Feinkopf (r); p134: Peter Aaron/Esto (t&br), Sharon Reisdorph (bl); p135: Peter Mauss/ Esto; p136: courtesy Tobias Grau; p137: Timothy Hursley/courtesy the architect (t), Luis Gordoa/courtesy the architect (b); p138: Jens Markus Lindhe; p140: Grant Mudford; p141: Courtesy Gaetano Pesce (t&bl), Benny Chan/Fotoworks (t&br); p142: Benny Chan/Fotoworks; p143: Paul Warchol (l), Michael Moran (r); p145: Michael Moran (t&bl), Kim Zwarts (t&br); pp146-47: Peter Aaron/Esto; p148: Steve Wrubel; p150: Richard Barnes; p151: Mark York/Mark York Photography; pp152-53: Timothy Soar; pp154-155: Roland Halbe; pp156-57: Fotografie Scagliola/Brakke; p158: Nick Merrick/Hedrich Blessing (tl); p159: Paul Warchol; pp160-161: Paul Warchol; p162: Christian Richters; p163: Christian Richters; pp164-65: Paul Warchol; p166: Mario Ermoli; p167: David Churchill **Civic** p169: Philippe Ruault; p170: Christian Kandzia; p171: ©Wolfram Janzer; p172: Hiroyuki Hirai (t&bl), Courtesy ISON (t&br); p173: Hélène Binet; p174: Benny Chan/Fotoworks; p175: ©David Sundberg/Esto (tl), Michael Moran (t&br); 176: Timothy Hursley; p177: Herman van Doorn, Lock Images/GKF (tl), Michael Mathers (t&br); p178: Paolo Rosselli, Studio di Fotografia; p179: Hans Werlemann/Hectic Pictures; p180: Richard Barnes (tl), Philippe Ruault (all others); p182: Romon Viñoly (t), Rafael Viñoly Architects (b); p183: Paul Warchol; p184: Adam Monk/courtesy the architects; p185: Peter Aaron/Esto; p186: Tadeuz Jalocha; p187: Tim Griffith/Esto; pp188-89: Michael Moran; p190: Timothy Hursley; p191: Henrich Helfenstein; p192: Pedro Sánchez Albornoz; p193: Gerald Zugman; p194: ©ADAGP/Dominique Perrault/Georges Fessy; p195: Courtesy the British Library; p196: Grant Mudford; p197: Christian Richters; p198: Bill Timmerman/courtesy the architect; pp199-201: Christian Richters; p202: Oscar Ferrari; p203: Roderick Coyne (t&bl), ©Jeff Goldberg/Esto (tr), ©Peter Mauss/Esto (br); pp204-205: Philippe Ruault; pp206-207: Margherita Spiluttini; p208: Nacása & Partners; p210: Jens Markus Lindhe; p211: Hiroshi Ueda; p212: John Gollings (t), Peter Bennetts (b); p213: Richard Bryant/Arcaid; p214: ©Duccio Malagamba; p215: Roland Halbe; p216: Christian Kandzia; p217: Nigel Yound/courtesy Foster + Partners; pp218-19: ©Scott Frances/Esto; p220: Hisao Suzuki (t&bl), SVA Archive/courtesy the architect; p221: Michael Moran; p222: Hisao Suzuki; p223: Jussi Tiainen; pp224-25: Christian Richters/©Netherlands Embassy Berlin **Religious** p227: Jussi Tainen; p228: Pino Musi/©Studio Architecture Mario Botta; p229: Enrico Cano (br), Pino Musi/©Studio Architecture Mario Botta (all others); p230: courtesy the architect; p231: Roland Halbe; pp232-33: Simone Rosenberg; p234: Jan Olav Jensen (l), Jiri Havran/Per Bernsten (r); p235: Christian Richters; p236: Paul Warchol (t&bl), Francesco Colarosi (tr); p237: Mitsumasa Fujitsuka; p238: Christian Richters; p239: Tim Griffith; p240: ©Julius Shulman and David Glomb; p241: ©Mitsuo Matsuoka (tl), Florian Holzherr (tr), Toshiharu Kitajima (br); p242: ©Aga Khan Trust for Culture (l), ©Wolfgang Hoyt/Esto (r); p243: Lourdes Legorreta; p244: Guy Welborne/courtesy the architect; p245: Richard Barnes; p246: Jan Staller; p247: ©Scott Frances/Esto; p248: Christian Richters; p249: Katsuhisa Kida; p250: Hisao Suzuki; p251: Shinkenchiku-sha; p252: Courtesy Uribe de Bedout Architects; p253: Jussi Tainen; p254: Timothy Hursley; p255: Timothy Hursley (t), Alberto Fonseca (b); p256: ©Mitsuo Matsuoka; p257: ©Werner Huthmacher; p258: ©Aga Khan Trust for Culture; p259: Andrew Garn; p260: ©Aga Khan Trust for Culture (tl), ©Mitsuo Matsuoka (tr), ©Tadao Ando (br); p261: Courtesy Candian Centre for Architecture, Montreal **Cultural** p263: Paul Warchol; p264: Christian Richters/courtesy Renzo Piano Building Workshop; p265: ©Michel Denancé; p266: Jens Weber (tr&bl), Achiv Bunz (tl); p267: Shinkenchiku-sha; pp268-69: Timothy Hursley; p270: ©Michel Denancé; p271: ©Mitsu Matsuoka; p272: Roland Halbe; p273: Philippe Ruault (l), Yasuaki Yoshinaga/©Issey Miyake Inc.; p274: Robert Harding Picture Library/Nigel Francis (l), Katsuaki Furudate (tr), Yasuhiro Ishimoto (br); p275: Nigel Young/courtesy Foster + Partners; p276: Hiroshi Ueda (l), Jimmy Cohrssen (tr), Kudo Photo (br); p277: Lydia Gould Bessler (t), Tom Powell (b); p278: James D'Addio (t), Brad Feinknopf (b); p279: Scott Frances/Esto, ©J.pGetty Trust; p280: Morley von Sternberg; p281: Paul Warchol; p282: Richard Barnes (tl&r), Jeffrey Goldberg/Esto (br); p283: Margherita Spiluttini; p284: Michael Moran (t&bl), Dan Cornish/Esto, courtesy Gluckman Mayner Architects; p285: Bernhard Kroll/ASP; pp286-87: Margherita Spiluttini; pp288-89: ©David Joseph; p290: Mary Ann Sullivan (l), Lourdes Legorreta (r); p291: Pino Musi/©Studio Architect Mario Botta; pp292- 93: Mitsumasa Fujitsuka; p294: Shinkenchiku-sha; p295: Philippe Ruault; p296: Peter Mauss/Esto (t&bl), Ralph Richter (tr), Peter Tahl (br); p297: Mahendra Sinh; p298: Christian Richters; p299: Sebastián Sepúlveda; p300: Michael Moran; p301: Studio Hollein/Arch. Sina Baniahmad; pp302-303: Grant Mudford; p305: ©Hans Werlemann; pp306-307: Christian Richters; p308: ©Jeff Goldberg/Esto (l), Duccio Malagamba (r); p309: Bitter & Bredt; p310: Margherita Spiluttini; p311: ©Christian Richters/Esto (tl), ©Jeff Goldberg/Esto (t&br); p312: Enrico Cano/courtesy Renzo Piano Building Workshop (t), Moreno Maggi/courtesy Renzo Piano Building Workshop; p313: Lara Swimmer/Esto; p314: Kunsthaus Graz/LMJ Graz/Niki Lackner (t&bl), Roland Halbe (t,m&br); p315: Duccio Malagamba **Retail** p317: ©Todd Eberle; p318: Christoph Kicherer; p319: Paul Warchol; p320: Paul Warchol; p321: Volker Seding/courtesy the architect; p322: Davies + Starr/courtesy Moss; p323: C. Weber/courtesy Starck Network; p324: Paul Warchol; p325: Peter Aaron/Esto; pp326-27: Matteo Piazza; p329: Nacása & Partners; p330: Ramon Prat; p331: Nacása & Partners; p332: ©Jeroen Musch (t), Damir Fabijanic Photography (b); p333: ©Morgane Le Gall; p334: Paul Warchol; p335: Jimmy Cohrssen/Daicho Ano, ©Louis Vuitton Malletier, France (t&br); p336: Tomoko Imai/courtesy the architects; p337: Frank Hülsbömer; p338: Catherine Wagner; p339: Courtesy Comme des Garçons; p340: Jen Fong; p341: Andrea Martiradonna; pp342-43: André Lichtenberg/Marcel Wanders studio; p344: ©Jeroen Musch; p345: Yael Pincus; p346: Nacása & Partners; p347: David Grandorge; p348: Tuca Reinés (t), Alvaro Poroa (b); p349: Woo Il Kim/Sug K; p350: Paul Warchol/courtesy Carlos Miele; p351: Alberto Ferrero; p352: Paul Warchol; p353: Philippe Ruault; p354: ©Todd Eberle; p355: AB Rogers Design; p356: ©OMA; p357: ©OMA (l), ©Lydia Gould (r); p358: Nacása & Partners; p359: Richard Davies/©Future Systems **Restaurants and Bars** p361: Nacása & Partners; pp362-63: Richard Bryant/Arcaid; p364: Nikolas Koenig; p365: Claudio Silvestrin Archive; p366: Peter Mauss/Esto; p367: Åke E:son Lindman (l), Patrick Engqvist (t&br); p368: Richard Davies (t&bl); Gregory Goode (t&br); p369: Jeroen Musch; p37-73: Michael Moran; p374: Chen Shenghui; p375: Edward Hueber/Arch Photo; p376: Evan Dion; pp377-78: Tuca Reinés/courtesy Studio Arthur de Mattos Casas Architecture and Design; p379: Valerie Bennett; pp380-81: Paul Warchol; p382: Peter Paige; p384: ©Albi Serfaty/courtesy Aqua Creations; p385: ©Hélène Binet; pp386-87: Michael Moran; p388: Farshid Assassi/courtesy Morphosis; p389: ©Damien Hirst, courtesy Jay Jopling/White Cube (London); p390: Roger Dong/©2000 Condé Nast (l), Nicolla Borel/Archipress (t&br); p391: Nicolla Borel/Archipress; p392: David Joseph; p393: Eugeni Pons; p394: Barney Kulok (t&bl), courtesy Bernard Khoury (t&br); p395: John Butlin (t&bl), courtesy Starck Network (tr); p396: Eric Laignel; p397: ©Ken Hayden (t&bl), ©Néonata (tr), ©DR (br); p398: Ana Paula Carvalho (l), Luísa Ferreira (r); p399: Matti Pyykkö/courtesy the architects; p400: Ari Magg; p401: Emanuel Raab; p402: Nacása & Partners; p403: Marcus Gorts **Hotels** p405: Alberto Ferrero; p406: Tomio Ohashi; p407: courtesy Kandalama Hotel; p408: courtesy Singita Lebombo ; p411: Simon Freeman/courtesy Whitepod; p412: Luis Gordoa; p414: Courtesy Venetian Resort Hotel Casino; p415: Alessandro Anselmi (t), Franco Chimenti (bl&r); p416: Robert Polidori/courtesy Burj Al Arab; p417: Deidi van Schaewen; pp418-19: Courtesy Starck Network; p420: Courtesy Starck Network (t&bl), Bruno Augsburger (t&br); p421: Paul Warchol; p422: David Joseph; p423: Thomas Loaf (t), Todd Eberle (b); pp424-25: Tim Street-Porter; pp426-27: Nikolas Koenig; p428: Nicholas Démians d'Archimbaud (l), Simon Upton (r); p429: Todd Eberle; p430: Courtesy Palazzo Versace Gold Coast; p431: Christophe Bielsa/courtesy Hotel du Petit Moulin; p432: Leo Torri; p433: Courtesy Casa Camper/Factory PR; p434: Alberto Ferrero; p435: Courtesy 3 Rooms, 10 Corso Como (l), ©Christoph Kicherer (r); p436: Sebastiaan Westerweel (l), Inga Powilleit (r); p437: Alberto Ferrero; pp438-39: Martyn Thompson; pp440-41: Philippe Ruault; p442: Hiepler Brunier Architekturfotagrafie; pp444-45: Uwe Spoering; p446: Jimmy Cohrssen; p447: Nelson Kon (tr&l), Leonaardo Finotti (b); p448: Tuca Reinés/courtesy Studio Arthur de Mattos Casas Architecture and Design; p449: Álvaro Povoa; p450: Santi Caleca; p451: Rafael Vargas Fotografía; p452: Nacása & Partners; p453: Christian Richters; p454: Rob 't Hart; pp455-457: Rafael Vargas Fotografia **Therapeutic** p459: Courtesy Michael Young Studio; pp460-61: Kouji Horiguchi; pp462-63: Paul Ott; p464: Angelo Kaunat (t&bl), Gisela Erlacher (r); p467: Remco van Blokland/courtesy the architect; p468: Courtesy Fat; p469: Courtesy IDEO; p470: Tim Griffith; p471: John Durant (l), ©NBBJ/Matt Milios; p472: Keating Khang; p474: Duccio Malagamba; p475: Robert Canfield; p476: Paul Warchol; p477: Christian Richters; p479: Paul Tierney (l), ©Martin Charles; p480: Nelson Kon; p481: Margherita Spiluttini; p482: Joke Robaard with Maarten Theuwkens; pp483-85: Margherita Spiluttini; p486: Paul Tyagi; p487: Nicholas Kane/Arcaid; p488: Grey Crawford; p489: Etienne Clément; p490: Paul Mansfield; p491: Derk Jan Wooldrik/©Atelier van Lieshout; p492: Emilio Conti; p493: Courtesy Michael Young Studio; p494: Jeroen Musch; pp496-97: ©Andrew Bordwin Studio; p498: David Joseph; p499: Doug Fogelson (t), Eric Laignel (b); p501: Nacása & Partners.

Index